*THE AMERICAN FAMILY
IN SOCIAL-HISTORICAL PERSPECTIVE*

MICHAEL GORDON, EDITOR
THE UNIVERSITY OF CONNECTICUT

The American Family in Social-Historical Perspective

ST. MARTIN'S PRESS
NEW YORK

ACKNOWLEDGMENTS

p. 19: "The Comparative History of Household and Family," by
Peter Laslett. © 1971 by Peter N. Stearns. Revised by the author from the
Journal of Social History, Vol. IV, No. 1 (Fall, 1970), 75-87. Reprinted by
permission of the editor and the author.

p. 34: "The Stem Family and the Developmental Cycle of the
Peasant Household: An 18th-Century Austrian Example," by Lutz K.
Berkner. Reprinted with the permission of the author from the *American Historical Review,* LXXVII (April, 1972), 398–418.

p. 59: "Family, Household, and the Industrial Revolution," by
Michael Anderson. Reprinted with the permission of the author and
publisher from Peter Laslett (ed.), *Household and Family in Past Time*
(Cambridge: Cambridge University Press, 1972). Revised by author.

p. 77: "Family Structure in Seventeenth-Century Andover, Massachusetts," by Philip J. Greven, Jr. First published in *William and
Mary Quarterly,* Vol. 23 (1966), 234–256. A revised and expanded
version of this article has been incorporated in Mr. Greven's book:
Four Generations: Population, Land, and Family in Colonial Andover, Massachusetts (Ithaca, N.Y.: Cornell University Press, 1970) Reprinted by
permission.

p. 100: "Family and Community Structure: Salem in 1800," by
Bernard Farber. Excerpted and reprinted by permission from pp.
191–205, Chapter 6, "Conclusion: Family and Community Structure"
in *Guardians of Virtue: Salem Families in 1800* by Bernard Farber; ©
1972 by Basic Books, Inc., Publishers, New York.

p. 111: "Middle-Class Families and Urban Violence: The Experience of a Chicago Community in the Nineteenth Century," by Richard Sennett. Reprinted with the permission of the author and publisher from Stephen Thernstrom and Richard Sennett (eds.) *Nineteenth Century Cities: Essays in the New Urban History* (New Haven: Yale University Press, copyright © 1969 by Yale University Press), 386–420.

p. 136: "Patterns of Work and Family Organization: Buffalo's Italians," by Virginia Yans McLaughlin. Reprinted with the permission of the author and publisher from the *Journal of Interdisciplinary History,* II (Autumn, 1971), 299–314. Copyright © 1971 by the Massachusetts Institute of Technology and the *Journal of Interdisciplinary History.*

p. 152: "The Two-Parent Household: Black Family Structure in Late Nineteenth-Century Boston," by Elizabeth H. Pleck. Copyright © 1972 by Peter N. Stearns. Reprinted with the permission of the author and publisher from the *Journal of Social History,* VI (Fall, 1972), 1–31.

p. 180: "Infancy and Childhood in the Plymouth Colony," by John Demos. From *A Little Commonwealth: Family Life in Plymouth Colony,* by John Demos. Copyright © 1970 by Oxford University Press, Inc. Reprinted by permission.

p. 192: "The American Child As Seen by British Travelers, 1845–1935," by Richard L. Rapson. Reprinted with the permission of the author and publisher from the *American Quarterly,* XVII (1965), 520–534. Copyright, 1965, Trustees of the University of Pennsylvania. The dissertation upon which this article is based has been expanded into a book entitled, *Britons View America: Travel Commentary, 1860–1935* (Seattle and London: University of Washington Press, 1971).

p. 209: "Adolescence in Historical Perspective," by John and Virginia Demos. Reprinted with the permission of the authors and the National Council on Family Relations from the *Journal of Marriage and the Family,* XXXI (November, 1969), 632–638.

p. 224: "The Cult of True Womanhood: 1820–1860," by Barbara Welter. Reprinted with the permission of author and publisher from the *American Quarterly,* Vol. 18, No. 2, part 1 (1966), 151–174. Copyright, 1966, Trustees of the University of Pennsylvania.

p. 251: "Divorce in the Progressive Era," by William L. O'Neill. Reprinted with the permission of author and publisher from the

To Arthur W. Calhoun, who started all of this

Preface

From time to time a new field takes form or an older one receives a reinvigorating transfusion. During the past decade, the social history of the family, a much neglected field, emerged as a vital area which has attracted scholars from a variety of disciplines. The research they have already done not only sheds light on areas of which we were previously uninformed but also does much to dispel some favored myths about the family in past times. Yet, despite the relevance of the new historical investigation of the family to both the research and teaching of sociologists, materials in a readily accessible form for classroom use have been lacking. This volume has been created in the hope of rectifying that situation; it may be used not only as a text but also as an introduction to this rapidly developing and important field.

I have tried to bring together articles and sections of books that reflect all facets of the new history of the family. While my emphasis clearly is upon the American family, I have included some European and English material both to fill in gaps and to provide a comparative perspective. If the book has a unifying theme, apart from representing the broad sweep of American family history from the colonial era to the turn of the twentieth century, it can be found in the concept of modernization. Since the major portion of the introductory essay is devoted to the ramifications of this concept for family history, there is little need to elaborate upon it here, except to note that a key feature of the premodern setting is the centrality of family—and that even today the majority of the world's nations are not yet modernized. Therefore, by looking at the family in nations that have already undergone modernization, we should be able to learn something about the experiences of what Marion J. Levy describes as "latecomers," i.e., countries currently undergoing modernization, even though we must recognize that there are important differences between the "survivors" such as England, France, and the United States, which modernized gradually, and the "latecomers," which have often been subjected to an accelerated experience.

The selections that follow are organized into five sections, each focusing on a different aspect of family and kinship. To some extent, these categories are arbitrary, since in certain instances an article or chapter could have been placed in any of several sections; yet these categories do, I believe, provide useful perspectives.

In the first section, "The Family: Aspects of Domestic Life," we have what some might see as the heart of the book. There are three subsections: one dealing with European and English data, one concerned with the prevailing American experience, and one outlining some ethnic variations on this experience. These sections neatly convey the richness and variety of the new history of the family. From the selections here we see the danger of discussing all that went before the twentieth century as though it were a monolithic entity, with no variation between periods or groups. There is a considerable difference between the family that Philip Greven describes as characteristic of Andover, Massachusetts, in the early days of its settlement and the one that Richard Sennett sees as characteristic of middle-class Chicagoans during the time of the Haymarket riots. Bernard Farber's work indicates that significant class distinctions in family life existed during the Federal era, and Elizabeth Pleck and Virginia McLaughlin make similar points with regard to ethnic variations during the periods covered in their articles. There is no need to belabor the point of variation; the selections in this section make the points eloquently enough and have much to teach us about such diverse topics as household size, inheritance, contact with kin, and how all these factors varied during the years of this country's growth and development.

"Growing Up: Childhood and Youth" is the title of the second section, and the brevity of the section is indicative of the fact that this area has only begun to be explored. Scarcity notwithstanding, the selections do give us some sense of the kinds of changes and shifts that have occurred in these early periods of life. John and Virginia Demo's article, for example, deals with the development of adolescence both as a new stage of life and as a scientific concept. Apart from demonstrating generally how bound up in our own time are our notions of the stages of life, the authors point to a number of important ways in which the concept of adolescence is peculiarly a product of modern life. Adolescence, they maintain, could not have arisen had it not been for the extended period of economic dependence and education brought about by industrialization; and its concomitant of youth culture, they argue, is profoundly tied to urban life with its concentrations of large numbers of young people with similar life situations.

The fact that there is a section on women ("Women: Role and Relationships") but none on men may cause some raised eyebrows and provoke some suggestions that male chauvinism is at work here. I should like to think not, but, in any case, I would argue that the status of women has been more dramatically affected, at least potentially, by modernization than has the status of men. This is what the selections in this section portray, though, since most historians have been and continue to be men, it may not be surprising that they have considered their position less problematic than that of women. Perhaps no other section offers greater diversity than this one. It contains articles that deal with such diverse topics as vocation, divorce, and politics, and when these articles are related to those in the other sections, a vivid picture emerges of the social history of sex roles in American society.

The fourth section, "Sex: Behavior and Ideology," contains a good deal of information that readers not familiar with the field of family history will find to be both fresh and important to an understanding of long-term change in sexual mores and behavior. Edmund Morgan's classic article on Puritan sexuality and Daniel Smith's paper on the dating of the sexual revolution in this country make it evident that the Puritans were hardly as puritanical as some would have us believe and that there is an important distinction to be made between Puritanism and Victorianism. Furthermore, we shall see that shifts in patterns of premarital sexual behavior in this country cannot be thought of as unfolding in a linear fashion, but instead seem to follow a cyclical curve. Nonetheless, there does appear to be an increasing separation of sex from marriage, a phenomenom that is tied to the declining salience of the family in society—which, as we noted earlier, is in turn related to modernization. This section also includes Edward Shorter's work on European illegitimacy, which is notable, apart from its excellent data, for the author's attempt to deal theoretically with the emergence of different types of sexuality. The section ends with Ben Barker-Benfield's important essay on nineteenth-century American sexuality.

The final section, "Demographic Trends: Marriage, Birth, and Death," includes two articles that deal with vital statistics. Neither of them, however, can be thought of as bald demography, for their analyses of the demographic shifts that have characterized this nation from its settlement to its experience of modernization are informed by a solid social-historical sense. Taken together, these selections add another dimension to understanding of the aspects of family life that have been discussed earlier.

I should like to acknowledge some debts incurred while preparing this volume. The college department at St. Martin's Press should be applauded for having the courage to publish a book which some saw as too specialized for "today's market." A special debt is owed to Dan Smith of the University of Connecticut's history department; his insightful comments and useful suggestions did much to improve this book, though whatever failings it may have are entirely my own responsibility.

M. G.

Contents

Introduction   1

PART I   The Family: Aspects of Domestic Life   17

COMPARATIVE PERSPECTIVES   18
  1   The Comparative History of Household and Family
      Peter Laslett   19
  2   The Stem Family and the Developmental Cycle of
      the Peasant Household: An 18th-Century Austrian
      Example
      Lutz K. Berkner   34
  3   Family, Household, and the Industrial Revolution
      Michael Anderson   59

THE AMERICAN SCENE   76
  4   Family Structure in Seventeenth-Century Andover,
      Massachusetts
      Philip J. Greven, Jr.   77
  5   Family and Community Structure: Salem in 1800
      Bernard Farber   100
  6   Middle-Class Families and Urban Violence: The
      Experience of a Chicago Community in the
      Nineteenth Century
      Richard Sennett   111

ETHNIC VARIATIONS ON THE AMERICAN
SCENE 135

7 Patterns of Work and Family Organization: Buffalo's
Italians
Virginia Yans McLaughlin 136
8 The Two-Parent Household: Black Family Structure
in Late Nineteenth-Century Boston
Elizabeth H. Pleck 152

PART II Growing Up: Childhood and Youth 179

9 Infancy and Childhood in the Plymouth Colony
John Demos 180
10 The American Child As Seen by British Travelers,
1845–1935
Richard L. Rapson 192
11 Adolescence in Historical Perspective
John and Virginia Demos 209

PART III Women: Roles and Relationships 223

12 The Cult of True Womanhood: 1820–1860
Barbara Welter 224
13 Divorce in the Progressive Era
William L. O'Neill 251
14 Family, Career, and Reform: Women Leaders of the
Progressive Era
Richard Jensen 267

PART IV Sex: Behavior and Ideology 281

15 The Puritans and Sex
Edmund S. Morgan 282
16 Illegitimacy, Sexual Revolution, and Social Change
in Modern Europe
Edward Shorter 296
17 The Dating of the American Sexual Revolution:
Evidence and Interpretation
Daniel Scott Smith 321
18 The Spermatic Economy: A Nineteenth-Century
View of Sexuality
Ben Barker-Benfield 336

**PART V Demographic Trends: Marriage, Birth, and
Death** 373

    19 A Long View
*Wilson H. Grabill, Clyde V. Kiser, and Pascal K.
Whelpton* 374

    20 The Demographic History of Colonial New England
Daniel Scott Smith 397

Selected Bibliography 417
Index 423

*THE AMERICAN FAMILY
IN SOCIAL-HISTORICAL PERSPECTIVE*

Introduction

Recent developments within the field of history have a wealth of material that is of relevance and importance to sociologists. This is especially evident in the area of the social history of the family. The new concern on the part of historians with questions of family and kinship can, in part, be interpreted as the product of two, by no means widespread, shifts of emphasis: an emerging interest in common people and everyday life, and the diffusion into the discipline of quantitative techniques. These are interrelated phenomena. Farmers and laborers generally do not keep diaries or write family histories, and their role in "great" events often goes unrecorded or, at best, is set down by the hardly objective hand of their social "betters." Thus when an interest in history's inarticulate actors began to develop, it became necessary to look for new sources of data; and they were found in such places as church and civic records, governmental reports and surveys, and other similar aggregations of material. These sorts of data lend themselves to enumeration and statistical manipulation, and, not surprisingly, computer tapes have appeared where previously only index cards were to be found.

Another factor that has contributed to the development of historical investigation of the family is the blurring of interdisciplinary lines between sociology and history that has occurred during the 1960s and 1970s. This blurring has been particularly evident to those who study such topics as social mobility, urban growth, politics, and violence.[1] The writings of historians now include such concepts as *reference group, extended family,* and *total institution,* as well as theoretical frameworks derived from the writings of Talcott Parsons and Robert Merton, among others. In fact, the debt of history to sociology resides more in the realm of concepts and theory than in the adoption of quantitative techniques, most of which were developed by statisticians. Conversely, a growing number of sociologists now see the importance of long-term trend analysis and the relevance of historical data for their understanding of contemporary events. Furthermore, they have gained from historians an awareness of data sources that they previously ignored. Still, differences between the disciplines persist. For example, sociologists exhibit a much greater concern for generalization than for details of specific events, a proclivity that has often caused them to neglect the temporal limitations of their data while pursuing social laws.[2]

The social-historical study of the family is an area that lends itself well to the further melding of these disciplines, and, as we shall see, a fair amount of progress has already been made in this direction. The present volume brings together the fruits of this new family research, with a specific emphasis on material collected in the United States. I have not attempted to limit the selections to studies employing quantitative techniques. To have done so would have imposed an unnecessary parochialism and, more importantly, would have resulted in the omission of the significant contribution made to this field by scholars using more conventional methodologies. Indeed, in some instances, these latter works are the only materials available showing such qualitative aspects of family life as the *nature* of interpersonal relationships as distinct from simply the *number* of such relationships. Taken as a whole, the articles that follow should allow students of the family to see the extent and breadth of the work that historians and other social scientists have been producing in this area.

Until the past decade, if one wanted to know anything about the history of the American family he had very few places to turn. The only major work available was Arthur Calhoun's three-volume study tracing the development of the American family from the Colonial era to World War I.[3] While this was a pioneering, comprehensive, and influential piece of work, it suffered from many of the defects we generally associate with traditional historiography, e.g., a reliance on limited and often problematic sources that permit only highly qualified generalizations. Between the time of the publication of Arthur Calhoun's study and World War II, there was virtually no work of any scope done in this field.[4] In the 1940s two studies in the traditional historiographic mold did appear: Charles Ironside's dissertation on the Colonial family in New York, and Edmund Morgan's deservedly well-received and frequently quoted *The Puritan Family*.[5]

The development of a technique that was to provide an important vehicle for the growth of family history occurred in France.[6] Students of early populations have for the most part had to rely on census data, and these are only available for the last two centuries. This created a wall of sorts which was breached only after World War II, when a group of demographers interested in the historical study of fertility began, under the leadership of Louis Henry, to elaborate a method of data analysis that has since come to be known as *family reconstitution.*

> Family reconstitution is the bringing together of scattered information about the members of a family to enable its chief demographic characteristics to be described as fully as possible. The family reconstitution method is not new. Genealogists have for generations searched out the dates of birth and death of the partners to marriages of the rich, the wellborn, and famous, and have listed the dates of birth of their offspring and the dates of the marriages and deaths to establish lineages and relationships. The tracing of family histories and the recording of family histories of these sorts is actively prosecuted to this day. But it is only very recently that attempts have been made to apply this method to a sample of the families of a whole community by making use of parish registers as a source of information. Where this is possible the community's demographic history can be examined in greater detail and with greater precision than with any other method.[7]

Through the use of this technique, parish records in Western Europe and other areas have been made to yield quantities of data crucial to our understanding of trends not only in births and deaths, but also in age at marriage, bridal pregnancy, patterns of remarriage, and so on.

While it is generally agreed that the reconstitution or *nominal* method, as it is sometimes called, is hard to beat for accuracy and certainty, it is nonetheless a time-consuming and expensive procedure that is not suited to all problems in demographic or family history. An alternative methodology is aggregate data analysis, a technique that involves analyzing records at different points in time in order to develop a picture of trends. Here we are looking at numbers of events, e.g. births as they are distributed over time in particular populations, rather than, as in the reconstitution method, at these events as they occur in individual families. However, the reader should not conclude that these are mutually exclusive techniques.

> Aggregation, in fact, can often be a prelude to reconstitution, for with this comparatively rapid system of analysis, it is possible to pinpoint those areas and periods of population history which saw the most striking changes.[8]

The impact of these new methods of data analysis in some respects transcends the study of population trends. Indeed, it may be said that with some ingenuity and a great deal of hard work various bodies of existing data can offer new and relevant data to the historical study of the family. Wills, city registers, and other diverse sources help recreate past family life.

Another innovation that is just beginning to make a contribution to this field is what has come to be known as psycho-history. Psycho-history employs psychological and psychoanalytic principles and concepts in the analysis of historical materials, and it further illustrates the interdisciplinary borrowing that is increasingly taking place. While most psycho-history takes the form of biography, there are a number of instances of its application to issues relevant to the family. John Demos, for example, in his monograph on family life in the Plymouth colony, employs Erik Erikson's stages of life formulation to look at the process of growing up in seventeenth-century Massachusetts. This allows him to move beyond the realm of description, and he adopts a theoretical framework that gives coherence to what otherwise might have been bald narration. It should be kept in mind that psycho-history represents a different reading of history rather than a *new* methodology per se—it draws upon conventional sources but subjects them to a novel interpretation.[9]

We must recognize, however, that historians working with traditional sources and using traditional historiography have also made important contributions to the social history of the family. This is attested by the several examples of such works that have been included in this volume. Regrettably, as often happens when new paradigms are discovered, there are some who criticize those who do not adopt new techniques and points of view. These "data snobs" look down their noses at those whose findings are not quantifiable. Given the newness of this research area and the attacks that these hard-nosed historians have come under from their more humanistically oriented colleagues, this sort of snobbery is perhaps understandable, albeit hardly desirable. Ideally, the methodology that a scholar employs should reflect the kinds of questions he or she is asking, and, as we have indicated earlier, varied approaches should not be thought of as mutually exclusive. An excellent illustration of the value of this principle is found in the article in this volume by Daniel Smith on the dating of the sexual revolution in the United States. Professor Smith draws upon a variety of data sources in his attempt to look at trends in premarital sexual behavior. He uses record-matching studies of bridal pregnancies, government illegitimacy figures, analyses of sexual education literature, and historical essays. These sources taken together allow Smith to come to a conclusion that would not have been possible had he relied on any one source alone. Thus we see the importance of a catholic approach. This anthology should make clear that the new social history of the family is characterized by a healthy diversity and that a good part of its strength and importance as an emergent field resides in this diversity.

The Meaning of Modernization

Given the fact that this book has been prepared primarily as an introduction to family history for sociologists, it will be necessary to review some of the relevant sociological literature. This will provide a backdrop against which the findings presented later in the book can be viewed.

A theme that runs through the sociological literature on the family is the impact of modernization on this institution. Here, the term *modernization* encompasses much more than the replacement of cottage industry by the factory system of production; it involved profound and revolutionary changes that took place in Europe during the eighteenth and nineteenth centuries and that affected all aspects of society, from types of community in which people lived to the way in which they viewed the world. An informative scheme for exploring the nature and meaning of these changes is provided by Robert Nisbet in his important book, *The Sociological Tradition*.[10] This book is essentially a treatment of the emergence of sociology as a discipline during the nineteenth century, but it is Nisbet's thesis that sociology arose as a new way of seeing the world in response to the changes brought about by the resounding impact of what E. J. Hobsbawm has called the "dual revolution": the French Revolution and Industrial Revolution, which were occurring simultaneously.[11] Nisbet feels that the five basic concepts, or "unit-ideas," of the discipline (which, by the way, are still with us) get to the core of these changes. These are: Community, Authority, Status, the Sacred, and Alienation. Each of these concepts focuses on an aspect of social structure or culture that was in a state of flux during the nineteenth century; together they provide a composite picture of the alterations in Western society that have variously been referred to as the movement from *Gemeinschaft* to *Gesellschaft*—from organic to mechanical solidarity or, later, from folk to urban society, but perhaps most appropriately as modernization. Whatever the phrase employed, the basic issue is still dramatic social change, social change that both directly and indirectly affected the family. Let us look at each of these unit ideas in some detail.

The concept of *community* as it figured in the writings of sociology's "founding fathers" dealt with the quality of the individual's relationships to other people through group and associational involvement. Obviously, then, an important determinant of community becomes the degree to which a society is urbanized. While cities did exist long before industrial growth took place, they were scattered centers containing only a small proportion of the population. As markets grew and factories multiplied, the escalated need for labor created a veritable urban explosion. In England's industrial midlands, for example:

> The population of Preston in 1851 was 5.7 [times] what it had been in 1801 and Burnley, Ashton, Blackburn, Stockport, Rochdale, Bolton, and Bury had all grown by more than three times. The population of Preston, and also of Burnley, more than doubled between 1831 and 1851.[12]

The sociological implications of such dramatic shifts in population are far-ranging indeed. Most obviously, and this gets at the heart of the so-called Industrial Revolution, these shifts meant that for the first time in history agriculture and husbandry were dethroned as the major sources of production and social position. From the individual's point of view, it meant that the relatively insulated social existence possible in farm and village was now out of the question. Almost by definition, urban life involved what Richard Sennett has aptly called "contact points."[13] It is tempting, though dangerous, as Michael Anderson has shown us, to play down the maintenance of extended kin ties in an urban setting; but it does seem evident that the likelihood of living near nonkin was greater and that people were required to leave their homes to obtain services and items previously provided by the domestic unit. In short, these new rural migrants were forced to interact with strangers in settings that were alien to them. Yet, at the very center of the urban experience, and perhaps overriding all other factors, was a phenomenon that William Goode with his usual acuity describes so well:

> The city became the carrier of new ideologies, thus giving a moral validation to these alterations in social patterns. Thus, the urban-rural differences begin to *decline*, since the thinking of those who live in rural areas is shaped by the forces that urbanize the nation.[14]

The meaning of this will become clearer as we consider the other unit-ideas.

By directing our attention to issues of *authority*, Nisbet is referring not only to changes in government but also to more fundamental changes in the legitimation of power within the community. Quite correctly, he is going beyond the replacement of monarchies by legislative forms of government and considering more subtle and wideranging alterations.

> In traditional society authority is hardly recognized as having separate or even distinguishable identity. How could it be? Deeply embedded in social functions, an inalienable part of the inner order of family, neighborhood, parish, and guild, ritualized at every turn, authority is so closely woven into the fabric of tradition and morality as to be scarcely more noticeable than the air men breathe. Even in the hands of the king, authority in such a society tends to maintain this diffuse and indirect character. Such is the tendency of monarchical power to become submerged in the whole ethos of patriarchalism that the power of the king seems to its subjects as but little different from that exercised by fathers over sons, priests over communicants, and masters over apprentices. The entire weight of morality—which is typically the morality of duty and allegiance—makes authority an undifferentiated aspect of the social order, the government hardly more than a symbolic superstructure.[15]

Not surprisingly, then, the coming of new forms of national authority was associated with the questioning of authority in other spheres of life, and the family did not remain unscathed. Paternal authority, a relevant example, resided not only in the broad legitimating sources described by Nisbet but also in the basic control that a father could exercise over his son's vocational life chances. Where we find the intergenerational transmission of land intact, as in peasant societies, we find paternal authority to be strong; but in industrial societies a son no longer required—at least not to the same extent— the good offices of his father to obtain work. Thus he could assert his autonomy at the expense of his father's authority. To be sure, the effects of this liberating process were not equally felt in all segments of society. Among the wealthy, even after industrialization the inter- generational transmission of wealth and opportunity resulted in the maintenance of parental control over children and a dulling of indus- trialization's impact; yet here, too, the new ideology of equalitarian- ism ultimately weakened paternal dominance.

The weakening of paternal authority through the emergence of a broader division of labor is related in a fundamental way to questions of social stratification. In focusing on the unit-idea of *status,* Nisbet directs our attention to the preoccupation with the question of social class that is found in the writings of Marx, Weber, Tocqueville, and other early sociological lights. Clearly, the previously held picture of a continuous hierarchy was no longer adequate to describe social reality, and a debate now raged over the shape of the new stratification system. From the present point of view, the question of whether "class" or "status group" best describes it is not as significant as the fact that such issues has assumed importance at that time. In terms of the family, what is most relevant is that the new stratification— whether status group or class—permitted much more social mobility.

Stratification systems vary in the degree to which they permit mobility between strata. Estate systems such as that which character- ized medieval Europe (i.e., the nobility, clergy and commons) are generally thought of as allowing little interstrata movement, while current class or status sytems are seen as more permeable. Industriali- zation not only undermined agriculture as the primary vocational activity and source of social placement, but, as part of a broader institutional differentiation that was occurring in society, it created a multiplicity of jobs, that is, a division of labor much greater than anything that had previously existed. This meant that although a man might not move out of the *stratum* into which he was born during his own lifetime (vertical mobility), he might still move into a *job* which would involve a different occupational sub-culture and work sur- roundings while in the same stratum as his father's. This is *horizontal mobility.* What we must keep in mind is that such intergenerational discontinuity in the realm of work adds one more nail to the coffin of traditional society because of the potential for societal diversity, out- look, and life style that it introduces.

Since, as Nisbet so eloquently argues, sociology arose in the nineteenth century as a response to what were seen by some as crises in the realms of societal integration and social control, it is not surprising to find that there was a considerable amount of interest evidenced in religion. This concern with *the sacred* reflects what early sociologists saw as the increasing secularization of European society. Secularization is used to refer less to such things as church attendance than to the extent to which everyday life is infused with religious significance and the degree to which religious proscriptions and prescriptions affect behavior. Many nineteenth-century intellectuals, sociologists, as well as nonsociologists saw religion rapidly slipping into insignificance and in the process creating a situation of moral crisis, a theme which we hear echoed and reechoed in their writings. In terms of its immediate relevance for the family, we see this concern wih the loss of God manifested in the many social movements surrounding issues such as purity, prostitution, pornography, and so forth. In a sense we might say that the family, viewed as the cornerstone of society, was held to be the institution most vulnerable to the floodgates of irreligion that were apparently opening.

To this point, the four unit-ideas we have discussed deal more with the societal consequences of modernizaion than they do with the individual consequences. However, *alienation,* the last of the five unit-ideas dealt with by Nisbet, considers the personal impact of these dramatic changes. Given current perspectives it may be difficult to imagine just how profoundly social life was changed in the nineteenth century. For some, this change resulted in feelings of being cut off from the "self" and from a world that was rapidly undergoing modification before their eyes. Marx's early writings, for example, deal explicitly with what might be called "personal alienation" arising from man's being cut off from the products of his own labor. We should not emphasize solely the economic aspects of alienation. In even simpler terms, the growth in societal scale, with its concomitant impersonality and remoteness, fosters the feeling of isolation and detachment that we have come to identify as alienation. Yet, one must also remember that modernization is associated with the appearance of a degree of personal freedom never previously experienced by most people; perhaps freedom and alienation are best seen as opposite sides of the same coin.

When we look at the composite social picture of these five concepts, we can see how fundamental were the changes brought about by the two revolutions with which Nisbet deals. Obviously, the impact of these forces was not felt at all places at the same time. This country, for example, experienced its major industrial growth almost a century after England.[16] The later the modernization, the greater the ideological factor becomes—that is, whether these changes are regarded as right, proper, and even desirable. There are, of course, important and basic differences between a nation now emerging out of a colonial system of government and a primary economic system and England in the second half of the eighteenth century. Still, comparisons are not without value, and the historical data may provide considerable insights into present events.

The Impact of Modernization on the Family

No one has taken a closer, more reasoned, or better-documented view of the relationship between large-scale societal change and the resulting modification of family life than William Goode in his MacIver-award-winning book, *World Revolution and Family Patterns.* A major theme, if not *the* major theme, running through Goode's book concerns the pressure that the industrialization process places on the family to become smaller. However, Goode makes an important distinction between the nuclear and the conjugal family in discussing this.

> A major thesis of this volume is that most family systems of the world are moving toward the conjugal system. . . . However, an equally central thesis is that *no* family system as a whole may be called "nuclear" if by that is meant that the family system is reduced to the unit of parent and children. At a *minimum,* the members of each unit are tied to other units through a common member of a given nuclear family. . . . Thus, even in theoretical terms, a "nuclear" family system seems impossible without a great expenditure of ideological fervor and social energy and we may more properly refer to the *conjugal* family. Consequently, the widely held thesis that in the most industrialized nations, a genuinely nuclear family has come into existence, or is emerging, seems doubtful at best.[17]

The evidence contained in the present volume would seem to indicate that the movement in the direction of Goode's "conjugal family" occurred well before the Industrial Revolution. Evidence from England, for example, shows that the nuclear family (i.e., a family consisting of husband, wife, and dependent offspring) was the most prevalent form two centuries before industrialization.[18] Yet, industrialization did seem to undermine that period when landholding families became extended after the father retired and a son, often the eldest, married and took up residence in the paternal home. We must, however, recognize that this represented a rather brief period in the life cycle of the family; and for nonlandholding families, of which there were many in preindustrial Europe, this did not take place, a point which will be discussed at length by Lutz Berkner later in this book.

By making this distinction between nuclear and conjugal families, Goode forces us to direct our attention to the relationship between household units and broader kin networks. While, as we have already indicated, it seems safe to assume that modernization is not associated with a reduction in the categories of kin in the residential unit, the question still remains as to whether or not broader kin networks shrank in terms of both number and function.[19] Demos in his Plymouth study maintains that kin priorities then were similar to those now, but he has no data on the number of kin with whom individuals interacted or the reciprocal services demanded of them.[20] It is difficult to glean this sort of information from historical records. We can look at the number of kin available to an individual in a particular community, their dispersion over space, or the categories of kin named in wills, especially when no adult offspring are living; but the data yielded by such sources are often slim. Michael Anderson's findings on kin interaction during the height of England's industrialization do, however, indicate that extensive use of kin was made by those laboring in the mills, particularly by rural migrants. This suggests the functionality of kin even in this urban-industrial setting.[21] Perhaps the most appropriate way of looking at the question of the role of extended kin in the modern world is to conceptualize it in terms of options. As a result of the general societal differentiation that we discussed earlier, we now have specialists, such as contractors, policemen, and obstetricians, who provide formal services that may have been provided previously by kin. For many, then, kin interaction is now a matter of choice, while in past times and in many developing nations today it is a matter of necessity.

Goode's argument that industrialization results in a push toward a conjugal family rests on the notion that an industrial economy requires a mobile labor force—that people must be where the jobs are available. This means that family control over enterprise should be reduced—not only in terms of getting people to where the jobs are but also in terms of training people for jobs that suit their talents rather than the traditions of their family. Earlier, we noted that one important source of decline in paternal authority was the replacement by the factory of the family farm as the primary source of male employment; this may be seen as another way of looking at this process. In any case, the final result is that the family plays a reduced role in the occupational sphere. It is no longer an economically productive unit; instead, it becomes a unit of consumption.

Another important consequence of the industrial process has been the entry of women into the labor force.[22] Referring again to

Michael Anderson's superb study of Lancashire, we find that in Preston, one of the centers of the cotton industry, over 50 percent of the women over twenty were employed, only a very small majority (53 percent) in the cotton industry.[23] The entry of women into the work force in such large numbers was to have a variety of consequences. While from the very beginning of the industrial period women viewed their work as an extension of their roles as wives and mothers, nonetheless, the fact that they were bringing in the portion of the family's earnings that often made the difference between eking out an existence and starving gave them a leverage and independence that was probably absent in the preindustrial era. This leverage was apparent not only in marriage but in the premarital situation as well. There were, however, class differences here, differences which still persist. Women of the working class worked in much greater numbers than did middle-class women. The housewife, in the sense that we understand that term today, is a largely middle-class phenomenon created by industrialization.

One can go on and on looking at the specifics of social change wrought by the economic and political upheavals in the eighteenth and nineteenth centuries; the broad shape and implications of these changes have been discussed. The readings that follow seem to address themselves to the hope expressed by Goode a decade ago in concluding his study of the family and social change:

> This inquiry may also serve another function, the stimulation of historical research in the field of family study. Historians have neglected this area, being far more concerned with larger economic or political processes. Also, the difficulty of obtaining adequate data has undoubtedly made such inquiries less attractive. By historical research we do not mean merely references to historical events or reading history books, but genuinely archival investigations, and specifically the testing of sociological propositions with historical data.[24]

It does seem that to some extent this intention was realized, as is indicated by the numerous quotations of Goode's work in the articles included herein. These articles provide the elaboration and clarification that Goode felt was so desperately needed, but by no means are all the facts in. Much more research needs to be done before we can get a truly valid picture of family and kinship in previous eras, if, indeed, this will ever be possible. It is reassuring to know that this work is being done by scholars throughout the world, and that there is a growing interest in the social history of the family. Perhaps ten years from now many of the questions raised in this book will be answered. There is room for optimism!

A Final Note

Above all else, one thing is both implicit and explicit in the articles that follow: that the preindustrial history of the family is not static. Sociologists have too often fallen prey to the misconception that all that came before industrialization was a monolithic entity. In fact, Philippe Ariès, in what is perhaps the most influential book written in the area of family history in the past decade, makes the point that many of the changes usually associated with industrialization were set in motion as early as the twelfth century, when, in his view, the family began its "retreat" from society, a retreat that may have culminated in the situation described below by Richard Sennett.[25] Be that as it may, there are no shortages of examples of variation in various aspects of family life prior to the industrial era. For example, Daniel Smith and Edward Shorter both show that nonmarital pregnancies have varied in a nonlinear fashion since the seventeenth century.[26] This should not allow us to ignore the fact that there have indeed been periods of stability, but we must remember that these have been only periods, not the whole of history.

Notes

1   Representative examples of such work are to be found in Stephen Thernstrom and Richard Sennett, eds., *Nineteenth Century Cities: Essays in the New Urban History* (New Haven: Yale University Press, 1969); and Seymour M. Lipset and Richard Hofstadter, eds., *Sociology and History: Methods* (New York: Basic Books, 1968).

2   For general discussions of the relationship between history and sociology, see Kai T. Erikson, "Sociology and the Historical Perspective," *American Sociologist* 5 (November 1970): 331–38; and the reviews of Lipset and Hofstadter, *Sociology and History,* by Philip Abrams and David J. Rothman in *Past & Present* no. 52 (August 1971): 118–34.

3   There is also George E. Howard, *A History of Matrimonial Institutions,* 2 vols. (Chicago: University of Chicago Press, 1904), but the focus here is legalistic and the concern is as much with British patterns as it is with American.

4   There was one study of the Puritan family published during this time, but it relies almost exclusively on literary sources. See Levin L. Schücking, *Die Puritanische Familie* (Leipzig: B. G. Teubner Verlag, 1929).

5   Charles E. Ironside, *The Family in Colonial New York* (New York: Columbia University Press, 1942); and Edmund S. Morgan, *The Puritan Family* (Boston: Boston Public Library, 1945). See also Bernard Bailyn, *Education in the Forming of American Society* (Chapel Hill: University of North Carolina Press, 1962).

6   For a history of this movement, see Pierre Goubert, "Historical Demography and the Reinterpretation of Early Modern French History: A Research Review," *Journal of Interdisciplinary History* 1 (Autumn 1970): 37–48. Varied examples of the work of this school and other similar research are to be found in the special issue of

Daedalus 97 (Spring 1968), which is devoted to "Historical Population Studies." It should be kept in mind that these scholars are not essentially interested in the family; nonetheless, students of the family have benefited from their methodological innovations.

7   E. A. Wrigley, "Family Reconstitution," in E. A. Wrigley, ed., *An Introduction to English Historical Demography* (London: Weidenfeld and Nicolson, 1966), p. 96.

8   D. E. C. Eversley, "Exploitation of Anglican Parish Registers by Aggregative Analysis," in Wrigley, *Introduction,* p. 44. Eversley does note that it is difficult to do reconstitution in areas where only a small number of family and first names are found.

9   For other examples of psycho-history, see David Hunt, *Parents and Children in History* (New York: Basic Books, 1970); Peter Loewenberg, "The Psychohistorical Origins of the Nazi Youth Cohort," *American Historical Review* 76 (December 1971): 1457–1502; and Bruce Mazlish (ed.) *Psychoanalysis and History* (New York: Grosset and Dunlap, 1971). Also see the theme issue devoted to "Psychoanalysis and History" of the *Journal of Interdisciplinary History* 2 (Spring 1972).

10   Robert A. Nisbet, *The Sociological Tradition* (New York: Basic Books, 1966).

11   E. J. Hobsbawm, *The Age of Revolution, 1789–1848* (New York: Mentor Books, 1964).

12   Michael Anderson, *Family Structure in Nineteenth-Century Lancashire* (Cambridge: Cambridge University Press, 1971), p. 33.

13   Richard Sennett, *The Uses of Disorder* (New York: Alfred A. Knopf, 1970).

14   William J. Goode, *World Revolution and Family Patterns* (New York: The Free Press, 1963), p. 375.

15   Nisbet, *Sociological Tradition,* p. 108.

16   The point has often been made that while the United States was behind England in such measures as the percent of population employed in industry, in terms of other measures (e.g., literacy) she shows evidence of modernization before industrialization actually took place. See Richard Brown, "Modernization and the Modern Personality in Early America," *Journal of Interdisciplinary History* 2 (Winter 1972): 201–28.

17   Goode, *World Revolution,* pp. 70–71.

18   On this point see the articles published in Peter Laslett and Richard Wallis (eds.), *Family and Household in Past Time* (Cambridge: Cambridge University Press, 1972).

19   With regard to categories of personnel in the residential unit, an issue in which growing interest has been shown is that of the role of boarders and lodgers during the nineteenth and early twentieth centuries. See John Modell, "Strangers in the Family: Boarding and Lodging in Industrial America," paper read at the Clark University Conference on the Family, Social Structure, and Social Change, April 27–29, 1972; and the article by Sennett included in this volume.

20   John Demos, *A Little Commonwealth* (New York: Oxford University Press, 1970), p. 124.

21   Anderson, *Family Structure*.

22   For a general treatment of this topic, see Ivy Pinchbeck, *Women Workers and the Industrial Revolution, 1750–1850* (London: Frank Cass, 1969).

23   Anderson, *Family Structure*, pp. 24–25.

24   Goode, *World Revolution*, pp. 366–67.

25   Philippe Ariès, *Centuries of Childhood: A Social History of Family Life* (New York: Vintage, 1962).

26   See their contributions to this volume in the section on sexual behavior.

PART I

The Family:
Aspects of Domestic Life

Comparative Perspectives

Peter Laslett's summary and analysis of the contributions made to a conference on the size and structure of families in past times provides an exceptionally valuable beginning for this, the key section of the book. One point seems to have emerged most clearly for Laslett: that the extended family was by no means the offspring of industrialization and that in England and other nations the nuclear family was the prevalent form for several centuries before industrialization. One does, however, get the feeling that in making this point, the author may have too easily brushed aside some of the structural variations that have existed over time. Lutz Berkner in another article included in this section indicates that one of the reasons Laslett did not find more three-generation stem families in England may be because the data used by the Cambridge Group did not, for the most part, take family life cycle into consideration, a point on which we will have more to say below. Furthermore, research on nineteenth-century and early twentieth-century American cities has revealed that boarders, roomers, and lodgers, some of whom may have been extended kin, were present in the residential units of this time to a much greater extent than they are now. Yet, Laslett's basic point goes unchallenged: that there is certainly more continuity than discontinuity in the structure of preindustrial and industrial families.

PETER LASLETT

1 The Comparative History of Household and Family

In September 1969, there was a meeting at Cambridge on the obscure and rather difficult subject of the size and structure of household and family in past times. Organized by the Cambridge Group for the History of Population and Social Structure, its object was to explore what had so far become known in the small number of countries where records had been shown to exist for this study, and where work was already in progress. Five areas were eventually selected, and attention had to be confined for the most part to the last five hundred years or so. This in spite of the fact that historians and social scientists have been interested in the family and household for earlier periods than this, especially in Europe in ancient and medieval times.[1]

Discussion was limited in another and perhaps even more important way. Attention was directed to *family* defined as the elementary society of man, wife, and children, and to *household* as the co-residing group, that is the elementary family with the addition of kinfolk, servants, lodgers, and attached persons of all kinds—if present. The family in its many other senses—and their variety is one of the obstacles to analysis—came into the discussion again and again; the family as a descent group, as all offspring of a marriage (dead or alive, resident or nonresident), the family as kin and affines of ego, and so on. But the first object was to relate these wider definitions to the co-resident, domestic group itself. Accordingly, linkages *between* whole households had to be left on one side. So also were relations between elementary families, or relationships of a familial kind between members of different families or households.[2]

The reason for this exclusiveness was not simply the overriding necessity of defining a particular part, and a crucial part, of the enormous area of possible discussion and speculation. It was to give historical and geographical perspective, crosscultural perspective indeed, to a particular conclusion which has been arrived at during the past few years by the Cambridge Group itself. This was the recognition that in England the conjugal or nuclear family had been the standard form for the co-residential domestic group over the whole period in question, that is from the late sixteenth century. Not only was the English family and household relatively small in preindustrial times, its structure was remarkably simple, except for one thing. Servants abounded, in town and countryside; men, women, boys, and girls who had left the parental household to live unmarried, as full members of the domestic, co-residential group of a master, an employer. Servants, and decidedly not residential kin, accounted for most of the difference in size and structure between households.

In view of the persisting prejudice in favor of supposing that the nuclear family was the product of industrialization, it was certainly interesting to know it had been the ordinary arrangement in the first country to be industrialized. This had been so for many generations and perhaps for many centuries before that elusive process began—

or before the English had begun to colonize North America. The Cambridge Group was eager to place this conclusion in its proper perspective.

All the evidence went to show that the extended household was uncommon, indeed quite rare, in the preindustrial England of this era. Some three-generational households existed, just about the same number as in the England of the 1960s, but neither vertical nor lateral extension was at all frequent. Parents did not live with their married children, nor bachelors or spinsters with their married brothers or sisters, all that much more often than they do today. Resident kin of all kinds other than offspring formed less than a twentieth of the population. Though they were commoner at the highest social levels, the composition of the households of the English aristocracy and gentry, insofar as they have been analyzed, does not seem to bear out the view that any form of the extended family existed as an ideal type among them. Such arrangements as the stem family, whereby one son stays behind to carry on the family undertaking, and if he marries brings his wife to live with the parents, is difficult to detect in the data. As far as I can see, this form of the co-residential domestic group, which has been much discussed by anthropologists and sociologists since the time of Le Play, was quite uncharacteristic of traditional England, at least after the Middle Ages.[3]

Did these things make England exceptional among the societies of the past? Could it be that it was because the English had always lived in this peculiarly individualistic, personally responsible fashion, where every marriage meant a new household, that England had been the first to adopt individualistic attitudes, capitalist organization and the industrial way of life?

In order to answer the questions raised by such surprising possibilities as these, it was essential to know how far England has been typical of Western society as a whole in her social structural history, and how far the development of the West had diverged from that of the rest of the world. Not much progress would be expected over such a vast field from an exchange confined to a few localities. Obviously the form of the domestic group in preindustrial England was not all that exceptional, since social anthropologists and sociologists have always recognized that the nuclear family is found in many societies, among the Eskimos, for example. They realize too that even in societies where other familial forms are dominant or common, the nuclear family is present in considerable quantity.

Nevertheless, in order to put English society into historical as well as comparative social perspective, we had to find out as much as we could about how much England differed from her closest continental neighbor, France, in these respects and how far these two differed from the nearest social structure characterized by the large-scale domestic group. This was believed to be that area of southeast Europe where the *zadruga* (which I shall discuss later) was dominant until the twentieth century—that is, Serbia, now part of Yugoslavia. It was even more important to be able to contrast these European societies with Japan, a society entirely removed from the European scene, but which has been the first non-European society to enter the industrial era.

As for the final comparison, we particularly wanted to discover what happened to family and household when they were shifted three thousand miles west to North America, into an arena of what proved to be immeasurable plenty and opportunity. Did this transference bring into being something more like the extended family among English speaking people not as an ideal institution but as an ordinary arrangement?

It must be said that this question will have to be answered with a decided negative. This in spite of the most interesting single fact reported to the meeting: that the eighteenth-century American colonial household had a mean size greater than that of England or of France, and was as large as if not larger than that reported either for Serbia (Belgrade) or for Japan at the same period. This new item of social knowledge arose almost incidentally from a discussion whose original occasion, as we have seen, was to illuminate a particular conclusion about a particular society in past time. It belonged in fact rather to the second and much more important purpose of the meeting, which was to do what was possible to establish a framework in evidence of this kind, limited as it is, for comparative familial sociology over time as well as from place to place. It will surprise no social scientist to learn that at the very outset this project raises more problems than it resolves. Intriguing, challenging, critical problems they turn out to be, too. It seems to be settled, for example, that the *size* of households is in any community not a good indicator of their *structure*. It does not follow from mean size of households being large, therefore, that their structure is complex (see *H.F.P.T.*, p. 54) and this has only been clearly recognized since the conference.

Even the English case, which had seemed straightforward enough, if a little surprising, was radically changed by the first paper written for this gathering. It transpires that mean size of household in England was almost unaffected by industrialization. At a figure of 4.75 or somewhat below, this ratio appears to have been fairly constant from the late sixteenth to the beginning of the twentieth century. Not only was mean household size unaltered by the changes in economic and social organization which went on over these years, it seems to have been resistant to demographic fluctuations as well. Even the distribution of households by size, a far more revealing measure than an average, appears not to have shifted in England until well after the middle of the nineteenth century. And to cap it all, a tendency has now been detected in the English data which may make it possible to prove the exact reverse of the conventional proposition about industrialization and the structure of the household. In those communities where we have so far been able to compare their composition in preindustrial times with their composition during the process of industrialization itself, it can be shown that households became *more,* not *less,* extended. The tendency is quite well documented, and indicates the point at which the English household was most complex was between 1850 and 1880, though even then the great majority of all households were simple in their structure (*H.F.P.T.,* p. 61 and Laslett's article in *Annales* of June 1972, where tables to illustrate this point are included).

So difficult are problems of data in this field that the paper which contained these conclusions about the constancy in household size, a paper which is already in print,[4] had to be based on only one hundred documents listing the inhabitants of English communities between the years 1574 and 1821. Other contributions to the discussion of the English family and household at Cambridge showed how, by the middle of the nineteenth century, some divergence from the figures for this earlier period is detectable, but on the whole surprisingly little apart from the increase in complexity.[5] The proportion of three-generational households seems to have begun to rise slightly from 6 percent or less, characteristic of the earlier period, and the proportion of servants to fall sharply from the formidable figure of some 13 percent of the whole population. There was an increase in the number of resident kin and of lodgers, though the number of children tended to stay the same, or even to fall. These tendencies appear to have been quite marked in the rapidly industrializing town of Preston, Lancashire, and it will be noticed that they also point rather in the direction of an increase in the complexity of the domestic group than otherwise.

The delegates from the distinguished French school of historical demography, who included Louis Henry,[6] the doyen of the whole activity, agreed that the belief in the extended family as the ordinary condition of the domestic order in Europe before industrialization was almost as much of a myth for France as it was for England. English estimates of proportions of resident children, kin, servants, etc., were apparently acceptable for France, where rather less has so far become known. But certain differences seem to have existed, and some of them may turn out to be important.

A well-known French social structural historian, Pierre Goubert, has recently committed himself to the view that a small minority of French households were extended in structure as late as the eighteenth century, and some of them were very large. He described these as survivals, and as confined to particular towns and regions.[7] A southern French village in 1644 was analyzed in meticulous detail for the meeting, and it showed more extended family characteristics than any we know in England, with a mean household size of 5.48.[8]

Nevertheless, the knowledge that we have so far does nothing to justify a view of pre-Revolutionary France which would place her in that immobile state of kin-dominated, extended family organization which seems sometimes to be associated with the condition which precedes the passing of traditional society. At the Cambridge Group, we have been able to examine the familial structure of two French communities in the late eighteenth century, and it is clear that the differences from the English counterparts are of minor order.[9] Perhaps Corsica in the 1770s is hardly regarded as French, but it might well be expected to have even more signs of traditional, extended family organization. Yet mean household size in Ajaccio in the year when Napoleon Bonaparte was born there was no higher than 4.3, and, with certain fascinating exceptions, familial organization seems to have been nuclear all over Corsica.[10]

The wild island in which Napoleon Bonaparte grew up did not, however, have the smallest mean household size yet known for western Europe at the time. That record belongs at present to an area of the province of Holland, the most advanced part of the United Netherlands, where in the eighteenth century mean household size was as low as 3.7 in the countryside and could be even lower in the towns.[11] This is a good fifth lower than in preindustrial England and two-fifths lower than in the United States in 1790. The structure of Dutch households was even simpler than in England in some of the provinces, and the proportion of resident kin less than half the tiny proportion found in the latter country. The fall in the number of servants and growth in the number of lodgers found in industrializing Lancashire in 1851 is already to be seen in Holland in the early eighteenth century, where the economy was innovative but certainly not industrial in the factory sense.

We turn to the contrast in these respects between the historical development of far western Europe with that of Serbia in far eastern Europe; there was less agreement than might have been expected among the experts, and the picture of a culture dominated by large-scale households continuous over time was not as clear as had been hoped. One authority doubted whether the *zadruga* was in fact a characteristic of the Serbian social system, since for her it was predominantly an Austrian legal institution. Though he was able to produce evidence to show that large and complex households were quite usual in Serbia in 1528, another authority insisted that the *zadruga* was a process, not a static institution, that very large households to be found at any time were all due to split up as their life cycle proceeded into smaller households, which might or might not themselves eventually become complex and extended.[12]

These differences of opinion, and the tendency for the *zadruga* to take on a somewhat mythical form to suit the *gemeinschaftliche* dogma of socialist beliefs, raised issues that came up again and again during these interchanges. Did the concept *household* have a constant meaning from country to country and culture to culture? Were numerical comparisons accordingly too simple-minded to be wholly significant? This especially in view of the cycle of the life in the domestic group, which must differ in size and structure from the time of the marriage of the couple which creates it, through the childbearing period, and so on to the stage when children leave and parents die.[13] It cannot be said that much progress was made with these problems, but there was no doubt that the Balkan familial structure illuminated that of the West by its vivid contrast. An expert on peasant organization in this region and elsewhere has shown that a village in Serbia in 1863 had a mean household size of 8.26 and nearly half of its population in households of ten persons and more.[14] There were 35 percent of multigenerational households and a complication of kinship relationships within the domestic groups entirely foreign to traditional England.

Perhaps even more interesting for comparison with England was the evidence from the city of Belgrade in 1733–1734, not only for the structure of households, many of which were wonderfully complex although mean size was well below six, but for the relative age of spouses. Husbands in Belgrade in the mid-eighteenth century were on average over ten years older than their wives. In England this age gap has never to our knowledge been on average more than four years, and some wives have always been older than their husbands, a circumstance apparently pretty well unknown in eastern Europe.[15] What is more, it was reported from the brilliant Renaissance city of Florence for the date 1427 that mean age at marriage was 32 to 33 years for males and that there was a gap between spouses of 14.5 to 15.5 years.

The remarkable communication which contained this information was derived from a fiscal document which can be made to yield evidence on household size and structure for a wide area around Florence at this time.[16] Although it might well be supposed that with girls of 16½ marrying men of 32 the extended family must have been common—for how could a child bride have been expected to keep house for a mature, active man—over 80 percent of all households in Florence were nuclear. In the Tuscan countryside over a third of the households were multiple in some way; yet, even there, mean households size seldom rose above 5. In the cities where most people lived it was not much bigger than in eighteenth-century Holland, at a figure varying between 3.5 and 4.4, with 3.9 in Florence itself. It ought perhaps to be added that the formidable problems of interpreting the document makes these figures minimal ones and that, as in England and everywhere else, the richer and more privileged the family, the larger the household.

This historical information from eastern and southern Europe does serve to bring out the peculiarities of the household in western Europe. It is made to seem relatively large, and the early American family enormous. But this does little toward understanding why in England industrialization had so little effect on size of household. The evidence from Japan did bear on that issue, however, in a very striking way.

Akira Hayami of the department of economics at Keio University in Tokyo presented the most ambitious paper to the conference, basing it on no less than 382 detailed census-type documents relating to the 38 communities making up one Japanese county and stretching from 1671 to 1870, that is, over the whole Tokugawa era.[17] It seems unlikely that any other country in the world will yield such an archive to the historical sociologist, and it must be remembered that Japan was innocent of what we think of as industrialization over the whole period.

Hayami found that the mean size of household declined steadily from 7.04 to 4.25; that the variance went down in an equally even and impressive fashion, until at the end there was rather less variation than in the English sample; that the more advanced the area within the county was economically, the smaller and less variable the mean size of household, and the sooner it reached the standard mean size and variance; that structural change was indeed from extended to nuclear, the decline in size being due to a large number of related variables, the most important a progressive fall in households with more than one married couple, together with the departure of both resident kin and of servants.

This arresting analysis shows that although, as in England, industrialization can apparently occur without much affecting size of household and its variance, considerable change can take place in the household size and structure within a society without strictly "economic" industrialization coming about. Indeed, it almost looks as if

Japan were preparing itself for eventual industrialization by bringing household size and even household structure into line with the English. To say this, of course, is to assume precisely what is here under criticism, that the nuclear family and industrialization are necessarily connected. But even a whole county may be an unreliable guide to the entire area of a country if only because it is a particular locality, and it has to be said that another Japanese contributor took a somewhat different view of the data and the problem. Speaking as an anthropologist, Miss Chie Nakane of Tokyo University asserted that the household had never been as big or as complex as Japanese historians believed. In this view Japanese development resembled that for England, where household size and structure have been standard and fairly constant, but with the difference that the custom of keeping the successor to the house at home after his marriage made the Japanese household somewhat larger.[18]

Behind this inconsistency may have stood one more difference over what constituted a household in the minds of the men of the past who produced the data. The same reservation has to be made in respect to the American evidence, though in many ways it is the most straightforward. Figures from the United States census show that the mean size of household was 6.61 persons in 1790, persons per household excluding slaves being 5.8. Though it progressively declined thereafter it did not fall to the traditional English standard of 4.75 until 1900.[19]

The presence of extended-kin relationships and several married couples within the large American household has not yet been demonstrated. Although it was asserted at the conference that they must have been there, and that these, along with high fertility, not the presence of servants, accounted for the size being larger than the European, subsequent research has failed entirely to confirm this suggestion. Those accustomed to European conditions find it difficult to believe that conventional servants (as distinct from slaves) can have been so scarce in colonial America as is often supposed.

But there seems no doubt that the household in the true, raw, frontier settlement was actually smaller than in the maturer communities, and that the effect of slavery was far-reaching indeed. In 1790 South Carolina had the smallest size of elementary family though it was huge by European standards at 5.42 persons apiece. But if all slaves had been resident with the families of their masters, mean household size in this state would have been 9.51, the largest in the colonies. In the Charleston district the figure reaches 25.85, 31.12, 47.95 in three of the parishes.

These groups cannot, of course, be taken as co-residential for comparative purposes. Interesting psychological consequences may follow from the fact that fertility seems to have been so high, groups of children so large, the average household so big and yet living room so cramped in early America.[20] In the state of Rhode Island, however, it seems clear that these conditions had gone for the most part by 1875, and extended family characteristics were few, though they were not all that much reduced between 1875 and 1950, which accords with the available English evidence.[21]

If the evidence for the size of the colonial American household cannot yet be matched with a great deal of reliable data on its structure, then there seems to be some prospect of showing from demographic data whether it was predominantly of the extended type. The proof will come, it is hoped, from the most promising, if at present only tentative, set of inquiries which were discussed at Cambridge. This was the project of modeling the family and household in mathematical terms, using as parameters both demographic and structural variables. Fertility, mortality, expectation of life, age at marriage, propensity to stay in the parental home after marriage, relative frequency of widows and eldest sons taking over the headship of the household after the death of the master are some of them. Most important seems to be age at the time of succession to headship of household, a statistic unfortunately not easily recoverable from historical data.

In the view presented by John Hajnal of the London School of Economics to the conference, even crude attempts at modeling the household in this way may imply that constancy in household size is to be expected over time, even rather long periods of time, rather than changes.[22] A point of the first importance is that both mortality and fertility have only a moderate effect on household size in all seemingly realistic models, but fertility is always more important than mortality. A demographer actually communicated figures for expected household size given various values for some of the parameters mentioned.[23] Nuclear or stem families appear to reach the dimensions found in colonial America only under high expectations of life, and with fertility on a prodigious scale.

Attempting to show how far the extended family existed as a substantial institution, then, has already led to a complicated and challenging discussion over many cultural areas and in many historical periods. An unexpected difficulty was one which came to be called the problem of the straw man, the tendency to set up a fallacy no one holds in order to demolish it. The anthropologists at Cambridge found the discussion somewhat puzzling and irrelevant from time to time because they were not conscious of ever having subscribed to any such statements about the extended family as were being so enthusiastically attacked.

It has indeed proved quite difficult to show who it is who has in his head the sentimental picture of grandfathers, aunts, and uncles sitting round the cottage fire with grandchildren, cousins, and second cousins all under the mastership of the patriarchal head of a biological family. Nevertheless, as William Goode has insisted, "the classical family of Western nostalgia" has affected attitudes to ourselves and our families today as well as attitudes to our past and that of other cultures in the world.[24] We have come across other vague and unformed but obstinate misbeliefs several times already during the life of the Cambridge Group, and have been requested to concede that nobody really believes in any such thing. We have been told, for example, that no one seriously supposed that all peasant girls used to marry in their teens, which they certainly did not do in England. Or that our peasant ancestors were for the most part entirely unaware of the means of controlling family size, which now seems certain not to have been the case. But whatever the truth of these things, the establishment of a comparative, empirical, historical sociology of the family is surely worth the manufacture and conflagration of one or two straw men.

Notes

This is a revision of an article which appeared in the *Journal of Social History,* Vol. IV, No. 1 (Fall 1970). Peter Laslett is a founding member with E. A. Wrigley of the Cambridge Group for the History of Population and Social Structure. The Cambridge interchange was made possible by a grant to the Cambridge Group from the Calouste Gulbenkian Foundation of Lisbon, London branch. Most of the papers, with some others, appear in a volume entitled *Household and Family in Past Time,* introduced and edited by Peter Laslett, with the assistance of Richard Wall, Cambridge University Press, 1972 (referred to here by the initials *H.F.P.T.*). The introduction to that volume contains a general analysis of the issues presented by the history of the co-resident domestic group, together with a system of classification and ideographic representation making possible fairly precise comparisons between period and period, and country and country. This system, with some extra tables, has already been published separately in France (*Annales, Economies, Societies Civilisations,* 27 Annee, 1972, June) and may well appear shortly both in Italian and in Spanish. The editor of *Annales,* Andre Bursiere, himself wrote an account of the conference. See "Le colloque de demographie historique de Cambridge, La famille 'reduite' une realite ancienne et planetaire" (*Annales:* 24 Annee, No. 6, pp. 1423–1426).

1   For recent discussion of what evidence there is, see *H.F.P.T.* and references, especially for Europe, the work of Mols, and for England, the work of J. C. Russell (e.g., *British Medieval Population,* Albuquerque, 1948).

2   It is essential to recognize that sets of relationships between separate co-residential domestic groups, or between individuals located in such groups, cannot

be analyzed by the examination of the dimensions and membership of the domestic co-residential groups themselves. Such relationships can only be tackled with the use of additional data which were discussed incidentally during the meeting now being reported. Research has since begun at Cambridge to recover the kin relations between families in preindustrial communities, but it looks as if it will have to be undertaken in select villages in France, perhaps in Italy and in Japan, and that firm results for England may never be forthcoming. The earliest outcome (March 1972) indicates that in a northern French parish in the late eighteenth century, density of kin relations was of the same order as that in an English working-class suburb in the 1950s.

3   The present state of the evidence seems to me to make the existence of the stem family somewhat problematic in England, even in the medieval period and earlier. Whatever may have been the position before the parish register era (mid-sixteenth century on) demographic data after that time failed to show signs of one son, whether oldest or youngest, delaying marriage until he succeeded to the family plot, and listings of inhabitants reveal no tendency for such a successor to bring his wife home to his parents' household to dwell with them until succession. Even arrangements for the retirement of parents to a particular room in the house or cottage on the tenement, which are common in wills, are hard to find in the sixteenth century and later when actual living patterns can be examined. These retirement arrangements seem to be the strongest support for the existence of this kind of familial pattern in the classic exposition of the peasant social structure in medieval England, that is George Homans, *English Villagers of the Thirteenth Century* (Harvard 1940). The impression left at this early stage of the investigation is that such sociological descriptions as Arensberg and Kimball, *Family and Community in Ireland* (Harvard, 1940) are less appropriate models for preindustrial peasant life than has been supposed heretofore. On the whole issue of the stem family, see Laslett's introduction to *H.F.P.T.*, section 3, *The Stem Family,* and especially the section *Le Play and the history of the domestic group.* The use of listings of inhabitants, the prime source of household structure in earlier times, is complicated by the domestic cycle, which is also discussed at length. But the tables appended to Laslett's introduction, and the others appearing in the article in *Annales* (1972,3) go to show that even allowing for the domestic cycle, stem family arrangements were only a common occurrence in the Japanese materials amongst all those examined at the Cambridge conference and since.

4   See Peter Laslett, "Size and Structure of the Household in England over Three Centuries, I. Mean Household Size in England since the 16th Century," *Population Studies* 23, no. 2 (July 1969), now chapter 4 of *H.F.P.T.* The reader should take note that the preceding two paragraphs, together with the later ones dealing with U.S. colonial evidence, have been considerably revised and extended since their original publication in 1970. It was stated in the earlier version that households in colonial America may have been more complex than those in Europe. In *H.F.P.T.* it is shown however, that the colonial household, in spite of its huge size, was exceedingly simple in composition, perhaps the simplest yet known to sociological history. Richard Wall, of the Cambridge Group, contributed to the conference a study of literary references to household size in England over the same period, which bore out the evidence of listings of inhabitants (*H.F.P.T.* chapter 5).

5   Contributions to the conference of Michael Anderson (Dept. of Sociology, University of Edinburgh), *Household Structure and the Industrial Revolution: Preston in Comparative Perspective, H.F.P.T.* chapter 7; Alan Armstrong (Dept. of History, Uni-

versity of Kent at Canterbury), *A Note on the Household Structure of Mid-Nineteenth Century York in Comparative Perspective, H.F.P.T.* chapter 8; Carol Pearce (Centre for Research in Social Sciences, University of Kent at Canterbury), *Ashford, Kent, 1840–70: A Socio-Demographic Study.*

6 Louis Henry of L'Institut National d'Etudes Demographiques in Paris (INED) was the perfecter of the technique of recovering vital statistics from the parish registers known as family reconstitution, whose importance to the demographical and social structural history is made plain in E. A. Wrigley, *Population in History* (World University Library. U.S. ed.; New York: McGraw Hill, 1969). Henry sets out the French methods of analyzing family and household structure in his *Manuel de Demographie Historique* (Paris: Droz, 1967). But in France the history of the domestic group, as distinct from demographic history, has not been much studied until very recently.

7 See Pierre Goubert, "La famille francaise au XVIIIe siecle" in *Saggi di demografia storica*, ed. M. Livi Bacci (Florence, 1969; Dept. of Statistics, University of Florence, Serie Ricerche Empiriche, No. 2), being the transcript of a lecture given in 1968. Unfortunately this distinguished French scholar, whose famous monograph *Beauvais et les Beauvaisis* (Paris, 1960) is an early landmark in the historical study of social structure, could not be present at Cambridge. His article contains no references, and subsequent inquiries in France and in Italy have so far (Feb. 1960) failed to provide any, or any clear confirmation, of the location and exact constitution of these patriarchal households.

8 Contributions to the conference of Jean-Noel Biraben (INED), *The Inhabitants of Montplaisant in 1644 (H.F.P.T.* chapters 8 and 9). The footnote on page 15 draws attention to the difficulty of being quite confident that the Montplaisant document actually represented the structure of households there in 1644.

9 Work in progress for the Cambridge Group, reported on by Valerie Smith at this conference, shows that the domestic group in which the French peasantry lived their lives was closely similar in size and structure to that in England, at least in the Pas-de-Calais and in the late eighteenth century. The data consist of successive listings of inhabitants giving annual descriptions of every household and person for twelve successive years in each of two villages in the 1760s to 1780s; see Peter Laslett's note in *Annales de demographie historique, 1968* (Paris: Sirey, 1968). There are the documents now being analyzed by M. Emmanuel Todd at Cambridge to determine kinship networks. Social structural statistics from one of the listings are included in the tables of *H.F.P.T.*

10 Contribution to the conference of Jacques Dupaquier and Louis Jadin of L'Ecole Pratique des Hautes Etudes, 6me Section, Paris (EPHE), Centre de Recherche Historique (*H.F.P.T.*, chapter 11).

11 Contribution to the conference of A. M. van der Woude, of the University of Wageningen in Holland, *H.F.P.T.*, chapter 12. Size and structure varied in this heterogeneous urban and rural economy in the seventeenth and eighteenth centuries, but households were uniformly smaller than in England at the time and even simpler in their composition.

12 Mrs. Lorraine Baric, of the Dept. of Sociology, University of Salford, England, who has written on Anglo-Saxon kinship as well as Serbian familial and social structure; Eugene Hammel of the Dept. of Anthropology, University of California,

Berkeley. His contribution on the document of 1528 (*H.F.P.T.*, chapter 14), analyzed in a remarkably attractive and versatile way, has since been extended into a more general review of the importance of the large-scale household over the last four centuries.

13   Contribution to the conference of Jack Goody, of the Dept. of Anthropology, Cambridge University, supported by other members of the department, Meyer Fortes and Edmund Leach. See Jack Goody, ed., *The Developmental Cycle in Domestic Groups,* Cambridge Papers in Social Anthropology No. 1 (1958).

14   Report to the conference of Joel Halpern, of the Dept. of Anthropology, University of Massachusetts. Figures from this settlement are held at the Cambridge Group and will appear in *Orasac, a Village in Serbia,* Case Studies in Cultural Anthropology Series (New York: Holt, Rinehart). Chapter 16 of *H.F.P.T.* is a numerical comparison for some social structural variables of Orasac with other villages in the same area at the same date.

15   Contribution to the conference of Peter Laslett and Marilyn Clarke of the Cambridge Group, *H.F.P.T.*, chapter 15, being a series of tables of familial and social structure examining from various viewpoints a census-type document which provides quite exceptional detail.

16   Contribution to the conference of Christiane Klapisch of the EPHE, Paris (*H.F.P.T.*, chapter 16). This must be compared with the work in print of David Herlihy, of the Dept. of History, University of Wisconsin, with whom Mme. Klapisch is working on this document, e.g., "Vieillir a Florence au Quattrocento," *Annales, E.S.C.*, 1969. Herlihy has recently shown that the "stem family" characteristics which Kalpisch discusses as characterizing these households can be related to the much more definite symptoms of that family form described by Lutz Berkner in "The stem family and the development of the domestic cycle in the peasant household," *American Historical Review,* April 1972.

17   Paper composed with Noboku Uchida, *H.F.P.T.*, chapter 18. Compare Akira Hayami, "Aspects demographiques d'un village Japonais," *Annales, E.S.C.*, 1969.

18   This contribution should be compared with her recent book *Kinship and Economic Organisation in Rural Japan* (London, 1967). Subsequent analysis at Cambridge of a listing of a Japanese community (Nishinomiya Issaicho in 1713, see the tables in *H.F.P.T.*) and others supplied by both Nakane and Hayami goes to show that the degree of complication in their structure was of a higher order from what is found in Europe, even when the household size was small.

19   Contribution to the conference of Philip Greven of the Dept. of History, Rutgers University, N.J., *H.F.P.T.*, chapter 20.

20   Contribution of John Demos, of the Dept. of History, Brandeis University (*H.F.P.T.*, chapter 21). Compare his book *A Little Commonwealth: Family Life in Plymouth Colony* (New York, 1970). There was one other contribution of a psychological character from Philippe Aries of France, suggesting from funeral inscriptions and wills that the attitude to the family had changed fundamentally in the early eighteenth century. This was published in *New Society* (London) in Oct. 1969.

21   Contribution to the conference (*H.F.P.T.*, chapter 22) of Edward Pryor, of the Dept. of Sociology, University of Ontario, London, Canada.

22   Communication not committed to paper. Repeated reference was made at the conference, however, to Hajnal's article "European Marriage Patterns in Perspective," Glass and Eversley, Eds., *Population in History* (London, 1965). The thesis here is that the lower age of marriage and lower proportion of celibates in southern and eastern Europe would as late as the 1900s be accompanied by a greater tendency toward extended households than in northern and western Europe.

23   Contribution to the conference of Thomas Burch, of the Population Council, since published in *Demography,* Vol. 7, Feb. 1970, (*H.F.P.T.*, chapter 2). Since 1969 Professor Hammel of Berkeley has initiated a research project on the computer simulation of populations over time, taking account both of demographic and social structural variables. The Cambridge Group is collaborating in this enterprise, which is of obvious significance to the subject matter of the present article.

24   Professor Goode of the Department of Sociology, Columbia University, developed these and other points for the conference with considerable force. It is certainly clear that not all historians can plead guiltless to having expressed in print their assumption that the extended family is a common characteristic in the European past. Perhaps the most straightforward expression of this misbelief is to be found in the introduction of Peter Laslett, ed., *Patriarcha and Other Political Works of Sir Robert Filmer* (Oxford: Blackwell, 1949).

This is, in virtually every respect, a model piece of research. It presents new and important findings and relates them to fundamental issues in the existing literature. Berkner maintains that part of the reason why Laslett and other members of the Cambridge group did not find three-generation stem families more prevalent in preindustrial England was that they did not take a family life-cycle approach. Since peasant families tend to be extended only during the period when the father has retired and a son marries and takes over the farm, we cannot get an accurate reading of how common this form was unless we follow families through the various phases of their life cycle. Berkner also makes another important point by suggesting that in England the number of landholding families may have already begun to decline by the end of the seventeenth century independently of industrialization, and this would have had a depressing effect on the number of stem families present in agricultural communities even if a life cycle were considered. This article very clearly conveys just how difficult it is to sort out the pieces of data that will ultimately give us a coherent picture of preindustrial family life.

LUTZ K. BERKNER

2 The Stem Family and the Developmental Cycle of the Peasant Household: An 18th-Century Austrian Example

There has been a widely held sociological theory that the nuclear family structure is linked to the development of modern Western society.[1] By "nuclear" is meant a man, his wife, and their unmarried children, if any; this becomes "extended" if their household also includes children or some other kin. It is commonly thought that kinship ties were stronger in the past, but it has never been very clear exactly from what previous form the modern nuclear family has emerged. This is hardly the fault of sociologists, who until recently could turn to virtually no historical family studies that would meet the standards of modern scholarship.[2] Only in the last few years have we seen an increase in the number of serious works on the family by historians, and we now have some excellent regional monographs[3] and one general survey, Peter Laslett's *The World We Have Lost*.[4] From his statistical studies of early censuses, Laslett has concluded that in England the nuclear family has always predominated and that there is so little evidence of extended or stem families in the past that theories claiming a shift to a nuclear pattern in modern times cannot be empirically validated.[5] Before we accept this revision as true for Western Europe as a whole, I would like to add two notes of caution: first, that the stem family did and does exist as an important part of the social structure in many parts of rural Western Europe,[6] and second, that the stem family structure does not necessarily emerge from empirical studies of demographic statistics unless the developmental cycle of the family and household are taken into consideration in the analysis. This will be illustrated by an examination of the eighteenth-century peasant stem family in the Waldviertel, a region of Lower Austria bordering on Bohemia and Moravia.

The term stem family was coined by the sociologist Frédéric Le Play to describe a specific type of extended family organization in

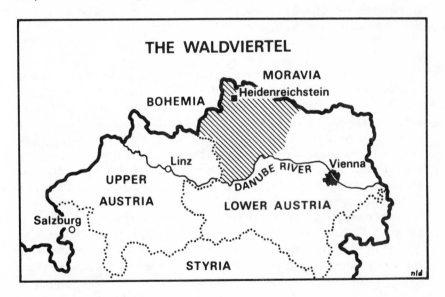

which only one child marries while remaining at home to inherit the family property and the other children either leave to establish their own families elsewhere or stay in the household as celibates.[7] Although Le Play assumed that the father would either maintain or share the ownership of the family farm until he died, he could also transfer the property to the heir and retire. In Austria it was retirement that formed the cornerstone of the stem family organization.

In 1763 the manor of Heidenreichstein in the Waldviertel took a census of households in its thirty-six villages.[8] Heidenreichstein was a small market town of ninety houses and a manorial castle, surrounded by a scattering of very small peasant villages that rarely contained more than thirty houses. This was an area of concentrated nuclear villages and open fields, although at the end of the seventeenth century some new scattered settlements appeared. Although 729 households belonged to the manor, we will only be concerned with the 651 (90 percent) "peasant" households. By "peasant" (Bauer) we mean the property-holding head of a farming household who was regarded as "neighbor" (Nachbar) in the community, a person who enjoyed political rights in the village and economic privileges in the common lands and forests.[9] This excludes servants and lodgers, who, as we shall see, were considered part of the peasant's household, as well as 51 households of landless laborers living in "common houses" owned by the village and 27 households of persons who were not directly involved in peasant farming.

Based on an analysis of the peasant households enumerated in this census, what follows will examine first the life cycle of an individual peasant householder, then the extended family, and finally the composition of the entire household of peasants, servants, and lodgers.

There were three major stages in the life cycle of the peasant householder: son and heir, head of the household (Hausvater), and retired parent (Ausnehmer). According to the land laws, the peasant holding (behaustes Gut) was impartible, but the inheritance customs in Lower Austria insured equal division of family property among all the children. Only one of them, the heir chosen by the parents, actually received the house and the land while the other children were compensated in money payments. Since the holding was usually held as common property by the man and his wife, when one of them died the other retained half of the property and the children divided the value of the other half, which they held as legal claims on the farm. The heir became a householder by making a settlement with the surviving parent and assuming the debts caused by his brothers' and sisters' claims.[10]

Often an elderly peasant couple would sell the farm to the heir and go into retirement *(ins Ausnahm gehen)*. In some areas of Austria there was a special little house set aside for the retired parents; in the Waldviertel a room *(Stübl)* was generally built onto the house.[11] A legal contract of sale effected the transfer between parents and heir. The amount to be paid was usually staggered to ease the burden of payment and to provide an annual income for the retired parents. The contract was full of specific rights and privileges reserved for the parents as long as they lived. These included the right to live in a room rent-free, the use of certain pieces of land, and the provision of specified amounts of grain, fodder, and wood every year.[12]

When, for example, Joseph and Anna Maria Pichler decided to retire in October 1784 they drew up a contract with their son Johann and his bride Gertraud, selling them their house and fields for 100 florins. Joseph deducted 20 florins from the price as a wedding gift to his son and asked that the rest be paid in installments of 20 florins every *Michaeli* (September 29). As a retirement settlement *(Ausnahm)* they reserved the right to live in the *Stübl* rent-free for the rest of their lives, the use of a small piece of meadow and a section of the garden to grow cabbage and potatoes, and a yearly supply of seven bushels of wheat, thirty-two batches of hay, and two piles of wood.[13]

Why should a father make such specific demands and insist on their being put into a legal contract when he was dealing with his own son? As an *Ausnehmer,* the parent relinquished all legal authority over his farm. The reservations in the contract were all he had left of his former possessions. And the only guarantees he had to these rights and to the payments due him were the good will of his son and a legal contract with very specific details in it. The fact that the peasants invariably chose to include the details of their rights in the contract suggests a common-sense awareness of the frailty of such agreements without any legal guarantees. The classic literary illustration for this concern is Emile Zola's *La Terre,* in which a peasant partitions his lands among his sons, expecting them to support him in his old age. One after another the children fail to live up to the agreement, refuse to make their payments to the father, and ignore the wishes of the man who has lost his authority and is now at the economic and physical mercy of his ungrateful children.

There must have been severe psychological strains within the peasant family after the change of ownership. The very existence of separate living quarters, the *Stübl*, is an indication of the conscious awareness of the tension that was bound to develop between the old parents, stripped of the economic power and the authority that they had always had over their children, and the young couple, exercising their independence for the first time.[14] The retiring peasants in the Waldviertel had no illusions about the tranquility of future relations with their children. When Michel and Maria Redl in Taures retired in 1779 they reserved the usual right to free lodging within the house they were selling to their son and his wife, but in the contract it was noted that "if they cannot agree with one another, then they would build a separate room onto the house."[15] A similar phrase, or a clause stipulating that if the parents could no longer live in the house the son would pay for their rent elsewhere, was often written into the contracts.[16]

Eighteenth-century family relationships among the Waldviertel peasants were probably no different from those described by a local folklorist in 1926:

> Although people say "Respect your Elders," when the parents go into retirement they are often not treated the way they should be. The fault usually lies on both sides. The "Old Ones" often don't like the daughter-in-law or the way the young ones run the farm. The "Young Ones" in return don't always quietly accept the grumblings of the "Old Ones" and once a strained relationship has developed, it usually cannot be overcome. The young ones who take over the farm with debts on it also find the retirement settlement very burdensome, for they must still "pay off" their parents and siblings. The old ones are not very considerate in their demands. Although they help out with the work, the need to hire servants adds another financial burden. From all of this we see that the young peasant "ain't got nothin' to laugh about."[17]

If retirement really meant so much trouble, why was it such a common practice? As the peasant got older and his physical capabilities declined, the option of exchanging the drudgery of hard farm labor for a small fixed income undoubtedly looked increasingly more desirable. At the same time he was feeling rising pressures from his son the heir who was becoming old enough to marry and head the household and who wanted to start doing things right for a change. Since the heir had no source of income he could not get married without the parents' permission, which was ordinarily not granted while the father remained head of the household. The sons therefore either waited for the father's retirement or left home to establish their own households. This conflict is expressed in some folksongs that were sung in the Waldviertel at the beginning of this century.

> Voda, wann gibst ma denn's Hoamatl
> Voda, wann loszt ma's vaschreibn?
> s'Dirndl is gwoxn wia's Groamatl,
> Lede wülls a nimmer bleibn.

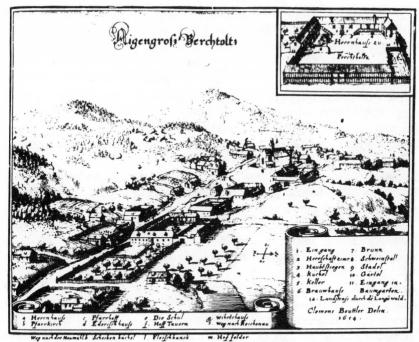

A seventeenth-century sketch of Gross Pertholz, a village in the northwestern Waldviertel near the Upper Austrian border. The quadrangular farmhouses situated in a line along both sides of a single street are typical for the whole region. The large farmhouse detailed in the insert, with its own brewery and somewhat pretentious formal garden, is the seat of a petty manor with rights over seven peasant holdings in the village. From Caspar Merian, *Topographia Windhagiana* (Frankfurt a.M., 1656), pt. 2 between pages 2 and 3, which is bound as "Anhang III" in Mathaeus Merian, *Topographia Provinciarum Austriacarum* (Frankfurt a.M., 1649; reprint Kassel, 1963).

[Father, when ya gonna gimme the farm,
Father, when ya gonna sign it away?
My girl's been growin' every day,
And single no longer wants to stay.]

Voda, wann gibst ma denn's Hoamatl,
Voda, wann gibst ma denn's Haus,
Wann gehst denn amol in dein Stüberl ein,
Und grobst da bra Eräpfoln aus?

[Father, when ya gonna gimme the farm,
Father, when ya gonna gimme the house,
When ya gonna retire to your room out of the way,
And dig up your potatoes all day?][18]

If a peasant normally married around age 25 and a son who would live to adulthood was born within the next three years, this son would be ready to marry and take over the farm when his father was in his late fifties, and the farm would change hands every thirty years or so with a minimum of domestic friction. This seems in fact to have been the usual pattern.[19] But many householders died before a son was old enough to marry, and then the widow would either run the farm by herself or remarry. Given the high mortality of the century, remarriage must have been rather common, since married couples headed 96 percent of the 651 households. The rest were headed by 19 widows, 5 widowers, and 2 young unmarried men. While there were still young children in the family, both widows and widowers were likely to remarry. But when there was a son old enough to take over the farm, a widow would probably choose to retire whereas a widower would probably remarry.[20]

Simon Riener retired in 1768, when he was 55 years old, after having worked his farm in the village of Eberweis for thirty-three years. Both of his daughters had already married and his son, Johann, who was only 20, had just picked a bride. Simon's farm was worth 200 florins when he owned it; three years after he transferred it to his son, Simon died with only 10 florins to his name. Sebastian Böhmmesser, who lived across the street, died when his son Leopold had already turned 19. But instead of letting him take over, the widow Maria Böhmmesserin kept title to the farm for six years. When Leopold married at age 25, she sold him the farm for only 40 florins, although it was worth 200. Matthias Küpfel, a few houses away, was not so lucky. His father held onto the farm until he was 65, and Matthias did not marry until he was in his late thirties.[21]

In fact only half of the peasants over the age of 58 recorded in the 1763 Heidenreichstein census had retired; half of them were still active heads of households. Three-quarters of these (46 out of 61) either had no sons or only had sons under 25 living in the household, so the pressure to retire had not yet reached its peak. Although the majority of older peasants conformed to the normal pattern of giving up the farm by the time the heir was 25, seven peasant householders lived with a married son or daughter who had not yet taken over ownership of the farm. These men, as well as the eight peasants who were living with unmarried sons between 30 and 40, were no doubt feeling strong pressure to retire.

We are rather far from the romantics' picture of the happy extended family of father and married son, working side by side and sharing a common income. When the son married, the father usually relinquished control of the farm. At its transfer he retired and worked only the garden plots he had reserved for himself. The son managed the farm alone but furnished a specific amount of goods and money to his parents every year, not necessarily out of devotion but because he had contracted to do so. They lived in the same house, but usually in separate quarters. And if there were no separate accommodations, the agreement often provided for building them if and when the family could no longer live together in harmony.

Families go through developmental cycles as the individuals who compose them go through their life cycles. A census taken at a given point in time takes a cross-section and gives a static picture of households and families that the historian or sociologist can sort out into types. We can count so many extended families, so many nuclear. But rather than being types these may simply be phases in the developmental cycle of a single family organization. There may be a normal series of stages that appear only rarely in a population because they last for only a short period of the family's cycle or in some cases do not appear at all. From this point of view, the extended family is merely a phase through which most families go.[22] Since there is a good chance that the parents will still be alive, when a young couple marries, they begin their marriage in an extended family. In time the parents die, and the now middle-aged couple spend their years in a nuclear family. When one of their sons marries and brings his wife into the household the family becomes extended again. And so forth. When a census reveals a low frequency of stem families it is tempting to conclude that stem families are rarely found in the society at any period in time. But it is just as possible to conclude that most families simply happen to be in the nuclear phase at the particular time the census is taken. In fact modern demographic studies have shown that the nuclear phase predominates in most societies, and this is the reason why the extended family household is seldom found as the modal or average type in any population.[23]

In this Waldviertel census of 1763 only 25 per cent of all peasant households included any kin and could be considered extended. But if we examine the type of family while controlling for the age of the head of household,[24] the extended family emerges as a normal phase in the developmental cycle of the peasant household (see table 1). In the households headed by a man between 18 and 27, 60 per cent are extended families, in those headed by men 28 to 37, 45 per cent are extended. Then the percentage of families with retired parents or celibate siblings drops sharply, and the percentage of those with married sons starts to rise, reaching 12 per cent in the final age group. In short, when the head of the household was under 40, in the years when we would expect to find his parents still alive and his brothers and sisters too young to leave home, half of the families were extended. In those households headed by men over 58 a small propor-

TABLE 1. TYPE OF PEASANT FAMILY BY AGE OF MALE HEAD OF HOUSEHOLD

Type of Family	Age of Male Head of Household					
	18–27	28–37	38–47	48–57	58–90	Total
Extended: Parents or	60%	45%	19%	5%	3%	
Unmarried Siblings	(26)	(78)	(39)	(7)	(2)	152
Extended: Married Child	0%	0%	1%	4%	12%	
	(0)	(0)	(2)	(5)	(7)	14
Nuclear	40%	55%	80%	91%	85%	
	(17)	(94)	(168)	(121)	(52)	452
Total	43	172	209	133	61	618

tion lived with a married child. But as none of these married sons or daughters had children who were more than two years old, the status of "married son" probably lasted only a few years before the parents retired. Hence the heir would be placed in a younger age category as a householder whose parents lived with him.

The composition of the extended group itself goes through a cycle: the elderly couple may retire and turn over the farm to the eldest son while another child is still living at home. If the census is taken at that point in time, we find a complete stem family. Two years later the child may have left home and the retired father may have died, leaving only a widow. The evidence for the presence of a stem family has vanished, but the stem family organization remains nevertheless. Although from the developmental point of view there can be no such thing as a "true" percentage of stem families in any population, we can gauge the importance of the stem family organization by examining the composition of the extended family groups (see table 2). If there is a large proportion of married children, retired couples, or widowers, there is strong evidence of a stem family structure. In this Austrian case they represent over half of the extended families and thirteen per cent of all households. The presence of a widow or unmarried elderly siblings is ambiguous by itself, but given the strong evidence of the stem family from the census and legal sources it is very likely that they represent the end of the life cycle of a stem family group.

The significance of the total percentage of stem families is further increased if we consider the effects of the high mortality prevailing everywhere in eighteenth-century Europe. The only sure empirical evidence of a stem family is the presence of an elderly couple living in the same household with one married child and his family. But considering the low life expectancy of the period this is an unrealisti-

Extended Group	Number	% of Extended	% of Total Population
Married Child	14	8%	2%
Retired Couple	57	35	9
Retired Widower	17	10	2
Retired Widow	59	36	9
Unmarried Sibling	19	11	3
Total	166	100%	25%

cally stringent criterion. Certainly few children would have had living grandparents. In fact two theoretical calculations of family composition under preindustrial demographic conditions estimate respectively that only 27 or 29 per cent of the families could contain three generations.[25] In this light the proportion of stem families found in this Austrian census seems quite high.

There are not only demographic limitations to the formation of stem families, but also economic limitations, for they can exist only on farms that produce enough income to support three generations. On the large farm the peasant could make a comfortable retirement arrangement with his oldest son and could afford to retire early, so the rich farms were the most likely to include retired parents and also to be owned by very young householders. Of the small number of men who already headed a household before age 28, over half (9 out of 17) owned farms paying the highest taxes. It is not surprising, therefore, to find that there is a distinct difference between the family structure of the rich and the poor: 15 percent of the poorer as opposed to 34 to 42 percent of the richer farms showed evidence of a stem family organization (see table 3).

TABLE 3. TYPE OF PEASANT FAMILY BY VALUE OF FARM PROPERTY

Type of Family	Value of Farm Property (in florins)[a]				
	1–49	50–149	150–249	250–349	350+
Extended	15%	15%	34%	35%	42%
Nuclear	85%	85%	66%	65%	58%
Number of Cases	56	27	53	34	36

[a] Figures for property value are found in NOLA, Theresianische Fassion 870 (Heidenreichstein). This land survey of 1752 was used as the basis of tax assessments for the rest of the century. The value of the family's property has been determined for Heidenreichstein and seven villages, or about one-third of the peasant households in the census.

The Stem Family and the Peasant Household

If the family owns no land at all the extended family will rarely be found: relatives were living with only 2 out of 109 lodger families and with one out of the 51 families of landless laborers who lived in village-owned houses. This tends to support the view that the small nuclear family has always been more common among the poor and the landless classes as their only practical means of existence.[26] Hence the presence of a stem family in any particular household depends both upon the age of the head of the household and the size or value of the farm. The older the householder the less likely that his parents will still be alive; the smaller the farm the less likely that it can support a stem family at all.

Laslett's argument denying the existence of the stem family in England is based largely on aggregate demographic statistics. He finds that only 10 percent of households in one hundred English parishes in his sample were extended families, and he concludes that "the stem family is scarcely in evidence at all."[27] I have tried to show that aggregate census data indicates only the proportion of stem families in the extended phase at a given time, but that the significance of this proportion cannot be evaluated without taking into account the age structure of the population and the distribution of wealth.

On the one hand, Laslett's figures on household composition have not been broken down into age-specific categories although family structure is closely linked to the age of the head of household or some other indicator of the family life cycle. On the other hand, while the literature on stem families has always assumed its link to specific social strata, in particular the landed peasantry, only half of Laslett's sample is made up of agricultural households, and many of these would not fit the category of landed peasants. Since the sample is so heavily weighted against the peasantry, it is not surprising that the proportion of stem families is so low. Laslett's own figures show that laborers are less likely to live in extended families than yeomen (8 percent as compared with 17 percent) and Tranter's excellent study of cottager families in Cardington also found only 8 percent living with relatives.[28] A community with few peasants composed instead of cottagers, agricultural laborers, and other poor classes, is not likely to have a stem family organization, because poverty makes it difficult to form such families. Drake's figures for three villages in Norway in 1801 underline the point: the households of peasant farmers had 26, 34, and 49 percent extended families compared to 6, 12, and 14 percent for crofters.[29]

England was, of course, the first European country to experience a substantial decline in its peasant population, and the process took place during the same period as Laslett's censuses, from the sixteenth to the nineteenth centuries.[30] Recent studies have shown that during this same period the village population in many parts of Germany shifted from a majority of landed peasants to a majority of cottagers. The absolute number of peasants remained stable but declined as a proportion of the whole population as the number of cottagers and gardeners multiplied.[31] A particularly dramatic case was Saxony, where the percentage of cottagers in the population increased sixfold from 5 percent in 1550 to 30 percent in 1750, while the proportion of peasants was cut in half, falling from 50 to 25 percent.[32] Given the strong relationship between wealth and family structure one would expect to find a shift in family organization parallel to these changes in society. Specifically, the proportion of stem families in the population should have declined as the proportion of peasants decreased.

So it may be that there was indeed a transition from stem to nuclear families in parts of Western Europe, but not in the sense that the classes who lived in stem families ceased to do so. It is more likely that the absolute number of landed peasants—with whom stem families are associated most strongly—has remained stable or declined, while the size of the landless and poor classes has dramatically increased. Hence the "emergence of the nuclear family" may represent the increase in the proportion of those social classes that have not at any time been associated with a stem family organization. Gregory King's estimates for 1688 already indicate that less than one quarter of the families of England were freeholders or farmers. Far from showing that peasant stem families were never prevalent in the past, Laslett's statistics may simply confirm that the shift from a peasant society had already occurred in England by the end of the seventeenth century.[33]

Although they are often identical in fact, the family and the household must be analyzed separately since the household can also include nonfamily members. On the manor of Heidenreichstein in 1763 servants and lodgers were found in nearly half (46 percent) of all the peasant households, and their presence can also be explained in terms of the developmental cycle. A servant (Knecht or Dirn) was someone employed by the family in whose house he dwelt, sharing their food and shelter as part of his wages. A lodger (Inwohner) was also a resident, but was not usually a steady employee of the householder and had to pay for his lodging. Lodgers were ordinarily landless laborers, working somewhere in the community, but might at times be hired by the families with which they lived. Servants and lodgers are not always easy to tell apart. The servant was an addition to the labor supply of a particular household; the lodger was a potential supplement to the labor supply of all households in the commu-

The Stem Family and the Peasant Household   *45*

nity.[34] Servants were found in about one-third of the households (31 percent), lodgers in one-fifth (19 percent), and 5 percent of the households had both.

Less than 10 percent of servants were over thirty and there were only two cases of a married *Knecht*. But 95 percent of the people listed as lodgers were over thirty and 75 percent lived with a child or a spouse. At first it would seem that we are talking about the same people at different stages in their life cycle: a lodger was an older servant who had married. Why bother with the distinction? In the first place, we will show that the presence of servants in a household was determined by different conditions than was the presence of lodgers, and, second, servants were not really a social class.

Servants should not be viewed as a distinct social class, but as young persons engaged in certain economic functions in another person's household for a limited period of time. They could be either children of lodgers or of landed peasants, and this was what determined a servant's social class.[35] For children of peasants, especially girls and nonheirs, a few years as a servant *(in Dienst)* was a normal part of growing up. If there were more children than were necessary to work the farm, some of them would be sent off to work elsewhere until they had earned sufficient money to marry or until they received their inheritance portion.[36] For children of lodgers the years spent as servants began earlier, and many of them remained servants or day laborers for the rest of their lives.[37]

The legal definition of the household was very precise in Austria: it meant all people living in the same house under the authority of the head of the household, whether or not they were members of the family. Moreover, as Otto Brunner has pointed out in his marvelous essay on the concept of the household in European history, the word family was not commonly used in German until the eighteenth century—before that people spoke of belonging to a house or a household.[38] The *Universal Lexikon* (1735), for example, defined the family as "a number of persons subject to the power and authority of the head of household either by nature or by law"[39]—"nature" referred to children, "law" to wife and servants. The idea that the entire household and not only the nuclear family group was the real basis of the peasant family organization was championed in the mid-nineteenth century by the German sociologist Wilhelm Riehl, who, like Le Play, idealized the big happy peasant family. Riehl described the social unit that he felt was rapidly disappearing in the modern world as the entire household [*das ganze Haus*], which since ancient times includes not only the natural members of the family, but also all those voluntary members and workers called *Ingesinde* [servants]. In *das ganze Haus* the blessing of the family is extended to whole groups of people otherwise without families; they are drawn, as if by adoption, into the moral relationship of authority and piety.[40]

In the peasant household servants were not simply employees, they were part of the family. Even at the beginning of this century a local folklorist of the Waldviertel noted that servants were counted as part of the family and usually ate with the family out of the same pot.[41] For Riehl this was a crucial fact, for

in many peasant villages a single circumstance—whether or not the entire household, including the servants, eat at the same table—is sufficient to settle whether the relation of master and servant has become a purely legal affair or whether it is still somewhat patriarchal; whether old customs have disappeared entirely or whether they have been maintained and developed.[42]

We have no way of knowing what the normal relationship between servants and masters was in the eighteenth century, but there is considerable evidence that it has never been as harmonious as romantics like Riehl would have us believe.[43] Certainly the oral agreement to work for a peasant was more than morally binding, for it was considered a legal contract and usually ran for only one year at a time. The local village laws were full of restrictions and regulations concerning servants. They could not leave before one full year was up, nor could they be dismissed without good reason. A common regulation prevented peasants from stealing servants from one another by offering higher wages. The lack of trustworthiness credited to servants is indicated by the laws that forbade the purchase of anything from a servant until the buyer checked with the master to see that it was not stolen.[44]

Some of the personal antagonisms of the peasant-servant relationship are expressed in the "Knechtslied," a widespread Austrian folksong first written down in the early nineteenth century. The first part of the song lists the peasant's complaints: servants are too expensive, never work hard enough for their pay, and spend their time chasing after girls and the peasants' own wives. In the Waldviertel only the second part of the song, in which the servant answers, was common.[45]

Harr narischa Baua	You stupid old peasant,
Was fallt da denn ein	Your mind is half gone.

| Und wann dir die Knecht ztheua san | If a servant's too costly, |
| So stellst du Koan ein. | Then don't take one on. |

Baua du hast es	Peasant, don't you have
Nöt guat in dein Lei?	A rich enough life?
Wann ma aussi in d'Arbeit gehn,	While I go out to work,
Bleibst bei dein Wei.	You stay home with your wife.

Und wann i in's Gasseln geh,	And when I go courting,
Eiferst du glei,	Your jealousy's rife,
Und i geh zu mein Diarndl	But I go to my sweetheart
Und nöt zu dein Wei.	And not to your wife.

Landless persons had a difficult time living in a society whose membership was defined in terms of landownership. They were not allowed to marry or settle in a village without community approval. When they lost positions they often had little recourse other than begging until they found other jobs. In fact the authorities saw little difference between vagabonds and unemployed servants, and the poor laws of the eighteenth century were mostly concerned with rounding up the "roaming beggars and other riffraff without masters" in order to send them back to the village of their birth.[46] Old Johann Hechenberber, for example, had worked for 60 years in villages near Heidenreichstein, as a servant for 19 years in the town of Vitis, 26 years in Rupprechts, 4 years in Gopprechts, 9 years in Klein Poppen, and one year in Seyfritz and as a cowherd for one year in Dietweis. After all these years of service he was unable to find work in his old age and was arrested for begging.[47]

The servants' main function in the peasant household was as a labor substitute for children. This means that servants were more likely to be found in households with no or few children or in households headed by a young couple whose children were not yet old enough to work. In the villages of the Waldviertel in 1763 the number of servants in a household was negatively related to the number of children in the peasant's family (Pearsonian correlation coefficient, $r = -.17$),[48] the age of the oldest son ($r = -.16$), and the age of the head of the household ($r = -.19$) (see table 4).

The Russian economist Chayanov pointed out the importance of the family life cycle in explaining the economic behavior of peasants. He showed that during the first half of a peasant family's life cycle the economic well-being of the family declines as each new child adds to consumption but not to the output of the farm. During the second half of a family's history, as the children one after another reach working age, there is a proportional rise in economic well-being. In Russia,

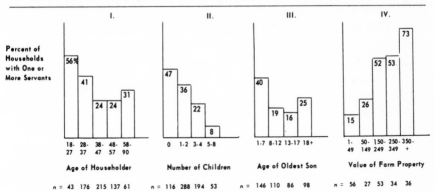

where the land was constantly being transferred and redistributed, the amount of land farmed by a peasant family rose and fell with the phases of the life cycle.[49]

In Austria the peasant holding was impartible and was transferred en bloc from generation to generation. The amount of land belonging to a family remained relatively constant,[50] but the amount of labor provided by the family went through the same cycle described by Chayanov, creating a labor shortage in the first years of the family's existence. The obvious solution was to expand the labor force by hiring servants in the early years of marriage to replace the labor of retired parents and the brothers and sisters who had left the farm and to do the work for which the children were still too young. As the children grew up they replaced the servants and even created a labor surplus on the small farms, which is why many of them became servants in other households in their teens. In Russia, where few peasant families kept servants, stability was achieved by expanding or contracting the size of the farm. In Austria, where the land was impartible, it was achieved by hiring or dismissing servants.[51]

The relationship of the Austrian peasant family's life cycle to the amount of labor available in the household can be shown by estimating the amount of standard labor units contributed by each family member. Householders and grown servants would add a full labor unit, a wife added somewhat less, especially during the childbearing years, and children added increasing fractions as they grew up.[52] Table 5 depicts a hypothetical cycle to show the importance of servants in maintaining the stability of the household labor supply.

The presence of servants in a household was positively related to

The Stem Family and the Peasant Household   *49*

TABLE 5. LABOR UNITS AVAILABLE IN HOUSEHOLD AT DIFFERENT PHASES OF FAMILY LIFE CYCLE

| Years of Family's Existence | Peasant Householder | Standard Labor Units Contributed | | | | | |
		Wife	Son	Daughter	Total Family	Servants	Total Household
0 Marriage	1	.8	—	—	1.8	1	2.8
1–12 Years of Childbearing	1	.4	—	—	1.4	1	2.4
12–20 Young Children	1	.8	.5	.5	2.8	—	2.8
20–30 Older Children	1	.8	1.0	.8	3.6	—	3.6

Adapted from S.H. Franklin, *The European Peasantry: The Final Phase* (London, 1969), 19.

the value of the property ($r = +.56$). The richer peasants were the most likely to need servants and could most afford to hire them (see table 4: IV). Within each economic group, the inverse relationship between servants and children still holds, but there is a steady increment as the property value increases. Servants were not kept by poor peasants if they had more than one child or by middling peasants if they had more than two children, and rich peasants were least likely to keep a servant if they had three or more children (see table 6). Servants were a labor substitute for children within each economic group, but the labor requirements of the farm obviously increased proportionally to its value and size.

One-fifth of peasant households included a lodger. Ordinarily there was only one lodger or lodger family per household, but fourteen households had two, and one household even had three. Three-quarters of the lodgers lived with a spouse or a child: over half were married couples, about one-quarter consisted of single parents with children, and another quarter were single individuals, almost all of them women. While the unmarried servant clearly functions as a labor substitute for children in the household, the economic role of the lodger is not so clear, because we do not know whether any particular

Lutz K. Berkner

50

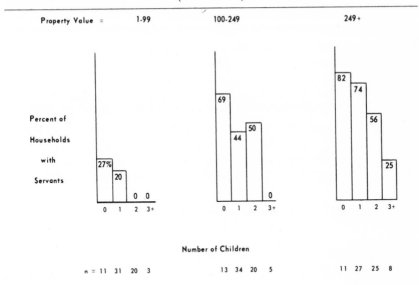

lodger exclusively or even primarily worked for the peasant in whose household he lived. The lodger could fulfill two opposite economic needs for the peasant: rentpayer or laborer. As someone who paid rent but did not work for the peasant in whose house he resided, he was a source of income for the household and served as a complement to the labor supply of the whole community, providing extra help wherever it was needed in the village. But sometimes the lodger was really an employee of the household where he resided and had the same function as any servant.[53] Because the lodger could be either a profit (as a rentpayer) or a cost (as a paid worker) to the household, there is no clear linear relationship between the presence of lodgers and the number of children in a family, the age of the head of the household, the age of the oldest son, or the value of the property. (No correlations are significant.)

The only significant indicator for the presence of a lodger in a household is the absence of an extended family ($r = -.13$). It would seem that the main reason for a lodger's being found in a household was that there was a room available to house one. A lodger could be taken in when the parents died and the Stübl was empty. Lodgers were half as likely to be found in households of extended families (10 percent) as in those of nuclear families (23 percent). The reverse is true for servants, who were half as likely to be found in nuclear families (26 percent) as in extended families (47 percent). Householders with retired parents needed servants because parents did not continue to participate fully in farmwork once they had retired. And servants, who slept with the children, did not take up a room in the house.

The fixed space available for lodging, the fixed farm size that requires a constant labor force, and particularly the stem family organization explain why the mean household size was so stable throughout the developmental cycle of the household. Grandparents die as children are born: servants leave as children grow older; the heir remains to begin his own family while his parents retire and his siblings depart. As a result the mean household size varies only from a high of 5.76 to a low of 5.42 persons over the entire household cycle (see table 7). This stability in size throughout the developmental cycle of the household is probably a distinguishing feature of a stem family structure, since we would expect nuclear family households to begin small, reach their peak size when the parents are in their forties and all the children have been born, and then decline in size again as the children leave home.[54] Even using this developmental approach, mean household size has limited usefulness as a measure of household or family structure.[55] The mean household size was nearly the same at every stage of the life cycle in these Austrian villages, but the underlying social composition of the household varied considerably.

The social structure of this Austrian peasant society has been described in terms of the three parallel developmental cycles of the individual, the family, and the household. The phases of the *individual's* cycle are: son and heir; head of household; retired parent. The critical events in his life cycle are his marriage and the transfer of authority through retirement or inheritance. The *family* cycle is formed by the concurrence of the individual cycles of successive generations that constitute the stem family. The phases of the stem family

TABLE 7. MEAN HOUSEHOLD SIZE BY AGE OF MALE HEAD OF HOUSEHOLD

Household	Age of Male Head of Household					
	18–27	*28–37*	*38–47*	*48–57*	*58–90*	*All*
Mean Household Size						
(Number of Persons)	5.65	5.68	5.67	5.76	5.42	5.63
Number of Households	43	176	215	137	61	651

NOTE: Discrepancies in the totals in tables 1, 2, and 7 result from the fact that there were 19 households headed by females and 14 households whose family composition could not be determined. Table 2 includes both groups (n = 651), table 7 excludes female heads (n = 632), and table 1 excludes both (n = 618).

Lutz K. Berkner

alternate between extended and nuclear: the parents retire and the heir marries; the parents die and the heir heads a nuclear family; the heir retires and his son marries. The determinants of the phases are demographic events—marriages, births, and deaths. The developmental cycle of the *household* is dependent upon the phases of the family cycle and the presence or absence of nonfamily members. The typical phases are: an extended family with servants and young children; a nuclear family without servants and with older children; a nuclear family with lodgers or an extended family without them. The determinants are the economic need to maintain a stable labor force on the farm and the availability of living space.

As the composition of the household changed, personal relationships within it were affected. Only the head of the household had full legal rights, and with them came complete authority over all the other members. The children in the household were thus legally and financially dependent upon the father until, in a contract, he arranged for their marriage or succession. When land is the main or only source of wealth and authority, and when the amount of land is limited, there are sure to be struggles for its control: struggles among children to become heirs, between parents and children over the transfer of authority. When farm labor is relatively scarce, required only seasonally, and paid for from the earnings of peasants with marginal incomes, there are sure to be conflicts between peasants and servants. These social strains are reflected in laws limiting servant wages to the going rate, forbidding anyone from stealing his neighbor's servants, and forbidding servants from leaving a farm without permission. Dissatisfaction shows up in folk songs in which the farmer complains of his servant's laziness, disobedience, and immorality and is answered by the servant's song complaining of the peasant's enjoyment of a comfortable life at his expense. The peasant's entire household may have looked like a big happy family, but it was held together by legal restrictions imposed in the peasant community and by the limited opportunities offered by the rural economy.

Notes
   A version of this article was presented at the annual meeting of the American Historical Association, Dec. 29, 1971, in New York City. The research was supported by the Foreign Area Fellowship Program and a grant for computer time from the Joint Center for Urban Studies of M.I.T. and Harvard. I wish to thank Franklin Mendels, Thomas Cohen, Robert Brenner, Joel Halpern, and Philip J. Greven, Jr. for their helpful suggestions and Noel L. Diaz for preparing the map.

   1   William J. Goode, *World Revolution and Family Patterns* (New York, 1963) is a comprehensive survey of this thesis with many important qualifications, some of which are summarized in the preface to the paperback edition (1970).

2 As was pointed out by William J. Goode, *The Family* (Englewood Cliffs, 1964), 105.

3 For example, Philip J. Greven, Jr. *Four Generations: Population, Land, and Family in Colonial Andover, Massachusetts* (Ithaca, 1970); John Demos, *A Little Commonwealth: Family Life in Plymouth Colony* (New York, 1970); Michael Drake, *Population and Society in Norway, 1735–1865* (Cambridge, 1969); Anne Zink, *Azereix: La vie d'une communauté rurale à la fin du XVIIIe siècle* (Paris, 1969); and the too-little-known masterpiece by Rudolf Braun, *Industrialisierung und Volksleben: Die Veränderungen der Lebensformen in einem ländlichen Industriegebiet von 1800 (Zurcher Öberland)* (Erlenbach-Zurich, 1960), a portion of which has been translated by David Landes (David Landes, ed., *The Rise of Capitalism* [New York, 1966], 53–64).

4 Peter Laslett, *The World We Have Lost* (New York, 1965; 2d ed., London, 1971). Page references are to the first edition.

5 *Ibid.*, 89–92. This has been restated with additional evidence in Peter Laslett, "Size and Structure of the Household in England Over Three Centuries," *Population Studies,* 23 (1969): 199–223. The same point, illustrated with statistical evidence from Switzerland, was made earlier by Emil J. Walter, in "Kritik einiger familiensoziologischer Begriffe im Lichte der politischen Arithmetik des 18. Jahrhunderts," *Schweizerische Zeitschrift für Volkswirtschaft und Statistik,* 97 (1961): 64–75.

6 Conrad Arensberg and Solon Kimball, *Family and Community in Ireland* (Cambridge, Mass., 1940), is probably the most often cited description of a stem family system. Zink, *Azereix,* 234–40, describes the stem family in the French Pyrenees in the eighteenth century and Pierre Bourdieu, "Célibat et condition paysanne," *Études rurales,* nos. 5–6 (1962): 32—135, discusses the same area in more recent times. Jan Stehouwer, "Relations Between Generations and the Three-Generation Household in Denmark," in Ethel Shanas and Gordon F. Streib, eds., *Social Structure and the Family: Generational Relations* (Englewood Cliffs, 1965), 142–62, presents some contemporary statistics on the frequency of three-generation families in Europe.

7 Frédéric Le Play, *L'Organisation de la famille* (Paris, 1871), is the classic work. A historical application of Le Play's family types can be found in George C. Homans, *English Villagers of the Thirteenth Century* (Cambridge, Mass., 1941), 109–222.

8 This census, which is the basis of all the statistics in this article, is in the private Schlossarchiv Heidenreichstein, 13/1 (Seelenbeschreibung 1763). I wish to thank Graf Christian Kinsky for his kind permission to use this archive, which is located in the tower of the old castle in the town of Heidenreichstein.

9 Otto Brunner, *Land und Herrschaft: Grundfragen der territorialen Verfassungsgeschichte Österreichs im Mittelalter* (4th ed.; Vienna, 1959), 256–59; Helmuth Feigl, *Die niederösterreichische Grundherrschaft vom ausgehenden Mittelalter bis zu den theresianisch-josephinischen Reformen* (Vienna, 1964), 122–43.

10 Helmuth Feigl, "Bäuerliches Erbrecht und Erbgewohnheiten in Niederösterreich," *Jahrbuch für Landeskunde von Niederösterreich,* n.s. 37 (1965–67): 161–83; Feigl, *Grundherrschaft,* 66–73.

11 Heinrich Rauscher, "Volkskunde des Waldviertels," in Eduard Stepan, ed., *Das Waldviertel,* 3 (Vienna, 1926): 11; Arensberg and Kimball, *Family and Community,* 135, note that in Ireland a "west room" was set aside for parents at their retirement.

Lutz K. Berkner   54

12 The contracts, many of which are available in the Niederösterreichische Landesarchiv (hereafter NOLA), were copied into the *Kaufprotokolle* kept by the manor. There were similar contracts in other countries. For France, see Patrice Higonnet, *Pont-de-Montvert* (Cambridge, Mass., 1971), 21–22, 49; for colonial Massachusetts, see Greven, *Four Generations,* 84, 95, 143–44, 242–43.

13 NOLA, B.G. Litschau, Herrschaft Heidenreichstein, no. 66 (Kaufprotokolle 1774–86), fol. 395.

14 Peter Rosegger, *Volksleben in Steiermark* (Leipzig, 1914), includes a chapter, "Das Ausnahmshäusel," that gives a good picture of the psychological tensions involved in peasant retirement in Austria. Arensberg and Kimball *(Family and Community,* 115–40) discuss the same problem in Ireland, Zink *(Azereix,* 234–48), in southern France, and Greven *(Four Generations,* 133–38), in colonial Massachusetts.

15 NOLA, B.G. Litschau, Herrschaft Heidenreichstein, no. 66 fol. 187.

16 *Ibid.,* fol. 127. Zink, *Azereix.* 235, 237, quotes comparable stipulations in French contracts.

17 Rauscher, "Volkskunde," 22.

18 *Ibid.,* 99.

19 Based on a number of family histories put together from the Dienstbuch, the Kauf-, Inventur- and Heiratsprotokollen, and the Theresianische Fassion for Heidenreichstein, all in the NOLA.

20 There were eight times as many widows as widowers under the age of 58. A similar custom of peasant retirement and the resulting high ratio of widows to widowers is noted in Drake, *Norway,* 116.

21 NOLA, Theresianische Fassion 870 (Heidenreichstein), fols. 409, 401, 412; NOLA, B.G. Litschau, Herrschaft Heidenreichstein, no. 1 (Dienstbuch, 1715–74), fols. 409, 401, 412, no. 101 (Inventursprotokolle, 1754–74), fol. 307.

22 Meyer Fortes's introduction to Jack Goody, ed., *The Developmental Cycle in Domestic Groups,* Cambridge Papers in Social Anthropology, no. 1 (Cambridge, 1958), is an excellent discussion of this fundamental concept, which is also touched on by Goode, *World Revolution,* 371.

23 Thomas K. Burch, "Some Demographic Determinants of Average Household Size: An Analytic Approach," *Demography,* 7 (1970): 61, and "The Size and Structure of Families: A Comparative Analysis of Census Data," *American Sociological Review,* 32 (1967): 347–63.

24 Elsewhere Burch has warned "that the relationship of family structure to age of head is so strong that the age of head (or some other measure of family life cycle stage) ought to be controlled for in any empirical study of typical family forms or of group differences in family structure." Thomas K. Burch, "Comparative Family Structure: A Demographic Approach," *Estadistica,* 26 (1968): 291. The possibilities of the method are fully demonstrated by Paul Glick, *American Families* (New York, 1957).

25 E. A. Wrigley, *Population and History* (New York, 1969), 131–34; David V. Glass, introduction to *London Inhabitants Within the Walls 1695,* London Record

Society (London, 1966), xxxiv, n. 1. Using slightly different assumptions, Wrigley estimates 29 percent and Glass 27 percent three-generation families in the population. Furthermore, Marion J. Levy, Jr. has theorized that *no* society would have more than 50 percent extended families. Levy, "Aspects of the Analysis of Family Structure," in Ansley J. Coale *et al.*, *Aspects of the Analysis of Family Structure* (Princeton, 1965), 40–63.

26   Goode, *World Revolution,* 12–13, 17; Walter, "Kritik," 65–66.

27   "Size and Structure," 218. Laslett restates this in "The Comparative History of Household and Family," *Journal of Social History,* 4 (1970): 77 and n. 3.

28   "Size and Structure," 220, 222; N. L. Tranter, "Population and Social Structure in a Bedfordshire Parish: The Cardington Listing of Inhabitants, 1782," *Population Studies,* 21 (1967): 269–70.

29   Drake, *Norway,* 116.

30   H. J. Habakkuk ("La disparition du paysan anglais," *Annales: E.S.C.,* 20 [1965]: 649–63) argues that the major decline came between 1660 and 1740. The literature concerning this controversial subject is conveniently summarized in the Economic History Society pamphlet by G. E. Mingay, *Enclosure and the Small Farmer in the Age of the Industrial Revolution* (London, 1968).

31   Günther Franz, *Geschichte des deutschen Bauernstandes vom frühen Mittelalter bis zum 19. Jahrhundert* (Stuttgart, 1970), 214–27 and the literature cited there.

32   Based on figures from Karlheinz Blaschke, *Bevölkerungsgeschichte von Sachsen* (Weimar, 1967), as printed in *ibid.,* 220.

33   King's figures are printed in Laslett, *World,* 32–33. Eighty-five percent of Laslett's censuses are post-1688. See "Size and Structure," 204–05. In the introduction to Peter Laslett, ed., *Household and Family in the Past Time* (Cambridge: Cambridge University Press, 1972), Mr. Laslett replies to some of the points made in this article.

34   Brunner, *Land und Herrschaft,* 316; Feigl, *Grundherrschaft,* 104, 126; Hertha Hon-Firnberg, *Lohnarbeiter und Lohnarbeit im Mittelalter und zur Beginn der Neuzeit* (Baden-Wien, 1935), 8–10, 76–79; Wolf Helmhard von Hohberg, *Georgica curiosa* (Nuremberg, 1716), bk. 1: 72. This is a famous handbook of household economy written by a petty noble of the Waldviertel in 1682 and described in the stimulating book by Otto Brunner, *Adeliges Landleben und europäischer Geist: Leben und Werk Wolf Helmhards von Hohberg 1612–1688* (Salzburg, 1949).

35   Karlheinz Blaschke, "Soziale Gliederung und Entwicklung der sächsischen Landbevölkerung im 16. bis 18. Jahrhundert," *Zeitschrift für Agrargeschichte und Agrarsoziologie,* 4 (1956): 146.

36   Karl S. Kramer, *Bauern und Bürger im nachmittelalterlichen Unterfranken* (Würzberg, 1957), 155. In the marriage records of the parish in Heidenreichstein there are many examples of girls *in Dienst* in the town returning to their village to marry.

37   Feigl, *Grundherrschaft,* 24, 130.

38   Otto Brunner, "Das 'ganze Haus' und die alteuropäische 'Ökonomik' " in

his *Neue Wege der Verfassungs- und Sozialgeschichte* (2d ed.; Göttingen, 1968), 108, 111.

39   "Familia," in *Grosses Vollständiges Universal Lexikon* (Halle, 1732–50), 9: col, 205.

40   Wilhelm Riehl, *Die Familie* (Berlin, 1854), 147.

41   Rauscher, "Volkskunde," 22.

42   Riehl, *Die Familie,* 150. This translation is from Pitrim Sorokin *et al., A Systematic Source-book in Rural Sociology* (Minneapolis, 1931), 2: 95.

43   All of this must be considered in the context of an older sociology that was concerned with the decline of *Gemeinschaft* and with the replacement of personal relationships by contractual ones. But the myth of the happy life on the family farm is hard to kill and long continued to be a mainstay of conservative sociologists such as Hans Günther, *Das Bauerntum als Lebensund Gemeinschaftsform* (Leipzig, 1939), 191–93. The harsher realities are described in J. Walleitner, *Der Knecht* (Salzburg, 1947).

44   Feigl, *Grundherrschaft,* 126–27; Rauscher, "Geschichte des bäuerlichen Wirtschaftsleben," in Stepan, *Das Waldviertel,* 7 (Vienna, 1937): 139–41. Kaiserlichen Akademie der Wissenschaften, *Österreichische Weisthümer* (Vienna, 1870–1913), vol. 8, a collection of village laws in the Waldviertel, shows evidence of these restrictions on nearly every page.

45   Hermann Strobach, *Bauernklagen: Untersuchungen zum sozialkritischen deutschen Volkslied* (Berlin, 1964), 182–87 gives the history and various versions of the "Knechtslied."

46   Feigl, *Grundherrschaft,* 84, 128–29; Hon-Firnberg, *Lohnarbeiter,* 79; August Rothbauer, "Bettlerunwesen im 17. Jahrhundert," *Das Waldviertel,* n.s. s (1959): 112–15.

47   Schlossarchiv Heidenreichstein 3/131 (Hauptvisitation der vagierende Gesindl 1724), which contains a number of interrogations of vagabonds.

48   The Pearsonian correlation coefficient *(r)* measures the direction and strength of a linear (straight line) relationship between two variables. It has a range of -1.0 to $+1.0$. Inverse relationships have a negative sign, and direct relationships have a positive sign. The closer the coefficient comes to -1 or $+1$, the stronger the correlation; the closer it comes to zero, the weaker the correlation. The significance level chosen (here .05) establishes which coefficients will be rejected as statistically not significant (ns).

Correlation Matrix of Variable Pairs ($n = 220$)

Variables:	*Value*	*Age*	*Children*	*Kin*	*Servants*
Prop. Value	+1.00				
Age of Householder	−.07ns	+1.00			
No. of Children	+.11ns	+.31	+1.00		
No. of Kin	+.18	−.34	−.16	+1.00	
No. of Servants	+.56	−.19	−.17	+.25	+1.00
No. of Lodgers	−.09ns	+.05ns	+.08ns	−.13	−.16

The Stem Family and the Peasant Household

49   A. V. Chayanov, *The Theory of the Peasant Economy,* ed. Daniel Thorner *et al.,* (Homewood, 1966), 55–69.

50   There were actually two kinds of land, the impartible peasant land *(behaustes Gut)* and the partible *Überland.* The latter represented 18 percent of the land in the manor, but half of the *Überland* was located in the town itself and owned by small holders. In the villages the sale of *Überland* allowed peasants to increase their holdings slightly, but the bulk of the peasants' wealth lay in the impartible holding. NOLA, Theresianische Fassion 870 *(Überland);* Feigl, *Grundherrschaft,* 59–62.

51   See Chayanov, *Peasant Economy,* 110–12.

52   S. H. Franklin, *The European Peasantry: The Final Phase* (London, 1969), 18–20.

53   Hon-Firnberg. Lohnarbeiter, 77–78; Feigl, *Grundherrschaft,* 128, 131.

54   My calculations of mean household size for three villages in the Norman Pays de Caux in 1793, where there was no peasant stem family structure, provide the following comparison (from Archives Départementales de la Seine-Maritime, L 1599):

Age:	20–29	30–39	40–49	50–59	60–
Size:	3.1	4.2	4.8	4.5	3.6

In a study of five communities Laslett has found a similar pattern in England, but with a peak of over six persons in the households headed by persons 40 to 49. Private correspondence.

55   Burch concludes that mean household size reflects fertility mainly and has little to do with extended family structure. "Size and Structure," 363.

A further testimonial to the complexity of the question of industrialization's impact on the family is Michael Anderson's article on households in Preston during the middle of the nineteenth century. Ironically, he discovered that in 1851 more families there had kin in residence than was true of the families recorded in Laslett's data on preindustrial England. To some extent, of course, this represents the "piling up" typical of rapidly growing cities. Who better to turn to than kin after making the move from the outlying rural regions to an industrial city? Yet, the reason for a higher incidence of three-generation families (involving older, often widowed parents) in Preston than in rural and current urban areas is to be found in the services these persons were able to perform for the family. In fact, Anderson argues that such kin were an economic asset to family resources, rather than a drain as they might be in another setting. An aged grandmother could free her daughter from child care and thus allow her to go off to work, as we know many women were doing at this time. Implicit in Anderson's work, and developed further in his monograph on this topic, is an "exchange theory" of kin interaction. In other words, Anderson is arguing that kin ties and kin contact will be maintained only where these kin can perform reciprocal services. Family life during the beginnings of industrialization may, then, represent a distinctive transitional stage, rather than a full-blown picture of later patterns.

MICHAEL ANDERSON

3 *Family, Household, and the Industrial Revolution*

Aims of the Paper

The Lancashire cotton towns in the middle of the nineteenth century were in many ways a half-way house between a predominantly rural pre-industrial England and the predominantly urban-industrial/-

commercial post-capitalist society of the present day. Communities like Preston, the town I shall be most concerned with here, had between a quarter and a third of their adult male population directly involved in factory industry. Because of the extensive use of child labor, however, a considerably higher proportion of the population were at one time or another of their lives employed in the dominant cotton textile industry. The domestic handloom sector still survived, but it was of ever-shrinking size. Of those not employed in industry, hardly any had agricultural occupations. The prosperity of the mass of the population of almost 70,000 was firmly linked to the cotton textile industry.

These communities were, then, firmly a part of the urban-industrial order, oases in the midst of a predominantly rural nation. In them were to be found all the problems which beset capitalist societies— cyclical unemployment, overcrowding, large families struggling on low wages, factory-working wives and mothers, and large immigrant populations. But this was still an early stage in the transition to the more integrated advanced industrial society we know today. The problems had emerged with full force but the social changes which were to ameliorate or remove them had not yet appeared. Thus bureaucratically organized social security provision for the old, the sick, the unemployed, the pregnant mother and the large family was minimal and only given at great social and psychological cost to the recipient. Bureaucratically organized community social welfare services were almost non-existent. Fertility control was only just beginning, and mortality was as high or higher than ever. Wages were low, primary poverty widespread, housing appalling and relatively expensive.

Obviously, these communities have particular interest to the social historian and the sociologist. By investigating their family and household structure we can perhaps get clues which will help us resolve the many paradoxes which appear when we compare pre-industrial England with the present day. Here I want to concentrate particularly on one of these.

Why, contrary to all that one might be led to expect by the predictions of the cruder, and even of many of the more sophisticated, proponents of the thesis of convergence of family structures with industrialization towards a conjugal type, has there apparently been a massive *increase* over the past two centuries in co-residence of married couples and their parents, and precisely how and when did it come about?

The remainder of this paper falls into two parts. The first presents some (necessarily selective) data on various aspects of household and family structure in Preston in 1851, and contrasts it, on the one hand, with some of the figures which Laslett has at various times made public from his investigations on pre-industrial England (e.g., Laslett, 1969), and, on the other, with recent data on British family structure, notably from the 1966 sample census and from Rosser and Harris's study of Swansea.[1] I have also included for comparison some figures for 1851 from my own data on the Lancashire agricultural villages where many of the migrants to Preston had been born. This area was, however, unlike most of the rest of rural England where the agriculture was based on large farms and outdoor day laborers. In rural Lancashire there was much more of an almost peasant-type subsistence family farm system, where what employed labor there was was mainly the indoor farm servant, marriage was late, many never married, and children remained at home into their twenties in the expectation of an inheritance of the farm or of a portion of the family estate (cf. Anderson, 1971, a, chapter 7).

The second part offers an interpretation of the trends which the first reveals. Many of these interpretations are necessarily rather speculative. We still do not have nearly enough studies of the family structure of factory towns in the nineteenth, let alone in the early twentieth, century to be able to make firm generalizations about the impact of the various facets of urban-industrial life. Nor do we have adequate descriptive data for pre-industrial rural England to support our crude data on co-residence. What data we have, however, seem compatible with the interpretations offered here.

The Preston data are taken from a 10 percent sample of houses from the enumerators' books of the 1851 census. The rural sample is not representative of any finite population. It was drawn with the object of comparing the family structure of those persons who had migrated to Preston from villages where more than half the 1831 population had been employed in agriculture, with the family types which were found in the villages from which they had come. A variable fraction stratified sample was therefore drawn so that the percentage of sample households taken from any one village was proportional to the percentage of all the migrants who had come from that village. Since, however, the family and household structure of these migrants turned out to be little different from that of the population as a whole, I shall here, for convenience, use it for comparisons with the whole Preston population.

Households are taken as "census families." Doubtful cases follow the rules outlined elsewhere (Anderson, 1972, c).

Historical Data

Table 1 shows the extent to which households were likely, at different points in the past, to contain persons outside the nuclear family of the head.[2]

The most marked differences which seem to emerge here are:

1. When compared with pre-industrial England, the larger proportion of households with kin in both 1851 samples, to a level well above the modern figure. This figure, indeed, approximates to that for pre-industrial England. The Lancashire rural sample is probably not typical of England as a whole, though Professor Williams's Ashworthy figure (between 31 percent and 34 percent) is actually higher (Williams, 1963, p. 218). Both Ashworthy and North Lancashire had a predominance of family farms and few farm laborers, and it was above all on these family farms that kin, particularly married children coresiding with parents, were to be found.[3]

2. The far larger number of households with lodgers in Preston, compared both with pre-industrial England and with Swansea. In Preston, lodgers made up 12 percent of the sample and over 20 percent of the twenty to twenty-four age group. The married couples in lodgings were largely young and with small families, and inmigrants were over-represented in their number (cf. Anderson, 1971, a, chapter 5).

3. Servants in Preston in 1851 already show signs of the ultimate decline to which this class was destined. Employment in the factories was, of course, not conditional on co-residence, and the opportunities it offered to the young made it difficult to recruit suitable children to

Table 1 Percentage of Households with Kin, Lodgers and Servants for Various Communities

	Kin	*Lodgers*	*Servants***
England and Wales 1966 (approx.)	10	†	0
Swansea 1960 (approx.)	10–13	<3	<3
Preston 1851	23	23	10
Rural 1851	27	10	28
Laslett 1564–1821	10	<1	29

*Servants include apprentices in Preston and the rural samples
†Figures not available

Table 2 Structure of the Families of Household Heads[4]

Family Type	England & Wales 1966 (approx.)	Swansea 1960 (approx.)	Preston 1851	Rural 1851	Laslett 1564–1821
No related person	17	10+	4	5	
Married couple only	24	22+	10	12	90
Parent(s) and unmarried child(ren) only	49	54+	63	56	
Parent(s) and married child(ren) but no other kin	5	9+	9	6	10
Parent(s) and married child(ren) with other kin	0	<5*	1	0	
Other combinations of kin	4		13	21	
All (percentage)	99	100	100	100	100
N =	1,533,954	1958	1240	855	..

*Some of this group are here because they have co-residing non-kin, since the figures for Swansea are for household structure, not structure of the families of the household heads.

service. Servants and apprentices made up 3 percent of the population.

In the rural sample servants made up 16 percent of the sample population aged over fifteen. By contrast with the towns, the number of men more or less equalled the number of women, and the 225 farm servants who were aged over fifteen made up 43 percent of the paid agricultural labor force in these age groups.

Table 2 turns attention to the structure of the families of household heads.

The markedly higher present-day figures for both Swansea and England and Wales as a whole are obviously the most striking features of this table.

Little difference appears in Table 2 in the proportion living without any relative in their household. The different distribution of childless couples compared with couples with unmarried children mainly reflects the fall in family size and the older age distribution of the Swansea population.

Other highly significant differences appear in the remaining rows. Laslett's communities have very few parent/married child households indeed (Laslett, 1969). By contrast, in Preston, 10 percent of all families were of this type, and Rosser and Harris's modern figures are at about the Preston level, though the figures for England and Wales as a whole are lower. Foster also found a 10 percent figure for Oldham (1967, p. 314). The urban-industrial revolution, then, seems, contrary surely to all expectations ten years ago, to have been associated with a considerable increase in co-residence of parents and married children. However, Foster's (1967) finding[5] that the comparable 1851 figures for Northampton and South Shields, both industrial towns, were only 5 percent and 4 percent respectively suggests that the issue is not as simple as it might at first appear. Further discussion of this issue appears below.

The other main point to emerge from Table 2 is the way in which "other kin" family types maintained or even increased their proportion in the urban industrial society, and only fell away in the past 100 years. This issue too is best discussed below. Suffice to note here that Foster found these "other kin" in 12 percent of Northampton families, 16 percent of Oldham families and 11 percent of South Shields families (1967, p. 314). Certainly this family type was a widespread phenomenon.

Just who these co-residing kin were is explored further in Table 3.

By far the most remarkable thing to modern eyes about both columns of Table 3 is the immense number of "parentless" children, 28 percent of all kin in Preston, and 42 percent in the rural sample. I have been unable to find any comparable tables for present-day communities, but a glance at the first column of Table 2 suggests that the figure is well under 5 percent. By contrast the proportion for pre-industrial England may well have been higher still, and can certainly have been little lower.

Thus in Preston, while there were also still large numbers of this "parentless" group so rare today, there was also a much larger number of the "new," "twentieth-century" group of one or two grandparents, or one or two married children and their families, and married siblings and their families. We appear, therefore, to have in Preston something of a halfway stage in the transition, with both pre-industrial and modern types of kinship superimposed.

Before trying to analyze just who these various groups were, and

Michael Anderson   64

Table 3 Relationship of Kin to Household Head
(Percentage of All Kin)

	Preston 1851		Rural 1851	
Father or father-in-law	3·3*		3·2†	
Mother or mother-in-law	5·7*		4·0†	
Married/widowed son or son-in-law	11·1		6·9	
Married/widowed daughter or daughter-in-law	12·3		5·9	
Grandchild with parents	13·7		10·9	
'Stem' family members		46·1		30·9
Unmarried siblings (married head)	9·1		8·4	
Unmarried siblings (unmarried head)	5·0		8·6	
Unmarried members of family of orientation		14·1		17·0
Married or widowed siblings or siblings-in-law	5·1		4·0	
Nieces/nephews with parents	4·3		2·2	
Married siblings and family		9·4		6·2
Nieces/nephews without parents	15·0		11·9	
Grandchildren without parents	13·3		30·2	
'Parentless' children		28·3		42·1
Uncles, aunts and cousins	1·4	1·4	2·0	2·0
Others	0·8‡	0·8	1·7§	1·7
All (percentage)	100·1	100·1	99·9	99·9
$N =$	513	513	404	404

*All widowed.

†All but one widowed.

‡Son-in-law's father, son-in-law's brother, grandmother, great nephew.

§Five not specified (probably nieces/nephews, siblings-in-law, or cousins) great-niece and her illegitimate child.

why they were co-residing, attention is perhaps usefully turned to Tables 4 and 5. Aggregate tables on family structure, such as Tables 2 and 3, can be rather misleading in a comparative perspective, because, given the typical English pattern where co-residence of married children and parents is mainly confined to the first years of marriage, and to the old age (particularly the widowhood) of the parents, such tables are highly sensitive to varying population age structures. Before proceeding further, then, it is instructive to look briefly at some tables where age or life-cycle stage are controlled.

Table 4 shows the co-residence patterns of the section of the community aged over sixty-five. The "Britain" figures are from the old people in a three industrial societies study (Stehouwer, 1965, p. 146).

The marked pattern of co-residence with children in Preston is particularly to be noted. Rather few old people there lived apart from a relative. Indeed, when the proportion of old people who could have had a child alive at all is estimated (and this figure is considerably below that for modern Britain and probably below the rural figure), it is obvious that well over 80 percent of those old people who had a child alive were, in Preston in 1851, in fact living with one or other of their children.[6]

Table 5 shows the residence patterns of the young childless couples.[7]

In Preston, as in Swansea, only just over half of all childless younger couples lived in households of their own and apart from their parents. In contrast to Swansea, however, where most of the rest lived with parents, over half of this group in Preston lived as lodgers in another household. (None in Preston co-resided in a household headed by a kinsman other than a parent.) Part of this difference may be due to the rather different criteria by which households are distinguished in the two studies, but there is no doubt that many of these lodger couples did, in fact, share a common table and would therefore have been classified as lodgers even by Rosser and Harris. Compared with Laslett's figures, in contrast, even the 16 percent who lived with parents are probably a very numerous body indeed.

Thus it seems likely that urban-industrial life of the cotton-town type markedly increased the proportion of wage-earner families in which parents and married children co-resided. It also markedly increased the alternative form of residence for the young married couple, living as lodgers with another family. Compared with pre-industrial England, however, the proportion of "parentless" children did not decline, and may even have increased somewhat. Twentieth-century urban life saw a marked reduction in this latter group but some considerable further increase in the co-residence of young married children and their parents, probably to some extent at the expense of the lodger group. But, in spite of this increase, more old people live

Table 4 Household Composition of the Over Sixty-Fives
(Percentage) Listing in Priority Order

	Married			Widowed, single and separated		
	Britain 1962	*Preston 1851*	*Rural 1851*	*Britain 1962*	*Preston 1851*	*Rural 1851*
Living with:						
Married child(ren)	6	16	13	27	41	26
Unmarried child(ren)	26	47	36	27	29	21
Spouse only	68	37	50	–	–	–
Other kin only	–	–	–	4	8	18
No related person	–	–	–	42	22	35
All (percentage)	100	100	99	100	100	100
N =	1022	70	143	889	124	106

Table 5 Residence Patterns of Childless Couples where the
Wife was Aged under Forty-Five (Percentage)

	Swansea 1960	*Preston 1851*	*Rural 1851*
Percentage living:			
In own household	57	58	80
Co-residing with parents	40	16	13
Other	3	26	7
All (percentage)	100	100	100
N =	97	158	46

alone today than in nineteenth-century Preston; possibly more do so
than did in pre-industrial England.

Interpretation of Data

I have argued elsewhere (Anderson, 1971, a, especially chapter
2) that, if we are to understand variations and changes in patterns of

Family, Household, and the Industrial Revolution   67

kinship relationships, the only worthwhile approach is consciously and explicitly to investigate the manifold advantages and disadvantages that any actor can obtain from maintaining one relational pattern rather than another, and I have outlined what I see as the main considerations which must be taken into account in any such approach. Here I want to go further and suggest, that, in the case of *co-residence,* a very special set of hypotheses, which consider only economic advantages and disadvantages, may be appropriate. In short, I am suggesting that any significant proportion of one group of actors in a society (say young married men) will generally only be found *co-residing* with another given class of kin (say widowed parents) if:

1. The time discounted, average life-span, economic advantages to most of them of doing so (bearing in mind that co-residence will normally imply some sharing of resources and support if necessary) outweigh or at least are not greatly exceeded by the economic disadvantages which they would suffer either directly from the kinsman, or from third parties, if they did not do so: and

2. If most of the other party would also receive net advantages calculated in the same way.

Conscious calculation of these advantages is seen in this approach as only occurring under rather special conditions;[8] generally norms develop to set a seal on conduct which is in line with these economic pressures. In highly stable and fairly prosperous societies (which the societies we are concerned with here were not), where the future is reasonably predictable, it can be shown, on the premises used, that norms would logically develop as a kind of insurance policy to provide at least for all who have relatives, some minimum standard of living provided by kin, except if assistance at this minimal level were seen as obtainable from some other outside agency.

There is no space to go further into this matter in this paper. Here I am mainly concerned with the principle as a conceptual framework which may help us to understand changes and differences in patterns of co-residence. To this detailed problem I now return.

"PARENTLESS" CHILDREN

Firstly, then, who were these parentless children who seem to have been present in a sizeable proportion of households over most of rural and urban England?

Some of the odd grandchildren were undoubtedly illegitimate sons and daughters of co-residing daughters, or, indeed, of daughters who had left home to marry or for other reasons.[9] It is now impossible except by reconstitution techniques to ascertain what this proportion might have been, but it does seem as if this was a fairly standard behavior pattern. A second group were children of orphaned parents, children who had lost one parent (particularly the mother), and also children of mothers who had remarried. In all these cases it seems to have been normal for relatives to take over the children, assisted often by a small parish allowance in return (Anderson, 1971, a, chapter 10). Children in this class undoubtedly make up a not inconsiderable proportion of the group as a whole. A third, and probably small, group are those who, though they had parents alive and living in the community, lived with aunts, uncles or grandparents to relieve the overcrowding in their own households or, possibly, to provide aged grandparents with some company and help around the house or in a small shop. Several cases which look very like this cropped up during the work on enumerators' books, and the phenomenon of "lending a child" is not unknown in modern working-class communities (cf., e.g., Young and Willmott, 1957, p. 38).

Certainly, for one reason or another, widows and single women were more than twice as likely to have such "parentless" kin in their households as were the rest of the population. Most of these young men and women were already earning and would thus be already keeping themselves and, indeed, probably making some useful contribution towards the family finances (about 80 percent were over ten years of age). Many more would soon be doing so in a society where child labor was the norm (and many of those who were sent out to work very young do indeed seem to have been being cared for by kin; cf., e.g., Parliamentary Papers, PP. 1833, XX, DI, 34, and see also Anderson, 1971, a, chapter 11). Many of the rest would have been the children of co-residing daughters who more than paid for their keep.

To this social welfare function, however, one must also add an important economic function of kinship which both overlapped with the first and also made its own independent contribution to the figures. In the nineteenth century it was above all through the agency of kin that one got a job.[10] Where one had a kinsman who had his own business or farm he might frequently offer a job directly, particularly to the sons of siblings who had fallen on hard times, and this would frequently involve co-residence (Anderson, 1971, a, chapters 9 and 10). Some of these kin are described in the occupation columns of the schedules as servants, while many so-called servants were almost certainly kin. Their status in the household was probably often little different from that of the non-relative who would otherwise have been given the place. The net cost, therefore, was probably minimal, the system meant that orphans and the children of destitute kin were provided for, and kin were probably easier to sanction, less likely to leave their jobs, and probably, therefore, more reliable.

In the towns, of course, most of the population were employees, but recruitment to jobs in the factories or in the laboring gangs was similarly influenced by kinship considerations. "Asking for" a job for kin was normal in the factory towns, and the employers used the kinship system to recruit labor from the country (Anderson, 1971, a, chapter 9). This process of drawing in kin from rural areas continued in London to the end of the nineteenth century at least.[11] Most of these kin were single, being especially siblings, and nieces and nephews. When they got to the town to the job their kinsman found for them, they had nowhere to live, so they normally lodged with him. This, then, is the second major source of "parentless" kin. It is also, surely, the reason why inmigrant couples (except significantly those from other factory towns) had almost as many siblings, nieces and nephews, and cousins in their households as did the Preston born (for details, see Anderson, 1971, a, chapter 10), and also, surely, the reason why it was above all the better paid factory workers—overseers and spinners and the like—who had these relatives in their homes (Anderson, 1971, a, chapter 10). These were the men with the greatest influence over factory recruitment.

In sum, then, in industrializing England, men continued to be able, and indeed possibly became more able, to perform functions for their kin which were to these kin a considerable economic advantage. They could, moreover, do this at minimum cost to themselves except sometimes in the rather short run. The twentieth century, by contrast, reduced the control of kin over jobs, and reduced the scale of migration of young single persons. At the same time orphanage decreased and the Welfare State cushioned the poor from the worst ravages of crises. In consequence this class of kin largely disappeared from British homes.

PARENTS AND MARRIED CHILDREN

To explain the co-residence of parents and married children in larger proportions in Preston and Oldham than in both pre-industrial England, and other nineteenth-century towns so far studied is a considerably more difficult problem. By contrast with the situation among the better-off farmers in rural Lancashire, a fairly simple economic explanation based on economic cooperation in a family enterprise and the promise of future rewards from it is clearly unsuitable (Anderson, 1971, a, chapter 7); by far the larger proportion of the population of Preston were employees, and, anyway, there was no clear association between socio-economic group, and parent/married child co-residence.

Rather, as I have argued at greater length elsewhere (Anderson, 1971, a, especially chapters 10–12), my interpretation requires that attention be turned to other aspects of urban-social life. In most working-class communities before the coming of the Welfare State, if someone survived to old age (and many did not), then he could look forward to a life of poverty. This was particularly true, perhaps, in the towns, where the cost of living, and also rents were higher. It seems probable then that old people, particularly widows, would in general have been best off if they could co-reside with married children. They would thus save on rent, and participate in the economies of scale of the common table. Young married couples, too, might benefit from sharing, because they, too, would save on rent. But, and this is the crucial point, nineteenth-century society and the society which preceded it were, in general, poor societies, societies where after one had done one's best for one's own nuclear family, there was little left for anyone else, unless that someone else could contribute to the family's resources in return. And, if one was young and newly married, to take an old person into one's household or to join the household of that old person meant that this person could not but be given some of these scarce resources now, and also in the future when one's family was larger and poverty loomed at the door; the old persons would probably need some help even if they were receiving a parish pittance. If one refused to take them in, the Guardians would usually make sure they did not die of want; indeed their standard of living would probably be little if at all lower. Usually, moreover, this person could not give much of use in return. This, I would argue, explains the reluctance of the population of most nineteenth-century towns, and probably also of nineteenth-century and indeed pre-industrial rural areas, to share with old people even when soon after marriage they could for a while afford to do so. It is much more difficult to eject someone than never to take them in.

In the cotton towns, however, the situation was different. Here, though poverty was widespread, it was a little less biting than elsewhere and it lasted for a shorter part of the life cycle (cf. Foster, 1967). The drain of a non-productive relative was thus anyway somewhat less severe. But, and this may have been the crucial issue, the relative could also substantially *increase the family income,* not usually by seeking employment in the labor market, but by caring for the children and home while the mother worked in the factory. In this way the mother could have child and home looked after better, and probably more cheaply, than by hiring someone to do so, and the income she brought in kept the relative and gave a considerable surplus to the family budget.

Thus, in these communities, the old person could be valuable, not a drain on family resources. Even if the wife did not work, the old person could frequently earn her keep by performing similar services for a neighbor who did. It is, then, perhaps not surprising that few old people lived alone.

By contrast, however, not all young married couples had parents alive, and many were inmigrants whose parents lived elsewhere. It was migrants in particular who lived in lodgings rather than with kin, though some actually brought their parents in to join them. Some others had many siblings still living at home, so here considerations of overcrowding prevented their co-residing, though many lived near by. It would thus seem that only a minority of young married couples, even in Preston, were physically able to co-reside.

One may then perhaps suggest more speculatively that in the later nineteenth and early twentieth centuries these advantages of co-residence continued in Lancashire and gradually spread elsewhere. The advantages to young married couples of co-residence if anything increased as housing continued to be in short supply. At the same time the decline in family poverty meant that, proportionally, the cash disadvantages to them of taking in dependent kin declined. At the same time family size began to fall. More space thus became available at home, and fewer other married siblings were competing for the right to co-reside. More people had parents available too, because inmigrants came to be a smaller proportion of the total population, and some decline in adult mortality set in.

On the other hand, this very stabilization of communities, together with the old-age pension, changed the situation for the old. They could live near their children, not with them,[12] and more and more could afford to pay rent for a home of their own. Their children anyway were younger and most had left home for a while before widowhood struck.

Thus, while more and more couples came to co-reside for a few years after marriage, the proportion of old people who wished to co-reside probably began to fall. Some detailed investigations of household structure in the early twentieth century are necessary before we can understand the full situation here. The changes brought about by the introduction of the old-age pension in 1908 may well have been particularly significant.

What evidence is there in support of this interpretation?

Firstly, it is possible to show that in Preston it was only those in more affluent states who took in kin who could not support themselves. In Preston, of all households whose family standard of living was estimated as being within 4s. of the primary poverty line, only 2 percent contained kin none of whom had a recorded means of support; of those with a standard of living 20s. and more above, the figure was 11 percent. By contrast 9 percent of the first group and 12 percent of the second contained kin at least one of whom was self-supporting.[13]

There is also considerable contemporary comment by members of the working class that the possibility of assistance to kin was severely circumscribed by the costs which it incurred, unless such kin could either bring in some income through employment, or unless the Poor Law authorities were prepared to pay them some relief (see Anderson, 1971, a, chapters 10 and 11). The Poor Law Commissioners of 1834 found a similar attitude to support of parents to be prevalent in many parts of rural England (e.g., PP 1834 XXVII, especially 54). In addition, calculating reactions of this kind to assistance to kin in situations of extreme poverty have been pointed out by my own research on pre-famine rural Ireland (Anderson, 1971, a, chapter 7), by Banfield in Italy (1958, especially p. 121), and by Sahlins as typical of primitive societies (1965, especially p. 165).

Secondly, there is also supporting evidence for the special interpretation which has been offered for the cotton towns. Just such an explanation was offered for the low Lancashire poor rates by the special commissioner sent to inquire into the state of Stockport in 1842 (PP 1842 XXXV, 7 and 77). Households with children under ten where the wife worked were three times as likely to have had a co-residing grandmother (Anderson, 1971, a). Some married couples actually took unrelated old people into their households rent free and all found to provide just such a service (cf., e.g., Waugh, 1881, p. 85; cited in Anderson, 1972, a, chapter 11), and others brought their parents in from the country (PP 1836 XXXIV, 25, 69; PP 1859 Ses 2, VII, 116; PP 1837–8 XIX, 309; and sample data). Booth's (1894) data on poor relief for the elderly, compiled at the end of the century, show markedly fewer old people in receipt of relief in areas where married women habitually worked.

Obviously, at this stage, such an interpretation remains speculative, but it does seem to offer considerable scope for future research. The problem is a complex one, and many factors are obviously involved which we are only gradually coming to understand.

Notes
1   General Register Office (1968); Rosser and Harris (1965). Neither of these sources present data in quite the form required for the purpose at hand, so some

estimates have had to be made. The data based on these two sources are, therefore, only approximate. For a fuller discussion of this point see the original version of this paper.

2   The figures for England and Wales are from General Register Office (1968, pp. 1–2). Those for Swansea are derived from Rosser and Harris (1965, p. 148). The figures in the original are for household, not family composition, and contain a 4 percent "other" category, which includes both co-residing non-kin, and families with kin other than married children and their children, and siblings. The figures for pre-industrial England are from Laslett (1969), except for the lodger figure which is from Armstrong (1968, p. 72).

3   For a fuller discussion and explanation, see Anderson (1971, a) chapters 3 and 7.

4   For comment on the Swansea figures see footnote 2. The pre-industrial figures are derived from Laslett (1969).

5   Firth (1964, p. 74) found that only 16 percent of his Highgate sample (though 30 percent of the middle class (Crozier, 1965, p. 17)) had co-residing kin, which suggests that in London, too, this family type was not as predominant as it was in Lancashire.

6   For details of the estimate, see Anderson (1972).

7   For Swansea, from Rosser and Harris (1965, p. 167).

8   These problems, together with those raised by the next sentence, and such problems as the determinants of rates of time discount, are discussed at some length in Anderson 1971, a).

9   For the detailed references in support of this statement see Anderson (1971, a, chapter 10).

10   For a detail discussion see Anderson (1971, a, chapter 9).

11   Perhaps the classic discussion of this kin-based migration and occupational recruitment service is in Booth (1892, pp. 132–5).

12   For a similar observation on modern communities, cf. Willmott and Young (1960, p. 43).

13   Cf. Anderson (1971, a, especially chapter 11). The method of calculating the standard of living is set out in Anderson (1972, b).

References

ANDERSON, M. (1971, a), *Family Structure in Nineteenth-Century Lancashire,* Cambridge University Press.

ANDERSON, M. (1972, b), "Sources and techniques for the study of family structure in nineteenth-century Britain" in E.A. Wrigley (ed.) *Nineteenth-Century Society,* Cambridge University Press.

ANDERSON, M. (1972, c), "Standard tabulation procedures for houses, households and other groups of residents, in the enumeration books of the censuses of 1851 to 1891," in E. A. Wrigley (ed.), *Nineteenth-Century Society,* Cambridge University Press.

ARMSTRONG, W. A. (1968), "The interpretation of the census enumerators' books for Victorian towns" in H. J. Dyos (ed.), *The Study of Urban History*, Edward Arnold.

BANFIELD, E. C. (1958), *The Moral Basis of a Backward Society*, Free Press.

BOOTH, C. (ed.) (1892), *Life and Labour of the People in London*, vol. 3, Macmillan.

BOOTH, C. (1894), *The Aged Poor in England and Wales*, Macmillan.

CROZIER, D. (1965), "Kinship and occupational succession," *Sociological Review*, new series, vol. 13, pp. 15–43.

FIRTH, R. (1964), "Family and kinship in industrial society," in P. Halmos (ed.), "The development of industrial societies," *Sociological Review Monograph*, no. 8, Keele.

FOSTER, J. O. (1967), "Capitalism and class consciousness in earlier nineteenth-century Oldham," Ph.D. thesis, University of Cambridge.

GENERAL REGISTER OFFICE (1968), *Sample Census, 1966, Household Composition Tables*, H.M.S.O.

LASLETT, T. P. R. (1969), "Size and structure of the household in England over three centuries: mean household size in England since the sixteenth century," *Population Studies*, vol. 23, pp. 199–223.

ROSSER, C. and HARRIS, C. C. (1965), *The Family and Social Change*, Routledge & Kegan Paul.

SAHLINS, M. D. (1965), "On the sociology of primitive exchange," in M. Banton (ed.), *The Relevance of Models for Social Anthropology*, Tavistock.

STEHOUWER, J. (1965), "Relations between generations and the three generation household in Denmark," in E. Shanas and G. F. Streib (eds.), *Social Structure and the Family: Generational Relations*, Prentice-Hall.

WAUGH, E. (1881), *Factory Folk During the Cotton Famine*, in *Works*, Haywood, vol. 2.

WILLIAMS, W. M. (1963), *A West Country Village: Family Kinship and Land*, Routledge & Kegan Paul

WILLMOTT, P., and YOUNG, M. (1960), *Family and Class in a London Suburb*, Routledge & Kegan Paul.

YOUNG, M. and WILMOTT, P. (1957), *Family and Kinship in East London*, Routledge & Kegan Paul; Penguin Books, 1962.

Parliamentary papers

1833 XX *First report of the . . . Commissioners . . .* [on] *the employment of children in factories . . . with minutes of evidence . . .*

1834 XXVII *Report from His Majesty's Commissioners for inquiring into the administration and practical operation of the Poor Laws.*

1836 XXXIV *Poor inquiry, Ireland; Appendix G. Report on the state of the Irish poor in Great Britain.*

1837–8 XIX *Report by the Select Committee of the House of Lords . . .* [on] *. . . several cases . . .* [arising from] *. . . the operation of the Poor Law Amendment Act . . ., with minutes of evidence. . . .*

1842 XXXV *. . . Evidence taken, and report made, by the Assistant Poor Law Commissioner sent to inquire into the state of the population of Stockport.*

1859 Ses 2 VII *Minutes of evidence taken before the Select Committee on irremoveable poor. . . .*

The American Scene

Philip Greven's prize-winning article provides us with a wealth of information on family life in seventeenth-century Andover, Massachusetts—a newly settled community in which families were literally hacking home sites from the wilderness. The thrust of the paper is directed at the relationship between fathers and sons, that is, the first generation born into the community. By current standards the extent of paternal control over a young man as he reached maturity was truly extraordinary. In order to start a family of his own it was necessary for him to obtain land for a home and farm, and the most direct avenue for achieving this was through the father. It appears that a typical father was fairly generous but insisted on exercising some degree of regulation over a son's life by stipulating that ownership would not be transferred formally until the father's death. Thus we find a situation that Greven quite correctly characterizes as standing somewhere between a nuclear and an extended family and that he chooses to call a "modified extended family." The extension here resides both in the proximity of a married son to the father and in the persistence of paternal dominance after marriage. Most discussions of the extended family regrettably neglect the element of authority in this family form and mistakenly focus only on structure. In fact, current-day class differences in the degree of family extension also have to be understood in terms of parental control over children's destinies, despite the fact that residential patterns are largely neolocal.

PHILIP J. GREVEN, JR.

4 Family Structure in Seventeenth-Century Andover, Massachusetts

Surprisingly little is known at present about family life and family structure in the seventeenth-century American colonies. The generalizations about colonial family life embedded in textbooks are seldom the result of studies of the extant source materials, which historians

77

until recently have tended to ignore.[1] Genealogists long have been using records preserved in county archives, town halls, churches, and graveyards as well as personal documents to compile detailed information on successive generations of early American families. In addition to the work of local genealogists, many communities possess probate records and deeds for the colonial period. A study of these last testaments and deeds together with the vital statistics of family genealogies can provide the answers to such questions as how many children people had, how long people lived, at what ages did they marry, how much control did fathers have over their children, and to what extent and under what conditions did children remain in their parents' community. The answers to such questions enable an historian to reconstruct to some extent the basic characteristics of family life for specific families in specific communities. This essay is a study of a single seventeenth-century New England town, Andover, Massachusetts, during the lifetimes of its first and second generations—the pioneers who carved the community out of the wilderness, and their children who settled upon the lands which their fathers had acquired. A consideration of their births, marriages, and deaths, together with the disposition of land and property within the town from one generation to the next reveals some of the most important aspects of family life and family structure in early Andover.

The development of a particular type of family structure in seventeenth-century Andover was dependent in part upon the economic development of the community during the same period. Andover, settled by a group of about eighteen men during the early 1640's and incorporated in 1646, was patterned at the outset after the English open field villages familiar to many of the early settlers. The inhabitants resided on house lots adjacent to each other in the village center, with their individual holdings of land being distributed in small plots within two large fields beyond the village center. House lots ranged in size from four to twenty acres, and subsequent divisions of land within the town were proportionate to the size of the house lots. By the early 1660's, about forty-two men had arrived to settle in Andover, of whom thirty-six became permanent residents. During the first decade and a half, four major divisions of the arable land in the town were granted. The first two divisions established two open fields, in which land was granted to the inhabitants on the basis of one acre of land for each acre of house lot. The third division, which provided four acres of land for each acre of house lot, evidently did not form another open field, but was scattered about the town. The fourth and final division of land during the seventeenth century occurred in 1662, and gave land to the householders at the rate of twenty acres

Philip J. Greven, Jr.   78

for each acre of their house lots. Each householder thus obtained a minimum division allotment of about eighty acres and a maximum allotment of about four hundred acres. Cumulatively, these four successive divisions of town land, together with additional divisions of meadow and swampland, provided each of the inhabitants with at least one hundred acres of land for farming, and as much as six hundred acres. During the years following these substantial grants of land, many of the families in the town removed their habitations from the house lots in the town center onto their distant, and extensive, farm lands, thus altering the character of the community through the establishment of independent family farms and scattered residences. By the 1680's, more than half the families in Andover lived outside the original center of the town on their own ample farms. The transformation of the earlier open field village effectively recast the basis for family life within the community.[2]

An examination of the number of children whose births are recorded in the Andover town records between 1651 and 1699 reveals a steady increase in the number of children being born throughout the period. (See Table I.[3]) Between 1651 and 1654, 28 births are recorded, followed by 32 between 1655 and 1659, 43 between 1660 and 1664, 44 between 1665 and 1669, 78 between 1670 and 1674, and 90 between 1675 and 1679. After 1680, the figures rise to more than one hundred births every five years. The entire picture of population growth in Andover, however, cannot be formed from a study of the town records alone since these records do not reflect the pattern of generations within the town. Looked at from the point of view of the births of the children of the first generation of settlers who arrived in Andover between the first settlement in the mid-1640's and 1660, a very different picture emerges, hidden within the entries of the town records and genealogies.[4] The majority of the second-generation children were born during the two decades of the 1650's and the 1660's. The births of 159 second-generation children were distributed in

TABLE 1

The Number of Sons and Daughters Living at the Age of 21 in Twenty-nine First-Generation Families

	0	1	2	3	4	5	6	7	8	9	10
Sons	0	1	2	3	4	5	6	7	8	9	10
Families	1	2	7	1	6	6	3	3	0	0	0
Daughters	0	1	2	3	4	5	6	7	8	9	10
Families	0	2	7	6	11	2	0	0	0	1	0

Family Structure in Seventeenth-Century Andover

decades as follows: 10 were born during the 1630's, either in England or in the towns along the Massachusetts coast where their parents first settled; 28 were born during the 1640's; 49 were born during the 1650's; 43 were born during the 1660's; declining to 21 during the 1670's, and falling to only 8 during the 1680's. Because of this pattern of births, the second generation of Andover children, born largely during the 1650's and the 1660's, would mature during the late 1670's and the 1680's. Many of the developments of the second half of the seventeenth century in Andover, both within the town itself and within the families residing there, were the result of the problems posed by a maturing second generation.

From the records which remain, it is not possible to determine the size of the first-generation family with complete accuracy, since a number of children were undoubtedly stillborn, or died almost immediately after birth without ever being recorded in the town records. It is possible, however, to determine the number of children surviving childhood and adolescence with considerable accuracy, in part because of the greater likelihood of their names being recorded among the children born in the town, and in part because other records, such as church records, marriage records, tax lists, and wills, also note their presence. Evidence from all of these sources indicates that the families of Andover's first settlers were large, even without taking into account the numbers of children who may have been born but died unrecorded. An examination of the families of twenty-nine men who settled in Andover between 1645 and 1660 reveals that a total of 247 children are known to have been born to these particular families. Of these 247 children whose births may be ascertained, thirty-nine, or 15.7 percent, are known to have died before reaching the age of 21 years.[5] A total of 208 children or 84.3 percent of the number of children known to be born thus reached the age of 21 years, having survived the hazards both of infancy and of adolescence. This suggests that the number of deaths among children and adolescents during the middle of the seventeenth century in Andover was lower than might have been expected.

In terms of their actual sizes, the twenty-nine first-generation families varied considerably, as one might expect. Ten of these twenty-nine families had between 0 and 3 sons who survived to the age of 21 years; twelve families had either 4 or 5 sons surviving, and six families had either 6 or 7 sons living to be 21. Eighteen of these families thus had four or more sons to provide with land or a trade when they reached maturity and wished to marry, a fact of considerable significance in terms of the development of family life in Andover during the years prior to 1690. Fewer of these twenty-nine families had large numbers of daughters. Fifteen families had between 0 and 3 daughters who reached adulthood, eleven families had 4 daughters surviving, and three families had 5 or more daughters reaching the age of 21. In terms of the total number of their children born and surviving to the age of 21 or more, four of these twenty-nine first-generation families had between 2 and 4 children (13.8 percent), eleven families had between 5 and 7 children (37.9 percent), and fourteen families had between 8 and 11 children (48.3 percent). Well over half of the first-generation families thus had 6 or more children who are known to have survived adolescence and to have reached the age of 21. The average number of children known to have been born to these twenty-nine first-generation families was 8.5, with an average of 7.2 children in these families being known to have reached the age of 21 years.[6] The size of the family, and particularly the number of sons who survived adolescence was a matter of great importance in terms of the problems which would arise later over the settlement of the second generation upon land in Andover and the division of the estates of the first generation among their surviving children. The development of a particular type of family structure within Andover during the first two generations depended in part upon the number of children born and surviving in particular families.

Longevity was a second factor of considerable importance in the development of the family in Andover. For the first forty years following the settlement of the town in 1645, relatively few deaths were recorded among the inhabitants of the town. Unlike Boston, which evidently suffered from smallpox epidemics throughout the seventeenth century, there is no evidence to suggest the presence of smallpox or other epidemical diseases in Andover prior to 1690. With relatively few people, many of whom by the 1670's were scattered about the town upon their own farms, Andover appears to have been a remarkably healthy community during its early years. Lacking virulent epidemics, the principal hazards to health and to life were birth, accidents, non-epidemical diseases, and Indians. Death, consequently, visited relatively few of Andover's inhabitants during the first four decades following its settlement. This is evident in the fact that the first generation of Andover's settlers was very long lived. Prior to 1680, only five of the original settlers who came to Andover before 1660 and established permanent residence there had died; in 1690, fifteen of the first settlers (more than half of the original group) were still alive, forty-five years after the establishment of their town. The age at death of thirty men who settled in Andover prior to 1660 can be determined with a relative degree of accuracy. Their average age at the time of their deaths was 71.8 years. Six of the thirty settlers died while in their fifties, 11 in their sixties, 3 in their seventies, 6 in their eighties, 3 in their nineties, and 1 at the advanced age of 106 years.[7] The longevity of the first-generation fathers was to have great influence on the lives of their children, for the authority of the first generation was maintained far longer than would have been possible if death had struck them down at an early age. The second generation, in turn, was almost as long lived as the first generation had been. The average age of 138 second-generation men at the time of their deaths was 65.2 years, and the average age of sixty-six second-generation women at the time of their deaths was 64.0 years. (See Table 2.[8]) Of the 138 second-generation men who reached the age of 21 years and whose lifespan is known, only twenty-five or 18.1 percent, died between the ages of 20 and 49. Forty-two (30.3 percent) of these 138 men died between the ages of 50 and 69; seventy-one (51.6 percent) died after reaching the age of 70. Twenty-five second-generation men died in their eighties, and four died in their nineties. Longevity was characteristic of men living in seventeenth-century Andover.

The age of marriage often provides significant clues to circumstances affecting family life and to patterns of family relationships which might otherwise remain elusive.[9] Since marriages throughout the seventeenth century and the early part of the eighteenth century were rarely fortuitous, parental authority and concern, family interests, and economic considerations played into the decisions determining when particular men and women could and would marry for the first time. And during the seventeenth century in Andover, factors such as these frequently dictated delays of appreciable duration before young men, especially, might marry. The age of marriage both of men

		Second-Generation		
TABLE 2		Ages at Death		

Ages	Males		Females	
	Numbers	Percentages	Numbers	Percentages
20–29	10	7.3	4	6.1
30–39	9	6.5	4	6.1
40–49	6	4.3	6	9.1
50–59	16	11.5	10	15.2
60–69	26	18.8	13	19.7
70–79	42	30.4	16	24.2
80–89	25	18.1	8	12.1
90–99	4	3.1	5	7.5
Total	138	100.0%	66	100.0%

Philip J. Greven, Jr.

and of women in the second generation proved to be much higher than most historians hitherto have suspected.[10]

Traditionally in America women have married younger than men, and this was generally true for the second generation in Andover. Although the assertion is sometimes made that daughters of colonial families frequently married while in their early teens, the average age of sixty-six second-generation daughters of Andover families at the time of their first marriage was 22.8 years. (See Table 3.) Only two girls are known to have married at 14 years, none at 15, and two more at 16. Four married at the age of 17, with a total of twenty-two of the sixty-six girls marrying before attaining the age of 21 years (33.3 percent). The largest percentage of women married between the ages of 21 and 24, with twenty-four or 36.4 percent being married during these years, making a total of 69.7 percent of the second-generation daughters married before reaching the age of 25. Between the ages of 25 and 29 years, fourteen women (21.2 percent) married, with six others marrying at the age of 30 or more (9.1 percent). Relatively few second-generation women thus married before the age of 17, and nearly 70 percent married before the age of 25. They were not as young in most instances as one might have expected if very early marriages had prevailed, but they were relatively young nonetheless.

The age of marriage for second-generation men reveals a very different picture, for instead of marrying young, as they so often are said to have done, they frequently married quite late. (See Table 4.) The average age for ninety-four second-generation sons of Andover families at the time of their first marriages was 27.1 years. No son is known to have married before the age of 18, and only one actually married then. None of the ninety-four second-generation men whose marriage ages could be determined married at the age of 19, and only

	TABLE 3		Second-Generation Female Marriage Ages
Age	Numbers	Percentages	
Under 21	22	33.3	24 & under = 69.7%
21–24	24	36.4	25 & over = 30.3%
25–29	14	21.2	29 & under = 90.9%
30–34	4	6.1	30 & over = 9.1%
35–39	1	1.5	
40 & over	1	1.5	
	66	100.0%	Average age = 22.8 years

| | TABLE 4 | | Second-Generation
Male Marriage Ages |
Age	Numbers	Percentages	
Under 21	4	4.3	24 & under = 39.4%
21–24	33	35.1	25 & over = 60.6%
25–29	34	36.2	29 & under = 75.6%
30–34	16	17.2	30 & over = 24.4%
35–39	4	4.3	
40 & over	3	2.9	
	94	100.0%	Average age = 27.1 years

three married at the age of 20. The contrast with the marriages of the women of the same generation is evident, since only 4.3 percent of the men married before the age of 21 compared to 33.3 percent of the women. The majority of second-generation men married while in their twenties, with thirty-three of the ninety-four men marrying between the ages of 21 and 24 (35.1 percent), and thirty-four men marrying between the ages of 25 and 29 (36.2 percent). Nearly one-quarter of the second-generation men married at the age of 30 or later, however, since twenty-three men or 24.4 percent delayed their marriages until after their thirtieth year. In sharp contrast with the women of this generation, an appreciable majority of the second-generation men married at the age of 25 or more, with 60.6 percent marrying after that age. This tendency to delay marriages by men until after the age of 25, with the average age being about 27 years, proved to be characteristic of male marriage ages in Andover throughout the seventeenth century.

Averages can sometimes obscure significant variations in patterns of behavior, and it is worth noting that in the second generation the age at which particular sons might marry depended in part upon which son was being married. Eldest sons tended to marry earlier than younger sons in many families, which suggests variations in their roles within their families, and differences in the attitudes of their fathers towards them compared to their younger brothers. For twenty-six eldest second-generation sons, the average age at their first marriage was 25.6 years. Second sons in the family often met with greater difficulties and married at an average age of 27.5 years, roughly two years later than their elder brothers. Youngest sons tended to marry later still, with the average age of twenty-two youngest sons being 27.9 years. In their marriages as in their inheritances, eldest sons often proved to be favored by their families; and family interests and paternal wishes were major factors in deciding which son should marry and

Philip J. Greven, Jr.   84

when. More often than not, a son's marriage depended upon the willingness of his father to allow it and the ability of his father to provide the means for the couple's economic independence. Until a second-generation son had been given the means to support a wife—which in Andover during the seventeenth century generally meant land—marriage was virtually impossible.

Marriage negotiations between the parents of couples proposing marriage and the frequent agreement by the father of a suitor to provide a house and land for the settlement of his son and new bride are familiar facts.[11] But the significance of this seventeenth-century custom is much greater than is sometimes realized. It generally meant that the marriages of the second generation were dependent upon their fathers' willingness to let them leave their families and to establish themselves in separate households elsewhere. The late age at which so many sons married during this period indicates that the majority of first-generation parents were unwilling to see their sons married and settled in their own families until long after they had passed the age of 21. The usual age of adulthood, marked by marriage and the establishment of another family, was often 24 or later. Since 60 per cent of the second-generation sons were 25 or over at the time of their marriage and nearly one-quarter of them were 30 or over, one wonders what made the first generation so reluctant to part with its sons?

At least part of the answer seems to lie in the fact that Andover was largely a farming community during the seventeenth century, structured, by the time that the second generation was maturing, around the family farm which stood isolated from its neighbors and which functioned independently. The family farm required all the labor it could obtain from its own members, and the sons evidently were expected to assist their fathers on their family farms as long as their fathers felt that it was necessary for them to provide their labor. In return for this essential, but prolonged, contribution to their family's economic security, the sons must have been promised land by their fathers when they married, established their own families, and wished to begin their own farms. But this meant that the sons were fully dependent upon their fathers as long as they remained at home. Even if they wanted to leave, they still needed paternal assistance and money in order to purchase land elsewhere. The delayed marriages of second-generation men thus indicate their prolonged attachment to their families, and the continuation of paternal authority over second-generation sons until they had reached their mid-twenties, at least. In effect, it appears, the maturity of this generation was appreciably later than has been suspected hitherto. The psychological consequences of this prolonged dependence of sons are difficult to assess, but they must have been significant.

Even more significant of the type of family relationships emerging with the maturing of the second generation than their late age of marriage is the fact that paternal authority over sons did not cease with marriage. In this community, at least, paternal authority was exercised by the first generation not only prior to their sons' marriages, while the second generation continued to reside under the same roof with their parents and to work on the family farm, and not only at the time of marriage, when fathers generally provided the economic means for their sons' establishment in separate households, but also *after* marriage, by the further step of the father's with-holding legal control of the land from the sons who had settled upon it.[12] The majority of first-generation fathers continued to own the land which they settled their sons upon from the time the older men received it from the town to the day of their deaths. All of the first-generation fathers were willing to allow their sons to build houses upon their land, and to live apart from the paternal house after their marriage, but few were willing to permit their sons to become fully independent as long as they were still alive. By withholding deeds to the land which they had settled their sons upon, and which presumably would be theirs to inherit someday, the first generation successfully assured the continuity of their authority over their families long after their sons had become adults and had gained a nominal independence.[13] Since the second generation, with a few exceptions, lacked clear legal titles to the land which they lived upon and farmed, they were prohibited from selling the land which their fathers had settled them upon, or from alienating the land in any other way without the consent of their fathers, who continued to own it. Being unable to sell the land which they expected to inherit, second-generation sons could not even depart from Andover without their fathers' consent, since few had sufficient capital of their own with which to purchase land for themselves outside of Andover. The family thus was held together not only by settling sons upon family land in Andover, but also by refusing to relinquish control of the land until long after the second generation had established a nominal independence following their marriages and the establishment of separate households. In a majority of cases, the dependence of the second-generation sons continued until the deaths of their fathers. And most of the first generation of settlers was very long lived.

The first generation's reluctance to hand over the control of their property to their second-generation sons is evident in their actions.[14] Only three first-generation fathers divided their land among all of their sons before their deaths and gave them deeds of gift for their portions of the paternal estate. All three, however, waited until late in their lives to give their sons legal title to their portions of the family lands. Eleven first-generation fathers settled all of their sons upon their family estates in Andover, but gave a deed of gift for the land to only one of their sons; the rest of their sons had to await their fathers' deaths before inheriting the land which they had been settled upon. Ten of the settlers retained the title to all of their land until their deaths, handing over control to their sons only by means of their last wills and testaments. For the great majority of the second generation, inheritances constituted the principal means of transferring the ownership of land from one generation to the next.[15] The use of partible inheritances in Andover is evident in the division of the estates of the first generation.[16] Twenty-one of twenty-two first-generation families which had two or more sons divided all of their land among all of their surviving sons. Out of seventy-seven sons who were alive at the time their fathers either wrote their wills or gave them deeds to the land, seventy-two sons received some land from their fathers. Out of a total of sixty-six sons whose inheritances can be determined from their fathers' wills, sixty-one or 92.4 percent received land from their fathers' estates in Andover. Often the land bequeathed to them by will was already in their possession, but without legal conveyances having been given. Thus although the great majority of second-generation sons were settled upon their fathers' lands while their fathers were still alive, few actually owned the land which they lived upon until after their fathers' deaths. With their inheritances came ownership; and with ownership came independence. Many waited a long time.

The characteristic delays in the handing over of control of the land from the first to the second generation may be illustrated by the lives and actions of several Andover families. Like most of the men who wrested their farms and their community from the wilderness, William Ballard was reluctant to part with the control over his land. When Ballard died intestate in 1689, aged about 72 years, his three sons, Joseph, William, and John, agreed to divide their father's estate among themselves "as Equally as they could."[17] They also agreed to give their elderly mother, Grace Ballard, a room in their father's house and to care for her as long as she remained a widow, thus adhering voluntarily to a common practice for the provision of the widow. The eldest son, Joseph, had married in 1665/6, almost certainly a rather young man, whereas his two brothers did not marry until the early 1680's, when their father was in his mid-sixties. William, Jr., must have been well over 30 by then, and John was 28. Both Joseph and William received as part of their division of their father's estate in Andover the land where their houses already stood, as well as more than 75 acres of land apiece. The youngest son, John, got all the housing, land, and meadow "his father lived upon except the land and meadow his father gave William Blunt upon the marriage with his daughter," which had taken place in 1668. It is unclear whether John lived with his wife and their four children in the same house as his parents, but there is a strong likelihood that this was the case in view of his assuming control of it after his father's death. His two older brothers had been given land to build upon by their father before his death, but no deeds of gift had been granted to them, thus preventing their full independence so long as he remained alive. Their family remained closely knit both by their establishment of residences near their paternal home on family land and by the prolonged control by William Ballard over the land he had received as one of the first settlers in Andover. It was a pattern repeated in many families.

There were variations, however, such as those exemplified by the Holt family, one of the most prominent in Andover during the seventeenth century. Nicholas Holt, originally a tanner by trade, had settled in Newbury, Massachusetts, for nearly a decade before joining the group of men planning the new town of Andover during the 1640's. Once established in the wilderness community, Holt ranked third among the householders, with an estate which eventually included at least 400 acres of land in Andover as a result of successive divisions of the common land.[18] At some time prior to 1675, he removed his family from the village, where all the original house lots had been located, and built a dwelling house on his third division of land. Although a small portion of his land still lay to the north and west of the old village center, the greatest part of his estate lay in a reasonably compact farm south of his new house. Holt owned no land outside of Andover, and he acquired very little besides the original division grants from the town. It was upon this land that he eventually settled all his sons. In 1662, however, when Nicholas Holt received the fourth division grant of 300 acres from the town, his eldest son, Samuel, was 21 years old, and his three other sons were 18, 15, and 11. The fifth son was yet unborn. His four sons were thus still adolescents, and at ages at which they could provide the physical labor needed to cultivate the land already cleared about the house, and to clear and break up the land which their father had just received. The family probably provided most of the labor, since there is no evidence to indicate that servants or hired laborers were numerous in Andover at the time. With the exception of two daughters who married in the late 1650's, the Holt family remained together on their farm until 1669, when the two oldest sons and the eldest daughter married.

By 1669, when Holt's eldest son, Samuel, finally married at the age of 28, the only possible means of obtaining land to settle upon from the town was to purchase one of the twenty-acre lots which were offered for sale. House-lot grants with accommodation land had long since been abandoned by the town, and Samuel's marriage and independence therefore depended upon his father's willingness to provide him with sufficient land to build upon and to farm for himself. Evidently his father had proved unwilling for many years, but when Samuel did at last marry, he was allowed to build a house for himself and his wife upon his father's "Three-score Acres of upland," known otherwise as his third division.[19] Soon afterwards, his second brother, Henry, married and also was given land to build upon in the third division. Neither Samuel nor Henry was given a deed to their land by their father at the time they settled upon it. Their marriages and their establishment of separate households left their three younger brothers still living with their aging father and stepmother. Five years passed before the next son married. James, the fourth of the five sons, married in 1675, at the age of 24, whereupon he, too, was provided with a part of his father's farm to build a house upon.[20] The third son, Nicholas, Jr., continued to live with his father, waiting until 1680 to marry at the late age of 32. His willingness to delay even a token independence so long suggests that personal factors must have played an important part in his continued assistance to his father, who was then about 77 years old.[21] John Holt, the youngest of the sons, married at the age of 21, shortly before his father's death.

For Nicholas Holt's four oldest sons, full economic independence was delayed for many years. Although all had withdrawn from their father's house and had established separate residences of their own, they nonetheless were settled upon their father's land not too far distant from their family homestead, and none had yet been given a legal title to the land where they lived. Until Nicholas Holt was willing to give his sons deeds of gift for the lands where he had allowed them to build and to farm, he retained all legal rights to his estate and could still dispose of it in any way he chose. Without his consent, therefore, none of his sons could sell or mortgage the land where they lived since none of them owned it. In the Holt family, paternal authority rested upon firm economic foundations, a situation characteristic of the majority of Andover families of this period and these two generations.

Eventually, Nicholas Holt decided to relinquish his control over his Andover property by giving to his sons, after many years, legal titles to the lands which they lived upon. In a deed of gift, dated February 14, 1680/1, he conveyed to his eldest son, Samuel, who had been married almost twelve years, one half of his third division land, "the Said land on which the said Samuels House now Stands," which had the land of his brother, Henry, adjoining on the west, as well as an additional 130 acres of upland from the fourth division of land, several parcels of meadow, and all privileges accompanying these grants of land.[22] In return for this gift, Samuel, then forty years old, promised to pay his father for his maintenance so long as his "naturall life Shall Continue," the sum of twenty shillings a year. Ten months later, December 15, 1681, Nicholas Holt conveyed almost exactly the same amount of land to his second son, Henry, and also obligated him to pay twenty shillings yearly for his maintenance.[23] Prior to this gift, Nicholas had given his fourth son, James, his portion, which consisted of one-third part of "my farme" including "the land where his house now stands," some upland, a third of the great meadow, and other small parcels. In return, James promised to pay his father three pounds a year for life (three times the sum his two elder brothers were to pay), and to pay his mother-in-law forty shillings a year when she should become a widow.[24] The farm which James received was shared by his two other brothers, Nicholas and John, as well. Nicholas, in a deed of June 16, 1682, received "one third part of the farme where he now dwells," some meadow, and, most importantly, his father's own dwelling house, including the cellar, orchard, and barn, which constituted the principal homestead and house of Nicholas Holt, Sr.[25] In "consideration of this my fathers gift . . . to me his sone," Nicholas, Junior, wrote, "I doe promise and engage to pay yearly" the sum of three pounds for his father's maintenance. Thus Nicholas, Junior, in return for his labors and sacrifices as a son who stayed with his father until the age of 32, received not only a share in the family farm equal to that of his two younger brothers, but in addition received the paternal house and homestead. The youngest of the five Holt sons, John, was the only one to receive his inheritance from his father by deed prior to his marriage. On June 19, 1685, Nicholas Holt, Sr., at the age of 83, gave his "Lovinge" son a parcel of land lying on the easterly side of "my now Dwelling house," some meadow, and fifteen acres of upland "as yett unlaid out."[26] One month later, John married, having already built himself a house upon the land which his father promised to give him. Unlike his older brothers, John Holt thus gained his complete independence as an exceptionally young man. His brothers, however, still were not completely free from obligations to their father since each had agreed to the yearly payment of money to their father in return for full ownership of their farms. Not until Nicholas Holt's death at the end of January 1685/6 could his sons consider themselves fully independent of their aged father. He must have died content in the knowledge that all of his sons had been established on farms fashioned out of his own ample estate in Andover, all enjoying as a result of his patriarchal hand the rewards of his venture into the wilderness.[27]

Some Andover families were less reluctant than Nicholas Holt to let their sons marry early and to establish separate households, although the control of the land in most instances still rested in the father's hands. The Lovejoy family, with seven sons, enabled the four oldest sons to marry at the ages of 22 and 23. John Lovejoy, Sr., who originally emigrated from England as a young indentured servant, acquired a seven-acre house lot after his settlement in Andover during the mid-1640's, and eventually possessed an estate of over 200 acres in the town.[28] At his death in 1690, at the age of 68, he left an estate worth a total of £327.11.6, with housing and land valued at £260.-00.0, a substantial sum at the time.[29] Although he himself had waited until the age of 29 to marry, his sons married earlier. His eldest son, John, Jr., married on March 23, 1677/8, aged 22, and built a house and began to raise crops on land which his father gave him for that purpose. He did not receive a deed of gift for his land, however; his inventory, taken in 1680 after his premature death, showed his major possessions to consist of "one house and a crope of corn" worth only twenty pounds. His entire estate, both real and personal, was valued at only £45.15.0, and was encumbered with £29.14.7 in debts.[30] Three years later, on April 6, 1683, the land which he had farmed without owning was given to his three-year-old son by his father, John Lovejoy, Sr. In a deed of gift, the elder Lovejoy gave his grandson, as a token of the love and affection he felt for his deceased son, the land which John, Jr., had had, consisting of fifty acres of upland, a piece of meadow, and a small parcel of another meadow, all of which lay in Andover.[31] Of the surviving Lovejoy sons only the second, William, received a deed of gift from the elder Lovejoy for the land which he had given them.[32] The others had to await their inheritances to come into full possession of their land. In his will dated September 1, 1690, shortly before his death, Lovejoy distributed his estate among his five surviving sons: Christopher received thirty acres together with other unstated amounts of land, and Nathaniel received the land which his father had originally intended to give to his brother, Benjamin, who had been killed in 1689. Benjamin was 25 years old and unmarried at the time of his death, and left an estate worth only £1.02.8, his wages as a soldier.[33] Without their father's land, sons were penniless. The youngest of the Lovejoy sons, Ebenezer, received his father's homestead, with the house and lands, in return for fulfilling his father's wish that his mother should "be made comfortable while she Continues in this world."[34] His mother inherited the east end of the house, and elaborate provisions in the will ensured her comfort. With all the surviving sons settled upon their father's land in Andover, with the residence of the widow in the son's house, and with the fact that only one of the sons actually received a deed for his land during their father's lifetime, the Lovejoys also epitomized some of the principal characteristics of family life in seventeenth-century Andover.

Exceptions to the general pattern of prolonged paternal control over sons were rare. The actions taken by Edmund Faulkner to settle his eldest son in Andover are instructive precisely because they were so exceptional. The first sign that Faulkner was planning ahead for his son came with his purchase of a twenty-acre lot from the town at the annual town meeting of March 22, 1669/70.[35] He was the only first-generation settler to purchase such a lot, all of the other purchasers being either second-generation sons or newcomers, and it was evident that he did not buy it for himself since he already had a six-acre house lot and more than one hundred acres of land in Andover.[36] The town voted that "in case the said Edmund shall at any time put such to live upon it as the town shall approve, or have no just matter against them, he is to be admitted to be a townsman." The eldest of his two sons, Francis, was then a youth of about nineteen years. Five years later, January 4, 1674/5, Francis was admitted as a townsman of Andover "upon the account of the land he now enjoyeth," almost certainly his father's twenty acres.[37] The following October, aged about 24, Francis married the minister's daughter. A year and a half later, in a deed dated February 1, 1676/7, Edmund Faulkner freely gave his eldest son "one halfe of my Living here at home" to be "Equally Divided between us both."[38] Francis was to pay the town rates on his half, and was to have half the barn, half the orchard, and half the land about his father's house, and both he and his father were to divide the meadows. Significantly, Edmund added that "all my Sixscore acres over Shawshinne river I wholly give unto him," thus handing over, at the relatively young age of 52, most of his upland and half of the remainder of his estate to his eldest son. The control of most of his estate thereby was transferred legally and completely from the first to the second generation, Edmund's second and youngest son, John, was still unmarried at the time Francis received his gift, and waited until 1682 before marrying at the age of 28. Eventually he received some land by his father's will, but his inheritance was small compared to his brother's. Edmund Faulkner's eagerness to hand over the control of his estate to his eldest son is notable for its rarity and accentuates the fact that almost none of his friends and

Philip J. Greven, Jr.   92

neighbors chose to do likewise.[39] It is just possible that Faulkner, himself a younger son of an English gentry family, sought to preserve most of his Andover estate intact by giving it to his eldest son. If so, it would only emphasize his distinctiveness from his neighbors. For the great majority of the first-generation settlers in Andover, partible inheritances and delayed control by the first generation over the land were the rule. Faulkner was the exception which proved it.

Embedded in the reconstructions of particular family histories is a general pattern of family structure unlike any which are known or suspected to have existed either in England or its American colonies during the seventeenth century. It is evident that the family structure which developed during the lifetimes of the first two generations in Andover cannot be classified satisfactorily according to any of the more recent definitions applied to types of family life in the seventeenth century. It was not simply a "patrilineal group of extended kinship gathered into a single household,"[40] nor was it simply a "nuclear independent family, that is man, wife, and children living apart from relatives."[41] The characteristic family structure which emerged in Andover with the maturing of the second generation during the 1670's and 1680's was a combination of both the classical extended family and the nuclear family. This distinctive form of family structure is best described as a *modified extended family*—defined as a kinship group of two or more generations living within a single community in which the dependence of the children upon their parents continues after the children have married and are living under a separate roof. This family structure is a *modified* extended family because all members of the family are not "gathered into a single household," but it is still an *extended* family because the newly created conjugal unit of husband and wife live in separate households in close proximity to their parents and siblings and continue to be economically dependent in some respects upon their parents. And because of the continuing dependence of the second generation upon their first-generation fathers, who continued to own most of the family land throughout the better part of their lives, the family in seventeenth-century Andover was *patriarchal* as well. The men who first settled the town long remained the dominant figures both in their families and their community. It was their decisions and their actions which produced the family characteristic of seventeenth-century Andover.

One of the most significant consequences of the development of the modified extended family characteristic of Andover during this period was the fact that remarkably few second-generation sons moved away from their families and their community. More than four-fifths of the second-generation sons lived their entire lives in the town which their fathers had wrested from the wilderness.[42] The first generation evidently was intent upon guaranteeing the future of the community and of their families within it through the settlement of all of their sons upon the lands originally granted to them by the town. Since it was quite true that the second generation could not expect to acquire as much land by staying in Andover as their fathers had by undergoing the perils of founding a new town on the frontier, it is quite possible that their reluctance to hand over the control of the land to their sons when young is not only a reflection of their patriarchalism, justified both by custom and by theology, but also of the fact that they could not be sure that their sons would stay, given a free choice. Through a series of delays, however, particularly those involving marriages and economic independence, the second generation continued to be closely tied to their paternal families. By keeping their sons in positions of prolonged dependence, the first generation successfully managed to keep them in Andover during those years in which their youth and energy might have led them to seek their fortunes elsewhere. Later generations achieved their independence earlier and moved more. It remains to be seen to what extent the family life characteristic of seventeenth-century Andover was the exception or the rule in the American colonies.

Notes

Mr. Greven is a member of the Department of History, Rutgers University.

1   Two notable exceptions to this generalization are Edmund S. Morgan, *The Puritan Family . . .* (Boston, 1956), and John Demos, "Notes on Life in Plymouth Colony," *William and Mary Quarterly,* 3d Ser., XXII (1965), 264–286.

2   For a full discussion of the transformation of 17th-century Andover, see my article, "Old Patterns in the New World: The Distribution of Land in 17th Century Andover," *Essex Institute Historical Collections,* CI (April 1965), 133–148. See also the study of Sudbury, Mass., in Summer Chilton Powell, *Puritan Village: The Formation of a New England Town* (Middletown, Conn, 1963).

3   The figures in Table I were compiled from the first MS book of Andover vital records, A Record of Births, Deaths, and Marriages, Begun 1651 Ended 1700, located in the vault of the Town Clerk's office, Town Hall, Andover, Mass. For a suggestive comparison of population growth in a small village, see W. G. Hoskins. "The Population of an English Village, 1086–1801: A Study of Wigston Magna," *Provincial England: Essays in Social and Economic History* (London, 1963), 195–200.

4   The most important collection of unpublished genealogies of early Andover families are the typed MSS of Charlotte Helen Abbott, which are located in the Memorial Library, Andover. The two vols. of *Vital Records of Andover, Massachusetts, to the End of the Year 1849* (Topsfield, Mass., 1912) provide an invaluable and exceptionally reliable reference for vital statistics of births, marriages, and deaths.

Philip J. Greven, Jr.   *94*

5   While this figure is low, it should not be discounted entirely. Thomas Jefferson Wertenbaker, *The First Americans, 1607–1690* (New York, 1929), 185–186, found that, "Of the eight hundred and eight children of Harvard graduates for the years from 1658 to 1690, one hundred and sixty-two died before maturity. This gives a recorded child mortality among this selected group of *twenty* percent." Italics added.

6   Comparative figures for the size of families in other rural New England villages are very rare. Wertenbaker, *First Americans,* 182–185, suggested that families were extremely large, with 10 to 20 children being common, but his data for Hingham, Mass., where he found that 105 women had "five or more children," with a total of 818 children "giving an average of 7.8 for each family," is in line with the data for Andover. The figures for seventeenth-century Plymouth are also remarkably similar. See Demos, "Notes on Life in Plymouth Colony," 270–271.

7   The town of Hingham, according to the evidence in Wertenbaker, *First Americans,* 181–186, was remarkably similar to Andover, since the life expectancy of its inhabitants during the 17th century was very high. "Of the eight hundred and twenty-seven persons mentioned as belonging to this period [17th century] and whose length of life is recorded, one hundred and five reached the age of eighty or over, nineteen lived to be ninety or over and three . . . attained the century mark."

8   Since the size of the sample for the age of women at the time of their death is only half that of the sample for men, the average age of 64.0 may not be too reliable. However, the evidence for Hingham does suggest that the figures for Andover ought not to be dismissed too lightly. "The average life of the married women of Hingham during the seventeenth century," Wertenbaker noted, "seems to have been 61.4 years." He also found that for their 818 children, the average age at the time of death was 65.5 years. "These figures," he added, "apply to one little town only, and cannot be accepted as conclusive for conditions throughout the colonies, yet they permit of the strong presumption that much which has been written concerning the short expectation of life for women of large families is based upon insufficient evidence." *Ibid.,* 184. The observation remains cogent. For the longevity of Plymouth's settlers, see Demos, "Notes on Life in Plymouth Colony," 271.

9   The most sophisticated analyses of marriage ages and their relationship to the social structure, family life, and economic conditions of various communities have been made by sociologists. Two exceptionally useful models are the studies of two contemporary English villages by W. M. Williams: *Gosforth: The Sociology of an English Village* (Glencoe, Ill., 1956), esp. pp. 45–49, and *A West Country Village, Ashworthy: Family, Kinship, and Land* (London, 1963), esp. pp. 85–91. Another useful study is Conrad M. Arensberg and Solon T. Kimball, *Family and Community in Ireland* (Cambridge, Mass., 1940). For the fullest statistical and historiographical account of marriage ages in the United States, see Thomas P. Monahan, *The Pattern of Age at Marriage in the United States,* 2 vols. (Philadelphia, 1951).

10   In Plymouth colony during the seventeenth century, the age of marriage also was higher than expected. See Demos, "Notes on Life in Plymouth Colony," 275. For a discussion of various historians' views on marriage ages during the colonial period, see Monahan, *Pattern of Age at Marriage,* I, 99–104.

11   See especially Morgan, *Puritan Family,* 39–44. For one example of marriage negotiations in Andover during this period, see the agreement between widow Hannah Osgood of Andover and Samuel Archard, Sr., of Salem, about 1660 in the *Records and Files of the Quarterly Courts of Essex County, Massachusetts* (Salem, 1012–21),

III, 463, cited hereafter as *Essex Quarterly Court.* Also see the negotiations of Simon Bradstreet of Andover and Nathaniel Wade of Ipswich, *New England Historical and Genealogical Register,* XIII, 204, quoted in Morgan, *Puritan Family,* 41.

12   Similar delays in the handing over of control of the land from one generation to the next are discussed by W. M. Williams in his study of Ashworthy, *West Country Village,* 84–98. Williams noted (p. 91) that "the length of time which the transference of control takes is broadly a reflection of the degree of patriarchalism within the family: the more authoritarian the father, the longer the son has to wait to become master."

13   The use of inheritances as a covert threat by the older generation to control the younger generation is revealed only occasionally in their wills, but must have been a factor in their authority over their sons. One suggestive example of a threat to cut off children from their anticipated inheritances is to be found in the will of George Abbot, Sr., who died in 1681, about 64 years old. Prior to his death, his two eldest sons and one daughter had married, leaving at home five unmarried sons and two unmarried daughters with his widow after his death. Abbot left his entire estate to his wife except for the land which he had already given to his eldest son. At her death, he instructed, his wife was to divide the estate with the advice of her sons and friends, and all the children, except the eldest, who had already received a double portion, were to be treated equally unless "by their disobedient carige" towards her "there be rasen to cut them short." Widow Abbot thus had an effective means for controlling her children, the oldest of whom was 24 in 1681. George Abbot, MS will, Dec. 12, 1681, Probate File 43, Probate Record Office, Registry of Deeds and Probate Court Building, Salem, Mass.

14   For deeds of gift of first generation Andover fathers to their second-generation sons, see the following deeds, located in the MSS volumes of Essex Deeds, Registry of Deeds and Probate Court Building, Salem, Mass.: Richard Barker, v. 29, pp. 115–116; Hannah Dane (widow of George Abbot), v.94, pp. 140–141; Edmund Faulkner, v.39, p. 250; John Frye, v.9, pp. 287–288; Nicholas Holt, v.6, pp. 722–723, 814–821; v.7, pp. 292–296; v.9, p. 12; v.32, pp. 130–131; v.34, pp. 255–256; Henry Ingalls, v. 14, pp. 40–41; John Lovejoy, v.33, pp. 40–41.

15   The intimate relationship between inheritance patterns and family structure has been noted and examined by several historians and numerous sociologists. George C. Homans, in his study of *English Villagers of the Thirteenth Century* (New York, 1960), 26, pointed out that "differences in customs of inheritance are sensitive signs of differences in traditional types of family organization." See Homans' discussions of inheritance in England, chs. VIII and IX. H. J. Habakkuk, in his article, "Family Structure and Economic Change in Nineteenth-Century Europe," *The Journal of Economic History,* XV (1955), 4, wrote that "inheritance systems exerted an influence on the structure of the family, that is, on the size of the family, on the relations of parents to children and between the children. . . ." Very little, however, has been written about the role of inheritance in American life, or of its impact upon the development of the American family. One of the few observers to perceive the importance and impact of inheritance customs upon American family life was the shrewd visitor, Alexis de Tocqueville. See, for instance, his discussion of partible inheritance in *Democracy in America,* ed. Phillips Bradley (New York, 1956), I, 47–51.

16   For further details, see the following wills: George Abbot, Probate File 43; Andrew Allen, Probate File 370; John Aslett, *Essex Quarterly Court,* IV, 409; William

Ballard, Administration of Estate, Probate Record, Old Series, Book 4, vol. 304, pp. 388–389; Richard Barker, Probate File 1708; Samuel Blanchard, Probate File 2612; William Blunt, Probate File 2658; Thomas Chandler, Probate File 4974; William Chandler, Probate File 4979; Rev. Francis Dane, Probate File 7086; John Farnum, Probate File 9244; Thomas Farnum, Probate File 9254; Edmund Faulkner, Probate File 9305; Andrew Foster, Probate Record, Old Series, Book 2, vol. 302, pp. 136–137 (photostat copy); John Frye, Probate File 10301; Henry Ingalls, Probate File 14505; John Lovejoy, Probate File 17068; John Marston, Probate File 17847; Joseph Parker, *Essex Quarterly Court,* VII, 142–144; Andrew Peters, Probate File 21550; Daniel Poor, Probate Record, vol. 302, pp. 196–197; John Russ, Probate File 24365; John Stevens, *Essex Quarterly Court,* II, 414–416; and Walter Wright, Probate File 30733. The Probate Files of manuscript wills, inventories, and administrations of estates, and the bound Probate Records, are located in the Probate Record Office, Registry of Deeds and Probate Court Building, Salem, Mass.

17   MS Articles of Agreement, Oct. 23, 1689, Probate Records, Old Series, Book 4, vol. 304, pp. 388–389 (photostat copy). For genealogical details of the Ballard family, see Abbott's Ballard genealogy, typed MSS, in the Memorial Library, Andover.

18   For Nicholas Holt's land grants in Andover, see the MS volume, A Record of Town Roads and Town Bounds, 18–19, located in the vault of the Town Clerk's office, Andover, Mass. For genealogical information on the Holt family, see Daniel S. Durrie, *A Genealogical History of the Holt Family in the United States . . .* (Albany, N. Y., 1864), 9–16.

19   Essex Deeds, v. 32, p. 130.

20   *Ibid.,* v. 7, pp. 292–296.

21   See *ibid.,* v. 6, pp. 814–815.

22   *Ibid.,* v. 32, pp. 130–131.

23   *Ibid.,* v. 34, pp. 255–256.

24   *Ibid.,* v. 7, pp. 292–296.

25   *Ibid.,* v. 6, pp. 814–816.

26   *Ibid.,* v. 9, p. 12.

27   For an example of a first-generation father who gave a deed of gift to his eldest son only, letting his five younger sons inherit their land, see the MS will of Richard Barker, dated Apr. 27, 1688, Probate File 1708. The deed to his eldest son is found in the Essex Deeds, v. 29, pp. 115–116. All of Barker's sons married late (27, 31, 35, 28, 28, and 25), and all but the eldest continued to be under the control of their father during his long life.

28   For John Lovejoy's Andover land grants, see the MS volume, A Record of Town Roads and Town Bounds, 96–98.

29   See John Lovejoy's MS inventory in Probate File 17068.

30   For the inventory of the estate of John Lovejoy, Jr., see *Essex Quarterly Court,* VIII, 56.

31   Essex Deeds, v.33, pp. 40–41.

32   This deed from John Lovejoy, Sr., to his son, William, is not recorded in the Essex Deeds at the Registry of Deeds, Salem, Mass. The deed, however, is mentioned in his will, Probate File 17068, wherein he bequeathed to William the lands which he already had conveyed to his son by deed. It was customary for such deeds to be mentioned in wills, since they usually represented much or all of a son's portion of a father's estate.

33   For the inventory to Benjamin Lovejoy's estate, see the Probate File 17048.

34   *Ibid.,* 17068. Provision for the widow was customary, and is to be found in all the wills of first-generation settlers who left their wives still alive. Generally, the son who inherited the paternal homestead was obligated to fulfill most of the necessary services for his mother, usually including the provision of firewood and other essentials of daily living. Provision also was made in most instances for the mother to reside in one or two rooms of the paternal house, or to have one end of the house, sometimes with a garden attached. Accommodations thus were written into wills to ensure that the mother would be cared for in her old age and would retain legal grounds for demanding such provisions.

35   Andover, MS volume of Ancient Town Records, located in the Town Clerk's office, Andover.

36   For Edmund Faulkner's land grants in Andover, see the MS Record of Town Roads and Town Bounds, 52–53.

37   Town meeting of Jan. 4, 1674/5, Andover, Ancient Town Records.

38   Essex Deeds, v. 39, p. 250. Only one other instance of the co-partnership of father and son is to be found in the wills of seventeenth-century Andover, but not among the men who founded the town. See the MS will of Andrew Peters, Probate File 21550.

39   The only instance of impartible inheritance, or primogeniture, to be found in the first generation of Andover's settlers occurred within the first decade of its settlement, before the extensive land grants of 1662 had been voted by the town. See John Osgood's will, dated Apr. 12, 1650, in *Essex Quarterly Court,* I, 239. Osgood left his entire Andover estate to the eldest of his two sons.

40   Bernard Bailyn, *Education in the Forming of American Society: Needs and Opportunities for Study* (Chapel Hill, 1960), 15–16. "Besides children, who often remained in the home well into maturity," Bailyn adds, the family "included a wide range of other dependents: nieces and nephews, cousins, and, except for families at the lowest rung of society, servants in filial discipline. In the Elizabethan family the conjugal unit was only the nucleus of a broad kinship community whose outer edges merge almost imperceptibly into the society at large." For further discussions of the extended family in England, see Peter Laslett, "The Gentry of Kent in 1640," *Cambridge Historical Journal,* IX (1948), 148–164; and Peter Laslett's introduction to his edition of *Patriarcha and Other Political Works of Sir Robert Filmer* (Oxford, 1949), esp. 22–26.

41   Peter Laslett and John Harrison, "Clayworth and Cogenhoe," in H. E. Bell and R. L. Ollard, eds., *Historical Essays, 1660–1750, Presented to David Ogg* (London, 1963), 168. See also H. J. Habakkuk, "Population Growth and Economic Development," in *Lectures on Economic Development* (Istanbul, 1958), 23, who asserts that "from

very early in European history, the social unit was the nuclear family—the husband and wife and their children—as opposed to the extended family or kinship group." See also Robin M. Williams, Jr., *American Society: A Sociological Interpretation,* 2d ed. rev. (New York, 1963), 50–57. For a contrasting interpretation of family structure in other 17th-century New England towns, see Demos, "Notes on Life in Plymouth Colony," 279–280.

42   Out of a total of 103 second-generation sons whose residences are known, only seventeen or 16.5 percent, departed from Andover. Five left before 1690, and twelve left after 1690. The majority of families in 17th-century Andover remained closely knit and remarkably immobile.

It is difficult to convey the richness of a research monograph by reprinting its summary chapter; yet, this is what we have had to do here. **Guardians of Virtue** *represents a contribution to the new social history of the family not only because it focuses on a period for which little other data are available but also because it is, along with Michael Anderson's study of Lancashire families, one of the first studies to look at historical data from the perspective of sociological theory. By comparing this selection with the preceding one by Greven and with Demos's chapter on childhood in the Plymouth colony, we can get some sense of the direction of change during the Federal era. Furthermore, Farber's work shows us the dangers of discussing change in the American family as though it were being experienced by all groups in the society in the same way and at the same rate. The distinctions that Farber makes among merchant, artisan, and laboring families should make this pitfall evident. Of further interest is his discussion of continuities between Salem families of 1800 and the American family today, and the extent to which class differences in family have persisted.*

BERNARD FARBER

5 Family and Community Structure: Salem in 1800

This study of Salem families around the year 1800 suggests the process by which Puritan doctrine eventually stimulated economic growth and modernization in an ethnically homogeneous community. The preceding analyses indicated ways in which family organization throughout the social order complemented the development of commercial enterprise. With the writings of Max Weber and Philippe Ariès as background, this chapter discusses the results of the analyses. While the findings are most relevant for helping us to understand the process of modernization, they also provide a context for observing the perseverance of earlier cultural models in contemporary society and for examining the emergence of new family patterns.

Weber and Ariès

Max Weber was interested in religion as a triggering mechanism which set off events ultimately shaping modern economic and political institutions. Although there were conflicting statements in Calvinist writings, Weber suggested that the influence of Protestantism lay in the congruence of its essential elements with the spirit of rational capitalism. His major interest was to demonstrate the motivational force of Calvinist Protestantism. Given this intention, Weber did not concern himself with ephemeral economic and political conditions involving technological change, war, revolution, or depression. Since Weber did not empirically examine the process by which Calvinistic norms became functionally autonomous, he may have misinterpreted the nature of Protestant influence on capitalism.

Weber's position that Puritan theology promoted the development of modern capitalism has been challenged by some historians. To Philippe Ariès, for example, religious ideology is peripheral in forwarding the evolution of modern social structure. Instead, Ariès emphasizes demographic and technological factors in his explanation of change. Taken together, however, the perspectives of Weber and Ariès may shed new light on an old problem in social causation.

The data on Salem show that by the Revolutionary era each social class, with its characteristic family form, provided its own unique contribution to a growing commercial spirit. Thus, the commercial spirit may be seen to emerge, not as the ideological property of a single social class, which is what Weber implies, but rather as an evolving consensus: an intermeshing of separate social classes having descended from the earlier federated community, which in turn had originated in Puritan theology.

The Puritan-Based Family Model

Around 1800, when Salem was at the height of its brief success as a seaport, it still held vestiges of Puritan family and kinship organization, modeled after the Old Testament patriarchal structure. The Puritan conception of the ancient Hebrew family embodied permissibility of first-cousin marriage, partible inheritance (with a double portion to the eldest son), solidarity between male relatives, and a conviction that conformity to the traditional norms of family life would enable the community to prosper.

With belief in a connection between family government and prosperity as the ideological core for both the Hebrew code and the Puritan ethic, it is understandable that the concept of family government came to be extended to the community. The Puritan community was regarded as analogous to the Hebrew tribe, with the "visible saints" as the "chosen people." Left unchecked, the American Puritans developed a federated community organization. Legitimized by "federal theology," community federation existed on two levels: (1) family government, which, through the parents, supervised conduct within the household unit, and (2) town government, which, through its overseers, supervised the conduct of family units. By dominating town government, the Puritan élite had privileges and power denied to families and individuals whose predestined state of grace was doubtful. This federated structure persisted long after the Puritan religious basis for community organization had died away.

It is Ariès's approach which captures those forces at work undermining relationships upon which the federated life-style was based. Ariès attributes the movement away from medievalism to the decrease in death rates of children, to the decline of apprenticeships as socializing agencies, and to the growth of occupationally oriented educational institutions. As Salem social structure became more highly differentiated with the passage of time, it manifested the changes in death-rates, apprenticeships, and schools which Ariès associates with modernization. By the end of the eighteenth century, diverse family forms could be identified in the three major social classes: the merchant class, the artisan class, and the laboring class. The following sections discuss the relationship of family organization within each class to the economic and political life of Salem around 1800.

THE MERCHANT CLASS

In the merchant class, the role of the patriarch as entrepreneur was emphasized. The merchant patriarchs sent out ships on long voyages, which sometimes took two or three years to complete. In the course of a single voyage, several ocean crossings at various parts of the world might take place. Ships loaded in Sumatra might unload in the Middle East or the Mediterranean before taking up another Far Eastern cargo for the voyage home. These long voyages pulled men away from their families and exposed them to a variety of exotic life-styles. The merchants made extensive use of unskilled and unbound labor, such as mariners and shoremen and introduced a highly rational organization in the division of labor in their shipping and commercial enterprises.

Since the patriarch-entrepreneurs took many risks in order to earn high profits, they had to find ways to minimize them. One way that they could minimize risks was to hire relatives whom they could trust. In families like the Crowninshields or the Derbys, sons, nephews, or the children of close friends often acted as sea captains or supercargoes or were given other positions of trust such as correspondents in distant lands. A second way was to pool capital in family partnerships, which apparently also symbolized a high degree of family solidarity. Third, they extended their sources of capital and trusted personnel by creating family alliances through marriage.

Certain characteristics of family life were more effective than others in fostering entrepreneurship. First of all, patriarchal authority helped to develop an effective division of labor in commercial enterprises. Second, partition of inheritance forced heirs to pool their resources, thereby encouraging family unity (at least symbolically). Third, first-cousin marriage and sibling-exchange facilitated the creation of alliances and partnerships in business and politics. Fourth, the designation of the eldest son as the primary heir or successor to the family headship (symbolized by the double portion of inheritance prior to the Revolution) facilitated the stability of the commercial enterprises past a single generation. Fifth, the creation of family alliances signified a strong emphasis upon kinship solidarity, which would then be translated into trust and expansion of the sources of investment capital.

While family organization in the merchant class was generally effective in fostering collective entrepreneurship, it produced other results as well. First, decisions in business sometimes caused merchants to question the competence and integrity of relatives (who were also their partners). Consequently, suspicion and distrust eroded family partnerships, which had been originally intended to symbolize solidarity. Second, coalitions between families were used not only for commercial endeavors but also for the formation of political factions. These factions tended to become separate social worlds, each with its own set of business arrangements and of intermarriages among first cousins and among sets of siblings. The formation of these factions split the community politically and socially, but still facilitated political control by the merchants and professionals over the artisans and laborers. The artisan who did not conform to deference-voting patterns found himself blacklisted in all firms associated with a particular faction (cf. Thernstrom, 1964). Furthermore, the factionalism of the merchant-professional class implies a conception of society as a highly unstable, competitive arena. The factions themselves were competitive enterprises which extended into almost all facets of family and community life and conflicted with the conception of an orderly federated community.

The dominance and life-style of the merchant-professional families rested on their success in shipping and commerce. The shipping industry in turn had a powerful influence on the entire social structure of Salem, an influence which was felt not only in its division of labor but also because of its demographic effects. Because of the high rate of fatalities from exotic diseases, there was a continual shortage of young men in Salem. This shortage made Salem a convenient locus of migration. Outsiders could not compete with the local artisans but did provide a reservoir of unskilled labor. In contrast, those persons who survived to become successful artisans and merchants had a long life expectancy, during which time they could continue to accumulate wealth and power for themselves and their heirs.

In brief, involvement in business enterprise brought power to merchant-class families, but it also created a divisiveness among them despite the gains that were made by pooling resources and by creating alliances. For the most part, these alliances were ephemeral; although ties with the extended family might not be completely broken (so that resources could again be pooled), conjugal families tended to be autonomous.

THE ARTISAN CLASS

The role played by artisan-class families in the development of business enterprise was different from that of the merchant class. The artisans' industry was still largely homebased but provided an arena for socializing children particularly suited to the pursuit of business enterprise.

As formulated by Max Weber, the needs of rational capitalism for the maximization of profit included (1) the presence of a pool of unbound labor and (2) the separation of household affairs from work. In both of these areas, the artisans restrained the progress of rational enterprise. Their economy, with its apprenticeship system, relied heavily upon bound labor. By collaborating with the merchant class on numerous issues, the artisans were able to mount enough power to keep down the numbers of unbound, skilled labor. As for the relationship between family and work, the artisans' households held apprentices as members, and noneconomic factors influenced interaction between master and apprentice. In taking on apprentices, artisans frequently favored relatives over others who might be more capable and efficient. All of these actions often ran counter to the emphasis on maximization of profit among artisans.

While the artisan family as an economic institution may have deviated from the norms of rational capitalism, the artisan family as a socializing agency did not. Even in early colonial days the artisan class supported greater conformity to the Puritan codes of conduct, while the merchants championed a more liberal position. The patriarch-artisans acted as guardians of Puritan-derived norms and values and tried to instill discipline and self-control in the young. Precisely because of their situation in which they controlled much cheap labor through apprenticeships, the patriarch-artisans were in a position to extol the virtues of hard work and to denounce the evil of indolence. They could justify these prescriptions not through base financial motives but by showing that the success of the unproven apprentice-relative was dependent upon internalizing such values. (As an analog, professors today exhort their graduate students to work hard as research assistants on the basis that the knowledge gained will enable the students to become masters of their academic field; the successful undertaking of the professor's research is only incidental.)

Findings relevant to the maintenance of artisan-class families and the apprenticeship system include the following: (1) the relative longevity of parents and the large number of children in need of apprenticeships, (2) the strong ties between male kin as suggested by the tendency toward first-cousin marriage with a blood-uncle's daughter, (3) the strong role of family symbolic property, such as a highly skilled occupation, which was then transmitted from one generation to the next among relatives, (4) the expectation that relatives would assist one another both in time of need and to ward off need, and (5) the tendency of individual members of the family to remain in the same general locale as their close relatives.

The above findings suggest that strong, stable extended-family relationships persisted in the artisan class long after the merchant families had fragmented themselves into numerous conjugal units. With extensive periods of apprenticeships and with emphasis on occupation as a family property, the young had little autonomy in their daily lives. The establishment of a public school system permitted the artisans' children to remain in their families of orientation longer. Yet, as the children grew older, they still faced an apprenticeship of several years. With children trained by relatives outside the conjugal family, extended families formed tight social networks, and the conjugal family did not achieve complete independence as a social unit.

Despite their dependence on relatives, the artisan families, rather than the more independent merchant families, inculcated in children the drive and skills needed for upward social mobility. This tendency calls into question the assumption by many sociologists that the small, isolated conjugal-family form is more appropriate than the close-knit extended family in fostering social mobility in industrial society. Sennett (1969) found a similar relationship between extended-family households and social mobility in Chicago during the period 1870–1890.

THE LABORING CLASS

The families making up the laboring class tended to deviate markedly from the norms upheld by the merchant and artisan classes. The laboring class was made up mainly of "strangers" to the community, outsiders to the body politic. It was not until the first decade of the nineteenth century that members of this class were accorded voting privileges. In the previous decades, they had even been warned out of town. This group, which contributed the day labor to the economy, constituted a marginal category of the population. The rationalization of the division of labor toward the end of the eighteenth century required just such a malleable population segment to meet the needs of the moment.

The undefined family organization of the laboring class allowed its members to become victims of circumstance. While the patriarch-dominated artisan class generally resisted encroachments on its skills and its domestic base, the loose mode of family organization in the laboring class left each member open to exploitation regardless of age or sex. Because of their lack of conformity, members were sometimes placed under the guardianship of the town overseers or were sent to the charity house. School attendance was low, and special-education programs failed to solve the problems of inadequate preparation in a school system which was geared to the needs of artisan families. In addition, the fragility of marital ties precluded the development of patriarchal authority; men in the laboring class died early, and widows generally remarried (and probably dominated) other lower-class men. In general, the lack of organized authority in the laboring-class families seems to have complemented the power of élite families in commercial enterprise and community organization.

The strong role of the community in the guardianship of children from laboring-class families must have interfered with the organization of the households as autonomous conjugal units. The participation by community authorities in decisions affecting the lives of family members among the poor and deviant blended family life and community life so that distinctions between them were easily lost. (Even today the easy access of social workers and other community representatives into the families of the poor and deviant may inhibit the development of strong family boundaries and may instead contribute to the disintegration of family units.) Moreover, since the age of family members in the laboring class meant little in the differentiation of occupational or familial roles, the lower-class family probably failed to develop a concept of parental guardianship to prepare children for adult life. Factors inhibiting the development of stable conjugal units made the poor and the deviant easy targets for exploitation.

CLASS AND CAPITALISM

The configuration of family life in the merchant, artisan, and laboring classes gave to Salem commercial enterprise its peculiar characteristics. The intense competition within the merchant class required the pooling of family resources and the creation of family alliances to embark on commercial ventures with some sense of security. Unintentionally, artisan families were responsible for the socialization of persons who were motivated in the extreme to strive for upward social mobility. The artisan class emphasized the instrumentality of family and kinship toward the achievement of security in livelihood and security in status. Finally, the frequently female-dominated family of the lower class allowed the further separation of domicile and economy which the development of commercial endeavor demanded. The loosely organized lower-class family made possible a pool of geographically mobile, unbound labor. Later studies of industralization in New England show that migrants and the old laboring class constituted the factory labor force; the artisans continued at their trades for some time, until the need for their skills finally died out.

In general, the findings of this investigation provide some support for Max Weber's contention that in the final analysis the Puritan ethic promoted the development of capitalistic enterprise in America. The differences in findings can be ascribed mainly to methods of analysis.

Weber's discussion of the ideal-type entrepreneur placed the ascetic, responding to his calling, at the very center of the Protestant ethic. He regarded firm dedication to acquisitiveness as an expression of worldly asceticism. Strong family ties would interfere with the cultivation of industriousness inherent in the calling and with the reinvestment of profits to make more profits. In short, Weber saw the family solely as an agency for consumption hindering the development of rational capitalism.

In *The Protestant Ethic and the Spirit of Capitalism*, Weber considered post-Revolutionary Massachusetts to be the archetype of the Protestant ethic in action. Yet in Salem at the height of its phenomenal success as a seaport, families were organized in ways which did not oppose capitalistic enterprise. In fact, the one successful merchant who most conformed to Weber's ideal typical entrepreneur was despised by the community for his subordination of family and friends to acquisitiveness. Contrary to Weber's position, the family functioned as an instrument rather than an obstacle in the development of rational capitalism.

It is ironic that the asceticism which Weber considered crucial to the spirit of capitalism was less characteristic of entrepreneurs than craftsmen, whose family ties were strongest. Weber himself points out that Benjamin Franklin's printing business was essentially a handicraft enterprise and that

> it was by no means the capitalistic entrepreneurs of the commercial aristocracy, who were either the sole or the predominant bearers of the attitude we have here called the spirit of capitalism. It was much more the rising strata of the lower industrial middle classes.

The role of the family thus seems to be central in the transition of Salem from a community with strong medieval overtones to a commercial town. Were it not for the Puritan heritage, the kinds of family organization in the various parts of the social structure would have been different. Were it not for the demographic and technological changes, the federated community structure might have persisted. Hence, Salem at the end of the eighteenth century represents an historic moment when the families as a group were able to marshall their material and ideological resources in ways which changed the shape of their society dramatically.

The Post-Revolutionary American Family

Ideas about the family derived from Puritanism and based on biblical injunctions were diffused throughout the United States after 1800. Emigration to the West is apparent in many of the Salem genealogies. New England seaports became obsolete as large sailing vessels and steamships were built, and prosperous merchants migrated with their families to such commercial centers as New York and Philadelphia. Artisans and unskilled workers traveled southward and westward as well. Partly as a consequence of the decline of these seaports, the Puritan version of the biblical-based family model spread and influenced states outside of New England. Early Illinois marriage law was typical in the following Levitical norms. According to a footnote in the 1856 edition of *Illinois Statutes of a General Nature* (p. 739), "under the statute of 1819, males of the age of seventeen and females of fourteen, could be joined in marriage, "if not prohibited by the laws of God. 'A.' married the daughter of his sister, and the marriage was held to be within the Levitical degrees, and voidable, though not absolutely void." In other states, such as the Michigan statutes of 1857 (Vol. II, p. 950), marital proscriptions also adhered to the Levitical code, although no mention was made of a biblical reference.

The contemporary American family still bears some resemblance to its ancestor in Salem of 1790–1810. The similarity is apparent in the norms of family government, many ideas about marriage, and some socialization practices.

With regard to family government, studies of juvenile delinquency, mental illness, and other forms of deviance lay the blame on the family for the failure of its members to develop into responsible citizens in the community. The ideal of domestic control still dominates the thinking of many political leaders and educators. There appears to be a general consensus that the poor and their children are incompetent to manage their affairs; social workers, counselors, and other agents of welfare institutions are then brought in to assist them.

The biblical kinship structure upon which the Puritans modeled their family relationships has persisted in a modified form in modern society. Its close association with middle-class society even today is indicated in relationships among kin. Biblical kinship is characterized in part by the symbolic incorporation of a man or woman into his spouse's family of orientation. In eighteenth-century Salem, a man might use the terms "brother" and "brother-in-law" interchangeably in referring to his wife's sibling. Similarly, he might refer to his wife's mother as his "mother."

The perseverance of biblical kinship in contemporary middle-class families is suggested by the contrast in kinship terminology used to address in-laws in middle and lower socioeconomic groups. A study of kinship in a midwestern community indicates that middle-class young adults address their in-laws as "Mother" and "Father" when they feel close to them but address them by their first names when they feel more distant. The reverse is true for low socioeconomic classes, with the first name used to indicate a close tie. This usage of kin terms of address implies that a middle-class adult (regardless of motivation) acknowledges a status which he acquires in his spouse's family of orientation. This status is equivalent to that of his spouse and defines the married couple's relationship to their in-laws. For the lower class, however, kinship ties formed with affines represent merely formal relationships, whereas the *real* ties of married couples with in-laws are personal. As personal ties, the relationships with in-laws do not depend so much upon norms that govern status as on ways people relate to their in-laws as individuals. Hence, for the lower class, marital ties are not the gateway to a symbolic incorporation into one's spouse's family of orientation. Rather, as in the old Salem lower class, marital ties are relatively weak and bonds with maternal kin are frequently strong.

As in other aspects of family life, there appears to be some carryover of the Puritan-based model in areas of the socialization of children. In upper-class socialization, there is apparently emphasis upon moderation in child rearing; there is generally no attempt or "need" to inculcate strong motives of upward social mobility. For the middle classes, however, achievement motivation seems to be strong. This class focuses upon delayed gratification patterns, the suppression of eroticism which might interfere with achievement, and the recognition that effective authority (rather than a laissez-faire parent-child relationship) should exist. By contrast, lower class socialization places little emphasis upon delayed gratification, repression of eroticism, and the development of effective authority patterns; instead, lower-class families are plagued by many authority problems. Thus the general patterns in the socioeconomic variations of the Salem family seem to have persisted into modern urban society.

To the extent that norms governing the contemporary family resemble those pertaining to the Salem family of the period 1790–1810, the American kinship system can be said to retain the norms and values of the Puritan-based family as a cultural model.

As the editor of this book, I find myself in the position of including an article with which, in many respects, I take issue. Yet, despite my reservations, I consider this to be a valuable piece of historical sociology. In essence, Sennett tries to explain the response to the Haymarket Riot and subsequent disorders by looking at the family life of people living in the area. He sees two types of families there: those with a boarder, lodger, or kinsman in residence, which he describes as extended families, and the conventional nuclear families. He feels that the nuclear families, because of the absence of nonparental adults, were cut off from the larger world and that the "intensity" of life in such families created not only sons who were to prove less occupationally mobile than their counterparts in "extended" families but also fearfulness and hostility to anything strange or different. Some of Sennett's inferential leaps are truly monumental; nevertheless, he does give us some sense of what urban family life may have been like at this time through the imaginative use of a variety of data sources.

RICHARD SENNETT

6 *Middle-Class Families and Urban Violence: The Experience of a Chicago Community in the Nineteenth Century*

Unlike the other writers in this volume, I have sought in this essay to make historical judgments that cannot be proved in a rigorous way. Historians using sociological tools find in quantitative methods and constructs the possibility of achieving great precision in describing the past; for sociologists like myself who turn to the historical frame, a rather opposite possibility exists. For us, the complexities and contradictions found in the "actual time" of human life suggest ways in which abstract concepts can be made more dense and more subtle, and so less precise, in their evocation of men's experience.

This study seeks the hidden connections between two seemingly disparate phenomena in a quiet middle-class neighborhood of Chicago in the late nineteenth century: the family patterns of the people of the community and the peculiar response made by men living there to the eruption of violence in their midst. In imagining how the structure of family life was related to the character of men's reaction to violence, I have tried to recapture some of the subtlety of what it was like to be a middle-class city dweller during this era of rapid urban growth.

In the years 1886 and 1888 an epidemic of violence broke out in this quiet neighborhood of Chicago. The striking feature of this epidemic lay not in the violent events themselves but in the reaction of shopkeepers, store clerks, accountants, and highly skilled laborers to the disorder suddenly rampant among their sedate homes. Their reaction to violence was impassioned to an extent that in retrospect seems unwarranted by events; indeed it is the contrast between the limited character of the disorder and the sense residents had of being overwhelmingly threatened by anarchy that suggests that the response could have been a product of larger, seemingly unrelated social forces, such as the structure of family life.

The Community Setting

The scene of the disturbance, which I shall name Union Park, was an area centered on the near West Side of Chicago around a rather large park formally landscaped in the early 1850s. Like most of the middle and lower middle-class neighborhoods of American industrial cities in the later nineteenth century, the area was considered so nondescript that it was never given a special name, as were the richer and poorer sections of Chicago. Its people were the forgotten men of that era, neither poor enough to be rebels nor affluent enough to count in the affairs of the city. For a quarter century, from 1865 to 1890, Union Park epitomized that tawdry respectability of native-born, lower middle-class Americans that Dreiser was to capture in the early sections of *Sister Carrie,* or that Farrell would later rediscover in the bourgeois life of Catholic Chicago.

The beginnings of Union Park, when Chicago was a commercial town rather than a diverse manufacturing city, were much grander. For in the 1830s and 1840s it was a fashionable western suburb on the outskirts of town, separated by open land from the bustle of the business district and the noisome, unhealthy river at the heart of the city. A change in the pattern of commercial land investment, the filling in of a swamp on the edge of Lake Michigan by Potter Palmer, and the growth of a manufacturing district to the south of Union Park in the years after the Civil War led fashionable people to desert the old suburb for newer, more magnificent residences along the lake shore of Chicago. In their place, in the 1870s, came people of much lesser means, seeking a respectable place to live where rents and land were becoming cheap. Union Park for these new people was a neighborhood where they could enjoy the prestige of a once-fashionable address, and even pretend themselves to be a little grander than they were. "The social Brooklyn of Chicago," Mayor Harrison called it; "a place where modest women became immodest in their pretensions," wrote another contemporary observer of the area. For twenty-five years, the old holdings were gradually divided up into little plots, and native-born Americans—who were the bulk of the migrants to the cities of the Midwest before the 1880s—rented small brick houses or a half floor in one of the converted mansions.

During the middle 1880s, it was in modest, cheerless Union Park that a series of unexpected events broke out. A bloody encounter between laborers and police took place on its borders during the Haymarket Riot of 1886, to be followed eighteen months later by a series of highly expert robberies in the community, a crime wave that culminated in the murder of a leading Union Park resident. Union Park reacted by holding a whole class—the poor, and especially the immigrant poor—responsible for the course of unique and rather narrow events.

The Haymarket Bombing

> Certain people, mostly foreigners of brief residence among us, whose ideas of government were derived from their experience in despotic Germany, sought by means of violence and murder to inaugurate a carnival of crime. *F. H. Head, official orator at the unveiling of the Haymarket Square Statue for policemen slain in the riot, reported in the* Chicago Daily Tribune, *May 31, 1889, p. 5.*

During the 1870s and early 1880s the warehouse district of Chicago grew in a straight line west, across the Chicago River, up to the edge of Union Park. The haymarket constituted the farthest boundary of this district; it was the dividing line between the residences and neighborhood stores of Union Park and the warehouses of Chicago's growing central city. Haymarket Square itself was enclosed by large buildings and the Des Plaines Street Police Station was just off the Square. It was hardly a place to engage in clandestine activity, but, for a peaceful meeting, the Square was an ideal forum, since it could accommodate roughly 20,000 people.[1]

The common notion of what happened on May 4, 1886, is that a group of labor unionists assembled in Haymarket Square to listen to speeches and that, when the police moved in to break up the meeting, someone in the crowd threw a bomb, killing and wounding many policemen and bystanders. This account is true as far as it goes, but explains little of what determined the event's effect on the community and city in the aftermath.

The people who came to the meeting were the elite of the working class, those who belonged to the most skilled crafts;[2] they were hardly the "dregs" of society. The crowd itself was small, although it had been supposed that events in Chicago during the preceding days would have drawn a large gathering. On May 3, demonstrations had been organized in the southwestern part of the city against the McCormick Works, where a lockout of some union members had occurred. The police had responded with brutal force to disperse the crowd. Later that same night, at a number of prescheduled union meetings, it was resolved to hold a mass meeting at some neutral place in the city.[3]

A small group of Socialist union leaders, led by August Spies and Albert Parsons, decided the time was ripe for a mass uprising of laboring men; the moment seemed perfect for an expression of labor solidarity, when large numbers of people might be expected to rally to the cause as Spies and Parsons understood it—the growth of Socialist power. Haymarket Square was the obvious choice for a neutral site. Posters were printed in the early hours of the next day and spread throughout the city.

When Parsons and Spies mounted the speakers' rostrum the next night in Haymarket Square, they must have been appalled. Instead of vast crowds of militants, there were only a thousand or so people in the Square, and, as speaker after speaker took his turn, the crowd dwindled steadily. The audience was silent and unmoved as the explanations of the workers' role in socialism were expounded, though there was respect for the speakers of the kind one would feel for a friend whose opinions grew out of a different sphere of life. Yet as the meeting was about to die out, a phalanx of policemen suddenly appeared on the scene to disperse the crowd.

Why the police intruded is the beginning of the puzzle we have to understand. Their reaction was totally inappropriate to the character of what was occurring before their eyes; they ought rather to have breathed a sigh of relief that the meeting was such a peaceful fiasco. But, as the civil riots of a later chapter in Chicago's history show, it is sometimes more difficult for the police to "cool off" than the demonstrators. In any event, just as the Haymarket meeting was falling apart, the police moved in to disperse it by force, and thus brought back to life the temporary spirit of unity and of outrage against the violence at McCormick Works that had drawn crowd and orators together.

The knots of men moved back from the lines of police advancing toward the speaker's stand, so that the police gained the area in front of the rostrum without incident. Then, suddenly, someone in the crowd threw a powerful bomb into the midst of the policemen, and pandemonium broke loose. The wounded police and people in the crowd dragged themselves or were carried into the hallways of buildings in the eastern end of Union Park, drugstores, like Ebert's at Madison and Halstead and Barker's on West Madison, suddenly became hospitals with bleeding men stretched out on the floors, while police combed the residences and grounds of Union Park looking for wounded members of the crowd who had managed to find shelter, under stoops or in sheds, from the police guns booming in the Square.[4]

Reaction of the Middle Class

As the news spread, small riots broke out in the southwestern part of the city, with aimless targets, but they were soon dispersed.By the morning of May 5, the working-class quarters were quiet, though the police were not. They, and the middle-class people of Chicago, especially those living in Union Park, were in a fever, a fever compounded of fear, a desire for vengeance, and simple bewilderment.

It is this reaction that must be explored to gauge the true impact of the Haymarket incident on the Union Park community. The first characteristic of this reaction was how swiftly an interpretation, communally shared, was formed; the middle-class people of Union Park, and elsewhere in Chicago, were moved immediately by the incident to draw a defined, clear picture of what had happened, and they held onto their interpretation tenaciously. Today it is easy to recognize, from the location of the meeting next to a police station, from the apathy of the crowd, from the sequence of events that preceded the bombing, that the Haymarket incident was not a planned sequence of disorder or a riot by an enraged mob, but rather the work of an isolated man, someone who might have thrown the bomb no matter who was there. The day after the bombing, these objective considerations were not the reality "respectable" people perceived. Middle-class people of Chicago believed instead that "the immigrant anarchists" were spilling out of the slums to kill the police, in order to destroy the security of the middle class themselves. "Respectable" people felt some kind of need to believe in the enormity of the threat, and in this way the community quickly arrived at a common interpretation.

The enormity of the perceived threat was itself the second characteristic of their reaction. The color red, which was taken as a revolutionary incitement, was "cut out of street advertisements and replaced with a less suggestive color."[5] On the day after the riot a coroner's jury returned a verdict that all prisoners in the hands of the police were guilty of murder, because Socialism as such led to murderous anarchy, and anyone who attended the meeting must have been a Socialist. Yet this same jury observed that it was "troublesome" that none of those detained could be determined to have thrown the bomb. Anarchism itself was generalized to a more sweeping level by its identification with foreign birth; the "agitators" were poor foreigners, and this fact could explain their lawlessness. For example, the *Tribune* reported that on the day after the Haymarket Riot police closed two saloons

> that were the headquarters of the foreign-speaking population, which flaunts and marches under the red flag, and heretofore they were the centers of a great throng of men who did little but drink beer and attend the meetings in the halls above.[6]

On May 5 and 6, the police were engaged in a strenuous effort to determine where the "anarchist" groups lived, so that the population as a whole might be controlled. On May 7, and this was the view to prevail henceforward, they announced that the residences of most anarchists must be in the southwestern portion of the city, the immigrant, working-class area.[7]

The assigning of the responsible parties to the general category of "foreigner" excited even more panic in Union Park. It was reported in the *Tribune* of May 7 that a fear existed in the community that lawless marauders would again erupt out of the proletarian sector of the city and terrorize people in the neighborhood of the riot.[8] These fears were sustained by two events in the next week.

First were reports of the deaths, day after day, of policemen and innocent bystanders who had been seriously wounded by the bomb on May 4, coupled with a massive newspaper campaign to raise money for the families of the victims. Second, and by far more important, fear of renewed bombing was kept alive by the phantasies of a Captain Schaack of the Chicago police who day by day discovered and foiled anarchist plots, plans to bomb churches and homes, attempts on the lives of eminent citizens. Such were the horror stories with which the middle-class people of Chicago scared themselves for weeks.

Some kind of deep communal force engendered in the people of Union Park an immediately shared interpretation of what objectively was a confused event; this same communal force led men to escalate the metaphors of threat and challenge involved in this one event. As events a year later were to show, the force that produced these two characteristics of response was also to prevent the men of Union Park from being able to deal with future violence in an effective way.

Burglaries and Murder

On Thursday, February 9, 1888, the *Chicago Tribune* gave its lead space to the following story:

> Amos J. Snell, a millionaire who lived at the corner of Washington Boulevard and Ada Street, was shot to death by two burglars who entered his house and made off with $1,600 worth of county warrants and $5,000 in checks. The murder was committed at about 2 A.M. and discovered by a servant at about 6:30 A.M.[9]

Snell had been a resident of the area since 1867, when he built a home in Union Park and bought up many blocks of desirable real estate around it.

The murder of Snell climaxed a tense situation in Union Park that had existed since the beginning of the year 1888. Since New Year's Day, "between forty and fifty burglaries have been committed within a radius of half a mile from the intersection of Adams and Ashland Avenues," the Editor of the *Tribune* wrote the day after Snell's death. The police counted half this number; it appears that the burglars had a simple and systematic scheme: to loot any household goods, such as furs, silver plate, jewelry, or bonds left in unlocked drawers. Occasionally some of the property was recovered, and occasionally a thief was arrested who seemed to have been involved, but the operation itself was remarkably smooth and successful.[10]

How did people in Union Park react to these burglaries, and what did they do to try to stop them? The reaction of the community was much like the reaction to the Haymarket bombing: they felt involved at once in a "reign of terror," as the *Tribune* said,[11] that was none of their doing—they didn't know when the danger would strike again or who would be threatened. Most of all, they didn't know how to stop it.[12] Once again, the level of fear was escalated to a general, sweeping, and impersonal level.

Before the Snell murder, the citizens of the community had tried two means of foiling the robbers, and so of quieting the fears within their families. One was to make reports to the police, reports which the editor of the *Tribune* claimed the police did not heed. The citizens then resorted to fortifying their homes, to hiring elderly men as private night guards, but the thieves were professional enough to deal with this: "somehow or other the burglars evaded all the precautions that were taken to prevent their nocturnal visits."[13]

After the Murder: A Change in Communal Attitudes

The Snell murder brought public discussion of the robberies, and how to stop them, to a high pitch. Especially in Union Park, the vicinity of Snell's residence, the community was "so aroused that the people talked of little else than vigilance committees and frequent holdings of court . . . as a panacea for the lawless era that had come upon them."[14] Gradually, the small-town vigilante idea gave way to a new attitude toward the police, and how the police should operate in a large city. "It is no use," said one member of the Grant Club, the West Side club to which Snell himself had belonged, "to attempt to run a cosmopolitan city as you would run a New England village."[15] He meant that the police had up to that time concentrated on closing down gambling houses and beer parlors as a major part of their effort to keep the town "respectable" and "proper." Thus they didn't deal effectively with serious crimes like robbery and murder because they spent too much time trying to clean up petty offenses; the main thing was to keep the criminal elements confined to their own quarters in the city. In all these discussions, the fact of being burgled had been forgotten. The search turned to a means of separatism, of protection against the threatening "otherness" of the populace outside the community.

Such views were striking, considering the position of Union Park. The community's own physical character, in its parks and playgrounds, was nonurban, designed in the traditions of Olmstead and Vaux; the people, as was pointed out repeatedly in the newspaper account, were themselves among the most respectable and staid in the city, if not the most fashionable. Yet here were the most respectable among the respectable arguing for abandoning the enforcement throughout the city of a common morality. The petty criminals outside the community's borders ought to be left in peace, but out of sight. Union Park existed in a milieu too cosmopolitan for every act of the lower classes to be controlled; the police ought to abandon the attempt to be the guardians of all morality and instead concentrate on assuring the basic security of the citizens against outbursts of major crime.

Richard Sennett

What Union Park wanted instead, and what it got, was a garrison of police to make the community riotproof and crimeproof. The police indeed abandoned the search for the killers, and concentrated on holding the security of Union Park, like an area under siege. In this way, the original totally suburban tone of the parks and mansions was transformed; this respectable neighborhood felt its own existence to be so threatened that only a state of rigid barriers, enforced by a semimilitary state of curfew and surveillance, would permit it to continue to function.

The effect of the riot and the train of burglaries and murder was to put the citizens in a frame of mind where only the closure of the community through constant surveillance and patrolling would reassure them. Indeed, the characteristics of their reaction to violence could only lead to such a voluntary isolation: everyone "knew" immediately what was wrong; and what was wrong was overwhelming; it was nothing less than the power of the "foreigner," the outsider who had suddenly become dominant in the city. Isolation, through garrisons and police patrols, was the only solution.

Union Park held onto its middle-class character until the middle of the 1890s; there was no immediate desertion by respectable people of the area in the wake of the violence: where else in a great city, asked one citizen, was it safe to go? Everywhere the same terror was possible.

The contrast between the limited character of civil disturbance and the immediate perception of that disturbance as the harbinger of an unnameable threat coming from a generalized enemy is a theme that binds together much research on urban disorders.

Until a few years ago, riots were taken to be the expression of irrational, and directionless, aggression. The "irrationality of crowds," and similar explanations of crowd behavior as an innate disorder, was first given a cogent interpretation in the industrial era in the writings of Le Bon,[16] for whom the irrational brutality of crowds was a sign of how the "psychology" of the individual becomes transformed when the individual acts in concert with other people. According to Le Bon, the crowd releases a man from the self-reflective, rational restraints that normally operate when a person is alone or with one or two other people. The anonymity of mass gatherings reinforces the desire each one has to cast off these rational, individual restraints, and encourages men to express more violent traits without fear of personal detection. It is the social psychology of the massive gathering to be unrestrained, Le Bon wrote, the psychology of the individual to prescribe rules for himself.[17]

This image of crowds was as congenial to many of the syndicalists on the Left (though not Sorel) as it was to the fears of bourgeois people like those in Union Park. The difficulty with the image is that, for the nineteenth century at least, it seems not to fit the facts of crowd behavior.

Thanks to the pioneering work of George Rudé and Charles Tilly,[18] it has been possible to ascertain that, in the urbanizing of English and French populations during the early nineteenth century, popular rebellions and crowd activities possessed a high degree of rationality; that is to say, the crowds acted to achieve rather well-defined ends, and used only as much force as was required to make their demands prevail. Though the work of Rudé and Tilly seems contradicted by the extensive researches of Louis Chevalier[19] on Parisian lower-class behavior during the nineteenth century, there are enough points of agreement, in looking at crowd behavior where violent coercion is involved, to rule out the "unrestrained frenzy" Le Bon saw in crowds that made them useless as a social tool to gain definite, common goals.[20] What is important in Le Bon's work, for the present purpose, was his *expectation* that this unrestrained frenzy would result from group action by the lower class.

For it is this same split between middle-class expectation of blind anarchy and the actual limitations on working-class disorder that characterized the Haymarket incidents, the same split between a reign of terror sensed during the later burglaries and the actual routine narrowness of these crimes.

The problem of the Union Park experience was the citizenry's inability to connect the facts seen to the facts as elements of what people knew was a correct interpretation. Expecting "seething passions" to erupt hysterically, the middle-class people of Chicago and their police were somehow immune to the spectacle they should have enjoyed, that of the workers becoming bored with the inflammatory talk of their supposed leaders. The expectations of a seething rabble had somehow to be fulfilled, and so the police themselves took the first step. After the shooting was over, the respectable people of Chicago became in turn inflamed. This blind passion in the name of defending the city from blind passion is the phenomenon that needs to be explained. A similar contradiction occurred in the series of robberies a half a year later as well. As in the riot, the facts of the rationality of the enemy and his limited purpose, although acknowledged, were not absorbed; he was felt to be something else, a nameless, elusive terror, all-threatening. And the people reacted with a passion equal to his.

This mystifying condition, familiar now in the voices heard from the "New Right," is what I should like to explain, not through a sweeping theory that binds the past to the present, but through a theory that explains this peculiar reaction in terms of strains in the family life of the Union Park people. What I would like to explore —and I certainly do not pretend to prove it—is how, in an early industrial city, the fears of the foreign masses by a middle-class group may have reflected something other than the actual state of interaction between bourgeoisie and proletariat. These fears may have reflected instead the impact of family life on the way the people like those in Union Park understood their places in the city society.

Studies of overreaction to limited stimuli have centered, for the most part, on the idea of a "frustration-aggression syndrome." This ungainly phrase was given a clear definition in one of the early classic works of American social psychology, *Frustration and Aggression* (1939). The authors wrote that

> aggression is always a consequence of frustration. More specifically . . . the occurrence of aggressive behavior always presupposes the existence of frustration and, contrariwise, the existence of frustration always leads to some form of aggression.[21]

Applied in terms of social class, this frustration-aggression syndrome implies that when a group fails to achieve goals it desires, or when it is unable to maintain a position it covets, it becomes aggressive, and searches out objects on which it can blame its failure. This simple, clear idea Parsons[22] has applied to the formation of the Nazi party in Germany: the fall in status in the 1920s of fixed-income, middle-class groups breeding an aggressive desire to get back at their enemies, without knowing, or really caring, who they were. Lipset[23] has incorporated elements of the same idea in his essay on working-class authoritarianism in the United States after the Second World War. And of course the concept is now used to explain the hostility of lower middle-class whites toward blacks: the whites who have failed to rise high in the economic system they believe in are said to make blacks "aggression objects" of the frustration they themselves have suffered.[24]

If it is true, as this syndrome of frustration-aggression suggests, that in the character one ascribes to one's enemy lies a description of something in one's own experience, the nature of the fear of lower-class foreigners among Union Park families might tell something about the Union Park community itself. The Union Park men, during the time of the riot and robberies, accused their chosen enemies of being, first, lawless anarchists, which was transmuted, secondly, to being pushed by their base passions outside the bounds of acceptable behavior, which resolved itself, finally, to being emotionally out of control. If the poor were reasonable, if they were temperate, ran the argument, these violent things would not have come to pass.

What about the Union Park people themselves, then? Were they masters of themselves? A study I have recently completed on the family patterns of the Union Park people during the decades of the 1870s and '80s may throw some light on the question of stability and purposefulness in their lives: it is the dimension of stability in these family patterns, I believe, that shaped sources of the reaction to violence.

Intensive Family Life

In 1880, on a forty-square-block territory of Union Park, there lived 12,000 individuals in approximately 3,000 family units. These family units were of three kinship types: single-member families, where one person lived alone without any other kin; nuclear families, consisting of a husband, wife, and their unmarried children; and extended families, where to the nuclear unit was added some other relative—a brother or sister of the parents, a member of a third generation, or a son or daughter who was married and lived with his spouse in the parental home. The most common form of the extended family in Union Park was that containing "collateral kin," that is, unmarried relatives of the same generation as the husband or wife.

The dominant form of family life in Union Park was nuclear, for 80% of the population lived in such homes, with 10% of the population living alone in single-member families, and the remaining 10% living in extended family situations. A father and mother living alone with their growing children in an apartment or house was the pervasive household condition. There were few widowed parents living with their children in either nuclear or extended homes, and though the census manuscripts on which my study of the year 1880 is based were inexact at this point, there appeared to be few groups of related families living in separate dwellings but in the same neighborhood.

Is this nuclear-family dominance a special characteristic of middle-class life in this era? At the Joint Center for Urban Studies, I was fortunate in working with other researchers in this field to coordinate census measures of class and family form that could be used comparatively across different studies.[25] Comparison with these other studies, as well as within the limited range of social groups in Union Park, convinces me that this kind of family form was not a middle-class phenomenon. Within Union Park, the 80% dominance of the nuclear families held in lower social strata (of which enough existed to measure and test statistically, since the population as a whole was so large —about 25% of the community fell into a working-class category, excluding the servants in the homes of the other 75%) and through-out the range of middle-class groups. In Lynn Lees' data on an Irish working-class district in London in 1860, it similarly appeared that about 80% of her community's population lived in nuclear family configurations, 10% in single-member families, and 10% in extended families, virtually the same distribution as was found in Chicago's Union Park in 1880.

Again, the *outer* limits on the size of families in Union Park did seem to be the product of a special class condition. Contrary to the stereotype of the sprawling families of the poor, in Union Park the size of poor families was in its contours similar to the size of the wealthier ones: few families were larger than six members, among rich or poor. Similarly, comparison of family sizes in Union Park to the poor Irish of Lynn Lee's study or to the middle-class area of St. Pancras in London reveals the limits on family size in the three areas to have been the same.

Since family studies of nineteenth-century cities are at this date in a primitive stage, the body of future research may show these present examples to be "sports" or explainable by circumstances re-searchers do not now understand. Yet it does now seem more fruitful to concentrate on the *function* of nuclear families or on the *function* of families of restricted size in middle-class communities in the great cities of the nineteenth century, rather than to try to locate the condi-tions of peculiarly middle-class life in the *structural* existence of these family types.

What I did find to be true in Union Park was the following: over the course of time internal conditions of family structure and of family size tended to lead to similar family histories. Nuclear families had characteristic histories similar to the experience of smaller families having from two to four kin members in the 1870s and '80s. Extended families, on the other hand, had histories similar to the experience of the minority of families with four to six kin members during these decades. What made this process subtle was that nuclear families did not tend to be smaller, or extended larger. Family size and family kinship structure seemed rather to be independent structures with parallel internal differences in functioning.

Why and how this was so can be understood by assessing the patterns of the generations of the dominant group of nuclear, small-size families during the year 1880. These families were marked, in the relations between husbands and wives, parents and children, by strong patterns of family cohesion. Whether rich or poor, the young men and women from such homes rarely broke away to live on their own until they themselves were ready to marry and found families, an event that usually occurred when the man was in his early thirties. The families of Union Park, observers of the time noted, were extremely self-contained, did little entertaining, and rarely left the home to enjoy even such modest pleasures as a church social or, for the men, a beer at the local tavern. The small family, containing only parents and their immediate children, resisted the diverse influences of either other kin associations or extensive community contacts. This was the mode of family life that dominated Union Park numerically. These families can be called "intensive families," and their life histories contrasted to families of larger size or more complex kinship. The intensive families would seem to epitomize a defined order of stability among the people of Union Park, Yet, Lynn Lees and I have found some functional differences between Chicago and London in families of this general character.

Instability Through Separation or Desertion

In most census collections in the United States and Britain, the official tabulations of divorce are very low, because the formal breaking of the marital tie was considered a disgrace to both partners. But, as Talcott Parsons has demonstrated,[26] these official figures are misleading, since a great deal of unofficial divorce through separation or desertion occurred, at a higher rate, Parsons thinks, than in our own time. One means of detecting this hidden marital disorder in the census is to locate the individuals who were officially married but living without a spouse in the family. This measurement lets in a certain number of "beachhead migrants," men who have come to the city in advance of their families to establish a job and find a house, but in Union Park such men were less common in this category than spouses who were married, living with their children, but not with their husbands (or wives).[27]

In Union Park the number of families involved in such a break was about 10%. But in London, in the middle-class district of St. Pancras, the incidence of such marital separation was one-half of this, or 5%; in the lower-class Irish district Lynn Lees studied, there were less than a third as many marital separations of this type. In all three communities, of course, the official rate of divorce was nearly zero.

The explanation for this comparatively high incidence of marital break in Union Park is obscure, since there are now so few other comparative measures of family conditions behind the official statistics to use. In terms of these Chicago and London communities themselves perhaps the best thing to be said is the simplest: the higher incidence of marital break occurred in a city whose development was exclusively in the industrial era; the lower incidence of such a break occurred in a city for whom industrial production and large bureaucratic enterprises were but one chapter in a very long history.

Work Mobility and Family Stability

Added to this kind of family instability in the community as a whole, my study of intergenerational mobility in work and residence from 1872 to 1890 revealed a complicated, but highly significant pattern of insecurity in the dominant intensive families when compared to the smaller group of less intensive families.[28]

In the nuclear-family homes and in the smaller families the fathers were stable in their patterns of job holding, as a group, over the course of the eighteen years studied; roughly the same proportions of unskilled, skilled, and white-collar workers of various kinds composed the labor force of these nuclear fathers in 1890 as in 1872. Given the enormous growth of Chicago's industrial production, its banking and financial capital, retail trade volume, as well as the proliferation of the population (100% increase each ten years) and the greatly increasing proportion of white-collar pursuits during this time, such stability in job distribution is truly puzzling. Further, this pattern of job holding among the fathers of intensive families was not shared by the fathers in extended families or fathers of larger families living in Union Park. They were mobile up into exclusively bureaucratic, white-collar pursuits, so that by 1890 virtually none of these fathers worked with their hands. Within the range of white-collar occupations, the extended-family fathers and the large-family fathers gradually concentrated in executive and other lesser management pursuits and decreased their numbers in shopkeeping, toward which, stereotypically, they were supposed to gravitate.

Now the differences between fathers and sons in each of these family groups were even more striking. I found the sons in the dominant family homes to be, unlike their fathers, very unstable in their patterns of job holding, with as much movement down into manual pursuits over the course of the eighteen years as movement up within the white-collar occupations. Following the lead of Blau and Duncan,[29] we might be tempted to explain this pattern of dispersion simply as regression-toward-the-mean of higher status groups intergenerationally. But the sons of extended and large families did not move in this mixed direction. Rather, they followed in the footsteps of their fathers into good white-collar positions, with almost total elimination of manual labor in their ranks over the course of time. This pattern occurred in small-family sons versus large-family sons and in nuclear-family sons versus extended-family sons. The difference in the groups of sons was especially striking in that the starting distribution of the sons in the occupational work force was virtually the *same*, in the measure of family form and in those of family size. Thernstrom has pointed out in the conference discussions for this volume that economic aid between generations of workers ought to manifest itself more at the beginning point of the careers of the young rather than when the older generation has retired and the young have become the principal breadwinners. In Union Park, the fact that both extended-family and nuclear-family sons, both large- and small-family sons, began to work in virtually the same pursuits as their fathers, but then became distinctively different in their patterns of achievement, strongly suggests that something *beyond* monetary help was at work in these families to produce divergences in work experience in the city.

The residence patterns of the generations of the intensive and less intensive families also bears on the issues of stability and instability in the lives of the people of Union Park. Up to the time of violence in the Union Park area, the residence patterns of the two kinds of families, in both the parents' and the sons' generations, were rather similar. In the wake of the violence it appears that, within the parents' generation, there was significant movement back into the Union Park area, whereas for the half decade preceding the disturbances there was a general movement out to other parts of Chicago. It is in the generation of the sons that differences between the two family groups appeared. In the wake of the violence, the sons of large families and of extended families continued the processes of residential break from Union Park initiated during the early years of the 1880 decade. The sons from intensive families did not; in the years following the violence they stopped migrating beyond the boundaries of the community they had known as children, and instead kept closer to their first homes.

Two Theories of Intensive Family Stability

In my study of Union Park,[30] I tried to explain these differences in work experience and in residence in terms of patterns of family life and child nurturance for bourgeois people in a new, immensely dynamic, disordered city. In so doing, my researches led me into a debate that exists between the work of the sociologist Talcott Parsons and the cultural historian Philippe Ariès.[31] For Parsons has argued that the small nuclear family is an adaptive kinship form to the industrial order; the lack of extensive kin obligations and a wide kin circle in this family type means, Parsons has contended, that the kinship unit does not serve as a binding private world of its own, but rather frees the individual to participate in "universalized" bureaucratic structures that are urban-wide and dynamic.[32] Aries has challenged this theory by amassing a body of historical evidence to show that the extended kinship relationships in large families, at least during the period he studied, were actually less sheltering, more likely to push the individual out into the world where he would have to act like a full man on his own at an early age, than the intense, intimate conditions of the nineteenth-century home. In intensive homes, the young person spent a long time in a state of independence under the protection and guidance of his elders. Consequently, argues Aries, the capacity of the young adult from small nuclear homes to deal with the world about him was blunted, for he passed from a period of total shelter to a state in which he was expected to be entirely competent on his own.[33] Aries' attack has been supported for contemporary American urban communities by a variety of studies, the most notable being those of Eugene Litwak and Marvin Sussman, and it has been supported for English cities by the work of Peter Willmott and Elizabeth Bott.[34]

The data I have collected on Union Park during the early stages of Chicago's industrial-bureaucratic expansion clearly are in line with the argument made by Aries. The young from homes of small scale or from homes where the structure of the family was nuclear and "privatistic," in Aries' phrase, had an ineptness in the work world, and a rootedness to the place of their childhood not found to the same degree among the more complex, or larger-family situations. (I have no desire to argue the moral virtues of this rootedness to community or failure to "make it" in the city; these simply happened to be the conditions that existed.) But the context of these Union Park families as new urbanites, in a new kind of city form, alters the meaning of stability and shelter leading to instability in the next generation among the intense family households. For it is clear that the nineteenth-century, privatistic, sheltering homes Aries depicts, homes Frank Lloyd Wright describes in his *Autobiography* for his early years in Chicago, homes that observers of the time pointed to as a basic element in the composition of the "dull respectability" of Union Park, could easily have served as a refuge themselves from the confusing, dynamic city that was taking shape all around the confines of Union Park. It indeed seems natural that middle-class people should try to hold onto the status position they had in such a disrupting, growing milieu, make little entrepreneurial ventures outside their established jobs, and withdraw themselves into the comfort and intimacy of their families. Here is the souce of that job "freeze" to be seen in the mobility patterns of fathers in intense-family situations; the bourgeois intensive family in this way became a shelter from the work pressures of the industrial city, a place where men tried to institute some control and establish some comforting intimacies in the shape of their lives, while withdrawing to the sidelines as the new opportunities of the city industries opened up. Such an interpretation of these middle-class families complements, on the side of the home, the interpretation Richard Hofstadter has made of the middle classes politically, in the latter part of the nineteenth century. He characterizes them as feeling that the new industrial order was not theirs, but had passed them by and left them powerless.[35] It is this peculiar feeling of social helplessness on the part of the fathers that explains what use they made of their family lives.

Confusion in the Desire for Stability

What makes this complex pattern of family stability-instability significant for wider social orientations are the values about work to be found in the middle classes of this era. For here the idea of seizing opportunities, the idea of instability of job tenure for the sake of rising higher and higher, constituted, as John Cawelti has described it,[36] the commonly agreed-upon notion of how sure success could be achieved at this time among respectable people; in the same way, this chance-taking path was presented, in the Horatio Alger novels and the like, as the road into the middle class itself. One should have been mobile in work, then, for this was the meaning of "opportunity" and "free enterprise," but in fact the overwhelming dislocations of the giant cities seem to have urged many men to retreat into the circle of their own families, to try simply to hold onto what they knew they could perform as tasks to support themselves, in the midst of the upheaval of urban expansion.

This is deduction, to be sure, and perhaps it is characteristic of sociologists dealing with history that they speculate where historians would prefer to remain silent and let the ambiguities stand. Yet the body not only of Union Park data, but the memoirs, fictional portraits, and secondary studies of this period seem to me to indicate that such an internally contradictory response to urbanization among the heads of middle-class families is the means by which the differences in social mobility between kinds of families can be explained. Conditions of privacy and comfort in the home weakened the desire to get ahead in the world, to conquer it; since the fathers of the intensive families were retreating from the confusions of city life, their preparation of their sons for work in Chicago became ambiguous, in that they wanted, surely, success for their sons, yet shielded the young, and did not themselves serve as models of successful adaptation. The result of these ambiguities can be seen directly in the work experience of the sons, when contrasted to the group of sons from families which, by virtue either of family form or size, were more complex or less intense. Overlaid on these family patterns was a relatively high rate of hidden marital breakdown in Union Park—one in every ten homes —while the expectation was, again, that such breakdown must not occur, that it was a disgrace morally.

These contradictions in family process gave rise, I believe, to the characteristics of Union Park's reaction to violence during the years 1886 to 1888.

The Feeling of Threat Generated by the Family Experience

In the older version of the "frustration-aggression" syndrome it was assumed that if a social group failed to achieve a certain goal, it searched for an enemy to punish. But the goals of these middle-class people in Union Park were themselves self-contradictory: they wanted success in the work of the city and yet they didn't want it, given the definition of success at that time as an entrepreneurial grasping of opportunities rather than the fruit of plodding and routine service. The goals for the home were also contradictory: they wanted a stable shelter from the confusion and terror of the city, yet somehow they expected their sons, growing up sheltered, to be able to make it in that city world, and the sons of the dominant family groups seemed unable to do so. Divorce was a disgrace, yet there is evidence that one out of every ten of the neighborhood families were involved in a marital separation or desertion, a voluntary condition as opposed to the involuntary break of widowhood. Thus, because the goals of these middle-class people were bred of an equal desire to escape from and succeed in the city, the possibility of a wholly satisfying pattern of achievement for them was denied. The contradictory nature of the family purpose and products was innately frustrating so that a family impulse in one direction inevitably defeated another image of what was wanted. This meant that the sources of defeat were nameless for the families involved; surely these families were not aware of the web of self-contradictions in which in retrospect they seem to have been enmeshed; they knew only that things never seemed to work out to the end planned, that they suffered defeats in a systematic way. It is this specific kind of frustration that would lead to a sense of being overwhelmed, which, in this community's family system, led easily to a hysterical belief in hidden, unknown threats ready to strike at a man at almost any time.

Feeling of Threat and Perceptions of Violence

What I would like to suggest is that this complex pattern of self-defeat explains the character of the Union Park reaction to violence. For the dread of the unknown that the middle classes projected onto their supposed enemies among the poor expressed exactly the condition of self-instituted defeat that was the central feature of the family system in Union Park. And this dread was overwhelming precisely because men's own contradictory responses to living in such a city were overwhelming. They had defined a set of conditions for their lives that inevitably left them out of control. The fact that there was in Union Park a desire to destroy the "immigrant anarchists" or to garrison the neighborhood against them, as a result of the incidents of violence, was important in that it offered an outlet for personal defeats, not just for anger against lawbreakers. This response to violence refused to center on particular people, but rather followed the "path of hysterical reaction," in Freud's phrase, and centered on an abstract class of evildoers. For the fear of being suddenly overwhelmed from the outside was really a sign that one was in fact in one's own life being continually overwhelmed by the unintended consequences, or "latent consequences" as Merton calls them, of what one did.[37] By blaming the urban poor for their lawlessness, these middle-class people were expressing a passion for retribution that had little to do with riots or thefts. The retribution was rather in the nature of what Erikson calls a "cover object" for hostility, an expression of inability to deal with the issues of one's own life, of mobility and stability in the city: the fear in these middle-class people was that if they were to act entrepreneurially in the work world they might be destroyed, yet their desire was to make it big suddenly. The desire to escape to the safety of the simple home of father, mother, and children became, unexpectedly, a crippling shield when the sons went out into the world.

This dilemma, expressed in the terrible fear of attack from the unbridled masses, was also related to the fear of falling into deep poverty that grew up in urban middle-class families of this time. To judge from a wide range of novels in the latter half of the nineteenth century there was a dread among respectable people of suddenly and uncontrollably falling into abject poverty; the Sidwells in Thackeray's *Vanity Fair* plummet from wealth to disorganized penury in a short space of time; Lily Bart's father, in Edith Wharton's *Age of Innocence*, is similarly struck down by the symbol of entrepreneurial chance in the industrial city, the stock market. This feeling of threat from the impersonal, unpredictable workings of the city economy was much like the sense of threat that existed in the Union Park families, because the dangers encountered in both cases were not a person or persons one could grapple with, but an abstract condition, poverty, or family disorder that was unintended, impersonal, and swift to come if the family should once falter. Yet what one *should* do was framed in such a self-contradictory way that it seemed oneself and one's family were always on the edge of survival. In this way, the growth of the new industrial city, with its uncertainties and immense wastes of human poverty not all to be dismissed as personal failures, could surely produce in the minds of middle-class citizens, uneasy about their own class position, living out from the center of town, the feeling that some terrible force from below symbolized by the poor, the foreigner, was about to strike out and destroy them unless they did something drastic.

The demographic reaction among most of the families to the eruption of violence bears out this interpretation of events. With the exception of the upwardly mobile, extended-family sons, most family members did not try to flee the community as a response to the threats of riot and the organized wave of crime. The demographic movement mirrored a renewed feeling of community solidarity in the face of violence, a solidarity created by fear and a common dread of those below. Again, it is significant that the group that did not show this pattern of "sticking out the trouble" is the generation of young family members who lived in more complex family circumstances than the majority, and who achieved, on the whole, greater occupational gains than the majority.

The relations between family life and the perception of violence in this Chicago community could be formed into the following general propositions. These were middle-class families enormously confused in what they wanted for themselves in the city, considered in terms of their achievements in the society at large and in terms of their emotional needs for shelter and intimacy; their schema of values and life goals was in fact formed around the issues of stability and instability as goals in a self-contradictory way. The result of this inner contradiction was a feeling of frustration, of not really being satisfied, in the activities of family members to achieve *either* patterns of stability or mobility for themselves. The self-defeat involved in this process led these families naturally to feel themselves threatened by overwhelming, nameless forces they could not control, no matter what they did. The outbreak of violence was a catalyst for them, giving them in the figure of the "other," the stranger, the foreigner, a generalized agent of disorder and disruption.

It is this process that explains logically why the people of Union Park so quickly found a communally acceptable villain responsible for violence, despite all the ambiguities perceived in the actual outbreaks of the disorders themselves; this is why the villain so quickly identified was a generalized, nonspecific human force, the embodiment of the unknown, the outside, the foreign. This is why the people of Union

Park clung so tenaciously to their interpretation, seemed so willing to be terrorized and distraught.

If the complex processes of family and social mobility in Union Park are of any use in understanding the great fear of disorder among respectable, middle-class urbanites of our own time, their import is surely disturbing. For the nature of the disease that produced this reaction to violence among the industrial middle classes was not simply a matter of "ignorance" or failure to understand the problems of the poor; the fear was the consequence, rather, of structural processes in the lives of the Union Park families themselves. Thus for attitudes of people like the Union Park dwellers to change, and a more tolerant view of those below to be achieved, nothing so simple as more education about poor people, or to put the matter in contemporary terms; more knowledge about Negroes, would have sufficed. The whole fabric of the city, in its impact on staid white-collar workers, would have to have been changed. The complexity and the diversity of the city itself would need to have been stilled for events to take another course. But were the disorder of the city absent, the principal characteristic of the industrial city as we know it would also have been absent. These cities were powerful agents of change, precisely because they replaced the controlled social space of village and farm life with a kind of human settlement too dense and too various to be controlled.

And it comes to mind that the New Right fears of the present time are as deeply endemic to the structure of complex city life as was the violent reaction to violence in Union Park. Perhaps, out of patterns of self-defeat in the modern middle classes, it is bootless to expect right-wing, middle-class repression to abate simply through resolves of goodwill, "education about Negroes," or a change of heart. The experience of these bourgeois people of Chicago one hundred years ago may finally serve to make us a great deal more pessimistic about the chances for reason and tolerance to survive in a complex and pluralistic urban society.

Notes

1   Henry David, *The Haymarket Affair* (New York, 1936), p. 198.

2   See Foster Rhea Dulles, *A History of American Labor* (New York, 1949), passim.

3   *Chicago Daily Tribune,* May 4, 1886, pp. 1, 2.

4   See the full account in the *Chicago Daily Tribune,* May 5, 1886, p. 1.

5   David, p. 226.

6   *Chicago Daily Tribune,* May 6, 1886, p. 3.

7   *Chicago Daily Tribune,* May 7, 1886, p. 8.

8   Ibid.

9   *Chicago Daily Tribune,* February 9, 1888, pp. 1–2.

10   Ibid., p. 4.

11   Ibid., pp. 1–2.

12   See the statements of the Union Park fathers in *Chicago Daily Tribune,* February 9, 1888, p. 2.

13   *Chicago Daily Tribune,* February 9, 1888, pp. 1–2.

14   Ibid.

15   Ibid.

16   G. Le Bon, *The Crowd: A Study of the Popular Mind* (London, 1909).

17   It is interesting that Le Bon was led by this route into looking later in his life for a different set of psychological "instincts" in crowds than in individuals.

18   George Rudé, *The Crowd in History, 1730–1840* (New York, 1954) and Charles Tilly, *The Vendée* (Cambridge, Mass., 1964).

19   L. Chevalier, *Classes Laborieuses et Classes Dangeureuses* (Paris, 1958).

20   I understand Chevalier is now more convinced of the "rationality" hypothesis. See, as one indication of this, the writings on Belleville in L. Chevalier, *Les Parisiens* (Paris, 1967).

21   J. Dollar, L. Doob, J. Miller, E. Mower, J. Sears, et al., *Frustration and Aggression* (New Haven, 1939), p. 1.

22   See "Democracy and Social Structure in Pre-Nazi Germany" in Parsons, *Essays in Sociological Theory* (rev. ed., Glencoe, Ill., 1954).

23   See Seymour Martin Lipset, *Political Man,* Pt. I, Chap, 4 (New York, 1960).

24   This theory, widely expressed in the press by amateur sociologists, explains the phenomenon neatly as a whole, but explains nothing of the particulars of class jealousy or fear.

25   Stephan Thernstrom and Lynn Lees, work in progress (description to be found in Joint Center *Bulletin* of 1968). The measures are also relatable to the social class categories used by D. V. Glass in his study of intergenerational social mobility in Britain; Part III of *Social Mobility in Britain,* D. V. Glass, ed. (London, 1954).

26   Talcott Parsons and Robert Bales, *Family,* Chap. 1 (Glencoe, Ill., 1955).

27   See Charles Tilly, *"Migration to an American City"* (unpublished manuscript on file at Joint Center for Urban Studies) for an excellent discussion of migration patterns.

28   There were, of course, no two-generation households in the single-member families.

29   P. Blau and O. D. Duncan, *The American Occupational Structure* (New York, 1967).

30   *Families Against the City* (Cambridge, Mass., 1970).

31   Phillipe Ariès, *Centuries of Childhood* (New York, 1965).

32   Parsons and Bales, Chap. 1.

33   Bernard Wishy, in *The Child and the Republic* (Philadelphia, 1967), has material relevant to this idea for America in the late nineteenth century.

34   See Sennett, *Families Against the City,* Chap. 9, for a review of this literature.

35   Richard Hofstadter, *The Age of Reform* (New York, 1958).

36   John Cawelti, *Apostles of the Self-Made Man* (Chicago, 1965).

37   The Union Park situation was, in fact, a classic case of Merton's theory of latent consequences.

Ethnic Variations on the American Scene

Ethnic variation is another factor which contributes to the great diversity of American family history. Bernard Farber has sensitized us to the importance of looking at class differences in family life during periods of change, and here Virginia McLaughlin conveys the dangers of too readily assuming that all migrant groups respond similarly to their new homes in urban industrial centers. Buffalo's Italians at the beginning of the century did not appear to experience the family disorganization so frequently presented as the typical pattern for such immigrant groups. Males were able to maintain their traditional position of authority despite regular seasonal unemployment and the periods of family hardship it brought. One device employed by this group was keeping wives at home, rather than allowing them to undertake full-time factory employment. The women were not economically idle, however; they took in boarders and lodgers, by no means a negligible source of income, and engaged in homework industry. Thus, they were able to supplement family income while posing no real threat to traditional patterns of family authority and division of labor. McLaughlin notes that the family has generally been viewed as a dependent variable in the industrialization process; she, however, provides us with a study that brings out the value of recasting questions and hypotheses with the family as an independent variable.

VIRGINIA YANS McLAUGHLIN

7 *Patterns of Work and Family Organization: Buffalo's Italians*

In their discussions of industrialization and urbanization, some social scientists have described the family as a dependent variable. Implicitly or explicitly, they view technical and economic organization as the prime determinant of family organization.[1] Not surprisingly, power relationships within the family are also frequently considered to be dependent upon economic roles within the larger society. A common assumption, for example, is that because the industrial city offers work opportunities to women, they can become less reliant upon their husbands and fathers, especially if the latter are unemployed. And so, the argument continues, female employment outside the home encourages the decline of "traditional" family relationships in which the chief power and control reside with the male. In extreme cases, the unemployed male deserts his family altogether and female-headed households result.

Not all social scientists, of course, agree with this interpretation. Historians have a specific task in this dispute—to seek empirical evidence which will sustain or weaken generalizations concerning the dependent and causal relationships between the family, urbanization, and industrialization. As Goode put it, one of our difficulties is a "simple lack of information about the past history of family systems under varying conditions of urbanization and industrialization."[2]

In line with Goode's suggestion, this paper attempts to add to our knowledge of family history by examining the relationship between female occupational patterns and family organization among south Italians in Buffalo from about 1900 to 1930. It questions the idea that the family should be viewed simply as a dependent variable by demonstrating that female assumption of new economic functions did not necessarily alter family power arrangements or disrupt the "traditional" family.

Any historian attempting to deal with working-class families immediately confronts the problem of documentation. Until recently, scholars have relied upon the reports of reformers and social workers for evidence concerning "the inarticulate." Thus, we have viewed working-class history through a filter of middle-class values. In order to overcome this problem, as well as the scarcity of literary sources concerning the family, historians have increasingly relied upon manuscript censuses and other statistical data. Much, but not all, of the argument presented in this paper is based upon such evidence, and I should caution the reader concerning its limitations. With the help of census materials, we can inform ourselves about the percentage of husbandless families, of unemployed males, and of employed wives. On the basis of these formal indices, inferences can be drawn regarding possible power relationships within the family. Statistics concerning household organization, however, cannot tell us to what degree traditional arrangements were being strained without actually being eliminated, nor can they describe the quality and "normal" tensions of family life. The picture that emerges tends to be static: If the family were broken, we can assume conflicts occurred. But if a family remained together, we cannot conversely assume that it did so free of tension. This is a problem, especially with relatively stable groups such as Buffalo's south Italians, who did not exhibit extreme family pathology in the process of becoming assimilated into American society. Statistics simply do not permit absolute conclusions concerning conflict and change among Italian families remaining together. But female occupational arrangements can tell something about family power alignments. Buffalo's south Italians favored conservative female employment patterns, patterns which usually kept women working at home or under relatives' supervision despite possibilities of better pay and opportunities elsewhere. These occupational styles, it will be argued, are a strong indication that patriarchal control continued.

An examination of south Italian families within the context of one city, Buffalo, makes one thing abundantly clear. The usual question —"What is the impact of 'urban-industrial life' upon the family?"— is much too general, too imprecise. The class and ethnic identity of the families in question, as well as the type of city and range of industrial development existing in the communities under consideration, must be specified because each can play a critical part in determining the family's relationship to the social order. First, in some cases, ethnic background and associated cultural ideals had an important impact upon the way immigrant families responded to their new environment. Buffalo's south Italian women, for example, expressed, and acted upon, a decided preference for occupations which permitted minimal strain upon their traditional familial arrangements. In this way, Old World family values could continue to operate effectively even within an advanced industrial city such as Buffalo. Other options were available, and other ethnic groups took them. This clearly suggests that south Italian values played an important part in determining family work patterns; in other words, the family acted as an independent variable. Some may wish to argue that immigrant family values, not the family itself, were the prime determinant here. Such an argument makes a strict distinction between the family as a formal structure and the system of values, norms, rights, and obligations associated with it. Although such a distinction is useful in some cases, in this paper values and organization are considered together as parts of the family as a social institution.

In discussing the relationships between economic and familial organization, it should also be noted that actually available work opportunities define the perimeters of behavior. In a small city dominated by one industry, the relationships between family and economy should be relatively clear. In the early twentieth century, for example, Homestead, Pennsylvania was a typical steel mill town, offering work to men on a fairly regular basis. Women could find employment only occasionally. Therefore, the possibilities for varying family occupational patterns were obviously limited: In Homestead, the overwhelming majority of working-class families adopted the attitude that men should be the breadwinners and that women should contribute to the family economy through their housekeeping skills, and not by leaving the home to work.[3] In a cotton mill town, another type of one-industry city, we would expect to find women from needy families working; ethnic or cultural biases against female employment would probably be modified to meet the family's economic needs. In short, in one-industry towns, family occupational patterns would ultimately be determined by that industry regardless of cultural preferences. In larger, highly diversified manufacturing centers such as Buffalo, a variety of economic opportunities for both men and women existed; despite the city's emphasis on heavy industry women could, and did, find work. In such cities, the relationship between occupational patterns and family organization was, as we shall see, correspondingly much more complex. The nature of work opportunities permitted freer expression of cultural preferences concerning women's work role, and Old World family values could operate easily despite the urban-industrial context.

Finally, it should be emphasized that the subjects being considered, south Italian immigrants, were "working-class." I use that term here to refer not only to their occupational status as an unskilled, frequently unemployed group, but also to their relatively stable life style and culture, much of which represented a survival from traditional European peasant life.[4] In such families, the occupational positions of husband and wife are frequently related to family structure. Hence, our original question regarding the family's status as a dependent or an independent variable is raised once again. Most social scientists argue that working-class and lower-class family structures are dependent upon occupational arrangements. They frequently cite unusual work patterns, for example, as a cause for family disorganization. The Moynihan report is a case in point. It stressed male employment difficulties in conjunction with more stable female employment as a key cause for male desertion and consequent female control of the family.[5] Some historians similarly suggest that disrupted preindustrial work patterns upset family stability among first-generation immigrants. The move to industrial America supposedly caused radical changes in the traditional male-dominated family economy and hence forced a restructuring in family roles and relationships.[6]

Patterns of Work and Family Organization   *139*

Although this model appears logical enough, it is not in agreement with historical fact. Buffalo's south Italians provide a fine example. Because tradition bestowed upon the mother great prestige, authority, and power (frequently including control of the household budget), south Italian peasant family organization was not purely patriarchal. Male superiority and paternal control, however, were the norm. To this degree at least, the south Italian family resembled the traditional peasant form described by Handlin in *The Uprooted.*[7] The New World's industrial work patterns, however, did not destroy it. Specifically, women leaving the home to work did not necessarily cause an erosion of male control. This was true throughout the decades under consideration, despite the existence of certain female prerogatives in south Italian familial culture which could have emerged during times of family crisis, such as periods of male unemployment.

In southern Italy economic functions and family functions were closely integrated. Tradition required Italian men, the majority of them poor peasants without farms of their own, to support their families; children contributed their work in the fields or at home; wives ran their households, and, from this area, most of their rights derived. But the basis for each person's status within the family was *not* purely economic. Thus, strong cultural traditions sustained male authority despite seasonal or year-round unemployment. Although wife and children worked outside the home at harvest time in Sicily and more often elsewhere, the father's domination over family affairs remained unchallenged. Apparently this "family constellation" was strong enough to endure periods of male unemployment in America when women worked.[8] Consequently, family disorganization among Italians (measured by male desertion and non-support, at least) remained relatively rare, and female-controlled families were unusual. This appears more remarkable given the existence of certain female privileges in south Italian culture.[9] The point is that male authority did not depend entirely upon fulfillment of economic obligations; therefore, when a woman co-opted the male's economic function in whole or in part by becoming a wage-earner, she did not necessarily obtain greater bargaining power and so tip the balance of family authority in her favor.

Despite a potentially disruptive work situation, Buffalo's Italian men performed exceedingly well as husbands and fathers. Until the 1920s brought slightly improved conditions, the majority worked in low-paying construction, railroad, and other seasonal outdoor occupations; most were unemployed six or more months a year. This condition was not peculiar only to Buffalo Italians. Outdoor laborers all over the nation faced similar difficulties.[10] Frequently, construction work drew Italians away from the city and their families. In addition, the immigration process itself had caused temporary separations for many. Buffalo Italians, then, endured two conditions commonly associated with family breakdown and female domination—irregular male employment and temporary absence of the father from the household[11]—but the proportion of husbandless or female-headed families among them remained surprisingly low. Calculations based upon the 1905 New York State manuscript census reveal that only 4 percent of more than 2,000 first-generation families were headed by women with no spouse present.[12] And some of these were widows, not deserted wives. In 1908–09 Italians were the least likely Buffalo ethnic group to obtain welfare because of neglect or desertion by a family head. And, although the proportion applying for welfare had increased by the 1920s, the percentage giving desertion or non-support as their justification actually declined from 6 percent in 1908 to 4 percent in 1926.[13]

These figures dispute the notion that male unemployment or contact with industrial city life disrupted immigrant working-class families; they also invite comparison with other urban groups who did not fare as well. How can the south Italian family's relative stability be explained? Undoubtedly inherited ethnic traditions supporting male authority helped, but let us look elsewhere before coming to definite conclusions. The answer resides, at least partially, in long-term female employment patterns, for they, and not male unemployment, distinguished Italians from less stable working-class families.

The south Italian family's traditional work patterns and economic roles were not seriously disturbed after immigration to a modern industrial city. Most important of all, women's work roles were adapted to the new industrial situation. This resulted to some extent from Buffalo's peculiar occupational structure. Unlike other upstate cities, heavy industry and transportation dominated its economy. The city offered comparatively little in the way of light industrial production for unskilled women. But it should be emphasized that even though alternatives were available, Italians *preferred* specific types of labor—occupations on the fringes of Buffalo's industrial structure—where customary family relationships could be and were effectively maintained. This preference helps to explain why Italian immigrant families remained stable. There was for them a period of transition, a time of adjustment, rather than rapid family disorganization or reorganization. Thus there was a lot of room in some late nineteenth- and early twentieth-century cities for immigrant families who wished to avoid a head-on collision with the new way of life. It was not simply a case of occupational arrangements determining family organization; cultural preferences also played a part in determining patterns of work. In short, traditional family values acted as an independent variable, and the occupational opportunities of industrial cities provided enough variation for individual families to find work arrangements appropriate for their cultural needs.

Let us first turn to the occupational patterns of Buffalo's first-generation Italian women in the period preceding World War I. In 1905, for example, less than 2 percent of more than 2,000 wives reported to census-takers full-time employment which could have taken them from domestic concerns; some involved themselves in family enterprises which did not draw them permanently from the home or give them the status of independent wage earners. Only three women worked because their husbands were unemployed; only 1 percent of the working women had children. Clearly, in 1905 Italian women did not sacrifice child-rearing responsibilities for work and no trend toward female assumption of the role of chief provider existed. Most women who contributed to the family budget in this year did so by providing housekeeping services to roomers and boarders residing with their families. Twelve percent of all first-generation wives belonged to this category. The remaining 86 percent reported no occupation at all, but we know that several hundred women engaged in part-time work as part of family groups. They did so most commonly as migrant laborers in northwestern New York's canneries and vineyards during the summer. A smaller number worked in Buffalo's domestic industries.

Italian women and girls rarely left their homes unsupervised by relatives or friends to work either as housekeepers or as factory laborers. Buffalo's Irish, Polish, Swedish, and German women commonly sought employment as domestics in middle-class homes, but jealous Italian men would not permit their wives to work under another man's roof, no matter how serious the family's economic circumstances. For example, efforts of various organizations in Buffalo and elsewhere to interest Italian women in such positions failed to erode this Mediterranean attitude toward female honor. The women themselves preferred employment which would not separate them from their families; even second-generation Italians failed to find service occupations as agreeable as did those of other ethnic groups.[14] Italian husbands and fathers apparently appreciated the dangers of female employment outside the home. A National Federation of Settlements survey, noting that Italian parents tended to be more careful than most regarding their daughters' place of employment, cited parental concern for their children's morality as a reason.[15]

Buffalo Italians responded to economic need by removing male children from school and sending them to work so that the women could remain in a sheltered environment. The 1905 manuscript census reveals that sons and daughters under fifteen, for example, had an equal chance to remain in school. From the ages of fifteen to nineteen, they dropped out of school at the same rate—79 percent of the sons and 82 percent of the daughters left school or were not attending. But the sons generally entered the labor force, while the daughters remained at home. Boys withdrawn from school had to pay the price of restricted occupational mobility, which helps to explain the Italians' slow rise up the social ladder. Considerations of female honor restricted the girls' freedom and achievement. As a result, Italian women almost always worked within the confines of their homes or as part of a family group, especially before World War I. Most who labored did so only part-time or by the season. This continued to be true throughout the 1920s. If these occupational patterns are examined in detail, it becomes clear that they minimized strain upon the traditional family system.

An examination of the homework industry indicates that Italians were especially noted for their preference for this type of occupation, which also acted as a kind of shock absorber for other ethnic groups including, for example, Russians and Germans. There are a number of ways in which homework did not challenge Old World family organization. The mother's roles as arbiter of household organization and tasks and as disciplinarian and child-rearer were reinforced by her economic position as manager of the domestic undertaking, be it artificial flower-making, basting, or sewing. Because she still had not become, in the strict sense of the term, a wage-earner, she presented no clear threat to her husband's authority and power. The basic unit of homework industries continued to be just as it had been in the Old World—the family, not the individual. The seasonal nature of most homework industry meant that the wife and child were only sporadically occupied. Finally, and critically, the wife did not leave the home, and therefore did not abandon her important roles of childbearing and child-rearing. These two responsibilities clearly exceeded in importance any economic obligation, for homework wages were lower than those a woman could earn working full- or even part-time away from home. The similiarity between the family as a working productive unit in preindustrial southern Italy and in America under the homework system is striking.

Although some domestic manufacture existed in Buffalo and Italians worked in it, the women and their children earned better pay as migrant laborers on farms and processing sheds near Buffalo. The canneries, which also utilized the family as the basic work unit, permitted the same sort of easing of family members into a potentially disruptive work situation. Due to the immigrants' handling of the situation and the industry's special character, the Italian family was able to maintain its Old World complexion. Once again, although Italians preferred this kind of work, other ethnic groups in different parts of the nation engaged in it, probably for similar reasons.[16]

At first glance it seems surprising that conservative south Italian men would sometimes permit women and children to leave their Buffalo homes without husbands and fathers. The men sought and often obtained city construction jobs during the summer. South Italian mores, after all, required a husband to guard his wife with a jealous eye. In Italy, moreover, the wife who left home to work was viewed disapprovingly. But was going to the cannery really such a radical departure? In the first place, seasonal migration had not been an unusual experience for south Italian families. Laborers frequently followed harvests throughout the *Mezzogiorno*. Second, though many fathers remained in Buffalo, some found employment with their families as harvesters or as canning factory mechanics.[17] Third, the women and children did not drift as separate family members into the labor market. They were recruited, lived, and worked as a family under the close scrutiny of the Italian-American community of migrant workers, many of whom were close associates, *paesani*, and kin. Fourth, as was the case in Italy, the seasonal income earned by wives and children who ventured into migrant labor camps was never understood as a replacement of the father's wages, as earlier figures on low desertion and non-support rates indicated, but as a supplement. The Italian father did not relinquish his obligation to support his family; likewise, he did not forfeit his control and authority over it. Finally, like the domestic industries, the migrant labor camp permitted close integration of living and working quarters and therefore did not separate the family's productive from its child-rearing capacities. Here a close integration of economic and family functions, similar to those which existed in Italy, prevailed. In short, the initiation of women into the factory system did not necessarily cause disruption of the traditional south Italian family.

The seasonal and part-time character of female employment patterns also prevented disruption. In the pre-World War I era, when Italian males were most likely to be chronically unemployed, their wives were also likely to be unemployed for at least as long. If women contributed to the family budget the year round, they generally did so by keeping boarders, an activity which did not contribute to their social or financial independence. Rarely did the Italian wife provide greater financial stability than her husband. Cultural tradition prevented her from taking the one suitable readily available job for unskilled women which would have guaranteed more steady employment than her husband—work as a maid or domestic. The contrast with black women who continue to depend upon this important source of income is striking. Equally striking are the contrasting attitudes between Italian and Polish families toward women entering the work world. Unfortunately, none of the evidence presented in the following pages allows for class distinctions between ethnic groups. (Because the overwhelming majority of both Italians and Poles were unskilled laborers, the difficulty is not a serious one.)

Buffalo's Polish women eagerly sought work in factories and as domestics.[18] According to a 1910 survey of 146 Buffalo firms employing almost 11,000 individuals of Polish background, two Polish women found employment in the city's manufacturing and industrial establishments for every eight Polish men. If *all* Italian women who worked in all occupations—excluding those in cannery work and those with boarders in their households—are considered, the ratio for 1905 was only one to twenty.[19] Even granting a higher proportion of Polish women to men, these differences are significant. They were not peculiar to Buffalo alone. Butler, noting the relative unimportance of Italian women in Pittsburgh's industrial life, also emphasized cultural differences between Italian and Polish women. "The Polish women," she wrote in 1910, "have not the conservatism which keeps the Italian girl at home. They have not the same standard of close-knit family relations. There is a flexibility in their attitude toward life and toward their part in it."[20] In 1909 Tobenkin compared Chicago's Italian, Polish, Jewish, and Lithuanian girls and came to similar conclusions regarding the Italians' conservatism.[21] In New York City, Italian girls left domestic and personal service work to other ethnic groups and entered the factory. Still, they viewed factory work chiefly as an opportunity to learn a skill such as sewing, which they might keep up at home after marriage.[22]

During the war and pre-depression years when more Italian women began to leave their homes to work, Italian men were also more likely to be employed, or at least more likely to be earning higher incomes. Hence female employment did not represent a serious challenge to male authority at this time. Even after World War I female employment patterns had not changed radically, at least insofar as first-generation wives were concerned. An analysis of fifteen densely populated blocks in the Buffalo ward most heavily settled by Italians in 1925 indicated that although daughters had gone to work in silk factories, clothing trades, or offices, not one mother or wife in this district had left her home to work. Very few households in these blocks, moreover, contained boarders or lodgers, so the number of women contributing to family income in this way had actually declined.[23] Italian women continued to work in the canneries during the summer after the war, but, as I have argued, this work tended to sustain, not challenge, traditional family relationships.

Italians retained a cultural bias against female employment even among the second generation. A survey of all second-generation families in sixteen wards, once again including those most heavily populated by Italians, revealed that in 1925 only 12 percent had working wives (120 of 1,022). Moreover, these women were not forced to work because their spouses were unemployed or had deserted their family. Only one had no husband, and she may have been a widow. The remaining wives had employed husbands.[24] The evidence produced by the 1905 data and suggested by the 1925 samples is amply substantiated by other local and national sources.[25] In some cities, especially those with significant light industry, Italian women worked more often than they did in Buffalo, but even in these cases they tended to enter occupations which, like the canneries, assured the security and protection of working closely with fellow Italians or at least within Little Italy's confines.

Even if women entered factories in greater numbers, they could not have been the family's chief support. Italian female factory laborers, like most women in industry, tended to be irregularly employed. For example, in 1909 Odencrantz, known for her studies of women wage earners, found that one-half of a group of 1,000 New York City working girls held their jobs for less than six months, chiefly because most had seasonal occupations and their employers frequently discharged them.[26] Most of the light industries to which women flocked for employment, such as clothing, textiles, food, candy, and paper box manufacturing, responded to irregular seasonal demand. Employers in these trades could not afford to maintain a year-round labor force if they wished to maximize profits. The situation was worst in cities like Buffalo where heavy industry predominated.[27] Thus, even if other working-class ethnics took a more open-minded approach toward female labor than did Buffalo's south Italians, the nature of work opportunities for unskilled females in early twentieth-century America made it possible, albeit difficult, for them to supplant their husbands as chief breadwinners.

Why was family disorganization minimal and why were female-headed families rare among Italian-Americans? First, Italians had strong cultural and historical traditions regarding their women's role which survived long after emigration. The male continued to dominate in spite of his own unemployment and despite the existence of certain matriarchal privileges within the south Italian family. The conservatism of female employment patterns is clear evidence for continuing male domination. Male unemployment, furthermore, was not an entirely new experience for this group of former peasants any more than it was for other agricultural laborers, and the Italians withstood it as well in America as they did in Italy. Once in the United States, the peculiar occupational patterns of Italian women permitted the traditional family system to survive. Rather than permit their wives to leave the home, men who needed money resigned themselves "rather painfully" to daughters working in factories. The general disposition toward women's work, however, remained one of disapproval.[28] This attitude persisted well into the 1920s, and it had a considerable influence upon second-generation families, which looked unfavorably upon female employment.

More Italian women entered the labor force after World War I, but generally these were daughters, not mothers. By contributing to the family income, they merely fulfilled the proper function of children, and hence represented no challenge to their fathers' prestige and control. In any case, because daughters and sons—not wives and mothers—left the home to work, the latter had little opportunity to enhance their bargaining power within the family by way of significant economic contributions.

Although Buffalo's Italians differed in some ways from other working-class groups, on the basis of their experience it is possible to offer a few speculations regarding the white working-class of late nineteenth- and early twentieth-century America. Single and unmarried sons and daughters, not wives and mothers, were the most likely candidates in these families to supplement the male head's earnings. Most were not occupied full-time or year-round. The white working-class male family head, though poor and unemployed, therefore probably found himself in a stronger familial position than does today's urban unemployed male, who is forced to depend upon his wife's wages. In the case of blacks, of course, wives and mothers supposedly assumed year-round employment or at least significantly more stable positions than their husbands and so challenged male control and authority within the family. Further studies of white working-class families, especially those in which wives worked year-round and husbands remained unemployed, and of ethnic groups with strong matriarchal tendencies, are required to determine the relative importance of ethnicity, the slavery heritage, and employment patterns. The findings of this paper, however, caution against assuming, as Moynihan and others have, that partial or total female control of the economic function necessarily predicts family power arrangements. Furthermore, before applying Moynihan's matriarchal models of the past, we should examine historical evidence to see if matriarchal families existed. As TenHouten suggests, conceptual muddling has caused many scholars to confuse matriarchies with female-headed families, a structure in which no male is present.[29]

In conclusion, contrary to general descriptions of European immigrant adjustment, Buffalo's Italians suffered no immediate or radical disruption in family life. Although the Italian family had its share of poverty and unemployment, it did not develop a characteristic frequently associated today with lower-class life—a female-headed family system. In fact, there is little evidence of family disorganization among Buffalo's Italians. This is not to suggest that these Italians and their contemporaries were superior or more adaptable than today's urban minorities. First-generation European immigrants entered an industrializing economy and responded to it with the equipment of a traditional peasant background. Their historical experience as a class was strikingly different from today's urban workers.

We have moved throughout this discussion from the narrow focus of women's history to the broader realm of women, the family, and working-class culture. The seasonal, part-time, sporadic work patterns of wage-earning women stemmed partly from their sexual peculiarities, for most women dropped out of the labor market during the childbearing and child-rearing years. But the demands of a developing capitalist industrial economy for a cheap labor force which could be discharged periodically with a minimum of difficulty also explains their position. In this case the demands of employers and working-class cultural priorities coincided. The traditional, conservative character of this era's working-class culture advocated keeping women at home in order to avoid familial tensions, and in this manner worked toward providing the part-time labor force which employers sought.

We are now in a position to question clichés concerning the impact of industrialization and employment upon the family and woman's role. Probably no one generalization will hold for all women in all families everywhere. One can only plead for careful examination of women within the context of family life by class, ethnic group, region, city, and perhaps by religious background.

Notes

Virginia Yans McLaughlin is Assistant Professor of History at Princeton University. She is revising her dissertation, "Like the Fingers of the Hand: The Family and Community Life of First-Generation Italian-Americans in Buffalo, New York," for publication. This paper was originally presented before the American Historical Association, Boston, 1970. The author would like to thank Allen F. Davis and J. Stanley Lemons for their criticisms.

1 For a discussion of the relationship between the family, urbanization, and industrialization, see William J. Goode, *The Family* (Englewood Cliffs, N.J., 1964), 110; Sidney M. Greenfield, "Industrialization and the Family in Sociological Theory," *American Journal of Sociology,* LXVII (1961), 312–314.

2 William J. Goode, "The Process of Role Bargaining in the Impact of Urbanization and Industrialization on Family Systems," *Current Sociology,* XII (1963–64), I.

3 Margaret F. Byington, "The Family in a Typical Mill Town," *American Journal of Sociology,* XIV (1909), 648–659.

4 Herbert Gans, *The Urban Villagers: Group and Class in the Life of Italian-Americans* (Glencoe, 1962), 250, views working-class culture as a "continuation of European peasant culture." S. M. Miller and Frank Riessman, "The Working Class Subculture: A New View," *Social Problems,* IX (1961), 90, 95, correctly emphasize the distinction between working- and lower-class culture, a distinction of which the author is aware. Although white immigrants shared many of the hardships which today's urban poor experience, I think it is best to place them in the working-class category because of their traditional peasant background, much of which survived immigration.

5 Daniel P. Moynihan, "The Negro Family: The Case for National Action," in Lee Rainwater and William L. Yancey (eds.), *The Moynihan Report and the Politics of Controversy* (Cambridge, Mass., 1967), 41–124.

6 Oscar Handlin, *The Uprooted* (New York, 1951), 228ff., 239 takes this position.

7 *Ibid.;* Leonard Moss and Walter Thomson, "The South Italian Family: Literature and Observation," *Human Organization,* XVIII (1959), 38, quote an old Italian proverb testifying to the mother's importance: "If the father should die, the family would suffer; if the mother should die, the family ceases to exist." Although the two sources of authority were constantly clashing, the father was generally able to assert himself, "receiving his main support," according to Covello, "from the elevated status of the male in general." See Leonard Covello, "The Social Background of the Italo-American School Child: A Study of the Southern Italian Family Mores and Their Effect on the School Situation in Italy and America," unpub. Ph.D. thesis (New York University, 1944), 347.

8 Gans, *The Urban Villagers,* 240–241.

9 Covello, "Italo-American School Child," 328ff., 336, 378. See also Phyllis Williams, *South Italian Folkways in Europe and America* (New Haven, 1938), 76–77.

10 Amy Bernardy, "L'Emigrazione delle donne e dei fanciulli italiana," *Bolletino dell'Emigrazione* (1909), 17. Bernardy toured several eastern cities, including Buffalo, and noted the seasonal unemployment of Italian men. See also U.S. Department of Commerce, *Seasonal Operation in the Construction Industries: Summary of Report and Recommendations of a Committee of the President's Conference on Unemployment* (Washington, D.C., 1924).

11 Gans, *The Urban Villagers,* 240–241.

12   All figures cited are either from the New York State manuscript censuses of 1905 (Buffalo, 1905) and 1925 (unpublished census schedules) unless otherwise indicated. For a discussion of the accuracy of these censuses, see Virginia Yans McLaughlin, "Like the Fingers of the Hand: The Family and Community Life of First-Generation Italian-Americans in Buffalo, New York, 1880–1930," unpub. Ph.D. thesis (State University of New York at Buffalo, 1970), 450–455. A 10 percent sample check revealed that in no case did coding and key-punching errors exceed the reasonable range of 5 percent in any one variable; in most cases it remained well below that figure.

13   The 1908–09 figures are from United States Senate, *Reports of the Immigration Commission,* XXXIV, 61st Cong., 3rd Sess., *Immigrants as Charity Seekers,* I (Washington, D.C., 1911), 137. The 1926 figures were computed by the author from City of Buffalo Department of Public Welfare, *Annual Report of the Bureau of Public Welfare for Fiscal Year Ending June 30, 1927* (Buffalo, 1927). The Charity Organization Society did not aid persons of the Jewish faith, and, therefore, they are not included in the 1907–08 figures. The author is well aware that welfare agency statistics do not necessarily give the most accurate picture of family life. Nevertheless, it is not necessary to rely upon these alone. Other sources confirm family stability among Italians. See McLaughlin, "Like the Fingers of the Hand," 121ff.

14   This was a common attitude among Italians all over the United States. See, for example, Williams, *South Italian Folkways,* 36; Bernardy, "L'Emigrazione," 8. For efforts to interest Italian women in domestic service, see "Uncle Sam's Debt to the Italians," Utica *Pensiero Italiano* (Sept. 26, 1914), which discusses an Italian baroness who attempted to work with organizations and individuals in several cities, including Buffalo, to place Italian women in such positions.

15   Robert A. Woods and Robert J. Kennedy, *Young Working Girls: A Summary of Evidence from Two Thousand Social Workers* (Boston, 1913), 59, 23.

16   Alexander Cance, "Immigrant Rural Communities," *The Survey,* XXV (1911), 588; United States Senate, *Reports of the Immigration Commission,* III, 61st Cong., 2nd Sess., *Immigrants in Industries, Recent Immigrants in Agriculture,* II (Washington, D.C., 1911), 489–490, 801.

17   Maria Maddalena de Rossi, "Le donne ed i fanciulli italiani a Buffalo e ad Albion," in Segretariato femminile per la tutela delle donne e dei fanciulli emigranti, *Relazione* (Rome, 1913), 14.

18   United States Senate, *Recent Immigrants in Agriculture,* II, 491; John Daniels, "Polish Laborers and Their Needs," Buffalo *Express* (March 13, 1910), 7.

19   John Daniels, "Polish Wage Earners in Buffalo," Buffalo *Express* (March 6, 1910), 3, contains information on the Polish population. The Buffalo Italian data are based upon the New York State manuscript census for 1905.

20   Elizabeth Beardsley Butler, "The Working Women of Pittsburgh," *The Survey,* XXIII (1910), 573.

21   Elias Tobenkin, "The Immigrant Girl in Chicago," *The Survey,* XXIII (1909), 190.

22   Mary Van Kleeck, *Artificial Flower Makers* (New York, 1913), 32, 38.

23   New York State manuscript census, 1925.

24   *Ibid.,* Wards 12–27. Second-generation families were defined here as a family with an Italian name in which both spouses were born in the United States, in which the wife was born in the United States and the husband in Italy, or in which the husband was born in the United States and the wife in Italy. In every case, of course, in which the wife was born in the United States, she could have been of either non-Italian or Italian descent.

25   The following support the description of female employment: For the pre-war period, the infrequency of Italian female employment outside of the home is observed in Walter Goodale, "Children of Sunny Italy," Buffalo *Express* (Oct. 15, 1915), I. Post-war sources on Italian female employment include: H. E. Burber, *Industrial Analysis of Buffalo* (Buffalo, n.d.), no p.; Eleanor G. Coit, "An Industrial Study, Buffalo, New York" (unpub. paper, Business and Industrial Department, Young Women's Christian Association, 1922), 44; Young Women's Christian Association (Business and Industrial Department), "Further Data from the Industrial Study," *Buffalo Foundation Forum* (Nov., 1922), 12. For a national perspective, see Bernardy, "L'Emigrazione," 12, 50; Butler, "The Working Women of Pittsburgh," 571–572.

26   Louise Odencrantz, "The Irregularity of Employment of Women Factory Workers," *The Survey,* XXII (1909), 200.

27   Coit, "Industrial Study," 49; Business and Industrial Department, YWCA, "Some Facts Concerning Women in Buffalo Industries, A Study Bringing up to Date Certain Figures on the Employment of Women in 200 Industries" (unpub. paper, Buffalo, 1925), 6–7; Burber, *Industrial Analysis of Buffalo.* Each of the above indicate some of the major companies which employed women, most of which had highly seasonal employment cycles. Thomas W. Triller, "The History of the Development of the International Institute in Buffalo, New York," unpub. M.A. thesis (University of Buffalo School of Social Work, 1952), 4, quoting a report of Miss Ely (Nov. 1, 1919) to the International Institute for Women, notes that Buffalo's industry simply did not provide enough work for women.

28   Bernardy, "L'Emigrazione," 13.

29   Warren TenHouten, "The Black Family Myth and Reality," *Psychiatry,* XXXIII (1970), 154.

In the introduction to this volume it was pointed out that the growth of the new social history of the family had its roots partially in a new interest in history's "anonymous" actors. Perhaps no group has been more anonymous than this nation's black population. Research such as that done by Elizabeth Pleck becomes especially important, then, for it not only opens up new territory but also provides us with a basis for demythologizing much of the past of black Americans.

A theme that has stirred great controversy in sociological circles is the putative importance of female-headed homes in the black community. Daniel Moynihan, in his well-known and controversial report, has associated such matriarchal families with the "tangle of pathology" that is supposedly responsible for the economic hardship currently faced by many blacks. There has been a debate over the roots of this family form, and the answer frequently forthcoming has been slavery. Elizabeth Pleck's work, as well as that of Theodore Hershberg and Herbert Gutman, which she cites, seems to make suspect the view that the dehumanizing character of slavery, with its lack of respect for the integrity of the slave family, is the villain of the piece. This issue is hardly closed, both in terms of the origins of the form and its significance, but Pleck's work at least provides us with a good basis for further investigation.

ELIZABETH H. PLECK

8 The Two-Parent Household: Black Family Structure in Late Nineteenth-Century Boston

Once the most rural of American ethnic groups, Afro-Americans are now the most urban. Slavery, migration to the city and the adaptation to urban culture have had major effects on black life, yet we know little about the ways in which the most basic unit of black life, the family, was affected by these changes. Through research in the manuscript census schedules of the federal census for 1880 and other largely quantitative materials, I looked for answers to the following questions. What was the effect of migration on the black family? What was the occupational situation of black heads of household? How did urban and rural families differ in their adaptation to life in the city? How did literate and illiterate families differ? What family forms predominated? How frequent was "family disorganization," as reflected in an imbalanced sex ratio, frequent desertions by the head of household and large numbers of female-headed households?

We can learn a great deal about black family life from an examination of Boston in the late nineteenth century. The Hub was a major northern metropolis, with a large and diversified economy, which should have offered opportunities for unskilled but willing black workers. As a result of the long efforts of blacks and whites in the abolitionist movement, the city had no segregated institutions and a widely respected system of free public schools. Boston had acquired a reputation among blacks as "the paradise of the Negro," a city of unparalleled freedom and opportunity.[1] Since the black population was so small a percentage of the inhabitants of the city, the racial fears and animosities of the white population appeared, surfaced, but did not explode into major race riots like those in New York and Philadelphia during the Civil War. The large Irish and small black populations lived in an uneasy truce, with the two groups dwelling in close proximity in the west and south ends of the city. Unique in some ways, representative of major northern cities in others, Boston is an interesting city in which to study many facets of black family life.

The most typical black household in late nineteenth-century Boston included the husband and wife, or husband, wife, and children. This predominant household form prevailed among all occupational levels and among families of both urban and rural origins. By enlarging the household to include boarders, families from all occupational strata augmented the family income and provided homes for the large numbers of migrants in the population. This evidence from the manuscript census contradicts the commonly held association between "the tangle of pathology," "family disorganization" and the black family.

Before examining the composition of the black household, I will indicate how inferences were made about the origins and literacy of heads of household and I will discuss three aspects of social life in Boston—the transiency of the population, the depressing occupational position of black heads of household and the physical circumstances of life—which severely constrained family survival.

The Two-Parent Household   *153*

Comparison of Rural and Urban, Literate and Illiterate Heads of Household

In the analysis of one- and two-parent households which follows, the foreign-born heads of household were excluded since they offer too few cases for valid comparisons.[2] Comparing the northern- and southern-born heads of household, I looked for possible differences in urban and rural family adaptation to life in Boston. Since the manuscript census schedules indicate the state of birth of an individual, but not the city or area where the individual was born or raised, the comparison is imperfect. Although a majority of northern-born blacks lived most of their lives in urban areas, the northern-born category also included farmers from New England, townspeople from western Massachusetts, and settlers from the free black communities of Ohio. By further separating those born in Massachusetts (mostly natives of Boston) from the rest of the northern-born, I was able to discern differences between that part of the population which was born in Boston and that portion of the population which migrated into the city.

While most southern-born blacks were rural folk, that category also includes city-dwellers from Richmond, Baltimore, or Washington, D.C. Even more difficult to distinguish are those southern-born blacks who were urban in experience, if not in place of birth. But despite these qualifications, it seems useful to perceive the northern-born as essentially an urban group, and the southern-born as a rural group.[3]

The distinction between literacy and illiteracy may have been as important as the difference between urban and rural families. Seven out of ten black adults could read a few words and sign their names, the nineteenth-century standard of literacy. Even this minimal knowledge reflected a variety of skills which facilitated successful adaptation to urban life. Those without such skills—the illiterates—were more at a disadvantage than they were on the farm and more noticeable for their deficiency as well. Whole families headed by illiterates faced far greater difficulties in cities than those headed by literate parents.

In the South, illiterates tended to be ex-slaves.[4] (The equation of illiteracy and slave status would have been unnecessary had the Boston census takers directly enumerated the number of freedmen in the black population.) Under slavery, most blacks were not taught to read or write or were prevented from even learning. While there were exceptions, self-educated slaves (Frederick Douglass is the most well-known example), the opportunities for literacy were much greater for free blacks than for slaves. But before equating southern-born illiterates with ex-slaves, two important qualifications must be added. First, even the majority of free blacks, like the slaves, were untutored. Second, the number of illiterates was very low, far below any estimate we might make of the number of ex-slaves in the population.[5] Thus, while illiteracy appeared in both northern- and southern-born families, its presence among the southern-born, in addition, reflects the existence of ex-slaves in the population.

Geographic Mobility

From the 3,496 blacks living in Boston in 1870, the population grew ten years later to include 5,873 persons.[6] By 1910, the population had expanded three times to 13,654. In the same forty-year period, the white population grew over two and one-half times, and the foreign-born white population tripled. The metropolis was growing rapidly, and within the city the black population, although small in absolute number and size relative to the white population—never more than 2% of the total population throughout the period—was growing at a rate faster than that of the foreign-born immigrants.[7]

In the late nineteenth century the black population absorbed a large number of migrants. While a minority, 42%, of Boston's blacks in 1880 had been born in the North, a majority were strangers to northern life; 49% of the population was born in the South, while another 9% were born in foreign countries. Of the northern-born population, especially those born in Massachusetts, the majority probably were natives of Boston. Other northern-born blacks came from neighboring cities in the Northeast and a few were from rural areas in New England. For the foreign-born, their life in Boston was the culmination of the long journey from Nova Scotia, New Brunswick, or other parts of Canada, or the end of a long sea voyage from the West Indies. The largest group in the population, the southern-born, included migrants from the Upper South, especially Virginia.

These southern newcomers seem to contradict prevailing theories of migration to cities.[8] Rather than traveling short distances and settling at the first stop along the way, these migrants moved as much as five hundred miles from home, often passing through other urban centers. Why did these men and women make the long journey? The usual explanation of black migration to the North refers to Jim Crow segregation, racism, and declining economic opportunities in the South, combined with the expanding economy and the promise of a freer life in the North. Pushed out by southern conditions, pulled to the North, the land of golden streets and busy factories, the combination of push and pull factors explains the Great Migration, the period during and after World War I. The earlier movement, described by Carter Woodson as the migration of the Talented Tenth, represented a period when blacks were more "pulled" to the North than "pushed" from the South.[9] The absence of two factors—widespread agricultural depression and active recruitment of blacks by northern employment agents—further distinguished the earlier migration from the Great Migration of World War I. Despite the propaganda of some of their brethren and the appeals of some southern whites, the black emigrant was above all looking for a better life in the northern city. One migrant was Ella Beam, a young woman who left the South Carolina Sea Islands for Boston.

> She stated that she did not leave home on account of hard times. When she left, her father was doing well on the farm. There were several boys in the family, so she was rarely called upon to go into the fields. She felt, however, that she was not especially needed at home. The fact that she manifested sufficient initiative to take the course at the training school [domestic science] is perhaps indicative of the courage and energy of a young woman who wanted to better her condition. She had been in Boston only one year when she received a simple job caring for children in the home of a Melrose family.[10]

For the most part, the migrants included young adults above the age of twenty, very few of whom came with their families. In households headed by a southern-born parent, 72.1% of the oldest children in the family were born in the North. Among the oldest children of a Canadian parent, 60.7% had been born in the North. Six out of seven of the oldest children in West Indian families had been born in the North. Thus the migration from the South and from foreign countries included single individuals or couples, but in very few cases did the whole family make the move.

The story of migration does not end with the arrival of the newcomer in Boston. Instead of settling down, the transient frequently packed up and left. Evidence from several nineteenth-century cities in the Northeast indicates a high rate of black migration, generally higher than that of other groups. But in the South and West the rate of black out-migration was about the same as or a little lower than among other groups. Assuming this pattern is substantiated in further research, it indicates the absence of job opportunities for black workers in nearby southern areas, as well as the proximity of many cities in the urban Northeast where the transient could find employment.

An examination of Boston city directories reveals that only 25% of adult black males listed in the 1880 census were enumerated in the 1890 city directory, while 64% of a respective sample of adult white males in 1880 remained in the city ten years later.[11] The rate of persistence for blacks was very similar among all occupational levels, as Table 1 suggests, while the rate of persistence among white males decreased for lower-status workers.[12] Among blacks heading households, the rate of persistence was 31%, compared with the 25% overall figure. Adult sons residing at home, although few in number, were more transient than their fathers, since only 21% of them remained in the city for the decade 1880–1890.

High rates of turnover were common in other northeastern cities. In the depression years of the 1870's black out-migration occurred frequently among Poughkeepsie and Buffalo residents. Only one-third of the black workers in Poughkeepsie in 1870 remained in the city ten years later.[13] In a twenty-year trace of black adult males in Buffalo from 1855 to 1875, only 12% could be found.[14]

The northern pattern of high black out-migration and much lower out-migration for other groups is reversed in the South and West. In Atlanta, for example, blacks were much more likely to remain in the city than either foreign-born whites or native whites. Even more remarkable, within all occupational categories, the black departure rate was lower than that of native white and foreign-born immigrants.[15] For Birmingham, Alabama, the much higher rate of black persistence was the result of fewer opportunities elsewhere for black workers.[16] During the depression decade 1870–1880, in San Antonio, blacks, European immigrants and native whites had very similar rates of persistence—36% for blacks, 36% for European immigrants, and 35% for native whites—while the Chicano population was the most transient, with only 25% of the male population remaining there ten years later.[17] The question remains whether this pattern of south-

Table 1. Proportion of Adult Male Residents of Boston in 1880 Persisting There to 1890, by Racial Group, Household Status, and Occupational Level[a]

	(%) Overall Persistence Rate	(%) White Collar	(%) Skilled	(%) Unskilled and Service	N
White Residents[b]	64	72	63	56	1809
All Blacks	25	26	25	25	1992
Heads of household	31	35	28	32	1066
Sons	21	25	33	15	63

[a]The white-collar category includes professionals, clerical workers, and petty proprietors. Heads of household include black males in single-member households, as well as the more prevalent one- and two-parent households. Adult males were defined as those 21 and over. Sons include adult males residing at home. Persistence rates for women were extremely difficult to estimate because of name changes due to marriage and the incomplete city directory coverage given to women who were not heading households. There was no statistically significant relationship between occupational level and persistence for all blacks, nor was there a significant relationship for heads of households or sons.

[b]Data for white residents is from Stephan Thernstrom and Elizabeth H. Pleck, "The Last of the Immigrants? A Comparative Analysis of Immigrant and Black Social Mobility in Late Nineteenth-Century Boston," unpublished paper delivered at the annual meeting of the Organization of American Historians (April, 1970), p. 12.

ern black geographic stability was also reflected in long-lasting marriages and continuity of parental care for black children.

Occupational Structure

The occupational position of black heads of household placed a great strain on the black family. While the children of white immigrants moved up the occupational ladder, the black child, like his parent, remained fixed in a world of menial and temporary jobs. Eight occupations—waiter, servant, cook, barber, laborer, porter, laundress, and seamstress—accounted for 74% of all blacks at work in Boston in 1880. The largest group by far were the 858 servants who worked in white homes, hotels, and institutions. Two occupations, laundress and seamstress, were largely the preserve of single women and women heading households. The last hired and the first fired, blacks in late nineteenth-century Boston formed a surplus labor force at the bottom of society.

The concentration of blacks in unskilled and service occupations is demonstrated in Table 2. Overall, 86.7% of the total black work force consisted of unskilled and service workers, 7.2% of black workers held skilled positions, 2.9% performed clerical jobs or owned small shops, and 3.2% were professionals. Table 2 also includes the percentage of Irish workers in 1880 in each of these occupational status groups. An immigrant group of peasant origins, the Boston Irish were the white ethnic group which ranked lowest in the Boston social

Table 2. Occupational Level of Black Male and Female Heads of Household, Black Non-Heads of Household, and Irish, 1880

	Black Heads of Household[a]		Black Non-Heads of Household		All Blacks at Work	All Irish at Work[b]
	Male	Female	Male	Female		
Professional	(36)	(1)	(25)	(25)	(87)	(562)
	3.4%[c]	.6%	2.3%	2.9%	3.2%	1.6%
White Collar	(33)	(2)	(52)	(6)	(93)	(3333)
	3.1%	1.3%	4.8%	.7%	2.9%	9.6%
Skilled	(72)	(31)	(54)	(84)	(241)	(6880)
	6.8%	19.4%	5.0%	9.7%	7.2%	19.8%
Unskilled	(925)	(126)	(950)	(751)	(2752)	(23,970)
and Service	86.8%	78.8%	87.9%	86.7%	86.7%	68.9%
	(1066)	(160)	(1081)	(866)	(3173)	(34,745)

[a]Heads of household with no occupation were omitted from the head of household group.

[b]Derived from data in Carroll Wright, *Social, Commercial, and Manufacturing Statistics of the City of Boston* (Boston: Rockwell and Churchill, 1882), pp. 92–116.

[c]Column percentages sometimes do not add up to 100 due to rounding. The relationship between occupational level and household status (head of household vs. non-head of household) is significant at .030 with three degrees of freedom for males, significant at .002 with three degrees of freedom for females.

order. Except at the top of the occupational structure, where there was a slightly higher percentage of professionals among the black work force than among the Irish, Irish workers had much larger percentages of white-collar and skilled workers and much smaller percentages of unskilled and service workers than the black labor force. While 68.9% of the Irish were laborers, teamsters, hostlers, and other unskilled and service workers, 86.7% of blacks performed this low-status work. The classification of menial labor, moreover, tends to obscure the wage differences between the two groups. The black waiter and the Irish cotton mill operative both worked long hours at low pay, but the rewards were somewhat greater for the Irish worker than for his black counterpart.

Seven point two percent of all blacks earning wages and 19.8% of the Irish were skilled workers. Such work, particularly in the building trades, required apprenticeship training which was generally closed to blacks; even buying tools could be an expensive proposition for a black worker. The white-collar group, over three times as large among the Irish as among blacks, owed their jobs to the expansion of record-keeping, paper work, and sales in an industrial society. The new jobs in the Boston labor market—office personnel, sales clerk, even telephone and telegraph operator—employed some of the children of Irish parents, while job discrimination and lack of the proper educational qualifications closed this employment to the aspiring black worker. The figures for the white-collar group also reflected the larger proportion of petty proprietors among the Irish than among blacks.

For black professionals, Boston deserved its reputation as the city of the "Talented Tenth." The relatively large number of black lawyers, doctors, and other professionals, compared with the somewhat smaller Irish percentage, was the result of the attractiveness of the city to educated blacks from the South and other parts of the North, as well as the educational opportunities for the black elite in the New England area.

Thus the black child and the black parent faced more limited job opportunities than even the proletarian Boston Irish. How did the occupational situation of heads of household compare with that of the black worker with no family responsibilities? Although the head of household, in order to support dependents, needed to earn more money than the unattached black worker, Table 2 indicates that there were virtually no differences in occupational situation between blacks heading households and those not heading households. Among unskilled and service workers, one finds 86.8% of black heads of household and 87.9% of the unattached black workers.

Providing for a family was even more difficult for the widowed or deserted wife. Female-headed households included 22 women with no occupations and 105 women at work, most of them in unskilled and service jobs. The skilled category in Table 2, which includes 18% of female workers, is the result of the large number of black seamstresses among females heading households.

Black workers, including male heads of household, female heads of household, and workers with no family responsibilities, were concentrated in the lowest ranks of the occupational structure. While there were slight differences in occupational level for heads of household as compared with all other workers, heads of household, in general, were no more occupationally diverse than other black workers.

Conditions of Life

In vast new areas of Boston, large frame houses with plenty of rooms, indoor plumbing, and spacious backyards were being built for the middle class. But the streetcar suburbs of late nineteenth-century Boston were restricted to whites. In 1880, about 42% of the black population lived in the West End (sometimes referred to as "Nigger Hill"), a conglomeration of tiny alleyways and sidestreets on the seamy side of Beacon Hill. Tenement commissioners visiting the area described filthy streets, polluted air, overcrowded housing, dirty cellars, unsanitary water closets, poor drainage, and unsafe buildings.[18]

> At No. — Anderson Street is a little court. Here a single water closet in a small shed, the bowl filled and in abominable condition, was the only accommodation in this line for eight or ten families of colored people, besides the hands in a stable and a couple of little shops.[19]

Since the tenement rooms were crowded, poorly heated and ventilated, children played in the street. Playing stickball in the summer and using Anderson and Phillips streets as ski slopes in the winter, black children made the most of their urban environment.[20] But street play also resulted in children being crushed under the wheels of fast-moving teams of horses.

The poor physical conditions and the inability of parents to provide an adequate family income resulted in sickness and sometimes death for black children. Mission workers from a settlement in the West End found "a young girl, whose only bed was two broken chairs placed between the cooking stove and the door. She was dying with consumption and was left all day with the care of a two-year-old child, tied into a chair beside her, while its mother was at work." In the same neighborhood, they found a poor black child "who shared the floor with the rats and mice on a cold winter's night."[21] These cases were probably the most dramatic, not the typical circumstances of black poverty in the West End. The mission workers, no doubt, chose examples which would underline the importance of their work and the need for hospital care for their clients.

Individual human tragedies like the deaths of these two children are hidden in the high death rates in the Boston black community. Although the birth rate for blacks was higher than for whites, the number of deaths was so great that deaths generally exceeded births. In fact, 1905–1910 was the first five-year period since the Civil War when the black birth rate was higher than the death rate.[22] Year after year, the city registrar reported more black deaths than births. In 1884, the registrar speculated that "there can be no question that, so far as the limited field furnished by this city affords the means of judging, were accessions from without to cease, the colored population would, in time, disappear from our community."[23] Arguing that the "colored" race was unsuited to northern climates, he concluded: "In short, it would not be too much to say, that were all opposing obstacles of every kind, and in every direction, to the entire liberty of the colored race removed, and they were allowed to seek and occupy any position they were qualified to fill, they would instinctively and inevitably gravitate to southern and congenial latitudes as naturally as water seeks its own level."[24]

As a result of poor diet, extremely high rates of infant mortality and deaths for mothers in childbirth, and the frequent incidence of tuberculosis and contagious diseases, the mortality rate for the black population in 1886 was 41 per 1000, almost twice the white rate.[25] A black person who grew up in the West End recalled that on Sundays after church his family discussed the number of deaths in the neighborhood and which of the neighbors were dying of consumption.[26] Diseases connected with childbirth accounted for the slightly higher death rate among black females than among black males. In 1890 the death rate per 1000 for white males in Boston was 15.86, for black males, 32. Among white females in mortality rate was 24 out of 1000, while black females died at the rate of 35 for every 1000.[27]

The death rate was highest among children under one year of age, and higher still among male children. But significant reductions in infant mortality for both whites and blacks led to a sharp decline in the death rate in the first decade of the twentieth century. From 1900 to 1910, the death rate for white children under one year of age fell from 189 per 1000 to 185, while the black death rate dropped from 322 to 294.[28] These figures were comparable to the mortality rates in other northern and western cities.[29]

The high death rate among adults created a large number of

widowed persons. About one-third of women aged 41–50 and a little less than half of women aged 51–60 lost their husbands. Either as a result of migration or in consequence of a higher rate of remarriage, the census takers found only about one-third as many widowers as widows. Some of the widows remarried, others went to live with relatives, and the remaining women made up the bulk of one-parent households in the black community.

The death of both parents left about 17% of black children homeless in Boston in 1880. These orphans were a much larger part of the population in late nineteenth-century cities than were the black youngsters in 1968 (one out of ten) who were not living with one or both parents.[30] Homeless black children, in most cases, lived with relatives or friends, for few such children found their way into asylums and homes for foundling children. Discrimination by public institutions combined with the desire of black families to adopt black children meant that few black children without parents became wards of the state.

Family Structure

The high death rate and overcrowded, unsanitary tenements, the transiency of the population, and the low occupational position constitute the kinds of pressures often cited as the causes of family disorganization. But several quantitative indicators—the sex ratio, the small number of one-parent households, the infrequency of desertion, and the adaptation of the household to include large numbers of migrants —suggest that the black family structure maintained its organization despite the many depressing aspects of life in Boston.

Several statistics are useful gauges of the nature of family life. One such statistic is the sex ratio, the number of males per one hundred females in the population. A frontier area, with a ratio of males to females of ten to one, or even higher, would have little family life. For everyone who chooses to marry, a stable ratio of males to females would theoretically insure the selection of a mate. Another arrangement of sex ratio, a small male population and a large female population, is said to produce a society with few stable marriages and high rates of illegitimacy, desertion, delinquency and female-headed households. These theoretical possibilities, reasonable in the abstract, have less meaning in concrete historical situations. Even in societies with quite similar sex ratios, great deviations can occur in patterns of sexuality, marriage, and family life. Still, for a population on the move, such as the black population over the last one hundred years, the possibility of imbalanced sex ratios due to large numbers of migrants is an important consideration in assessing the framework of family life.[31]

In fact, among blacks in late nineteenth-century Boston, parity of the sexes existed, as the third column of Table 3 discloses. The overall sex ratio in 1880 was 102.9, though much higher—121—for the marriageable age group (25 to 44). In two other age groups, the very young and the very old, there were more females than males, reflecting the differential mortality of the sexes. The preponderance of males in the 25 to 44 age group stems from the relatively greater economic opportunities drawing adult migrants to the city. Many of these males were "beachhead" migrants, husbands who sent for their wives after they had established themselves in Boston.

When the black sex ratio is contrasted with the sex ratio of the foreign-born and native white populations, we find greater imbalances in the two white groups. For all native whites in 1880 the sex ratio was 95.7, while it was much lower—79.4—for foreign-born whites. Among young adults, Table 3 indicates that there were 96 native white males for every one hundred females, and 83.8 foreign-born white males for every one hundred females. The larger number of adult females in the foreign-born white group reflects the presence of adult working women, usually employed as domestic servants and factory workers, some of whom were earning enough money to finance their dowries.

Throughout the last decades of the nineteenth century, there were slightly more males than females in the black population of Boston. Only in 1910 did the census takers find the reverse. Many young adult females, migrants to Boston, created this surplus of females in the population.[32]

The second important statistic for assessing the possibilities of family life is the number of married persons deserted by their spouses. Even though parity in the sex ratio suggests the necessary environment for stable family life, it is still quite possible that a high number of desertions would modify this conclusion. The number of desertions was determined by tabulating all those married persons in the census record who were not living with their spouse. Of those deserted by their spouses, there were 157 females, about 11% of all married

Table 3. Sex Ratios for Native Whites, Foreign-Born Whites, and Blacks, 1880[a]

	Native White	Foreign-Born White	Black
All Ages	95.7	79.4	102.9
25–44	95.9	83.8	121.0

[a]Derived from data in Carroll Wright, *Social, Commercial, and Manufacturing Statistics*, pp. 94–95.

women, and 167 males, about 13% of all married men in this category. The figures for males, as we noted earlier, were probably increased by the large number of men awaiting the arrival of their wives. In a middle-class district of late nineteenth-century Chicago, where few of the desertions could be explained as the result of large numbers of migrants, about 11% of households included a deserted wife or husband.[33]

What seems impressive in these figures for blacks in Boston is the low rate of desertion and separation, given the extremely high rate of out-migration, even among heads of household, and the dismal occupational prospect that blacks faced. W. E. B. DuBois discussed some of the causes of desertion and separation among blacks in Philadelphia.

> The economic difficulties arise continually among young waiters and servant girls; away from home and oppressed by the peculiar lonesomeness of a great city, they form chance acquaintances here and there, thoughtlessly marry and soon find that the husband's income cannot alone support a family, then comes a struggle which generally results in desertion or voluntary separation.[34]

As a result of death, desertion, or voluntary separation, 18% of black households came to be headed by one parent. In nine out of ten instances the one parent was a female. In assessing one- and two-parent households, I included households in which there were no children present as well as those with children. If childless couples were excluded, we would be unable to examine households of young couples, that is, future parents, as well as those households where grown offspring had moved away.

How did one- and two-parent households differ? Without substantial historical evidence, it would be foolhardy to apply present-day, widely questioned theories about the "tangle of pathology" associated with one-parent households.[35] Regrettably, I have found no qualitative evidence which bears on the issue of how members of the black community viewed the one-parent household.

Nevertheless, there was an important economic difference between the one- and two-parent households. Although precise income figures are not available for black households, black males enjoyed higher wages than black females. In consequence, a family dependent on a woman's wages almost always lived in poverty. The yearly wage among female domestic servants, for example, was half the wage of male domestic servants.[36] Moreover, given the concentration of female heads of household in the most poorly remunerated occupations, overall income levels between male- and female-headed households were even more disparate. In many two-parent households, the husband's wage was supplemented by both the wife's earnings from domestic service or laundry work and rent money from the boarder. Without these several income sources, the one-parent household was at an even greater disadvantage. Lacking the wages or unpaid labor of a wife, even the one-parent household headed by a male suffered economically.

From an analysis of the manuscript census schedules, three important distinctions emerged among two-parent households in the black community. First, there were proportionately more two-parent households among migrants to Boston than among native Bostonians. Second, the proportion of two-parent households among rural blacks was greater than among urban blacks. Finally, literate blacks headed two-parent households more often than illiterate blacks.

As we observed above, the early movement of blacks to Boston brought persons especially attracted to the advantages of the northern city. Both those heads of household from the rural South and those northern heads of household from outside Massachusetts revealed large and almost identical proportions of two-parent households, 83.3% and 83.4% respectively, while native Bostonians contributed fewer two-parent households. Given the many theories about the disruptive nature of migration, we might expect a higher percentage of one-parent households among the newcomers to the city than among the long-established urban blacks. But Table 4 reveals that the percentage of two-parent households among the two migrant streams of the population was significantly greater than among black Bostonians. Thus, the stereotype of disruptive migration does not fit the situation of blacks in late nineteenth-century Boston.

The combined effects of rural origins and long-distance movement away from family and friends made southern-born, rural migrants to Boston a distinctive group. We can compare the effect of

Table 4. One- and Two-Parent Households, by Place of Birth of the Head of Household[a]

	Born in Mass.	Born in North[b]	Total born in North	Born in South	N
One-Parent	(36)	(27)	(63)	(136)	(199)
	27.1%	16.6%	21.3%	16.7%	18.0%
Two-Parent	(97)	(136)	(233)	(676)	(909)
	72.9%	83.4%	78.7%	83.3%	82.0%
	(133)	(163)	(296)	(812)	(1108)

[a]This table omits foreign-born heads of household, heads of household with no place of birth, and single-member households. The relationship between place of birth and household status is significant at .02, with two degrees of freedom.
[b]Does not include Massachusetts

rural origins on the household by contrasting rural heads of household (the southern-born) with urban heads of household (the northern-born). As we note in Table 4, slightly more two-parent households occurred among rural than among urban heads of household, 83.3% as opposed to 78.7%. If we assume that a majority of the southern-born blacks were freedmen, the large number of two-parent households among them is even more remarkable. The common argument, that the abrupt transition from rural to urban life created indelible strains on the black family, does not hold for late nineteenth-century Boston. If anything, we find the reverse of this common proposition. It is clear from column four of Table 4 that households in which both parents were present were more frequent among rural than among urban black heads of household.

Even greater than variations between urban and rural households were variations within these two types of households. Table 5 bears on this issue, differentiating urban and rural blacks according to the literacy of the head of household. For both urban and rural heads of household, a literate black was more likely to head a two-parent household than an illiterate. The percentage of two-parent households dropped from 86.5% of southern-born literates to 75.7% among illiterates from the same region, and from 80.1% among northern-born literates to only 68.6% among illiterates born in the North. Although these northern-born illiterate heads of household were a very small group, only eleven persons, nevertheless it is striking that a larger percentage of one-parent households was found among them than among any other group in the population.

Table 5. One- and Two-Parent Households, by Place of Birth and Literacy of the Head of Household, 1880[a]

	Literate	Illiterate	Total
Northern-Born One-Parent	(52) 19.9%	(11) 31.4%	(63) 21.3%
Northern-Born Two-Parent	(209) 80.1%	(24) 68.6%	(233) 78.7%
Southern-Born One-Parent	(77) 13.5%	(59) 24.3%	(136) 16.7%
Southern-Born Two-Parent	(492) 86.5%	(184) 75.7%	(676) 83.3%
	(830)	(278)	(1108)

[a]Table omits foreign-born heads of household, heads of household with no place of birth, and single-member households. The relationship between literacy and household status was significant at .180 with one degree of freedom for the northern-born, significant at .001 with one degree of freedom for the southern-born.

If slavery permanently weakened family ties among blacks one would expect to find greater numbers of one-parent households among the ex-slaves. To be sure, there were fewer two-parent households among ex-slaves (southern-born illiterates) than among southern-born literates, but the freedmen had two-parent households more often than northern-born heads of household who were also illiterate. Thus, among both northern- and southern-born heads of household, illiteracy was associated with higher proportions of one-parent households.

It is possible that the relationship between illiteracy and one-parent, generally female-headed households is only a statistical artifact, the consequence of a higher rate of illiteracy among females than males.[37] In order to test whether Table 5 described a spurious relationship, I compared the number of illiterates among two groups of women, female heads of household and those females living with their husbands in two-parent households. If higher rates of illiteracy among one-parent households in both the North and the South were merely the result of the fact that one-parent households were mostly female, we would expect to find roughly similar proportions of illiterates among married women living with their spouses and among females heading households. Instead, female heads of household were much more commonly illiterate than women living with their husbands. Significantly, more female heads of household than married females were illiterate; about one-fourth of married women were illiterate, while more than a third of females heading households could not read or write. Among the southern-born women, most of whom were born into slavery, the rate of illiteracy was much higher. However, the general pattern remained the same; while about one-third of married women were illiterate, almost half of females heading households were illiterate.

Whether or not illiterates thought less of themselves than blacks who learned to read or write the numbers will never tell us. What is clear, however, is that for both urban and rural heads of household there were significantly more one-parent households among the illiterates. Speculation might lead us to conclude that illiteracy was both a real handicap in an urban society and, in addition, a characteristic found among the most disadvantaged adults in the black community.

Migrants and native Bostonians, rural and urban adults, illiterate and literate persons differed significantly in the number of two-parent households they formed. Did differences appear as well in the composition of the household? A single individual or that person and boarders lived in one out of seven black households in Boston. These solitary adults were excluded from the analysis of household composition. The great majority of black households, as Table 6 indicates, consisted of nuclear families—usually husband and wife, or a husband, wife, and children, but occasionally a single parent and child. Families which added other relatives to the nuclear family, in what is termed an extended household, were 9.7% of all black households. Finally, about one out of three black households included boarders, and in a few cases boarders and relatives, in addition to parents and children. DuBois discovered roughly the same number of augmented households—that is, households with boarders—in late nineteenth-century Philadelphia.[38]

Virtually the same patterns of family composition existed among rural and urban blacks, as columns three and four of Table 6 disclose. In both cases the majority of households was nuclear, although a significant minority—about one-third—included boarders. Only when native Bostonians are separated from the rest of the northern-born do differences appear in the composition of the household. The household headed by a black person born in Boston was somewhat more likely to mix relatives or boarders in the home than a household headed by a migrant. However, the differences in household composition between blacks born in Massachusetts, other northern states, and the South are not striking. What is important, in fact, is the uniformity of household composition among migrant and stable, urban and rural heads of household.

It might be thought relatives were more frequent among the poorest families, huddling together because they could not afford to live by themselves. The figures in Table 7 demonstrate that this was not the case. Controlling for the occupational level of the head of household, the proportion of relatives increased among higher-status

Table 6. Nuclear, Extended, and Augmented Households, by Place of Birth of the Head of Household, 1880[a]

	Born in Mass.	Born in North[b]	Total born in North	Born in South	N
Nuclear	(68) 51.2%	(93) 57.1%	(161) 54.4%	(462) 56.1%	(623) 56.2%
Extended	(16) 12.0%	(15) 9.2%	(31) 10.5%	(80) 10.6%	(111) 10.0%
Augmented	(49) 36.8%	(55) 33.7%	(104) 35.1%	(270) 33.3%	(374) 33.8%
	(133)	(163)	(296)	(812)	(1108)

[a]This table omits foreign-born heads of household, heads of household with no place of birth, and single-member households. The relationship between place of birth and family structure shown in this table is not statistically significant.
[b]Does not include Massachusetts.

Elizabeth H. Pleck

Table 7. Nuclear, Extended, and Augmented Households, by Occupational Level of the Head of Household, 1880[a]

	Professional	White-Collar	Skilled	Unskilled	N
Nuclear	(19)	(16)	(49)	(558)	(642)
	52.8%	50.0%	57.6%	58.8%	
Extended	(7)	(6)	(8)	(84)	(105)
	19.4%	18.8%	9.4%	8.9%	
Augmented	(10)	(10)	(28)	(307)	(355)
	27.8%	31.3%	32.9%	32.3%	
	(36)	(32)	(85)	(949)	(1102)

[a]This table omits persons with no occupation and single-member heads of household. Heads of household from all places of birth are included. The relationship between occupation and family structure is not statistically significant.

heads of household, while the proportion decreased among lower-status households. Relatives may have been more welcome to join the family in higher-status households which could afford to sustain additional members. The George Ruffins (he was a lawyer and judge, she a prominent clubwoman and suffragist) absorbed into their home Mrs. Ruffin's niece, Daisy Nahar. In other cases, the presence of additional adult family members may have financed the education or supported the family business, which, in turn, resulted in the higher status of the head of household.

Relatives were more common in higher-status households, but lodgers appeared more often in lower-status households. The number of augmented households, as summarized in line three of Table 7, shows that about one-third of blue-collar households included a boarder, while slightly fewer boarders resided in professional and white-collar homes. Among households headed by unskilled and skilled workers, just as in the female-headed household, the lodger's rent money was often an essential part of the family budget. In response to the influx of southern migrants, the black family accommodated these lodgers, generally single women and men who worked as servants and waiters. The augmented household was a product of necessity, but it met the housing needs of the lodgers as well as provided additional income requirements of black families.

Nineteenth-century observers often described the "demoralizing" influence of lodgers on the household. DuBois exemplified this attitude, fearing that "the privacy and intimacy of home life is destroyed, and elements of danger and demoralization admitted" when the lodger entered the black home.[39] Given the desperate economic circumstances of black families, the boarder's rent money may have insured family survival rather than destroyed it. Moreover, boarders were common additions to higher-status households. The boarder in many cases became a "relative" of the family, in function if not in kinship. Richard Wright recalled that as a boarder he easily became a part of a Memphis home—more so than he liked, since a match-making mother was eager for the boarder to marry her daughter.[40]

Conclusion

This study of the black family in late nineteenth-century Boston views the black family structure at one point in time. Subsequent studies must trace the family over the years in order to fully comprehend changes in the household. If we want to learn about the acculturation of children in the black family, it is particularly important to employ a dynamic perspective. For example, while we know that about seven out of ten black children in Boston in 1880 lived in two-parent households, we do not know how many of these children spent their early years in such a household. Nor, for that matter, among the minority of children in 1880 who were missing both parents do we know whether their family situation affected their future, for better or worse. This kind of analysis can only be pursued through the tracing of individuals, a method extremely arduous to undertake given the mobility of the population.

Any study of black family life largely employing quantitative information represents only a point of departure for further analysis of black families. While the high number of two-parent households, 82% of all black households in Boston, indicates the existence of much greater family organization than has been generally assumed, we need evidence about the cultural context in which the urban black family operated. How were one- and two-parent households viewed? Were different values placed on marriage, the family, even desertion in the black community than in other groups? Did the addition of boarders and relatives endanger the intimacy of the home or create additional adult models for black children? Except in the few instances of family diaries and personal accounts, these questions may prove difficult, if not impossible, to answer through literary materials.

While there are limitiations to numerical analysis, it does allow for comparisons across time and space. How then did Boston compare with other cities? Perhaps one could argue that, despite the poverty-stricken condition of blacks in Boston, there was still some way in which Boston was, indeed, "the paradise of the Negro," if only because the situation of blacks in the South was so much worse. Although more studies need to be undertaken, overall figures from southern urban, southern rural, and northern urban centers in the late nineteenth century demonstrate a striking similarity in the percentages of two-parent households. Theodore Hershberg reports that in

Elizabeth H. Pleck   *170*

both 1880 and 1896 the two-parent household comprised 76% of all households among blacks in Philadelphia. He found roughly similar proportions of two-parent households in ante-bellum Philadelphia, where 77% of all black households were two-parent. Among a special group of about 87 slaves who had bought their freedom 91% formed two-parent households.[41] From the major work of Herbert Gutman on the black family, the two-parent household in 1880 appeared among 81% of Adams County, Mississippi, black households and 77% of Mobile, Alabama, black households.[42] In three urban areas in 1896, Atlanta, Nashville, and Cambridge, Massachusetts, Gutman found 77%, 85%, and 90%, respectively, of two-parent households.[43] It would be tempting here to contrast the relative effects on the black household of southern urban, southern rural and northern urban environments. But what we find in the few areas studied is greater variation within than between locales. All in all, the two-parent household was the prevailing family form in southern rural, southern urban, and northern urban areas.

The figures cited above, except in the case of antebellum Philadelphia, do not distinguish between native-born city dwellers and rural migrants to the city. Such an analytic strategy is vital to the study of the effects of city and country origins and the migration from one area to another on the black household.

How did migration to the city affect the black family? The standard texts on black history scarcely mention the migration of blacks to northern cities before the Great Migration of World War I. On the whole, the northward migration was a movement of single individuals or couples; in few cases did the whole family move north. After the migrants from the South or other parts of the North reached Boston, an incredible number of single individuals and families left the city. This movement out of Boston in some cases left behind deserted wives and husbands, but the rate of desertion was rather low given the lack of occupational opportunity for blacks in Boston and the general rootlessness of the black population.

In the work of DuBois and E. Franklin Frazier, migration to the city is viewed as a disruptive factor which weakened the family and produced large numbers of one-parent households. DuBois wrote that "as a whole, it is true that the average of culture and wealth is far lower among immigrants than natives, and that this gives rise to the gravest of the Negro problems."[44] What these writers generally meant by migration was the *transition* from rural to urban culture among southern migrants to the city. This disruptive transition was said to have been the source of desertion, delinquency, and female-headed households. Frazier, in his discussion of the "city of destruction," noted: "Family desertion among Negroes in cities, appears, then, to be one of the inevitable consequences of the impact of urban life on the simple family organization and folk culture which the Negro has evolved in the rural South."[45]

At least for late nineteenth-century Boston, quantitative evidence calls Frazier's thesis into question. Two-parent households were more frequent among both migrant *and* rural black heads of household. Such evidence can be interpreted in two ways. One explanation would reverse the Frazier argument: instead of migration and the transition from rural to urban culture weakening the black family, these influences strengthened it. Persons who had invested so much effort to leave family, friends, and familiar ways had a greater stake in establishing households once they were settled in the city. Also, the limited expectations of rural blacks may have meant that city life in the North was, indeed, a significant improvement over life in the rural South. Finally, the special character of this early migration might have distinguished the early newcomers to the city (both in ante-bellum Philadelphia and in Boston about fifty years later) from more recent city-bound blacks.

A second explanation of the differences in the number of two-parent households, offered by Theodore Hershberg, is that neither slavery nor migration but the urban environment produced greater numbers of one-parent households. Tremendous differences in wealth, poor health conditions for blacks in cities, the destructiveness of urban culture—all these are cited as the causes of "family disorganization" among blacks. Without more knowledge of the internal workings of black culture, of the values blacks placed on different family forms, it is impossible to know whether the one-parent, female-headed household was viewed by blacks as "family disorganization." The use of this value-loaded term generally presupposes a hierarchy of family types, with the male-present, nuclear, and patriarchal household representing the most-valued family form.[46]

Another danger in substituting one grand interpretation of "family disorganization" in place of another is that it may tend to obscure other important differences in family type and composition which do not appear between rural and urban, ex-slave and free-born blacks. Important differences between city dwellers and rural blacks must be noted. But in late nineteenth-century Boston the composition of the black household was similar for both rural and urban black heads of household. Moreover, significantly more one-parent households occurred among illiterate blacks from both rural and urban origins. The social meaning of illiteracy for blacks in the city remains enigmatic, but the discovery that the illiteracy of the head of

Elizabeth H. Pleck   *172*

household significantly altered the proportion of two-parent households hints at the existence of other fundamental social characteristics differentiating black households.

While variations in household composition and percentage of two-parent households which are associated with place of birth, illiteracy, and migration should be noted and considered, the similarities in two-parent households among diverse groups in the black population are even more striking. The evidence suggests a family pattern of nuclear, two-parent households which prevailed among migrant and rural black heads of household as well as among stable and urban black heads of household. Despite the existence of blacks at the lowest rung of the occupational ladder, most black children lived in homes where both parents were present, and black families generally included husband, wife, and children.

The presentation of these raw statistics forces us to challenge and revise previous conceptions about the black family. More lies hidden behind a high death rate, a transient population, and a poverty-stricken black community than the phrases "culture of poverty" or "family disorganization" convey. Our vision of the family as an institution which reacts to and reflects changes is oversimplified, while there seems little understanding of the family as an institution which itself produces changes in individuals and institutions. If the black family were merely the image of the social conditions of urban blacks, we would find a rootless, disorganized mosaic of families. Notions of "black matriarchy" and "the tangle of pathology" of the black family have captivated sociologists and historians alike, but now the task before us is to tell the rather different story of the complex organization and continuity of the black household.

Notes

Ms. Pleck is a graduate student in history of American civilization at Brandeis University. A Ford Foundation Dissertation Fellowship in Ethnic Studies financed the research cited in this article. The author's ideas about the black family have been greatly influenced by the comments and work of Herbert Gutman, whose forthcoming book on the black family should greatly enlarge our knowledge of the subject. The revision of this paper has benefited from the criticism of Stephan Thernstrom. The author is especially indebted to Joseph Pleck for writing the computer programs employed in this study, and for his aid in data analysis and the use of statistical techniques. Useful comments and suggestions for changes in this article were made by Gordon Fellman, Allan Kulikoff, John Demos, Doug Jones, and Peter Knights.

1 "Boston as the Paradise of the Negro," *Colored American Magazine,* Vol. VII, no. 5 (May, 1904), 309–17. For a similar view, see also W. E. Burghardt DuBois, *The Black North in 1901: A Social Study* (New York: Arno Press and the New York Times reprint, 1969), 10–19.

2   There were 139 households headed by a black person born in a foreign country. In 28 of the foreign-born households, the head of household was a single individual, living without kin or children. Excluded from all analysis concerning family were those interracial couples which included a white husband and a black wife. Interracial couples composed of a black husband and a white wife were included.

3   Marriage records, registered by the Division of Vital Statistics of the Commonwealth of Massachusetts, indicated race and exact place of birth for the bride and groom. Of the marriage partners listing Massachusetts as their place of birth in the 1870 vital records, five out of seven were born in Boston. Half of the remaining non-Bostonians were from Newburyport, Worcester, Cambridge, Lynn, and Salem. The largest group of southern-born brides and grooms were natives of Virginia; two out of five were from Petersburg, Richmond, and Norfolk. In the period when these brides and grooms were growing up in Virginia, none of these three towns could be considered "urban" by Boston standards. The largest city in Virginia in 1860 was Richmond, which at the time was only one-fifth the size of Boston. James M. McPherson, *The Negro's Civil War: How American Negroes Felt and Acted During the War for the Union* (New York: Vintage Books, 1965), Appendix B, p. 320.

4   I am indebted to Peter R. Knights for suggesting this use of the literacy category.

5   At first glance, it seems possible to estimate the number of southern slave migrants to Boston by taking the percentage of slaves in the states of the upper South just before the Civil War. Between one-half and two-thirds of the southern migrants to Boston in the late nineteenth century were from Virginia, whose population in 1860 consisted of about ten slaves to each free-born black. If black migration operated randomly, the southern black population in Boston consisted of about ten freedmen for every free-born black. But migration to the North after the Civil War was extremely selective. We cannot assume that freedmen and free blacks migrated in proportion to their numbers in the population.

If we make the assumption that literacy corresponds to free status for blacks in the South, we arrive at a probability that it was twenty-seven times as likely for a free-born person to move north as it was for an ex-slave. This proportion is derived by taking the proportion of free persons to slaves in the 1860 Virginia population, a ratio of one to nine, multiplied by the population of literates to illiterates in the black population of Boston in 1880, a ratio of three to one.

For the proportions of blacks from the upper South in Boston's black population, see John Daniels, *In Freedom's Birthplace: A Study of the Boston Negroes* (Boston: Houghton Mifflin, 1915), pp. 141, 468. For the number of ex-slaves in the Virginia 1860 population, see U.S. Bureau of the Census, *Negro Population of the United States, 1790–1915* (Washington, D.C.: U.S. Government Printing Office, 1918), Table 6, p. 57.

6   The statistics used in this paper are based on a total of 5,847 individuals found in the manuscript census schedules for Boston in 1880. The discrepancy between this figure and the official figure, 5,873, is due to mistakes I may have made in transcribing the manuscript schedules, as well as errors in the original tabulated figure.

7   Net migration increases indicate only a small part of the actual population turnover. Stephan Thernstrom estimated that nearly 800,000 persons moved into Boston between 1880 and 1890. Since the population streams of in-migrants and

out-migrants tended to cancel out each other, the total Boston population only increased from 363,000 in 1880 to 448,000 in 1890. Stephan Thernstrom and Peter R. Knights, "Men in Motion: Some Data and Speculations About Urban Population Mobility in Nineteenth-Century America," Tamara K. Hareven, ed., *Anonymous Americans: Explorations in Nineteenth-Century Social History* (Englewood Cliffs, N.J.: Prentice Hall, 1971), pp. 21, 25.

8 E. G. Ravenstein, "The Laws of Migration," *Journal of the Royal Statistical Society*, Vol. XLVIII (1885), pp. 167–227; Samuel A. Stouffer, "Intervening Opportunities: A Theory Relating Mobility and Distance," *American Sociological Review*, Vol. V (1940), 845–67.

9 Carter Godwin Woodson, *A Century of Negro Migration* (Washington, D.C.: The Association for the Study of Negro Life and History, 1918), pp. 162–66.

10 Clyde Kiser, *Sea Island to City* (New York: Columbia University Press, 1932), p. 170.

11 Thernstrom and Knights, "Men in Motion," p. 22.

12 These four-fold classifications of occupation were based on an eight-scale occupational code devised by Stephan Thernstrom for his study of occupational mobility in Boston. Since there were so few high-status black workers, professionals, large-scale proprietors, managers and officials and semi-professionals were collapsed into one category called professionals. The white-collar category included clerical and sales personnel, petty proprietors, and minor managers and lower level government officials. I maintained a distinctive category of skilled workers as Thernstrom did, but the semi-skilled, service, unskilled, and menial service groups were merged into one category called service and unskilled workers. I am indebted to Professor Thernstrom for providing me with this occupational code. For a more detailed explication of the code, see Peter R. Knights, *The Plain People of Boston, 1830–1960: A Study in City Growth* (New York: Oxford University Press, 1971), Appendix E, pp. 149–56.

13 Clyde Griffen, "Making it in America: Social Mobility in Mid-Nineteenth Century Poughkeepsie," *New York History*, Vol. II, no. 5 (October, 1970), Table II, p. 498.

14 Data cited in Thernstrom and Knights, "Men in Motion," p. 46.

15 Richard J. Hopkins, "Occupational and Geographic Mobility in Atlanta, 1870–1896," *Journal of Southern History*, Vol. XXIV (May, 1968), Table 6, p. 207.

16 Paul B. Worthman, "Working Class Mobility in Birmingham, Alabama, 1880–1914," Hareven, ed., *Anonymous Americans*, pp. 180–85.

17 Alwyn Barr, "Occupational and Geographic Mobility in San Antonio, 1870–1900," *Social Science Quarterly*, Vol. 51, no. 2 (September, 1970), Table 3, p. 401.

18 Horace G. Wadlin, *A Tenement House Census of Boston*, Section II (Boston: Wright and Potter, 1893), pp. 89–93.

19 Dwight Porter, *Report upon a Sanitary Inspection of Certain Tenements-House Districts of Boston* (Boston: Rockwell and Churchill, 1889), pp. 37–8.

20 Walter J. Stevens, *Chip on My Shoulder* (Boston: Meador Publishing Company, 1946), p. 22.

21 *New York Age* (June 15, 1889), p. 1.

22 Daniels, *In Freedom's Birthplace,* p. 472.

23 *Boston City Document No. 68* (1884), pp. 7–8.

24 *Ibid.,* p. 8.

25 *Boston City Document No. 100* (1887), p. 11.

26 Walter J. Stevens, *Chip on My Shoulder,* p. 18.

27 Frederick L. Hoffman, *Race Traits and Tendencies of the American Negro* (Publications of the American Economic Association, 1896), p. 47.

28 U.S. Census Bureau, *Negro Population, 1790–1915,* p. 32.

29 *Ibid.*

30 U.S. Bureau of the Census, *Current Population Reports,* Series P-20, No. 187, Tables 4 and 9; and *U.S. Census of the Population: 1960. Detailed Characteristics, U.S. Summary,* Tables 181, 182, and 185, as quoted in Paul C. Glick, "Marriage and Marital Stability Among Blacks," *The Millbank Memorial Fund Quarterly,* Vol. XLVIII, no. 2 (April, 1970), Table 8, p. 113.

31 The sex ratio does more than reflect differing economic opportunities for females and males in the city. Jacquelyne Jackson in a recent article also maintains that the sex ratio is related to the number of female-headed families. In states with high sex ratios in 1970, she found few female-headed families, but in states with low sex ratios, she found large numbers of female-headed familes. Massachusetts, with a sex ratio of 88.6 in 1970, had the highest number of black female-headed families of any state in the nation. Jacquelyne J. Jackson, "But Where are the Men?" *The Black Scholar,* Vol. 3, no. 4 (December, 1971), pp. 30–41.

32 U.S. Census Bureau, *Negro Population, 1790–1915,* p. 156.

33 Richard Sennett, *Families against the city: Middle Class Homes of Industrial Chicago, 1872–1890* (Cambridge, Massachusetts: Harvard University Press, 1971), p. 115.

34 W. E. B. DuBois, *The Philadelphia Negro* (New York: Schocken Books, 1967), p. 67.

35 Robert Staples, "Towards a Sociology of the Black Family: A Theoretical and Methodological Assessment, " *Journal of Marriage and the Family,* Vol. 33, no. 1 (February, 1971), pp. 119-30 contains a comprehensive review of current sociological literature on the black family and maintains a critical stance towards views which associate "the tangle of pathology" with the black family.

36 DuBois, *The Philadelphia Negro,* p. 448. For related income figures, see also the same work, pp. 173-8 and W. E. B. DuBois, *The Negro American Family* (Cambridge, Massachusetts: MIT Press, 1970), pp. 111–13.

37 Carroll D. Wright, *The Social, Commercial, and Manufacturing Statistics of the city of Boston* (Boston: Rockwell and Churchill, 1882), pp. 130–1.

Elizabeth H. Pleck

38 DuBois, *The Philadelphia Negro,* pp. 194, 164.

39 *Ibid.,* p. 194.

40 Richard Wright, *Black Boy: a record of childhood and youth* (New York: Harper, 1937).

41 Theodore Hershberg, "Free Blacks in Antebellum Philadelphia: A Study of Ex-Slaves, Free-Born and Socio-Economic Decline," *Journal of Social History,* Vol. 5, No. 2 (Winter 1971–1972), Table 1, and pp. 186 and 190. Mr. Hershberg kindly sent me a manuscript copy of this paper.

42 Herbert G. Gutman and Laurence A. Glasco, "The Negro Family, Household, and Occupational Structure 1855–1925, with special emphasis on Buffalo, New York, but including Comparative Data from New York, New York, Brooklyn, New York, Mobile, Alabama, and Adams County, Mississippi," (unpublished tables presented at the Yale Conference on Nineteenth Century Cities, November, 1968), Table XXI. Figures were computed from this table in order to derive a percentage of one- and two-parent households. Professor Gutman kindly allowed me to quote from his unpublished data.

43 *Ibid.,* Table XXVI. Figures for one- and two-parent households were computed based on data in this table.

44 DuBois, *The Philadelphia Negro,* 80.

45 E. Franklin Frazier, *The Negro Family in the United States* (Chicago: the University of Chicago Press, 1966), 255.

46 For example, these paragraphs can be found in the Moynihan Report. "But there is one truly great discontinutiy in family structure in the United States at the present time: that between the white world in general and that of the Negro American. The white family has achieved a high degree of stability and is maintaining that stability. By contrast, the family structure of lower class Negroes is highly unstable, and in many urban centers is approaching complete breakdown." Office of Policy Planning and Research, United States Department of Labor, *The Negro Family: The Case for National Action* (Washington, D.C.: U.S. Government Printing Office, 1965), 5.

PART II

Growing Up: Childhood and Youth

This chapter from John Demos's book on family life in Plymouth colony not only offers us a picture of childhood at that time but also provides us with an example of psycho-historical research. The author's findings seem to support Ariès's notion that childhood is a relatively modern concept, since in Plymouth the ages of six and seven marked an important transition to an adult-like status, at least as indicated by dress. Furthermore, he points out that the reigning conception of the relationship between parents and their children was one that placed a great deal of emphasis on breaking the will of the offspring. This theme is one that dies a very slow death in American child-rearing literature, since evidence of its persistence is found in the early decades of the twentieth century.

JOHN DEMOS

9 *Infancy and Childhood in the Plymouth Colony*

Surely no event in the life-cycle displays a greater difference between the conditions prevalent then and now than the first one— the crisis of birth itself. The usual setting, in its most general outlines, is easily imagined. Delivery would take place at home. Tradition has

180

it that the "inner room" . . . in the familiar house plan was also known as the "borning room," in reference to its special use in times of childbirth. There the mother was brought to bed, and there presumably she remained until she and her infant child were strong enough to venture forth into the household at large. Her attendants were older women experienced in such matters and acting in the role of midwives.

In our own culture childbirth normally presents few difficulties of any magnitude; but in the seventeenth century it was quite another story. We . . . note . . . the evidence that in one out of thirty deliveries the mother would lose her life,[1] or, stated another way, that every fifth woman in the Old Colony died from causes associated with childbirth. The mortality rate for newborn infants is more difficult to determine, but one in ten would seem a reasonable guess. These figures may seem surprisingly low when set alongside more traditional notions of life in the seventeenth century; but they nonetheless describe a very real danger. And this danger must have profoundly affected the perceptions of everyone directly involved in any given delivery.

When a baby was safely past the hazards of his first few days of life, he was doubtless incorporated quickly into the ongoing routine of his household. One major public event in which he took center stage was his baptism. Usually this occurred within six months of birth,[2] and on some occasions, particularly in wintertime, it must have been quite an ordeal. Otherwise, he enjoyed a continuing round of sleep and nourishment. The matter of how and where he slept is uncertain. Wooden and wicker cradles are among the most appealing artifacts of the seventeenth century to have come down to us today; but they are not found often in the inventory lists. Perhaps some of them were too crude and of too little value to bother with in adding up a man's estate. Perhaps, too, some other kind of makeshift bed was contrived for the newborn; or possibly he would for a short period sleep alongside his parents. It does seem that within a few months he was moved elsewhere—most likely to a trundle bed, which he might share with some of his older siblings. One rather gruesome notation in the Court Records serves to illustrate this type of arrangement. A small child of "about halfe a yeer old" had been "found dead in the morning . . . lying in bed with Waitstill Elmes and Sarah Hatch, the childs sister." An official board of inquest studied the matter and concluded that "either it was stiffled by lying on its face or accedentally over layed in the bed."[3]

The infant's clothing was probably quite simple. Previous studies of this subject have turned up no evidence of swaddling or otherwise binding the child so as to restrict his movement.[4] Some type of linen smock seems to have been standard dress for seventeenth-century babies; and doubtless, too, they were frequently under several layers of woolen blankets.

The baby's nourishment consisted, it appears, entirely of breast milk. The subject is not much discussed in any documents extant today, but there are occasional, incidental references to it.[5] There is also the indirect evidence which derives from the study of birth intervals. We touched on this matter briefly in an earlier section, but it deserves a more extended statement here. In the average family, we noted, children were spaced roughly two years apart (or a bit longer near the end of the wife's childbearing span). This pattern is consistent with a practice of breast feeding a child for about twelve months, since lactation normally presents a biological impediment to a new conception.[6] The exceptions can nearly always be explained in the same terms. When one finds an interval of only twelve or fifteen months between two particular deliveries, one also finds that the older baby died at or soon after birth. (Here there would be no period of breast feeding, to speak of, and hence nothing to delay the start of another pregnancy.)[7]

We can try to pull together these various bits of evidence bearing on infancy as customarily experienced in the Old Colony. And in doing so, we are left with the impression—no stronger word could be justified—that for his first year or so a baby had a relatively comfortable and tranquil time. The ebb and flow of domestic life must have been constantly around him: large families in small houses created an inevitable sense of intimacy. Often he must have been set close to the fireside for warmth. His clothing was light and not especially restrictive, yet the covers laid over him heightened his sense of protection. And most important, he had regular access to his mother's breast[8]— with all that this implies in the way of emotional reassurance, quite apart from the matter of sound physical nourishment. Illness was, of course, a real danger; the death rate for infants under one year seems to have been substantially higher than for any later age. But this fact may well have encouraged an attitude of particular concern and tenderness towards infants.

All such statements are highly conjectural, and so too is any impression we may try to form of the subsequent phases of a child's life. Still, with this strong word of warning, it seems worth proceeding somewhat further. Let us return once again to the writings of John Robinson, for a most arresting pronouncement on the requirements of the child by way of discipline: "And surely there is in all children . . . a stubborness, and stoutness of mind arising from natural pride, which must, in the first place, be broken and beaten down; that so the foundation of their education being laid in humility and tractableness, other virtues may, in their time, be built thereon . . . For the beating, and keeping down of this stubborness parents must provide carefully . . . that the children's wills and wilfulness be restrained and repressed, and that, in time; lest sooner than they imagine, the tender sprigs grow to that stiffness, that they will rather break than bow. Children should not know, if it could be kept from them, that they have a will in their own, but in their parents' keeping; neither should these words be heard from them, save by way of consent, 'I will' or 'I will not.' "[9]

Translated into the language of modern psychology this statement amounts to a blanket indictment of the child's strivings toward self-assertion, and particularly of any impulses of direct aggression. The terms "break" and "beat down" ("destroy" is also used further on) seem to admit of no qualification. Robinson urged, moreover, that this sort of discipline be started very early. It had to be accorded "the first place" in a whole sequence of socialization, because until the child's inherent "stubborness" was thoroughly restrained training in the more positive virtues would not really take hold.

Precisely what age Robinson had in mind here is not clear; but we may suspect that it was somewhere between one and two years. This, at any rate, is the period when *every* child develops the ability to assert his own will far more directly and effectively than was possible earlier. His perceptions of himself as apart from other people grow progressively sharper; his world is for the first time explicitly organized in terms of "I" and "you," "mine" and "yours." He makes rapid progress with muscular control and coordination, and thus gains new power to express all his impulses. Even today, with our much more permissive style of child rearing, the second year is a time for establishing limits, and often for the direct clash of wills between parent and child.[10] In all likelihood these first raw strivings of the infant self seemed to sincere Puritans a clear manifestation of original sin—the "fruit of natural corruption and root of actual rebellion against God and man," as Robinson himself put it. Such being the case, the only appropriate response from parents was a repressive one.

And there was more still. The second year of life was for many children bounded at either end by experiences of profound loss. Somewhere near its beginning, we have surmised, the child was likely to be weaned; and near its end the arrival of a new baby might be expected. All this would serve to heighten the crisis imposed by the crushing of the child's assertive and aggressive drives.

The pattern is striking in itself; but it gains added significance when set alongside an important theme in the *adult* life of the colonists —namely the whole atmosphere of contention, of chronic and sometimes bitter enmity, to which we have already alluded.[11] This point merits the strongest possible emphasis, because it serves to call in question some extremely venerable and widespread notions about Puritanism. It has long been assumed that the people of this time and culture were peculiarly concerned—were effectively "neurotic," if you will—about all aspects of sex. But there is now a growing body of evidence to the contrary (some of which will be examined shortly); and it might even be argued that the Puritans took sex more nearly in their stride than most later generations of Americans.[12] Perhaps, though, there was a *different* bugbear in their lives—and psyches— namely, a tight cluster of anxieties about aggression. To read the records of Plymouth, and also those of the other New England settlements, is to sense a very special sort of preoccupation with any overt acts of this character. Here, it seems, was the one area of emotional and interpersonal life about which the Puritans were most concerned, confused, conflicted.

John Robinson's thoughts are pertinent once again, right at this point. His *Works* contain a number of short essays dealing successively with each of the most basic human instincts and emotions; and the one entitled "Of Anger" stands out in a very special way. Robinson could find nothing at all to say in favor of anger—no circumstance which could ever truly justify its expression, no perspective from which its appearance was less than totally repellent. The imagery which he summoned to describe it is intensely vivid. Anger, he wrote, "God so brands, as he scarce doth any created affection"; for it "hath always evil in it." The "wrathful man" is like a "hideous monster," with "his eyes burning, his lips fumbling, his face pale, his teeth gnashing, his mouth foaming, and other parts of his body trembling, and shaking."[13]

But anger, of course, is not easily avoided: efforts to suppress it can succeed only partially and at a very considerable cost. This leads us back to the opening stages in the life of a Puritan child. If his experience was, first, a year or so of general indulgence, and then a radical turn towards severe discipline—if, in particular, his earliest efforts at self-assertion were met with a crushing counterforce—it should not be surprising to find that aggression was a theme of special potency in the culture at large. Patterns of this kind are usually mediated, to a great extent, by fundamental practices and commitments in the area of child-rearing.[14] The latter create what psychologists call a "fixation." Some essential part of the child's personality becomes charged with strong feelings of guilt, anxiety, fear—and fascination. And later experiences cannot completely erase these trends.

The developmental theory of Erik Erikson, more directly applied, helps to fill out this picture: it suggests quite powerfully certain additional lines of connection between infant experience and Puritan character structure. The time between one and two years forms the second stage in Erikson's larger developmental sequence, and he joins its characteristic behaviors under the general theme of "autonomy." "This stage," he writes, "becomes decisive for the ratio between love and hate, for that between freedom of self-expression and its suppression." Further: while the goal of this stage is autonomy, its negative side—its specific vulnerability—is the possibility of lasting "shame and doubt." It is absolutely vital that the child receive support in "his wish to 'stand on his own feet' lest he be overcome by that sense of having exposed himself prematurely and foolishly which we call shame, or that secondary mistrust, that 'double-take,' which we call doubt." If a child does not get this type of support—if, indeed, his efforts to assert himself are firmly "beaten down"—then a considerable preoccupation with shame can be expected in later life as well. At just this point the evidence on the Puritans makes a striking fit; for considerations of shame (and of "face-saving"—its other side) loom very large in a number of areas of their culture. Such considerations are manifest, for example, throughout the legion of Court cases that had to do with personal disputes and rivalries. Many of these cases involved suits for slander or defamation—where the issue of public exposure, the risk of shame, was absolutely central. Moreover, when a conviction was obtained, the defendant was normally required to withdraw his slanderous statements, and to apologize for them, *in public*. Note, too, that a common punishment, for many different types of offense, was a sentence to "sit in the stocks." Presumably the bite here was the threat of general ridicule.

A second point, more briefly: Erikson contends that each of man's early stages can be fundamentally related to a particular institutional principle. And for the stage we are now discussing he cites "the principle of *law and order*, which in daily life as well as in the high courts of law apportions to each his privileges and his limitations, his obligations and his rights." Surely few people have shown as much concern for "law and order" as the Puritans.[15]

Once established in the manner outlined above, the same style of parental discipline was probably maintained with little significant change for quite a number of years. The average child made his adjustments to it and became fully absorbed into the larger pattern of domestic life. With several older siblings on hand (or younger ones to come) he attracted no special attention. What concessions may have been made to his youth, what his playthings were, and what his games —if any—there is no way of knowing. All such details are hidden from us. As noted previously, however, the fact that children were dressed like adults does seem to imply a whole attitude of mind. The young boy appeared as a miniature of his father, and the young girl as a miniature of her mother. There was no idea that each generation required separate spheres of work or recreation.[16] Children learned the behavior appropriate to their sex and station by sharing in the activities of their parents. Habits of worship provide a further case in point: the whole family went to the same Church service, and the young no less than the old were expected to digest the learned words that flowed from the pulpit.

Yet this picture needs one significant amendment: it probably did *not* apply to the very earliest period of childhood. There is, for example, some evidence of a distinctive type of dress for children of less than six or seven years old.[17] Until this age boys and girls seem to have been clothed alike, in a kind of long robe which opened down the front. This garment, while generally similar to the customary dress of grown women, was set off by one curious feature: a pair of ribbons hanging from the back of the shoulders. The switch from this to the "adult" style of dress was quite a symbolic step, and must have been perceived as such by the children themselves.

One other kind of material bearing on the same aspect of development comes from the contracts of apprenticeship (or just plain "service"). Many of these applied to very young children—young, that is, by the standards which we might think appropriate. Six to eight seems to have been the most common age for such arrangements in Plymouth Colony. Here, then, we find a kind of convergence of the evidence, alerting us to the likelihood that the culture attached a very special importance to this particular time of life. Further "proof" is lacking,[18] but perhaps it was now that children began to assume the role of little adults. After all, if apprentices and servants were considered able to begin to work effectively at the age of six or seven, it seems reasonable to think that the same judgment might apply to children who remained at home.

In psychological terms there is nothing surprising about any of this. Indeed the culture was reacting in an intuitive way to inherent developmental changes that are widely recognized by behavioral scientists of our own time. A substantial body of recent research on "cognitive development" treats the period from six to eight years as a vital crux. The child leaves behind the disordered and "magical" impressions that characterize his earliest years and becomes for the first time capable of "logical thinking." He begins, for example, to understand cause and effect, and other such abstract relationships.[19] Emotionally, too, there are changes of great magnitude. According to psychoanalytic theory this is the period when the child effects a massive repression of his oedipal wishes for the parent of the opposite sex. He does so, in part, by identifying with the parent of the *same* sex— by trying, in short, to imitate various aspects of adult behavior and style.[20] More generally, he wishes to "learn to accomplish things which one would never have thought of by oneself, things which owe their attractiveness to the very fact that they are *not* the product of play and fantasy but the product of reality, practicality, and logic; things which thus provide a token sense of participation in the real world of adults."[21]

Virtually all cultures accord some special recognition to this stage of development. In complex (and literate) societies like our own it is the usual time for beginning school. Among "primitive" peoples the child starts now to master "the basic skills of technology"; he learns "to handle the utensils, the tools, and the weapons used by the big people: he enters the technology of his tribe very gradually but also very directly."[22] Naturally, this too is an important kind of "instruction," which capitalizes on the child's new mental and emotional capacities.

In this respect Plymouth probably was closest to the model of the primitive cultures. The training that began at the age of six or seven was, it seems, chiefly of a "technological" kind. The boy starting to work with his father at planting or fencemending, and the girl helping her mother with cooking or spinning or candlemaking, were both learning to master "the utensils, the tools, and the weapons used by the big people." But this society was at least partially literate, and it is possible that some training of a more academic sort was also begun about now. Perhaps there was a new intensity in the religious tutelage or "catechizing" provided for children; and perhaps they began to learn the "three R's." Unfortunately, however, such questions can be raised only in a speculative way since the historical record becomes at this point quite mute.[23]

But what of education in a more formal sense? Were there no *bona fide* schools for the children of Plymouth? A brief answer to this question would have to be negative, at least if one thinks in overall terms for the whole of the Old Colony period. For the first forty odd years of settlement there is only indirect evidence of the intent to found schools,[24] and no evidence at all of schools in actual operation. Later on, admittedly, the picture did start to change. In December of 1670, for example, John Morton appeared before the Plymouth town meeting and "proffered to teach the children and youth of the towne to Reade and write and Cast accounts on Reasonable considerations."[25] The following year he renewed his proposal and the townsmen responded with a plan to raise money "for and toward the Maintenance of the free Scoole now begun and erected."[26] Meanwhile the General Court was taking similar steps on a Colony-wide basis. A fishing excise was to be allocated to any towns that could show a school actually underway.[27] In 1673 this money was awarded to Plymouth. In 1681 it went partly to Rehoboth and partly to "Mr Ichabod Wiswalls schoole at Duxburrow." In 1683 it was distributed among five different towns: Barnstable, Duxbury, Taunton, Rehoboth, and Bristol.[28]

Thus the trend in these later years was generally in the direction of increased facilities for formal schooling. Yet not until long afterward—well into the eighteenth century—would it produce a really firm and widespread system. The town of Plymouth itself can be cited to illustrate the point. Its achievement in starting a school during the 1670s was apparently not sustained, for two decades later its citizens repeatedly went on record with directives that the selectmen "should Indeavor to get A schoolmaster to teach Children to Reade and write."[29] Education under these conditions was definitely a sometime thing.

The whole subject of education in the American colonies was somewhat misconceived until a fascinating essay by Bernard Bailyn (published in 1960) supplied a new and much more meaningful focus.[30] Bailyn was the first to point out that formal schools constituted only a small part of the total educational process, at least with the first generations of settlers. Indeed they formed a kind of appendage to other, far more important and more comprehensive agencies: the church, the community at large, and above all the family itself. This situation was to change radically before the end of the colonial period, owing to the corrosive effects of the New World environment on Old World habits and institutions. By the time of the Revolution the web of connections between family, church, and community was irrevocably broken, and schools were increasingly called upon to fill a part of the resultant social void.

But only the first part of Bailyn's story seems relevant to Plymouth Colony. To be sure, there were certain glimmerings of the cultural disruption to which he ascribes such importance; and near the end of the Colony's lifetime the process of institutionalizing education, the proliferation of schools, was clearly under way. But for most children of this period and place the major kinds of learning occurred at home. Here, in the context of the total household environment, values, manners, literacy, vocation were all transmitted from one generation to the next. The process was none the less real for being only partly conscious.

John Demos

Notes

1   *A Little Commonwealth: Family Life in the Plymouth Colony,* by John Demos (New York: Oxford University Press, 1970), p. 66.

2   Such at least is the impression one gains from examining the vital records of the Old Colony towns. In a considerable number of cases the records show both a date of birth and a date of baptism.

3   *Records of the Colony of New Plymouth, in New England,* ed. Nathaniel B. Shurtleff and David Pulsifer (Boston, 1855–61), VI, 45.

4   My authority in this matter is Earle, *Child Life in Colonial Days,* 21 ff., 34 ff.

5   For example, Lidia Standish, testifying in connection with a trial for fornication, spoke of herself as "a mother of many children my selfe and have Nursed many." Ms. deposition, in the "Davis Scrapbooks," III, 12, at Pilgrim Hall, Plymouth, Mass.

6   On the question of the relationship between lactation and fertility, see Robert G. Potter et al., "Application of Field Studies to Research on the Physiology of Human Reproduction," in *Journal of Chronic Diseases,* XVIII (1965), 1125–40.

7   There is one alternative explanation for these data which must at least be considered. It is just possible that the settlers maintained a taboo against sexual relations between husband and wife whenever the latter was nursing a child. A custom of this type has been noted among *many* preindustrial peoples in the world today. (For example: the Ojibwa and the Jivaro, among American Indian tribes; the Nuer, the Fang, and the Yoruba, all of Africa; the Trobriands and Samoans, in Oceania.) Specific documentation can be obtained by consulting the appropriate category (#853) in the Human Relations Area File. There is no evidence for such a practice in any European culture of the seventeenth century; but this is not the kind of thing that would likely show up either in written comment from the period, or in secondary works by modern historians.

8   Admittedly, to put it this way skirts one very important question: what *sort* of feeding schedule the infant experiences. It makes considerable difference, of course, both for his immediate comfort and for his later development whether (1) he can obtain the breast simply by crying out for it, or (2) his mother adheres to a firm timetable of feedings at fixed intervals, regardless of his own demands. But there is simply no way of ascertaining what was the usual practice in Plymouth Colony.

9   *The Works of John Robinson,* ed. Robert Ashton (Boston, 1851), I, 246–47.

10   These few sentences represent the briefest summary of a huge psychological literature. For a useful introduction to this literature, see Paul H. Mussen, John J. Conger, and Jerome Kagan, *Child Development and Personality* (New York, 2nd ed., 1963), ch. 7. The same overall viewpoint is apparent in a number of popular books as well—most notably, perhaps, in Dr. Benjamin Spock's famous *Baby and Child Care* (New York, 1945). And finally I would like to acknowledge a special debt in this connection to Alison Demos, age twenty-one months, for a vivid *personal* demonstration of "autonomy" and related themes. Any parent of a child about this age will know what I mean.

11   Demos, *op. cit.,* p. 49.

12   The only useful study of this matter is Edmund Morgan, "The Puritans and Sex," *New England Quarterly*, XV (1942), 591–607.

13   *The Works of John Robinson*, I, 226.

14   There is an enormous literature in anthropology, tending to bear out this point of view. And among anthropologists it is particularly associated with the work of the so-called "culture and personality" school. See, for example, Abram Kardiner, *The Psychological Frontiers of Society* (New York, 1945).

15   The material contained in these two paragraphs is drawn particularly from Erik Erikson, *Identity and the Life Cycle* (New York, 1959), 65–74. Re "shame" in Puritan child-rearing, note the following attributed to John Ward in Cotton Mather, *Magnalia Christi Americana* (Hartford, 1853), I, 522: "Of young persons he would himself give this advice: 'Whatever you do, be sure to maintain shame in them; for if that be once gone, there is no hope that they'll ever come to good.' " I am indebted to Nancy Falik for bringing this passage to my attention.

16   A word of caution must be entered here. It is quite possible that certain tasks around the house or farm were normally left to children—that, in short, there was some notion of "children's work." No concrete evidence survives; but if this was the case, it would indicate at least a limited recognition of difference between the child and the adult. Still, the basic lines of contrast relative to the pattern prevalent in our own period remain firm.

17   Earle, *Child Life in Colonial Days*, 41, 44. And, for an extended discussion of the same practice in Europe at this time, see Philippe Ariès, *Centuries of Childhood*, trans. Robert Baldick (New York, 1962), ch. 3.

18   Perhaps, though, there is a relevant datum in the Court's handling of bastardy cases. The usual practice was to oblige the father of an illegitimate child to pay a certain sum each week for maintenance, over a period of six or seven years. What would happen *after* this time is never indicated, but possibly it was felt that the child would then be able to earn his own keep, either in helping his mother and her family or in being "put out" to some foster family. See, for example, the case of Rebecca Littlefield vs. Israel Woodcock, *Plymouth Colony Records*, V, 161; and that of Elizabeth Woodward vs. Robert Stedson, *ibid.*, V, 181. Edmund Morgan, in *The Puritan Family* (New York, 1966), 66, calls attention to a statement by John Cotton that is also interesting in this connection. Cotton believed that it was perfectly normal for very young children to "spend much time in pastime and play, for their bodyes are too weak to labour, and their mind to study are too shallow . . . even the first seven years are spent in pastime, and God looks not much at it."

19   This is a central theme in many studies of cognitive psychology; but it is associated, above all, with the work of Jean Piaget. See, for example, Barbel Inhelder and Jean Piaget, *The Growth of Logical Thinking from Childhood to Adolescence*, trans. Anne Parsons and Stanley Milgram (New York, 1958).

20   Of course, the Oedipus complex has an absolutely central place in the whole psychoanalytic scheme, and the writings which deal with it are legion. But for a good short summary, see Otto Fenichel, *The Psychoanalytic Theory of Neurosis* (New York, 1945), chs. V, VI.

21   Erikson, *Identity and the Life Cycle*, 84.

22 *Ibid.,* 83.

23. Or at least there is no evidence for Plymouth. The case seems otherwise for Massachusetts Bay. Morgan's *Puritan Family,* 96 ff., quotes some interesting statements by various Massachusetts clergymen on the subject of the religious instruction of the child. The statements imply a rather limited and fragmentary approach to the youngest children, followed later on by a switch to a more intense and systematic program. They do not indicate the precise age at which this switch was appropriate, but one is tempted to make a guess of six or seven. And what was true of the one Puritan colony was likely also to be true of its Puritan neighbor, Plymouth.

24 The Marshfield Town Records show that at a meeting in 1645 there was discussion of a proposal to raise money "for one to teach school." Ms. collections, Clerk's Office, Marshfield, Mass. See also John A. Goodwin, *The Pilgrim Republic* (Boston, 1888), 494–95. Goodwin cites some early indications of an intent to found schools which I have not been able to trace.

25 *Records of the Town of Plymouth* (Plymouth, 1889), I, 115.

26 *Ibid.,* 124.

27 *Plymouth Colony Records,* V, 107–8.

28 *Ibid.,* 108; VI, 81; VI, 102–3.

29 *Records of the Town of Plymouth,* I, 224, 245.

30 Bernard Bailyn, *Education in the Forming of American Society* (Chapel Hill, N.C., 1960).

Richard Rapson employs British travelers' accounts to describe American children in primarily the last half of the nineteenth century. He interprets the frequent concern and dismay that the travelers expressed with the "precocity" of American children as an indication of a break from traditional patterns of parent-child relations. That is, he notes that certain changes were occurring in this country before they took place in Britain. Rapson sees the present cult of youth as having had its roots in the emphasis on equality between parents and children that he feels emerged during the nineteenth century. However, we must keep in mind that travelers' accounts are selective and tend to emphasize the unusual and the irregular rather than the mundane; therefore we must see them as descriptions that might suggest further research rather than the last word on the subject.

RICHARD L. RAPSON

10 The American Child As Seen by British Travelers, 1845-1935

While British travelers to American shores disagreed with one another on many topics between the years 1845 and 1935, they spoke with practically one voice upon two subjects: American schools and American children.[1] On the whole they thought the public school system admirable; with near unanimity they found the children detestable.

This adds up to a paradox, for if the innovation of free public education was, as most of these visitors contended, the best thing about America, surely some decent effect upon the schools' young charges should have been faintly discernible. Yet the British were not at all charmed by the youngsters, and the foreign observers had very few kind things to say in behalf of American children.

The paradox as stated must leave one unsatisfied. In any nation one should expect the child to stamp his impress upon the climate of the entire society; the detestable child should become the detestable adult. But especially in a nation which the British characterized by the term "youthful"—the epithet more often used in a complimentary rather than a deprecatory fashion—one would with reason expect to find some association between the word and the actual young people of the country.

There was no question as to what quality in the children did most to nettle the Englishmen. As David Macrae said in 1867: "American children are undoubtedly precocious."[2] In the same year, Greville Chester explained a little this theme, which appeared with more monotonous regularity than did any other in these books. "Many of the children in this country," he said, "appear to be painfully precocious—small stuck-up caricatures of men and women, with but little of the fresh ingenuousness and playfulness of childhood."[3]

Again in that same uneventful year of 1867, the Robertsons embellished this developing portrait thus:

> Their infant lips utter smart sayings, and baby oaths are too often encouraged . . . even by their own parents, whose counsel and restraint they quickly learn wholly to despise. It is not uncommon to see children of ten calling for liquor at the bar, or puffing a cigar in the streets. In the cars we met a youth of respectable and gentlemanly exterior who thought no shame to say that he learned to smoke at eight, got first "tight" at twelve, and by fourteen had run the whole course of debauchery.[4]

Every year American youth was similarly berated for its precocity. "Precocity" politely expressed the British feeling that American children were pert, impertinent, disrespectful, arrogant brats. But "precocious" meant more than that; it implied that American children weren't children at all. Three British mothers made this point. Therese Yelverton exclaimed that "in the course of my travels I never discovered that there were any American *children*. Diminutive men and women in the process of growing into big ones, I have met with; but the child in the full sense attached to that word in England —a child with rosy cheeks and bright joyous laugh, its docile obedience and simplicity, its healthful play and its disciplined work, is a being almost unknown in America."[5]

Daniel Boorstin in the introduction to a new edition of *A Lady's Life in the Rocky Mountains* wrote of how Isabella Bird "saw a society where, in a sense, everyone was young, yet where the most painful sight was 'the extinction of childhood. I have never seen any children, only debased imitations of men and women.' "[6] And Lady Emmeline Stuart-Wortley, before the Civil War, commented: "Little America is unhappily, generally, only grown-up America, seen through a telescope turned the wrong way. The one point, perhaps, in which I must concur with other writers on the United States, is there being no real child-like children here."[7]

Eyre Crowe tells how he and his traveling companion, William Makepeace Thackeray, came across a youngster reading a newspaper, "already devouring the toughest leaders, and mastering the news of the world whilst whiffing his cigar, and not without making shies at a huge expectorator close at hand."[8] The picture of the cigar-smoking cherub flashed recurrently in these accounts.

The visitors did not have to search far for an explanation—at least a superficial explanation—for this disconcerting childhood behavior. Although a few of them remarked at the leniency of the common schools and regretted the lack of corporal punishment handed out there,[9] many more felt that the only doses of discipline ever received by the child were administered, even if in small quantities, in the schoolrooms. No, it was unquestionably in the home that the child was indulged, and indulgence gave him his swagger.

His parents either could not or else chose not to discipline their offspring. To be sure, the school system was not blameless. Many, like Fraser, regarded the school "as an extension of the family," which, by its very effectiveness made matters more difficult for mother and father.[10]

> . . . it must be allowed that schools are robbing parents of the power to control their families. The school has drawn to itself so much of the love and veneration of the young that in the homes missing its spell they grow unruly. Parents are not experts in the management of children, nor have they the moral weight of an institution to back them up, hence they fail to keep up the smooth ascendancy of the school.[11]

P. A. Vaile blamed the American mother: "She is refusing to perform her part of the contract. First she 'went back' on raising her children, now she does not want to have any children at all."[12] Mrs.

Humphreys raged at "the conspicuous absence of maternal instinct as a feature of American marriages."[13]

Many others accused fathers, but usually with greater sympathy. After all, the father simply worked too hard all day to have much time, interest or energy to devote to his little ones. "The husband has his occupations, friends, and amusements."[14]

No matter which parent had to bear the burden of guilt, many an Englishman simply felt that home life in the United States just wasn't homelike; it lacked atmosphere, comfort, love, play and warmth. It never became the cozy, friendly hearth which imparted to a family a sense of kinship, identity or oneness. Long after young couples had forsaken the custom of dwelling in boarding houses or hotels and exposing their tiny ones to the dregs of society—a custom deplored by every Englishman—long after this, W. L. George, along with most others, refused to admit that Americans still had any idea as to what constituted a "real" home.

> The hard child [he said] suggests the hard home, which is characteristic of America. I visited many houses in the United States, and, except among the definitely rich, I found them rather uncomfortable. They felt bare, untenanted; they were too neat, too new . . . one missed the comfortable accumulation of broken screens, old fire irons, and seven-year-old volumes of the *Illustrated London News,* which make up the dusty, frowsy feeling of home. The American house is not a place where one lives, but a place where one merely sleeps, eats, sits, works.[15]

George may have been a bit unfair to expect to find "seven-year-old volumes of the *Illustrated London News*" lying about, but he had a right to notice the lack of age; it takes years for a family to implant its brand on a structure of brick and mortar.[16] Perhaps, as many visitors rightly pointed out, Americans were too much on the go, too mobile for them ever to fulfill George's requirements for homeness.[17] This nonetheless did not excuse the parents from their failure to bring up their children appropriately. Joseph Hatton, in 1881, begged the mothers and fathers to take their responsibilities as parents more seriously than they were and to realize, as any sensible person must, that their overindulgence of the child was "excessive and injurious."[18]

Little Fritz, a pretty little American boy who sat as the subject for one of Philip Burne-Jones' paintings, told his grandmother, in the artist's presence, "I'll kick your head!" After being chided and asked to apologize there was "dead silence on the part of Fritz." Finally, after some more pleading, Fritz relented and uttered "a few perfunctory and scarcely audible sounds, which were generously construed by the family as expressive of contrition and penitence; and Fritz started again with a clear record, for a brief period. His mother had absolutely no influence on him whatever, and she admitted as much."[19]

Other American parents admitted as much also; they were fully aware of their inability to control their little ones, but they just didn't know what to do about it. L. P. Jacks, in 1933, let an American mother speak her heart about her utter helplessness and frustration in a way that was rather revealing and even poignant:

> We mothers are rapidly losing all influence over our children, and I don't know how we can recover it. We have little or no control over them, whether boys or girls. The schools and the colleges take them out of our hands. They give them everything for nothing, and that is what the children expect when they come home. Their standards and their ideals are formed in the school atmosphere, and more by their companions than their teachers. They become more and more intractable to home influence and there is nothing for it but to let them go their own way.[20]

But the majority of the Britons did not accept either the influence of the schools or the social fact of mobility as sufficient explanations for the precocious child; they would have had little justification for disliking the child with the fervor they did and deploring the parents' follies so strongly if these impersonal forces accounted adequately for the situation.

They felt, rather, that causes ran deeper, in more insidious channels. Not only did the parents spoil their children, but they *wanted* to spoil them. Not only did the mothers and fathers put up with more than they should have, but they were actually proud of their babies. The Britons were especially distressed when they decided that parents felt, as a rule, not the least bit guilty over their own efforts or over the way their boys and girls were turning out. The travelers came not to the conclusion that American parents were unable to discipline their sons and daughters, but that they deliberately chose to "let them go their own way." This either infuriated the by now bewildered visitor, or else made him desperate to figure out just how this insanity could possibly reign.

William Howard Russell could not accept the excuse that the schools pre-empted parental power since "there is nothing in the American [school] system to prevent the teaching of religious and moral duties by parents at home; but it would seem as if very little of that kind of instruction was given by the busy fathers and anxious mothers of the Republic. . . ."[21]

Horace Vachell, as did many others, told a child story that turned into a mother story. It seems that one day the author was in the parlor of a ship filled with ailing people, including the author's own mother who was suffering with a bad headache. Into this sickly assemblage trooped our hero—a small American boy who decided to soothe the aches of all by playing on the bagpipes! "The wildest pibroch ever played in Highland glen was sweet melody compared to the strains produced by this urchin."[22] He naturally continued to play, louder than ever, despite the daggered glances hurled at him from all around the parlor; he stopped only when he tired. Then, instead of permitting sweet peace, "he flung down the pipes, walked to the piano, opened it, sat down, and began to hammer the keys with his feet."[23]

At this turn of events, our long-suffering author had had enough. " 'You play very nicely with your feet,' I ventured to say, as I lifted him from the stool, 'but some of these ladies are suffering with head-ache, and your music distresses them. Run away, like a good boy, and don't come back again.' "[24]

But Vachell's story did not end here because, in the final analysis, this is more of a mother tale than a child story. "The mother was furious. Had I been Herod the Great, red-handed after the slaughter of the Innocents, she could not have looked more indignant or re-proachful. I was interfering with the sacred rights of the American child to do what he pleased, where he pleased, and when he pleased."[25]

Vachell's first conclusion inevitably was that American children were unspeakable monsters, utterly lacking in "sense of duty, rever-ence, humility, obedience."[26] His second conclusion was, however, more interesting and more important, namely that parents actually "encourage the egoism latent in all children, till each becomes an autocrat."[27]

Once this appalling discovery had been verified, it occurred to the more curious of the Britons to raise the appropriate question: how could the American parents be proud of these diminutive devils?

Sir Edwin Arnold presented a question of this sort, in more general form, to one whom he regarded as an expert on this strange *genus Americanus:* Walt Whitman. " 'But have you reverence enough among your people?' I asked. 'Do the American children respect and obey their parents sufficiently, and are the common people grateful enough to the best men, their statesmen, leaders, teachers, poets, and "betters" generally?' "[28]

To this most fundamental of all inquiries Whitman responded: " 'Allons, comrade!, your old world has been soaked and saturated in reverentiality. We are laying here in America the basements and foundation rooms of a new era. And we are doing it, on the whole, pretty well and substantially. By-and-by, when that job is through, *we will look after the steeples and pinnacles.*' "[29]

Whitman and Arnold included childhood precocity within the larger framework of a new people refusing to pay homage to their betters, refusing to revere their "superiors." Such reverence constitutes one of the necessary ingredients of an aristocratically oriented society. Lack of that reverence suggests an egalitarian society, and these two distinguished men of letters were implying that the precocious child was symptomatic not merely of weak, stupid, willful parents, but rather of the pervasiveness in American society of the principle of equality. In fact no generalization about America was made more forcefully or repeatedly by the commentators en masse than that the thrust of the American belief in equality (understood as opportunity to rise more than as classlessness) was ubiquitous; it extended into every corner of the daily institutional fabric of American life— into the schools wherein all children had the right to a free education, into politics where all had the right to vote, into the enhanced place of women in American society, into the fluid class structure, into the churches wherein voluntary religion was the rule, and perhaps most astonishing of all, apparently even into the homes where little boys and little girls were granted unheard-of liberties.

Captain Marryat, as early as 1839, related a well-known example illustrating this last point:

Imagine a child of three years old in England behaving thus:—

"Johnny, my dear, come here," says his mamma.

"I won't," cried Johnny.

"You must, my love, you are all wet, and you'll catch cold."

"I won't," replies Johnny.

"Come, my sweet, and I've something for you."

"I won't."

"Oh! Mr.—, do, pray make Johnny come in."

"Come in, Johnny," says the father.

"I won't."

"I tell you, come in directly, sir—do you hear?"

"I won't," replies the urchin, taking to his heels.

"A sturdy republican, sir," says his father to me, smiling at the boy's resolute disobedience.[30]

In 1845 Francis Wyse generalized upon incidents like these, placing them in a broad social context. "There is seldom any very great restraint," he noted, "imposed upon the youth of America whose precocious intellect, brought forth and exercised at an early, and somewhat premature age, and otherwise encouraged under the

Richard L. Rapson   198

republican institutions of the country, has generally made them impatient of parental authority."[31]

Parental authority did not sensibly differ from any other exercise of power: royal, military, governmental or private. Americans had established their independence in rebellion against authority; they had rejected all artificially imposed forms of superiority; and they had proclaimed the equality of man. Surely these principles should extend to the family. Indeed, Jacks talked aptly of the way in which children had applied (with considerable parental approval) the Declaration of Independence to themselves.[32] And James Fullarton Muirhead, who composed one of the most informative chapters on this topic, formulated the grand generalization thus: "The theory of the equality of man is rampant in the nursery."[33] He referred to the infants as "young republicans," "democratic sucklings," "budding citizens of a free republic."[34]

Here then was another application of the theory of equality—one which even the friendly Muirhead could not get himself to smile upon. It "hardly tends," he patiently tried to explain, "to make the American child an attractive object to the stranger from without. On the contrary it is very apt to make said stranger long strenuously to spank these budding citizens of a free republic, and to send them to bed *instanter.*"[35]

One must, of course, sympathize with the British traveler as he suffered through each encounter with these young specimens of the New World. But their hate affair is as much beside the point as their love affair with the schools. Both child-rearing at home and the nationwide system of compulsory public education were faithful to the omnipresent force of equality, and the paradox which began this chapter turns out to be no paradox at all. The commentators liked what they saw in the classrooms because authority was being exercised. It was being exercised by teachers who wielded it in the interests of learning and morality. When the visitors confronted the child outside the schools and in the context of home and family they were appalled by what they believed to be the universal and inexcusable betrayal of authority by the parents.

This reversal in the roles of authority vis-á-vis children disoriented the observers to such an extent that many of them never realized that, just a few chapters before their excoriation of the American child, they had been blessing his development in the schoolrooms. Although the traveler frequently sensed that the "success" of the teachers and the indulgent "failures" of the parents were related to each other, and that both stemmed from the same peculiar general assumptions in which American society was rooted, not one of them ever managed to pose squarely the problem of how and whether dual authority *could* be exerted on the child, of just how parent and teacher *should* combine their efforts in child-rearing, given the public school system and the widespread assumption that the child was an equal partner in the family "team."

The origins of this dilemma may be traced back to colonial days when, under the pressure of new conditions, the familiar family pattern brought over from the Old World suffered major transformations affecting both child-rearing practices and the role of education.

The traditional family was the wide kinship group with the source of power vested in the father and extending outward to include not only wife and children, but cousins, other relatives and servants as well. The father was the chief educator, transferring the traditions of his culture and vocational training itself to his sons. But authority and traditionalism were, as revealed in an excellent study by Bernard Bailyn, inadequate for conditions in the New World where problems were new, land abundant, labor scarce and old solutions to old problems irrelevant.[36] In these circumstances "the young—less bound by prescriptive memories, more adaptable, more vigorous—stood often at advantage. Learning faster, they came to see the world more familiarly, to concede more readily to unexpected necessities, to sense more accurately the phasing of a new life. They and not their parents became the effective guides to a new world, and they thereby gained a strange, anomalous authority difficult to accommodate within the ancient structure of family life."[37]

While the details need not concern us here, the traditional family and educative pattern could not survive these challenges.

> By the middle of the eighteenth century the classic lineaments of the American family as modern sociologists describe them—the "isolation of the conjugal unit," the "maximum of dispersion of the lines of descent," partible inheritances, and multilineal growth—had appeared. The consequences can hardly be exaggerated. Fundamental aspects of social life were affected. In the reduced, nuclear family, thrown back upon itself, traditional gradations in status tended to fall to the level of necessity. Relationships tended more toward achievement than ascription. The status of women rose; marriage, even in the eyes of the law, tended to become a contract between equals. Above all, the development of the child was affected.[38]

One of the effects on the child cited by Bailyn concerned the passage of the child into society as "the once elaborate interpenetration of family and community dissolved." A result was that "the individual acquired an insulation of consciousness," a "heightened

... sense of separateness" from society, and particularly from the state which no longer could "command his automatic involvement."[39] Perhaps this is what the British meant by precocity.

A second result came as the Puritans transferred the primary educative responsibilities from "the maimed . . . family to formal instructional institutions, and in so doing not only endowed schools with a new importance but expanded their purpose beyond pragmatic vocationalism toward vaguer but more basic cultural goals."[40] Perhaps this explains why the British abused American parents.

The commentators who believed that parents must exercise authority over children were not pleased by what they saw in American families. In order to muster any kind words it was necessary to revise traditional conceptions of the family and accept a measure of equality in the home, accept the notion that the various family members could be close friends.

Dicey was one who was able to take this step. He concluded one of his volumes in 1863 in praise of "the great charm which surrounds all family relations in the North. Compared with Europe, domestic scandals are unknown; and between parents and their grown-up children, there exists a degree of familiarity and intimacy which one seldom witnesses in this country."[41]

There were other companions besides the parents and grown-up children. Growing boys and their fathers were companions, wrote Zincke in 1868. "In America the father never loses sight of his child, who thus grows up as his companion, and is soon treated as a companion, and as in some sort an equal."[42] Zincke went on to relate a pleasant incident he observed on a train between a fourteen-year-old boy and his father:

> They had long been talking on a footing of equality. . . . At last, to while away the time, they began to sing together. First they accompanied each other. Then they took alternate lines; at last alternate words. In this of course they tripped frequently, each laughing at the other for his mistakes. There was no attempt at keeping up the dignity of a parent, as might have been considered necessary and proper with us. There was no reserve. They were in a certain sense already on an equal footing of persons of the same age.[43]

Mothers and daughters were companions, Low maintained. "Daughters are much with their mothers, and they become their companions younger than they do in Europe. At an age when the French girl, for instance, is still demurely attending her convent, or the English girl is in the hands of her governess, her more emancipated sister across the Atlantic is calling with her mother on her friends, or assisting her in the drawing-room on her reception days."[44]

Sons and daughters received equal treatment, claimed Saunders. Whereas "in an English family, as a rule, the greatest consideration is shown to the boys," in America, if anything, "the wishes of the girls would be first listened to, and their education provided for." The boy, after all, "is as eager to start life on his own account as is a greyhound to rush after the hare." "In the matter of early independence both sexes are equal."[45]

Even husbands and wives were companions. While the wife "will not consent to being submerged by her children, she gives much of her time to them, and is still able to find time to be with her husband. The average American husband makes a confidante and a companion of his wife. . . ."[46]

The patriarchies and matriarchies of the past had been replaced by a family team composed of equals. The British perceived this family revolution as being directly parallel to the fundamental cultural difference between the New World which blurred distinctions and the Old which honored and preserved them. As Muirhead put it: "The reason —or at any rate one reason—of the normal attitude of the American parent towards his child is not far to seek. It is almost undoubtedly one of the direct consequences of the circumambient spirit of democracy. The American is so accustomed to recognize the essential equality of others that he sometimes carries a good thing to excess. . . . The present child may be described as one of the experiments of democracy."[47]

Americans enthroned their children not merely out of blind obedience to some social ethos which compelled them to do in the home something consonant with what the nation proclaimed to the world as its faith. Americans, as Zincke's story of the singing father and son so nicely shows, were often quite fond of their children, and rather than being harried or intimidated, they were not infrequently joyful parents. In fact, the Americans, according to the British, believed in their young ones in much the same way that they believed in their future. Let the youths' natural spirit triumph and they would not only participate in a grand future, but they would be the chief forgers of that future; the child was the future. Children could be heard as well as seen because they represented hope in "the land of youth." "Nowhere," said Muirhead, "is the child so constantly in evidence; nowhere are his wishes so carefully consulted; nowhere is he allowed to make his mark so strongly on society in general."[48] Richard DeBary chimed in that "America is wholly convinced . . . that the young child can take it all in. The child is given kingship and becomes the king."[59]

Richard L. Rapson

Those few Englishmen who thought well of American children praised precisely the same qualities which the detractors abominated. Arnold Bennett, for example, came across one "captivating creature whose society I enjoyed at frequent intervals throughout my stay in America. . . . [She] was a mirror in which I saw the whole American race of children—their independence, their self-confidence, their adorable charm, and their neat sauciness."[50] The reformer George Holyoake liked "the American habit of training their children to independence" more than he did England's "unwise domestic paternalism, which encourages a costly dependence."[51]

John Strathesk did not employ the term "precocious" in a deprecating manner when he decided that "the girls and boys of America are very frank, even precocious."[52] And Sir Philip Gibbs expanded upon this theme. "The children of America," he said, "have the qualities of their nation, simplicity, common sense, and self-reliance. They are not so bashful as English boys and girls, and they are free from the little constraints of nursery etiquette which makes so many English children afraid to open their mouths. They are also free entirely from that juvenile snobbishness which is still cultivated in English society, where boys and girls of well-to-do parents are taught to look down with contempt upon children of the poorer classes."[53]

It may be noticed that the adjectives used to depict the child are similar, whether used in delight or disgust: saucy, self-reliant, wild, spontaneous, immodest, independent, demanding, irreverent. It may furthermore be observed that they bear resemblance to adjectives which some Englishmen thought applicable to the young nation as a whole.[54] Some visitors also found the terms suitable for characterizing American adults as well.

The blurring of lines between young and old in the New World furnished an invitation to some British writers to caricature both American parents and children. But to Margaret Mead this leveling tendency forms an explicable part of a peculiarly national approach to child-rearing which she has called "third-generation American."[55] The American child, contends this anthropologist, is expected to traverse a course very different from his father's, and "with this orientation towards a different future for the child comes also the expectation that the child will pass beyond his parents and leave their standards behind him."[56] Thus "it comes about that American parents lack the sure hand on the rudder which parents in other societies display."[57] Or, approaching the matter from a different perspective than either the historian Bailyn or Miss Mead, Erik Erikson supports their findings when he writes that "the psychoanalysis of the children of immigrants clearly reveals to what extent they, as the first real Americans in their family, become their parents' cultural parents."[58]

As Erikson and many other psychologists have stressed, the high prestige accorded youth, understandable though it may be considering the abundant resources, the scarcity of labor, the virgin conditions, and the rapid pace of change in the egalitarian New World, is not without cost to Americans. The child himself has to pay a price for his exalted place; the compulsion to achieve, to succeed, can be taxing and perhaps ultimately futile. Unlike his Old World counterpart who begins life with a position of ascribed status which he knows is his own, the American child can never let up.

The society, too, has to pay a price for its cult of youth. It is paid not only in the primitive music, the puerile television and the domestic tyranny to which the adult world is exposed at the command of teenagers, and to which the adults meekly succumb. It is paid also in the sacrifice of wisdom, of standards, of permanence, of serenity under the frantic injunction to constantly "think young." The quiet contemplation of the past and the present is sacrificed when all must worship at the altar of the future.

The most repeated consensus at which the travelers arrived concerning the "American character" was that that character resembled, at heart, the character of a child. If there were no childlike children, if there were only miniature adults in "the land of youth," then the reverse was equally true—there were few adultlike adults; there were only adults trying to be young. "There are no old in America at all," said George Steevens in 1900.[59] By this he meant two things. First, that adult virtues are uncultivated in the New World; the American "retains all his life a want of discipline, an incapacity for ordered and corporate effort."[60]

Steevens' second meaning centered on the fate of those who were actually aged. "They are shouldered unmercifully out of existence," he claimed. "I found in New York a correspondence on the open question whether the old have any right to respect. Many of the public thought, quite seriously, they had no right even to existence."[61]

The dearest price of all is paid neither by the children nor by the society but by the adults who have to be "boys" at the office, who as parents must "live for their children," who as mature women must forever look and act like eighteen-year-olds, who as elderly must join the other aged in some zippy retirement community quarantined from the rest of mankind.

The cult of youth has perhaps permitted a more spontaneous family life to develop, and it has, no doubt, lent to our national life a special vigor and freshness. But in exalting childhood and early youth to the consummatory positions in life, it follows that maturity and old age should become anti-climactic. Indeed, in America, as one ages, one declines, and the reward of lower movie admission fees for "senior citizens" furnishes rather ineffectual solace. One can only guess at the extent to which the American fixation on the earlier stages of the life cycle is related to our tendency to deny the reality of old age and to put from our minds all thoughts of death. And it is not possible to do more here than to raise the question which then becomes inescapable: what kinds of spiritual reserves might this habit of mind take from the individual as he passes through life?[62]

Thirty years after his 1869 visit to America, the Rev. Mr. Macrae returned and noted that the "independence and precocious intellect of the American children" had not diminished; but he was "less struck with these features this time."[63] The reason he was less struck was precisely the same that made Harold Spender think better of the American children in 1920, twenty years after *his* first visit. "Our English child in the interval," said Spender, substituting his native land for Macrae's Scotland, "has become a little more American."[64] By the early years of the twentieth century, America's startling departure in raising children and in inflating the status of the youngsters in the family hierarchy was, like various other American innovations, becoming more general in the Old World also.

Notes

1   The evidence for this article derives from a reading of over 260 published books composed by Britons who wrote of the United States on the basis of visits made here between 1845 and 1935. The essay itself is drawn from my dissertation at Columbia, *The British Traveler in America, 1860–1935.* [Ed. note: The dissertation has been incorporated into the book *Britons View America: Travel Commentary, 1860-1935* (Seattle and London: University of Washington Press, 1971).]

2   Macrae, *The Americans at Home* (New York, 1952), p. 45. (First edition, Edinburgh, 1870).

3   Chester, *Transatlantic Sketches* (London, 1869), pp. 230–31.

4   William and W. F. Robertson, *Our American Tour* (Edinburgh, 1871), pp. 9–10.

5   Therese Yelverton, *Teresina in America* (London, 1875), I, 263. She also found them to be "insolent, unruly, and rude." *Ibid.,* p. 269. Oscar Wilde thought that little girls were more charming in their precocity than little boys. *Writings* (New York, 1907), III, 251.

6   Isabella Lucy Bird, *A Lady's Life in the Rocky Mountains.* The edition by Daniel Boorstin (Norman, Okla., 1960) was used, p. xxii. (First edition, London, 1875).

7   Stuart-Wortley, *Travels in the United States* (Paris, 1851), p. 67.

8 Eyre Crowe, *With Thackeray in America* (London, 1893), p. 21.

9 John Strathesk [John Tod], *Bits About America* (Edinburgh, 1887), p. 149; Richard DeBary, *The Land of Promise* (London, 1908), p. 131.

10 James Nelson Fraser, *America, Old and New* (London, 1910), p. 280.

11 *Ibid.,* p. 282.

12 P. A. Vaile, *Y., America's Peril* (London, 1909), p. 111.

13 Mrs. Desmond Humphreys, *America Through English Eyes* (London, n.d. [1913?]), p. 165.

14 *Ibid.,* p. 161. Horace Vachell said that in the West at least "you will find fathers and mothers the slaves of their children." *Life and Sport on the Pacific Slope* (New York, 1901), p. 74.

15 Walter L. George, *Hail Columbia!* (New York, 1921), p. 199.

16 At least "if ever so humble, the abodes in America are invariably neat and cleanly," claimed Alfred Pairpont in 1890 in *Rambles in America* (Boston, 1891), p. 166.

17 Said George Steevens, *The Land of the Dollar* (Edinburgh, 1897): "You cannot call a people who will never be happy ten years in the same place . . . home-loving in the English sense." p. 313.

18 Joseph Hatton, *Today in America* (New York, 1881), p. 7

19 Sir Philip Burne-Jones, *Dollars and Democracy* (New York, 1904), p. 36.

20 L. P. Jacks, *My American Friends* (New York, 1933), p. 149. Notice the young mother's stress on the influence which the peer-group culture held over her children.

21 William Howard Russell, *Hesperothen: Notes from the West* (London, 1882), II, 156.

22 Vachell, p. 80.

23 *Ibid.,* p. 80.

24 *Ibid.,* p. 80.

25 *Ibid.,* p. 80.

26 *Ibid.,* p. 79.

27 *Ibid.,* p. 79. One should bear in mind at all times the difficulties the travelers had of meeting representative American families since, as W. L. George candidly admitted, "truly representative families generally keep themselves rather to themselves." George, p. viii.

28 Sir Edwin Arnold, *Seas and Lands* (New York, 1891), pp. 78–79.

29 *Ibid.,* p. 79.

30   Quoted in Lawrence A. Cremin, *The American Common School* (New York, 1969), p. 217.

31   *America: Its Realities and Resources* (London, 1846), p. 295.

32   *My American Friends,* pp. 150–51.

33   Muirhead, *America, The Land of Contrasts* (London, 1902), p. 64. (First edition London, 1898).

34   *Ibid.,* pp. 63, 65.

35   *Ibid.,* p. 65.

36   Bernard Bailyn, *Education in the Forming of American Society* (Chapel Hill, N.C., 1960).

37   *Ibid.,* pp. 22–23.

38   *Ibid.,* pp. 24–25.

39   *Ibid.,* pp. 25–26

40   *Ibid.,* p. 27.

41   Edward Dicey, *Six Months in the Federal States* (London, 1863), I, 310.

42   Foster Barham Zincke, *Last Winter in the United States* (London, 1868), pp. 70–71.

43   *Ibid.,* p. 71.

44   A. M. Low, *America at Home* (London, 1905), p. 74.

45   William Saunders, *Through the Light Continent* (London, 1879), pp. 399–400. Also enlightening on these leveling tendencies in the home are J. Nelson Fraser, p. 246 and Harold Spender, *A Briton in America* (London, 1921), pp. 253–54.

46   Low, p. 82.

47   Muirhead, pp. 70–71.

48   *Ibid.,* p. 63.

49   DeBary, p. 128. "Young America does not sit at the master's feet and worship; it has definite opinions, which it deems as much deserving of hearing as other people's, and it gives them forth with the bold confidence born of youthful inexperience and immaturity," Emily Faithfull, *Three Visits to America* (Edinburgh, 1884), p. 89.

50   Arnold Bennett, *Your United States* (New York, 1912), pp. 147–48.

51   George Jacob Holyoake, *Among the Americans* (Chicago, 1881), p. 183.

52   Strathesk, p. 149.

53   Philip Gibbs, *Land of Destiny* (New York, 1920), p. 88.

54   Even Vachell, who told the story of the boy with the bagpipes, had to confess to the "originality, independence, pluck, and perspicuity" of the children (p. 83).

55 Margaret Mead, *And Keep Your Powder Dry: An Anthropologist Looks at America* (New York, 1942), p. 45.

56 *Ibid.,* p. 41.

57 *Ibid.,* p. 43.

58 Erik Erikson, *Childhood and Society* (2nd ed.; New York, 1963), p. 294.

59 George Steevens, p. 314.

60 *Ibid.,* p. 314.

61 *Ibid.,* p. 314.

62 The seeds of the thoughts in the above paragraph, and in many others in this paper, were planted by Richard Hofstadter, both in conversation and in an early draft of an as yet unpublished article called "Foreign Observers and American Children"—an article from which Professor Hofstadter was kind enough to let me read.

63 David Macrae, *America Revisited and Men I Have Met* (Glasgow, 1908), p. 24.

64 Harold Spender, p. 271.

John and Virginia Demos here effectively convey just how time bound conceptions of particular periods of life can be. Those of us living today too easily fall prey to the notion that what is now always was—and that certainly people in the past knew of and dealt with a period called "adolescence." The authors, however, maintain that the concept of adolescence arose as a result of the shift in population from rural to urban settings at the same time that the family was moving from a unit of production to a unit of consumption. Their discussion of the importance of the urban environment in laying the foundation for the emergence of a youth culture is particularly apposite, emphasizing how it was first necessary for youth in similar circumstances to be brought together in a situation that permitted interaction before a special set of values and norms could appear.

JOHN AND VIRGINIA DEMOS

11 *Adolescence in Historical Perspective*

The idea of adolescence is today one of our most widely held and deeply imbedded assumptions about the process of human development. Indeed most of us treat it not as an idea but as a *fact*. Its impact is clear in countless areas of everyday life—in newspapers, magazines, and books; in various forms of popular entertainment; in styles of dress and of language. Its causes and meaning have been repeatedly analyzed in the work of psychologists and sociologists. Its effects are endlessly discussed by teachers, social workers, officers of the law, and parents everywhere.

Yet all of this has a relatively short history. The concept of adolescence, as generally understood and applied, did not exist before the last two decades of the nineteenth century. One could almost call it an invention of that period; though it did incorporate, in quite a central way, certain older attitudes and modes of thinking. It will be our purpose in this paper to describe the roots and growth of the concept, to the point in the early twentieth century when it had become well established in the public consciousness. We shall limit our attention to developments in the United States, since adolescence was on the whole an American discovery.

We shall begin with a sketch of some common ideas about childhood and "youth" during the period 1800–1875, as revealed in two kinds of sources: (1) a rapidly developing literature of child-rearing advice, and (2) a large body of books and pamphlets directed to the young people of the country and bearing especially on their "moral problems." Then we shall summarize the activities of the "child-study movement" (beginning in about 1890) and in particular the work of the psychologist G. Stanley Hall, for there the concept of adolescence can be examined at its source. And finally we shall propose a hypothesis for drawing together these various types of material and above all for explaining the relationship between the *idea* of adolescence and the social phenomena to which it was a response. It is here that questions of family life will come most fully into view, since adolescence was, we believe, profoundly related to certain fundamental changes affecting the internal structure of many American homes. But this matter of the connection between "ideas" and "facts," between major cultural assumptions like adolescence and the social realities in which they develop, presents extremely tricky problems. It lurks as an uncomfortable presence behind most serious study that bears in one way or another on the history of the family. The difficulty lies in the nature of the evidence available to historians, which comprises for the most part a variety of written materials. It is much easier, therefore, to construct a history of ideas *about* the family than of the family as such.

The present paper cannot pretend to resolve such problems; indeed it may serve chiefly to illustrate them. But it is at least our intention to keep sight of the important distinctions. And if the bulk of our efforts are directed toward the realm of "ideas," it is only because this seems the logical way to begin.

The literature of child-rearing advice is one of the most revealing, and least exploited,[1] sources for the history of the American family. Its beginnings can be located in the early part of the nineteenth century; and it has been growing steadily, and changing in character, ever since. Before about 1825 relatively few books on child-rearing could be found in this country, and those that were available came chiefly from England.[2] In general, they were mild in tone and full of simple moral homilies strung endlessly together. They do not, in short, seem to have been directed to any very pressing needs or problems in the lives of their readers.

After 1825 the situation, for this country at least, changed rapidly. Child-rearing books by American authors began to appear, some of which went through numerous editions and sold many thousands of copies.[3] This development was owing to several different factors. In the first place it was related to a deepening interest in the fact of childhood itself as a distinct period of life and one which was little comparable to the years of maturity. Secondly, it expressed the broad impulse of nationalism that engulfed the country at this time. English books on child-rearing could no longer be regarded as suitable to American conditions. Finally, the new and authentically "native" literature on this subject reflected deep anxieties about the quality of American family life.[4]

Most of the concern which was evident in these books related to problems of authority. In one form or another they all imparted the same message: the authority of parents must be established early in a child's life and firmly maintained throughout the years of growth. Even the smallest infant reveals a "willfulness" that "springs from a depraved nature and is intensely selfish."[5] This must be suppressed by strict training in obedience, or it will rapidly develop beyond the possibility of control with dire implications for the later (adult) personality.

These injunctions seemed all the more necessary because—so many people thought—parental authority was steadily on the wane. In describing the average home, the writers of the child-rearing books repeatedly used words like "disorder," "disobedience," "licentiousness," and above all "indulgence" (i.e., of the children). Statements such as the following were typical:

> It must be confessed that an irreverent, unruly spirit has come to be a prevalent, an outrageous evil among the young people of our land. . . . Some of the good old people make facetious complaint on this.

. . . "There is as much family government now as there used to be in our young days," they say, "only it has changed hands."[6]

This seeming change in the traditional family pattern had other dimensions as well. Thus many authors noted the growth of a kind of "child-centered" attitude and condemned it out of hand. More and more parents, for example, appeared to feel compelled to show off their children before any and all guests. Similarly, there was in many households far too much concern with efforts to amuse and entertain the young.[7] Children who were often made the center of attention in this manner would inevitably become conceited and selfish. Another alarming development was the increasing tendency of children to seek social satisfactions outside of the family, among groups of their own peers. Mrs. Lydia Child, whose *Mother's Book* went through many editions, returned again and again to the theme that "youth and age are too much separated."[8] She and many of her contemporaries decried the "new custom" of holding parties exclusively for young people[9] and urged that parents should always be the closest friends and confidants of their children.

Lest it be imagined that Americans of the nineteenth century had no special concern whatsoever for the period which we now call adolescence (and which in their day was simply termed "youth"),[10] we must turn to another category of books that were written specifically *for* the "youth" of the time and about their particular problems. The general nature of these writings is implicit in their titles: *A Voice to Youth; How to be a Man; Papers for Thoughtful Girls; The Young Lady's Companion; On the Threshold; Lectures to Young Men.*

From all of these works there emerges quite clearly a sense of "youth" as a critical transition period in the life of nearly everyone. It is a time, first of all, when people are extremely impressionable, extremely open to a wide range of outside influences. It is—to quote from Joel Hawes's *Lectures to Young Men* (1832)—

> pre-eminently . . . the forming, fixing period. . . . It is during this season, more than any other, that the character assumes its permanent shape and color.[11]

Words such as "pliant," "plastic," and "formative" appear again and again in the discussions of youth.

Because of this characteristic openness, young people are vulnerable to many kinds of "danger." To begin with, boys and girls entering their teens experience a sudden and sharp upsurge of the "passions." They become highly emotional; their mood fluctuates unpredictably from exuberance to melancholy. Henry Ward Beecher, whose *Lectures to Young Men* were among the best known examples of the genre, declared:

> A young man knows little of life; less of himself. He feels in his bosom the various impulses, wild desires, restless cravings he can hardly tell for what, a sombre melancholy when all is gay, a violent exhilaration when others are sober.[12]

In keeping with their Victorian conventions, these writers never directly mentioned the physiological changes that occur at puberty, in particular the strong new change of sexual energy and tension. Occasionally one finds an allusion to "internal revolutions" and "occult causes, probably of a physical kind"[13]; but for the most part people were content to define youth in the above terms, that is, as a vast outpouring of the emotions.

As if to complement these disruptive changes within the personality, the world at large was full of "seductive temptations," of inducements to all manner of wicked and ruinous behavior. As Beecher said,

> These wild gushes of feeling, peculiar to youth, the sagacious tempter has felt, has studied, has practiced upon, until he can sit before that most capacious organ, the human mind, knowing every step and all the combinations.[14]

Here, then, was the wider, social dimension of the problems which confront the young person. The world lies in wait for him, and "ardent, volatile, inexperienced, and thirsting for happiness," he is

> exceedingly liable to be seduced into the wrong paths—into those fascinating but fatal ways, which lead to degradation and wretchedness.[15]

There are, at this stage of life, dangers both within and without.

Most of the material considered so far has been drawn from the period 1825–1850. As the years passed and the century neared its end, the picture of youth that we have been describing was embellished somewhat in certain important respects. Thus, for example, the sexual factor began to receive some attention.[16] And some writers were struck by a kind of aimlessness and indecision that seemed increasingly common among American young people. Theodore T. Munger, whose book *On the Threshold* was published in 1881, declared that

> Young men of the present years . . . are not facing life with that resolute and definite purpose that is essential both to manhood and to external success. . . . [They] hear no voice summoning them to the appointed field, but drift into this or that, as happens.[17]

Moreover, towards the end of the century, many writers identified the "dangers" and "temptations" which threatened youth directly with urban life. Something of this had been implicit from the beginning, but now it came clearly into the open.[18] The city loomed as the prime source of corrupting influences for the young. Its chaotic social and economic life, its varied population, its frenzied commercial spirit, and its dazzling entertainments were all sharply antagonistic to proper growth towards adulthood.

At roughly the same time, meanwhile, the formal concept of adolescence was receiving its first public expression. The immediate context of this development was a new movement for systematic "child study," inspired and guided by G. Stanley Hall. Hall was, of course, one of the major figures in the early history of American psychology. After a lengthy period of study in Germany, he became in 1881 a professor at Johns Hopkins, and six years later he accepted the presidency of Clark University. There he remained for the rest of his life, presiding over a wide range of research and teaching activities.

The aim of the child-study movement was to enlist large numbers of ordinary citizens in a broad effort to deepen both public and scientific understanding of human development. The mothers who belonged to the various local organizations were encouraged to keep detailed records of the behavior of their children and to participate in regular discussions about such records. They were also exposed to, and themselves reflected back, the major themes in Stanley Hall's own work—not least, his theory of adolescence.

The essentials of Hall's view of adolescence appeared in one of his earliest papers on psychology: "The Moral and Religious Training of Children," published in 1882 in the *Princeton Review.* The great point of departure, then as later, was the idea of "storm and stress," of severe crisis characterized by

> lack of emotional steadiness, violent impulses, unreasonable conduct, lack of enthusiasm and sympathy. . . . The previous selfhood is broken up . . . and a new individual is in process of being born. All is solvent, plastic, peculiarly susceptible to external influences.[19]

The suggestions contained in this article were subsequently elaborated in much greater detail by some of Hall's students at Clark. Efforts were made to link the adolescent "crisis" with a wide range of personal and social phenomena—with religious conversion, for example,[20] and with the rising rate of juvenile delinquency.[21] Hall himself provided the capstone to this whole sequence of activity, with the publication in 1904 of his encyclopedic work *Adolescence: Its Psy-*

John and Virginia Demos

chology, and Its Relations to Physiology, Anthropology, Sociology, Sex, Crime, Religion, and Education. It is impossible to summarize here the many ideas and vast assortment of data embraced therein, but certain underlying themes can at least be singled out. From the very start Hall's thinking had been profoundly influenced by Darwinism, and the psychology he proposed was explicitly bound to an evolutionary, or "genetic," model. He urged a kind of "archaeology of the mind," in which all the various stages in the development of human consciousness would be rediscovered and understood in their proper order.[22] A key link here was the theory known as "recapitulation," which affirmed that every individual "lives through" each of the major steps in the evolution of the race as a whole. Adolescence assumed a special importance in this scheme, for it represented (and "recapitulated") the most recent of man's great developmental leaps. The adolescent, Hall believed, reveals truly enormous possibilities of growth and "is carried for a time beyond the point of the present stage of civilization."[23] This is not, however, an easy situation, for it encompasses a variety of contradictions and "antithetic impulses." Among the impulses which Hall paired in this context were hyperactivity and lassitude, happiness and depression, egotism and self-abasement, selfishness and altruism, gregariousness and shyness, sensitivity and cruelty, radicalism and conservatism. Caught in the midst of so much change and conflict, the adolescent was bound to experience "storm and stress" more or less continuously.

Hall's work on adolescence quickly exerted a considerable influence in many different directions. Its impact was clear in general texts on psychology,[24] studies of education,[25] the new literature on child-rearing,[26] and a variety of books on child labor, religious training, vocational guidance, and the like.[27] Even critical comments showed the extent to which the idea of adolescence had captured the public imagination: there were those who complained that "we are today under the tyranny of the special cult of adolescence."[28]

Hall's reputation was, however, relatively short-lived. From the very beginning his theories of adolescence aroused at least some criticism. Men like E. L. Thorndike (himself an important figure in the history of American psychology), Charles H. Judd, and Irving King charged him with many forms of exaggeration and overstatement.[29] And after 1925 his work went rapidly into eclipse. Many scholars came to feel that it was unreasonable to view growth in terms of set "stages" of any kind whatsoever. Margaret Mead, in her famous study of Samoan children, tried to show that adolescent "storm and stress" are a function of certain *cultural* determinants.[30] By contrast, Hall was seen as the representative of an outmoded, wholly physiological orientation.[31] Moreover, his fervent, almost missionary approach to his subject, his florid writing, his long-range goal of race improvement—all this came to seem irrelevant, or even offensive, to later generations of psychologists.

Thus G. Stanley Hall has been largely forgotten, if not rejected outright. Yet, we suggest, he has left his mark all the same. Hall's critics denied the validity of considering personal growth in terms of "stages"; but we still regard adolescence in just such a context. His critics accused him of having greatly exaggerated "storm and stress" phenomena, and yet today more than ever we view adolescence in exactly those terms. In fact, the "special cult of adolescence" seems to have lost no strength at all. And it was Hall, more than anyone else, who fixed it in our imagination.

It would be easy to overstate the element of innovation in Hall's thinking. If we compare the kind of adolescence that he was describing with some of the ideas that were current just before his time,[32] we find a considerable degree of continuity. His achievement lay in reshaping certain aspects of popular belief about youth, combining them with some of the most exciting new ideas in science (i.e., evolution), gathering data on a large scale, and presenting the whole in a persuasive and meaningful fashion.

Yet certain questions about the rise of the concept of adolescence remain. What larger developments in American society did it reflect? To what popular attitudes, or needs, or anxieties, did it minister? We offer, in conclusion, the following very tentative suggestions—some of which we have simply lifted from contemporary thinking about adolescence in the fields of psychology and sociology.[33]

We propose, as a starting point, the long-term transformation of the United States from an agricultural into an urban and industrial society; for this change—which has, of course, been basic to so much of our history during the last 150 years—has exerted a profound influence on the structure of American families. Consider that most farm families are characterized by a high degree of internal unity. Children and adults share the same tasks, the same entertainments, the same friends, the same expectations. There is a continuum between the generations. The child appears not so much as a child per se but as himself a potential farmer; he is, then, a miniature model of his father. Such, we would argue, was the prevalent situation in nearly *all* the families of this country before the nineteenth century.

But when Americans began to move to the city, all this changed. City children, for example, do not often have a significant economic function within the family as a whole. (Or alternatively—as in the case of poor children employed as factory hands—their work is likely to be quite different from that of their parents.) Moreover, they are thrust into close proximity with other families and have the opportunity to form numerous contacts among their own peers. Thus there develops in the urban setting an important "discontinuity of age-groups."[34] Children and adults are much more obviously separated from each other than is ever the case in a rural environment.

This second configuration was starting to show itself in some American families during the early part of the nineteenth century, and perhaps it helps to explain the material presented in our opening section. Now—i.e., with the new, typically urban family structure—childhood as such is "discovered"; it is no longer feasible to regard children simply as miniature adults. Now, too, "child-centered" families become possible. The behavior of the young is increasingly seen as bizarre and also as appropriate to their particular time of life. A new tolerance for such behavior develops, and parental authority appears to weaken.[35] Finally, there is an obvious place for a literature on child-rearing.

Most cultures with sharp discontinuities of this kind possess a system of "age-grading," which defines the various steps in the transition from childhood to adulthood.[36] In many cases there are elaborate initiation rites to dramatize this change. But our society lacks such rites; ceremonies like confirmation and graduation exercises are losing whatever significance in this regard they once had. It is in such situations, as Kenneth Keniston has suggested, that a "youth culture" is likely to develop. "Youth culture" may be defined, somewhat carelessly, as institutionalized adolescence. It refers, of course, to the special way of life characteristic of large groups of young people of approximately the same age. It is more than a simple substitute for formal age-grading and initiation rites. It is not, Keniston writes,

> so obviously transitional . . . [but is] much more like a waiting period . . . a temporary stopover in which one can muster strength for the next harrowing stage of the trip.

Its pattern is "not always or explicitly anti-adult, but it is belligerently *non*-adult."[37] In many respects adulthood looks rather forbidding when compared with the life of a child, and youth culture reflects some reluctance to bridge this gap.

It is pertinent to recall at this point the deep concern of many nineteenth-century Americans about the growth of peer-group contacts. We suggest that these people were witnessing the rudimentary beginnings of a youth culture. Of course, there were none of the artifacts so prominent in our own modern-day youth culture (e.g., "rock 'n roll," "teen magazines," special kinds of dress, and so forth).

But the very fact of "wanting to be with and for [their own] kind"[38] was significant. By about 1900 the situation had become more clear. The many and varied writings on "gangs," on juvenile delinquency, and on vocational guidance all show some feeling for the special characteristics of a youth culture.

Keniston argues that a second kind of discontinuity—that between specific generations—is also important in the formation of youth culture. By this he means a clear separation between the parents and the children within an individual family. In such cases the situation of the parents offers no viable goal at which their children may aim. Intra-family conflict is likely to become chronic, and the adolescent is on his own in the formation of an identity. This pattern is characteristic of societies with a high rate of social change and a plurality of alternatives in regard to careers, moral codes, and life styles. The young person shrinks from such a bewildering array of choices and becomes part of the youth culture, where a clear-cut, if temporary, identity comes ready-made.

All of this seems to describe nineteenth-century America fairly well, especially the new life of the cities. Social and economic change was everywhere apparent; ambitions were high; there was an astonishing diversity of people, ideologies, occupations. The disparity between generations was assumed; it became, indeed, a part of the national mythology. Immigrant families presented an especially dramatic case in point, likewise those families in which the children of uneducated parents had the chance to go to school. Thus, once again, there was the youth culture.

The growth of the concept of adolescence was the final step in this long and somewhat devious process. It was the response to an observable fact—the fact of a youth culture, of many young people seemingly in distress (or at least behaving in ways that distressed their elders). Americans needed some means of understanding the problems of, and the problems created by, these young people. We have tried to show them groping toward such an understanding through much of the nineteenth century. And we have located, chiefly in the work of G. Stanley Hall, a kind of culmination of these efforts: the first comprehensive theory of adolescence in modern history.

Notes
1   We know of only three attempts to confront this material directly: Bernard Wishy, *The Child and the Republic,* Philadelphia: University of Pennsylvania Press, 1968; Robert Sunley, "Early Nineteenth-Century American Literature on Child-Rearing," in *Childhood in Contemporary Cultures,* ed. by Margaret Mead and Martha Wolfenstein, Chicago: University of Chicago Press, 1955, pp. 150–167; and Elaine

V. Damis, *The History of Child-Rearing Advice in America from 1800–1940,* unpublished honor's thesis, Radcliffe College, 1960.

2   See, for instance, Juliana Seymour, *On the Management and Education of Children,* London, 1754; and Miss Appleton, *Early Education,* London, 1821

3   Parallel to this increase in books on child-rearing, there developed at this time a new kind of magazine directed specifically to "mothers." *Mother's Magazine* and the *Mother's Assistant* were prominent examples. Both seem to have achieved a wide circulation within a very few years. The magazines, in turn, were closely related to the movement for "maternal associations." These societies, operating at the local level and devoting their energies largely to the discussion of child-rearing problems, became quite a vogue in the 1820s and 1830s. All of this demonstrates further the heightened interest in motherhood—and thus childhood—that characterized the period.

4   These anxieties were a matter of great complexity and wide ramifications. Indeed they must be understood as relating not only to conditions internal to the family but also to the wider social climate of the time. For some useful discussion of all this, see Bernard Wishy, *The Child and the Republic.*

5   H. W. Bulkeley, *A Word to Parents,* Philadelphia: Presbyterian Board of Publication, 1858, p. 12.

6   Warren Burton, *Helps to Education,* Boston: Crosby and Nichols, 1863, pp. 38–39. Similar observations can be found in the writings of foreign visitors to this country. See Arthur W. Calhoun, *A Social History of the American Family,* New York: Barnes and Noble, 1945, pp. 17–19, for some extensive discussion of this travel literature. See also Max Berger, *The British Traveller in America,* New York: Columbia University Press, 1943.

7   On this matter see, for example, Lydia M. Child, *The Mother's Book,* Boston: Carter, Hendee and Babcock, 1835, p. 94; and Burton, *op. cit.,* pp. 74–75, 92.

8   Child, *op. cit.,* p. 95.

9   See *ibid.,* p. 138; also *Mother's Magazine,* 1, pp. 42–45.

10   The word "adolescence" was known in the nineteenth century, but we have found only a very few cases of its use in the literature on child-rearing and "youth."

11   Joel Hawes, *Lectures to Young Men,* Hartford, Connecticut: Cooke & Co., 1832, p. 35. See also Child, *op. cit.,* p. 125.

12   Henry Ward Beecher, *Lectures to Young Men,* Boston: J. P. Jewett & Co., 1844, p. 21. Beecher actually delivered these lectures to an audience of young people in Boston before publishing them. Such was also the pattern for many of the other works of this kind. For a similar comment on the turmoil characteristic of youth, see Henrietta Keddie, *Papers for Thoughtful Girls,* Boston: Crosby and Nichols, 1860, p. 1.

13   Isaac Taylor, *Home Education,* New York: D. Appleton & Co., 1838, p. 131.

14   Beecher, *op. cit.,* p. 21.

15   John M. Austin, *A Voice to Youth,* New York: J. Bolles, 1838, p. 1.

16   See, for example, Elizabeth Blackwell, *Counsel to Parents on the Moral Education of Their Children,* New York: Brentano's Literary Emporium, 1879.

17   Theodore T. Munger, *On the Threshold,* Boston: Houghton Mifflin & Co., 1881, p. 5. See also William A. Mowry, *Talks with My Boys,* Boston: New England Publishing Company, 1885, pp. 30 ff.; and Philip S. Moxon, *The Aim of Life,* Boston: Roberts Brothers, 1894, pp. 11–29.

18   See, for example, Goerge H. Hepworth, *Rocks and Shoals,* Boston: American Unitarian Association, 1870; and Mowry, *op. cit.*

19   G. Stanley Hall, "The Moral and Religious Training of Children," in *Princeton Review* (January, 1882), pp. 26–48. This essay was later republished in a slightly revised form in *Pedagogical Seminary,* 1, pp. 196–210.

20   See E. D. Starbuck, *The Psychology of Religion,* New York: Ginn & Co., 1899; and an essay by the same author, "A Study of Conversion," in *American Journal of Psychology,* 8, pp. 268–308.

21   See Edgar J. Swift, "Some Criminal Tendencies of Boyhood: A Study in Adolescence," in *Pedagogical Seminary,* 7.

22   See G. Stanley Hall, *Adolescence,* New York: D. Appleton & Co., 1904, Vol. 2, pp. 61, 69.

22   See the "epitome" of Hall's theories by G. E. Partridge, *The Genetic Philosophy of Education,* Boston: Sturgis & Walton Co., 1912, p. 31.

24   For example, James R. Angell, *Psychology,* New York: H. Holt & Co., 1904. See especially p. 358.

25   See George H. Betts, *The Mind and Its Education,* New York: D. Appleton & Co., 1906; P. M. Magnusson, *Psychology as Applied to Education,* New York: Silver, Burdett and Company, 1913; and Arthur Holmes, *Principles of Character-Making,* Philadelphia: J. B. Lippincott Company, 1913.

26   See William McKeever, *Training the Boy,* New York: Macmillan Company, 1913; and *Training the Girl,* New York: Macmillan Company, 1914; also W. B. Forbush and Catherine M. Burrell, *The Mother's Book,* New York: The University Society, Inc., 1919.

27   See George B. Mangold, *Child Problems,* New York: The Macmillan Company, 1910; George A. Coe, *Education in Religion and Morals,* New York: F. H. Revell Company, 1904; and Meyer Bloomfield, *The Vocational Guidance of Youth,* Boston: Houghton Miffln Company, 1911.

28   Frank O. Beck, *Marching Manward,* New York: Eaton & Mains, 1913, p. 38.

29   See E. L. Thorndike, *Notes on Child-Study,* in *Columbia University Contributions to Philosophy, Psychology, and Education,* 8:3–4, p. 143; also Thorndike's article, "Magnitude and Rate of Alleged Changes at Adolescence," in *Educational Review,* 54, pp. 140–147. See too Charles H. Judd, *The Psychology of High School Subjects,* Boston: Ginn & Company, 1915; and Irving King, *The Psychology of Child Development,* Chicago: University of Chicago Press, 1903, pp. 222 ff.

30 Margaret Mead, *Coming of Age in Samoa,* New York: W. Morrow and Company, 1928.

31 On this point Hall was somewhat misrepresented. It is true that he regarded the critical changes in adolescence as proceeding from within; but he also spent much effort in analyzing various factors in our *environment*—which, he felt, greatly accentuated adolescent distress. See Hall, *Adolescence, op. cit.,* Vol. 1, pp. xv, 321 ff., 348 ff., 376 ff.; and Vol. 2, pp. 59–60.

32 *Ibid.,* pp. 5–8

33 We have tried to draw together ideas from several different sources, chief among them: Kenneth Keniston, "Social Change and Youth in America," *Daedalus* (Winter, 1962), pp. 145–171; Erik H. Erikson, "Youth: Fidelity and Diversity," *Daedalus* (Winter, 1962), pp. 5–27; Ruth Benedict, "Continuities and Discontinuities in Cultural Conditioning," in *Psychiatry,* 1, pp. 161–167; Kingsley Davis, "The Sociology of Parent-Youth Conflict," *American Sociological Review,* 5, pp. 523–535.

34 The phrase is Kenneth Keniston's. See his article cited above.

35 This may have been *only* a matter of appearance. The reality may have been quite different; indeed parental authority seems, if anything, stronger in the nineteenth century than in the eighteenth. But the fact that children were now more visible and more often approached on their own terms was interpreted by many observers as a symptom of decadence and loosened family bonds.

36 Ruth Benedict, "Continuities and Discontinuities in Cultural Conditioning," *Psychiatry,* 1, p. 165.

37 Keniston, *op. cit.,* p. 161.

38 William B. Forbush, *The Boy Problem,* Chicago: The Pilgrim Press, 1901, p. 20.

PART III

Women:
Roles and Relationships

Barbara Welter gives us some ideological background for the demographic picture Uhlenberg presents of mid-nineteenth-century American women. This period was truly the heyday of Victorianism, and the prudery and fastidiousness that we associate with this era are evident in the idealized and romantic picture held of women of the time. To be sure, this was a vision for the middle class, since those less fortunate economically had neither time nor means to elevate women to such a glass-covered pedestal. Yet, even among the middle class, as we shall see, this cult of true womanhood was to be short-lived. Rumbles were being heard in a number of places, some touched upon in the articles included in the section on sex. However, the fact that remnants of feminine idealization are still very much with us (e.g., women are still presented with the view that their own sexuality is more spiritual than man's rather imperious nature, or less aggressive and ambitious) attests to their durability. Now that many of those remnants have been raised to a conscious level and presented as having their roots more in ideology than physiology, perhaps they will finally disappear.

BARBARA WELTER

12 The Cult of True Womanhood: 1820-1860

The nineteenth-century American man was a busy builder of bridges and railroads, at work long hours in a materialistic society. The religious values of his forebears were neglected in practice if not in intent, and he occasionally felt some guilt that he had turned this new land, this temple of the chosen people, into one vast counting-house. But he could salve his conscience by reflecting that he had left behind a hostage, not only to fortune, but to all the values which he held so dear and treated so lightly. Woman, in the cult of True Womanhood[1] presented by the women's magazines, gift annuals and religious literature of the nineteenth century, was the hostage in the home.[2] In a society where values changed frequently, where fortunes rose and fell with frightening rapidity, where social and economic mobility provided instability as well as hope, one thing at least remained the same—a true woman was a true woman, wherever she was found. If anyone, male or female, dared to tamper with the complex of virtues which made up True Womanhood, he was damned immediately as an enemy of God, of civilization and of the Republic. It was a fearful obligation, a solemn responsibility, which the nineteenth-century American woman had—to uphold the pillars of the temple with her frail white hand.

The attributes of True Womenhood, by which a woman judged herself and was judged by her husband, her neighbors and society could be divided into four cardinal virtues—piety, purity, submissiveness and domesticity. Put them all together and they spelled mother, daughter, sister, wife—woman. Without them, no matter whether there was fame, achievement or wealth, all was ashes. With them she was promised happiness and power.

Religion or piety was the core of woman's virtue, the source of her strength. Young men looking for a mate were cautioned to search first for piety, for if that were there, all else would follow.[3] Religion belonged to woman by divine right, a gift of God and nature. This "peculiar susceptibility" to religion was given her for a reason: "the vestal flame of piety, lighted up by Heaven in the breast of woman" would throw its beams into the naughty world of men.[4] So far would its candle power reach that the "Universe might be Enlightened, Improved, and Harmonized by WOMAN!!"[5] She would be another, better Eve, working in cooperation with the Redeemer, bringing the world back "from its revolt and sin."[6] The world would be reclaimed for God through her suffering, for "God increased the cares and sorrows of woman, that she might be sooner constrained to accept the terms of salvation."[7] A popular poem by Mrs. Frances Osgood, "The Triumph of the Spiritual Over the Sensual" expressed just this sentiment, woman's purifying passionless love bringing an erring man back to Christ.[8]

Dr. Charles Meigs, explaining to a graduating class of medical students why women were naturally religious, said that "hers is a pious mind. Her confiding nature leads her more readily than men to accept the proffered grace of the Gospel."[9] Caleb Atwater, Esq., writing in *The Ladies' Repository,* saw the hand of the Lord in female piety: "Religion is exactly what a woman needs, for it gives her that dignity that best suits her dependence."[10] And Mrs. John Sandford, who had no very high opinion of her sex, agreed thoroughly: "Religion is just what woman needs. Without it she is ever restless or unhappy. . . ."[11] Mrs. Sandford and the others did not speak only of that restlessness of the human heart, which St. Augustine notes, that can only find its peace in God. They spoke rather of religion as a kind of tranquilizer for the many undefined longings which swept even the most pious young girl, and about which it was better to pray than to think.

One reason religion was valued was that it did not take a woman away from her "proper sphere," her home. Unlike participation in other societies or movements, church work would not make her less domestic or submissive, less a True Woman. In religious vineyards, said the *Young Ladies' Literary and Missionary Report,* "you may labor without the apprehension of detracting from the charms of feminine delicacy." Mrs. S. L. Dagg, writing from her chapter of the Society in Tuscaloosa, Alabama, was equally reassuring: "As no sensible woman will suffer her intellectual pursuits to clash with her domestic duties" she should concentrate on religious work "which promotes these very duties."[12]

The women's seminaries aimed at aiding women to be religious, as well as accomplished. Mt. Holyoke's catalogue promised to make female education "a handmaid to the Gospel and an efficient auxiliary in the great task of renovating the world."[13] The Young Ladies' Seminary at Bordentown, New Jersey, declared its most important function to be "the forming of a sound and virtuous character."[14] In Keene, New Hampshire, the Seminary tried to instill a "consistent and useful character" in its students, to enable them in this life to be "a good friend, wife and mother" but more important, to qualify them for "the enjoyment of Celestial Happiness in the life to come."[15] And Joseph M' D. Mathews, Principal of Oakland Female Seminary in Hillsborough, Ohio, believed that "female education should be preeminently religious."[16]

If religion was so vital to a woman, irreligion was almost too awful to contemplate. Women were warned not to let their literary or intellectual pursuits take them away from God. Sarah Josepha Hale spoke darkly of those who, like Margaret Fuller, threw away the "One True Book" for others, open to error. Mrs. Hale used the unfortunate Miss Fuller as fateful proof that "the greater the intellectual force, the greater and more fatal the errors into which women fall who wander from the Rock of Salvation, Christ the Saviour. . . ."[17]

One gentleman, writing on "Female Irreligion" reminded his readers that "Man may make himself a brute, and does so very often, but can woman brutify herself to his level—the lowest level of human nature—without exerting special wonder?" Fanny Wright, because she was godless, "was no woman, mother though she be." A few years ago, he recalls, such women would have been whipped. In any case, "woman never looks lovelier than in her reverence for religion" and, conversely, "female irreligion is the most revolting feature in human character."[18]

Purity was as essential as piety to a young woman, its absence as unnatural and unfeminine. Without it she was, in fact, no woman at all, but a member of some lower order. A "fallen woman" was a "fallen angel," unworthy of the celestial company of her sex. To contemplate the loss of purity brought tears; to be guilty of such a crime, in the woman's magazines at least, brought madness or death. Even the language of the flowers had bitter words for it: a dried white rose symbolized "Death Preferable to Loss of Innocence."[19] The marriage night was the single great event of a woman's life, when she bestowed her greatest treasure upon her husband, and from that time on was completely dependent upon him, an empty vessel,[20] without legal or emotional existence of her own.[21]

Therefore all True Women were urged, in the strongest possible terms, to maintain their virtue, although men, being by nature more sensual than they, would try to assault it. Thomas Branagan admitted in *The Excellency of the Female Character Vindicated* that his sex would sin and sin again, they could not help it, but woman, stronger and purer, must not give in and let man "take liberties incompatible with her delicacy." "If you do," Branagan addressed his gentle reader, "You will be left in silent sadness to bewail your credulity, imbecility, duplicity, and premature prostitution."[22]

Mrs. Eliza Farrar, in *The Young Lady's Friend*, gave practical logistics to avoid trouble: "Sit not with another in a place that is too narrow; read not out of the same book; let not your eagerness to see anything induce you to place your head close to another person's."[23]

If such good advice was ignored the consequences were terrible and inexorable. In *Girlhood and Womanhood: Or Sketches of My Schoolmates,* by Mrs. A. J. Graves (a kind of mid-nineteenth-century *The Group*), the bad ends of a boarding school class of girls are scrupulously recorded. The worst end of all is reserved for "Amelia Dorrington: The Lost One." Amelia died in the almshouse "the wretched victim of depravity and intemperance" and all because her mother had let her be "high-spirited not prudent." These girlish high spirits had been misinterpreted by a young man, with disastrous results. Amelia's "thoughtless levity" was "followed by a total loss of virtuous principle" and Mrs. Graves editorializes that "the coldest reserve is more admirable in a woman a man wishes to make his wife, than the least approach to undue familiarity."[24]

A popular and often-reprinted story by Fanny Forester told the sad tale of "Lucy Dutton." Lucy "with the seal of innocence upon her heart, and a rose-leaf on her cheek" came out of her vine-covered cottage and ran into a city slicker. "And Lucy was beautiful and trusting, and thoughtless: and he was gay, selfish and profligate. Needs the story be told? . . . Nay, censor, Lucy was a child—consider how young, how very untaught—oh! her innocence was no match for the sophistry of a gay, city youth! Spring came and shame was stamped upon the cottage at the foot of the hill." The baby died; Lucy went mad at the funeral and finally died herself. "Poor, poor Lucy Dutton! The grave is a blessed couch and pillow to the wretched. Rest thee there, poor Lucy!"[25] The frequency with which derangement follows loss of virtue suggests the exquisite sensibility of woman, and the possibility that, in the women's magazines at least, her intellect was geared to her hymen, not her brain.

If, however, a woman managed to withstand man's assaults on her virtue, she demonstrated her superiority and her power over him. Eliza Farnham, trying to prove this female superiority, concluded smugly that "the purity of women is the everlasting barrier against which the tides of man's sensual nature surge."[26]

A story in *The Lady's Amaranth* illustrates this dominance. It is set, improbably, in Sicily, where two lovers, Bianca and Tebaldo, have been separated because her family insisted she marry a rich old man. By some strange circumstance the two are in a shipwreck and cast on a desert island, the only survivors. Even here, however, the rigid standards of True Womanhood prevail. Tebaldo unfortunately forgets himself slightly, so that Bianca must warn him: "We may not indeed gratify our fondness by caresses, but it is still something to bestow our kindest language, and looks and prayers, and all lawful and honest attentions on each other." Something, perhaps, but not enough, and Bianca must further remonstrate: "It is true that another man is my husband, but you are my guardian angel." When even that does not work she says in a voice of sweet reason, passive and proper to the end, that she wishes he wouldn't but "still, if you insist, I will become what you wish; but I beseech you to consider, ere that decision, that debasement which I must suffer in your esteem." This appeal to his own double standards holds the beast in him at bay. They are rescued, discover that the old husband is dead, and after "mourning a decent season" Bianca finally gives in, legally.[27]

Men could be counted on to be grateful when women thus saved them from themselves. William Alcott, guiding young men in their relations with the opposite sex, told them that "Nothing is better calculated to preserve a young man from contamination of low pleasures and pursuits than frequent intercourse with the more refined and virtuous of the other sex." And he added, one assumes in equal innocence, that youths should "observe and learn to admire, that purity and ignorance of evil which is the characteristic of well-educated young ladies, and which, when we are near them, raises us above those sordid and sensual considerations which hold such sway over men in their intercourse with each other."[28]

The Rev. Jonathan F. Stearns was also impressed by female chastity in the face of male passion, and warned woman never to compromise the source of her power: "Let her lay aside delicacy, and her influence over our sex is gone."[29]

Women themselves accepted, with pride but suitable modesty, this priceless virtue. *The Ladies' Wreath,* in "Woman the Creature of God and the Manufacturer of Society" saw purity as her greatest gift and chief means of discharging her duty to save the world: "Purity is the highest beauty—the true pole-star which is to guide humanity aright in its long, varied, and perilous voyage."[30]

Sometimes, however, a woman did not see the dangers to her treasure. In that case, they must be pointed out to her, usually by a male. In the nineteenth century any form of social change was tantamount to an attack on woman's virtue, if only it was correctly understood. For example, dress reform seemed innocuous enough and the bloomers worn by the lady of that name and her followers were certainly modest attire. Such was the reasoning only of the ignorant. In another issue of *The Ladies' Wreath* a young lady is represented in dialogue with her "Professor." The girl expresses admiration for the bloomer costume—it gives freedom of motion, is healthful and attractive. The "Professor" sets her straight. Trousers, he explains, are "only one of the many manifestations of that wild spirit of socialism and agrarian radicalism which is at present so rife in our land." The young lady recants immediately: "If this dress has any connexion with Fourierism or Socialism, or fanaticism in any shape whatever, I have no disposition to wear it at all . . . no true woman would so far compromise her delicacy as to espouse, however unwittingly, such a cause."[31]

America could boast that her daughters were particularly innocent. In a poem on "The American Girl" the author wrote proudly:

The Cult of True Womanhood

Her eye of light is the diamond bright,
Her innocence the pearl,
And these are ever the bridal gems
That are worn by the American girl.[32]

Lydia Maria Child, giving advice to mothers, aimed at preserving that spirit of innocence. She regretted that "want of confidence between mothers and daughters on delicate subjects" and suggested a woman tell her daughter a few facts when she reached the age of twelve to "set her mind at rest." Then Mrs. Child confidently hoped that a young lady's "instinctive modesty" would "prevent her from dwelling on the information until she was called upon to use it."[33] In the same vein, a book of advice to the newly married was titled *Whisper to a Bride.*[34] As far as intimate information was concerned, there was no need to whisper, since the book contained none at all.

A masculine summary of this virtue was expressed in a poem "Female Charms":

I would have her as pure as the snow on the mount—
    As true as the smile that to infamy's given—
As pure as the wave of the crystalline fount,
    Yet as warm in the heart as the sunlight of heaven.
With a mind cultivated, not boastingly wise,
    I could gaze on such beauty, with exquisite bliss;
With her heart on her lips and her soul in her eyes—
    What more could I wish in dear woman than this.[35]

Man might, in fact, ask no more than this in woman, but she was beginning to ask more of herself, and in the asking was threatening the third powerful and necessary virtue, submission. Purity, considered as a moral imperative, set up a dilemma which was hard to resolve. Woman must preserve her virtue until marriage and marriage was necessary for her happiness. Yet marriage was, literally, an end to innocence. She was told not to question this dilemma, but simply to accept it.

Submission was perhaps the most feminine virtue expected of women. Men were supposed to be religious, although they rarely had time for it, and supposed to be pure, although it came awfully hard to them, but men were the movers, the doers, the actors. Women were the passive, submissive responders. The order of dialogue was, of course, fixed in Heaven. Man was "woman's superior by God's appointment, if not in intellectual dowry, at least by official decree." Therefore, as Charles Elliot argued in *The Ladies' Repository,* she should submit to him "for the sake of good order at least."[36] In *The Ladies Companion* a young wife was quoted approvingly as saying that she did not think woman should "feel and act for herself" because "When, next to God, her husband is not the tribunal to which her heart and intellect appeals—the golden bowl of affection is broken."[37] Women were warned that if they tampered with this quality they tampered with the order of the Universe.

The Young Lady's Book summarized the necessity of the passive virtues in its readers' lives: "It is, however, certain, that in whatever situation of life a woman is placed from her cradle to her grave, a spirit of obedience and submission, pliability of temper, and humility of mind, are required from her."[38]

Woman understood her position if she was the right kind of woman, a true woman. "She feels herself weak and timid. She needs a protector," declared George Burnap, in his lectures on *The Sphere and Duties of Woman.* "She is in a measure dependent. She asks for wisdom, constancy, firmness, perseverance, and she is willing to repay it all by the surrender of the full treasure of her affections. Woman despises in man every thing like herself except a tender heart. It is enough that she is effeminate and weak; she does not want another like herself."[39] Or put even more strongly by Mrs. Sandford: "A really sensible woman feels her dependence. She does what she can, but she is conscious of inferiority, and therefore grateful for support."[40]

Mrs. Sigourney, however, assured young ladies that although they were separate, they were equal. This difference of the sexes did not imply inferiority, for it was part of that same order of Nature established by Him "who bids the oak brave the fury of the tempest, and the alpine flower lean its cheek on the bosom of eternal snows."[41] Dr. Meigs had a different analogy to make the same point, contrasting the anatomy of the Apollo of the Belvedere (illustrating the male principle) with the Venus de Medici (illustrating the female principle). "Woman," said the physician, with a kind of clinical gallantry, "has a head almost too small for intellect but just big enough for love."[42]

This love itself was to be passive and responsive. "Love, in the heart of a woman," wrote Mrs. Farrar, "should partake largely of the nature of gratitude. She should love, because she is already loved by one deserving her regard."[43]

Woman was to work in silence, unseen, like Wordsworth's Lucy. Yet, "working like nature, in secret" her love goes forth to the world "to regulate its pulsation, and send forth from its heart, in pure and temperate flow, the life-giving current."[44] She was to work only for pure affection, without thought of money or ambition. A poem, "Woman and Fame," by Felicia Hemans, widely quoted in many of

the gift books, concludes with a spirited renunciation of the gift of
fame:

> Away! to me, a woman, bring
> Sweet flowers from affection's spring.[45]

"True feminine genius," said Grace Greenwood (Sara Jane
Clarke) "is ever timid, doubtful, and clingingly dependent; a per-
petual childhood." And she advised literary ladies in an essay on "The
Intellectual Woman"—"Don't trample on the flowers while longing
for the stars."[46] A wife who submerged her own talents to work for
her husband was extolled as an example of a true woman. In *Women
of Worth: A Book for Girls,* Mrs. Ann Flaxman, an artist of promise
herself, was praised because she "devoted herself to sustain her husband's genius and aid him in his arduous career."[47]

Caroline Gilman's advice to the bride aimed at establishing this
proper order from the beginning of a marriage: "Oh, young and
lovely bride, watch well the first moments when your will conflicts
with his to whom God and society have given the control. Reverence
his *wishes* even when you do not his *opinions.*"[48]

Mrs. Gilman's perfect wife in *Recollections of a Southern Matron*
realizes that "the three golden threads with which domestic happiness
is woven" are "to repress a harsh answer, to confess a fault, and to
stop (right or wrong) in the midst of self-defense, in gentle submission." Woman could do this, hard though it was, because in her heart
she knew she was right and so could afford to be forgiving, even a
trifle condescending. "Men are not unreasonable," averred Mrs. Gilman. "Their difficulties lie in not understanding the moral and physical nature of our sex. They often wound through ignorance, and are
surprised at having offended." Wives were advised to do their best
to reform men, but if they couldn't, to give up gracefully. "If any habit
of his annoyed me, I spoke of it once or twice, calmly, then bore it
quietly."[49]

A wife should occupy herself "only with domestic affairs—wait
till your husband confides to you those of a high importance—and do
not give your advice until he asks for it," advised the *Lady's Token.* At
all times she should behave in a manner becoming a woman, who had
"no arms other than gentleness." Thus "if he is abusive, never re-
tort."[50] *A Young Lady's Guide to the Harmonious Development of a Christian Character* suggested that females should "become as little children" and "avoid a controversial spirit."[51] *The Mother's Assistant and
Young Lady's Friend* listed "Always Conciliate" as its first commandment in "Rules for Conjugal and Domestic Happiness." Small won-

der that these same rules ended with the succinct maxim: "Do not expect too much."[52]

As mother, as well as wife, woman was required to submit to fortune. In *Letters to Mothers* Mrs. Sigourney sighed: "To bear the evils and sorrows which may be appointed us, with a patient mind, should be the continual effort of our sex. . . . It seems, indeed, to be expected of us; since the passive and enduring virtues are more immediately within our province." Of these trials "the hardest was to bear the loss of children with submission" but the indomitable Mrs. Sigourney found strength to murmur to the bereaved mother: "The Lord loveth a cheerful giver."[53] *The Ladies' Parlor Companion* agreed thoroughly in "A Submissive Mother," in which a mother who had already buried two children and was nursing a dying baby saw her sole remaining child "probably scalded to death. Handing over the infant to die in the arms of a friend, she bowed in sweet submission to the double stroke." But the child "through the goodness of God survived, and the mother learned to say 'Thy will be done.' "[54]

Woman then, in all her roles, accepted submission as her lot. It was a lot she had not chosen or deserved. As *Godey's* said, "the lesson of submission is forced upon woman." Without comment or criticism the writer affirms that "To suffer and to be silent under suffering seems the great command she has to obey."[55] George Burnap referred to a woman's life as "a series of suppressed emotions."[56] She was, as Emerson said, "more vulnerable, more infirm, more mortal than man."[57] The death of a beautiful woman, cherished in fiction, represented woman as the innocent victim, suffering without sin, too pure and good for this world but too weak and passive to resist its evil forces.[58] The best refuge for such a delicate creature was the warmth and safety of her home.

The true woman's place was unquestionably by her own fireside —as daughter, sister, but most of all as wife and mother. Therefore domesticity was among the virtues most prized by the women's magazines. "As society is constituted," wrote Mrs. S. E. Farley, on the "Domestic and Social Claims on Woman," "the true dignity and beauty of the female character seem to consist in a right understanding and faithful and cheerful performance of social and family duties."[59] Sacred Scripture re-enforced social pressure: "St. Paul knew what was best for women when he advised them to be domestic," said Mrs. Sandford. "There is composure at home; there is something sedative in the duties which home involves. It affords security not only from the world, but from delusions and errors of every kind."[60]

From her home woman performed her great task of bringing men back to God. *The Young Ladies' Class Book* was sure that "the domestic fireside is the great guardian of society against the excess of human passions."[61] *The Lady at Home* expressed its convictions in its very title and concluded that "even if we cannot reform the world in a moment, we can begin the work by reforming ourselves and our households—It is woman's mission. Let her not look away from her own little family circle for the means of producing moral and social reforms, but begin at home."[62]

Home was supposed to be a cheerful place, so that brothers, husbands and sons would not go elsewhere in search of a good time. Woman was expected to dispense comfort and cheer. In writing the biography of Margaret Mercer (every inch a true woman) her biographer (male) notes: "She never forgot that it is the peculiar province of woman to minister to the comfort, and promote the happiness, first, of those most nearly allied to her, and then of those, who by the Providence of God are placed in a state of dependence upon her."[63] Many other essays in the women's journals showed woman as comforter: "Woman, Man's Best friend," "Woman, the Greatest Social Benefit," "Woman, A Being to Come Home To," "The Wife: Source of Comfort and the Spring of Joy."[64]

One of the most important functions of woman as comforter was her role as nurse. Her own health was probably, although regrettably, delicate.[65] Many homes had "little sufferers," those pale children who wasted away to saintly deaths. And there were enough other illnesses of youth and age, major and minor, to give the nineteenth-century American woman nursing experience. The sickroom called for the exercise of her higher qualities of patience, mercy and gentleness as well as for her housewifely arts. She could thus fulfill her dual feminine function—beauty and usefulness.

The cookbooks of the period offer formulas for gout cordials, ointment for sore nipples, hiccough and cough remedies, opening pills and refreshing drinks for fever, along with recipes for pound cake, jumbles, stewed calves head and currant wine.[66] *The Ladies' New Book of Cookery* believed that "food prepared by the kind hand of a wife, mother, sister, friend" tasted better and had a "restorative power which money cannot purchase."[67]

A chapter of *The Young Lady's Friend* was devoted to woman's privilege as "ministering spirit at the couch of the sick." Mrs. Farrar advised a soft voice, gentle and clean hands, and a cheerful smile. She also cautioned against an excess of female delicacy. That was all right for a young lady in the parlor, but not for bedside manners. Leeches, for example, were to be regarded as "a curious piece of mechanism . . . their ornamental stripes should recommend them even to the eye, and their valuable services to our feelings." And she went on calmly to discuss their use. Nor were women to shrink from medical terminology, since "If you cultivate right views of the wonderful structure of the body, you will be as willing to speak to a physician of the bowels as the brains of your patient."[68]

Nursing the sick, particularly sick males, not only made a woman feel useful and accomplished, but increased her influence. In a piece of heavy-handed humor in *Godey's* a man confessed that some women were only happy when their husbands were ailing that they might have the joy of nursing him to recovery "thus gratifying their medical vanity and their love of power by making him more dependent upon them."[69] In a similar vein a husband sometimes suspected his wife "almost wishes me dead—for the pleasure of being utterly inconsolable."[70]

In the home women were not only the highest adornment of civilization, but they were supposed to keep busy at morally uplifting tasks. Fortunately most of housework, if looked at in true womanly fashion, could be regarded as uplifting. Mrs. Sigourney extolled its virtues: "The science of housekeeping affords exercise for the judgment and energy, ready recollection, and patient self-possession, that are the characteristics of a superior mind."[71] According to Mrs. Farrar, making beds was good exercise, the repetitiveness of routine tasks inculcated patience and perseverance, and proper management of the home was a surprisingly complex art: "There is more to be learned about pouring out tea and coffee, than most young ladies are willing to believe."[72] *Godey's* went so far as to suggest coyly, in "Learning vs. Housewifery" that the two were complementary, not opposed: chemistry could be utilized in cooking, geometry in dividing cloth, and phrenology in discovering talent in children."[73]

Women were to master every variety of needlework, for, as Mrs. Sigourney pointed out, "Needle-work, in all its forms of use, elegance, and ornament, has ever been the appropriate occupation of woman."[74] Embroidery improved taste; knitting promoted serenity and economy.[75] Other forms of artsy-craftsy activity for her leisure moments included painting on glass or velvet, Poonah work, tussy-mussy frames for her own needlepoint or water colors, stands for hyacinths, hair bracelets or baskets of feathers.[76]

She was expected to have a special affinity for flowers. To the editors of *The Lady's Token* "A Woman never appears more truly in her sphere, than when she divides her time between her domestic avocations and the culture of flowers."[77] She could write letters, an activity particularly feminine since it had to do with the outpourings of the heart,[78] or practice her drawingroom skills of singing and playing an instrument. She might even read.

Here she faced a bewildering array of advice. The female was dangerously addicted to novels, according to the literature of the period. She should avoid them, since they interfered with "serious piety." If she simply couldn't help herself and read them anyway, she should choose edifying ones from lists of morally acceptable authors.[79] She should study history since it "showed the depravity of the human heart and the evil nature of sin." On the whole, "religious biography was best."[79]

The women's magazines themselves could be read without any loss of concern for the home. *Godey's* promised the husband that he would find his wife "no less assiduous for his reception, or less sincere in welcoming his return" as a result of reading their magazine.[80] *The Lily of the Valley* won its right to be admitted to the boudoir by confessing that it was "like its namesake humble and unostentatious, but it is yet pure, and, we trust, free from moral imperfections."[81]

No matter what later authorities claimed, the nineteenth century knew that girls *could* be ruined by a book. The seduction stories regard "exciting and dangerous books" as contributory causes of disaster. The man without honorable intentions always provides the innocent maiden with such books as a prelude to his assault on her virtue.[82] Books which attacked or seemed to attack woman's accepted place in society were regarded as equally dangerous. A reviewer of Harriet Martineau's *Society in America* wanted it kept out of the hands of American women. They were so susceptible to persuasion, with their "gentle yielding natures" that they might listen to "the bold ravings of the hard-featured of their own sex." The frightening result: "such reading will unsettle them for their true station and pursuits, and they will throw the world back again into confusion."[83]

The debate over women's education posed the question of whether a "finished" education detracted from the practice of housewifely arts. Again it proved to be a case of semantics, for a true woman's education was never "finished" until she was instructed in the gentle science of homemaking.[84] Helen Irving, writing on "Literary Women," made it very clear that if women invoked the muse, it was as a genie of the household lamp. "If the necessities of her position require these duties at her hands, she will perform them nonetheless cheerfully, that she knows herself capable of higher things." The literary woman must conform to the same standards as any other woman: "That her home shall be made a loving place of rest and joy and comfort for those who are dear to her, will be the first wish of every true woman's heart."[85] Mrs. Ann Stephens told women who wrote to make sure they did not sacrifice one domestic duty. "As for genius, make it a domestic plant. Let its roots strike deep in your house. . . ."[86]

The fear of "blue stockings" (the eighteenth-century male's term of derision for educated or literary women) need not persist for nineteenth-century American men. The magazines presented spurious dialogues in which bachelors were convinced of their fallacy in fearing educated wives. One such dialogue took place between a young man and his female cousin. Ernest deprecates learned ladies ("A *Woman* is far more lovable than a *philosopher*") but Alice refutes him with the beautiful example of their Aunt Barbara who "although she *has* perpetrated the heinous crime of writing some half dozen folios" is still a model of "the spirit of feminine gentleness." His memory prodded, Ernest concedes that, by George, there was a woman: "When I last had a cold she not only made me a bottle of cough syrup, but when I complained of nothing new to read, set to work and wrote some twenty stanzas on consumption."[87]

The magazines were filled with domestic tragedies in which spoiled young girls learned that when there was a hungry man to feed French and china painting were not helpful. According to these stories many a marriage is jeopardized because the wife has not learned to keep house. Harriet Beecher Stowe wrote a sprightly piece of personal experience for *Godey's,* ridiculing her own bad housekeeping as a bride. She used the same theme in a story "The Only Daughter," in which the pampered beauty learns the facts of domestic life from a rather difficult source, her mother-in-law. Mrs. Hamilton tells Caroline in the sweetest way possible to shape up in the kitchen, reserving her rebuke for her son: "You are her husband—her guide—her protector—now see what you can do," she admonishes him. "Give her credit for every effort: treat her faults with tenderness; encourage and praise whenever you can, and depend upon it, you will see another woman in her." He is properly masterful, she properly domestic and in a few months Caroline is making lumpless gravy and keeping up with the darning. Domestic tranquillity has been restored and the young wife moralizes: "Bring up a girl to feel that she has a responsible part to bear in promoting the happiness of the family, and you make a reflecting being of her at once, and remove that lightness and frivolity of character which makes her shrink from graver studies."[88] These stories end with the heroine drying her hands on her apron and vowing that *her* daughter will be properly educated, in piecrust as well as Poonah work.

The female seminaries were quick to defend themselves against any suspicion of interfering with the role which nature's God had assigned to women. They hoped to enlarge and deepen that role, but not to change its setting. At the Young Ladies' Seminary and Collegiate Institute in Monroe City, Michigan, the catalogue admitted few of its graduates would be likely "to fill the learned professions." Still, they were called to "other scenes of usefulness and honor." The average woman is to be "the presiding genius of love" in the home, where she is to "give a correct and elevated literary taste to her children, and to assume that influential station that she ought to possess as the companion of an educated man."[89]

At Miss Pierce's famous school in Litchfield, the students were taught that they had "attained the perfection of their characters when they could combine their elegant accomplishments with a turn for solid domestic virtues."[90] Mt. Holyoke paid pious tribute to domestic skills: "Let a young lady despise this branch of the duties of woman, and she despises the appointments of her existence." God, nature and the Bible "enjoin these duties on the sex, and she cannot violate them with impunity." Thus warned, the young lady would have to seek knowledge of these duties elsewhere, since it was not in the curriculum at Mt. Holyoke. "We would not take this privilege from the mother."[91]

One reason for knowing her way around a kitchen was that America was "a land of precarious fortunes," as Lydia Maria Child pointed out in her book *The Frugal Housewife: Dedicated to Those Who Are Not Ashamed of Economy.* Mrs. Child's chapter "How To Endure Poverty" prescribed a combination of piety and knowledge—the kind of knowledge found in a true woman's education, "a thorough religious *useful* education."[92] The woman who had servants today, might tomorrow, because of a depression or panic, be forced to do her own work. If that happened she knew how to act, for she was to be the same cheerful consoler of her husband in their cottage as in their mansion.

An essay by Washington Irving, much quoted in the gift annuals, discussed the value of a wife in case of business reverses: "I have observed that a married man falling into misfortune is more apt to achieve his situation in the world than a single one . . . it is beautifully ordained by Providence that woman, who is the ornament of man in his happier hours, should be his stay and solace when smitten with sudden calamity."[93]

A story titled simply but eloquently "The Wife" dealt with the quiet heroism of Ellen Graham during her husband's plunge from fortune to poverty. Ned Graham said of her: "Words are too poor to tell you what I owe to that noble woman. In our darkest seasons of adversity, she has been an angel of consolation—utterly forgetful of self and anxious only to comfort and sustain me." Of course she had a little help from "faithful Dinah who absolutely refused to leave her beloved mistress," but even so Ellen did no more than would be expected of any true woman.[94]

Most of this advice was directed to woman as wife. Marriage was the proper state for the exercise of the domestic virtues. "True Love and a Happy Home," an essay in *The Young Ladies' Oasis,* might have been carved on every girl's hope chest.[95] But although marriage was best, it was not absolutely necessary. The women's magazines tried to remove the stigma from being an "Old Maid." They advised no marriage at all rather than an unhappy one contracted out of selfish motives.[96] Their stories showed maiden ladies as unselfish ministers to the sick, teachers of the young, or moral preceptors with their pens, beloved to the entire village. Usually the life of single blessedness resulted from the premature death of a fiancé, or was chosen through fidelity to some high mission. For example, in "Two Sisters," Mary devotes herself to Ellen and her abandoned children, giving up her own chance for marriage. "Her devotion to her sister's happiness has met its reward in the consciousness of having fulfilled a sacred duty."[97] Very rarely, a "woman of genius" was absolved from the necessity of marriage, being so extraordinary that she did not need the security or status of being a wife.[98] Most often, however, if girls proved "difficult," marriage and a family were regarded as a cure.[99] The "sedative quality" of a home could be counted on to subdue even the most restless spirits.

George Burnap saw marriage as "that sphere for which woman was originally intended, and to which she is so exactly fitted to adorn and bless, as the wife, the mistress of a home, the solace, the aid, and the counsellor of that ONE, for whose sake alone the world is of any consequence to her."[100] Samuel Miller preached a sermon on women: "How interesting and important are the duties devolved on females as WIVES . . . the counsellor and friend of the husband; who makes it her daily study to lighten his cares, to soothe his sorrows, and to augment his joys; who, like a guardian angel, watches over his interests, warns him against dangers, comforts him under trials; and by her pious, assiduous, and attractive deportment, constantly endeavors to render him more virtuous, more useful, more honourable, and more happy."[101] A woman's whole interest should be focused on her husband, paying him "those numberless attentions to which the French give the title of *petits soins* and which the woman who loves knows so well how to pay . . . she should consider nothing as trivial which could win a smile of approbation from him."[102]

Marriage was seen not only in terms of service but as an increase in authority for woman. Burnap concluded that marriage improves the female character "not only because it puts her under the best possible tuition, that of the affections, and affords scope to her active energies, but because it gives her higher aims, and a more dignified position."[103] *The Lady's Amaranth* saw it as a balance of power: "The man bears rule over his wife's person and conduct. She bears rule over his inclinations: he governs by law; she by persuasion. . . . The empire of the woman is an empire of softness . . . her commands are caresses, her menaces are tears."[104]

Woman should marry, but not for money. She should choose only the high road of true love and not truckle to the values of a materialistic society. A story "Marrying for Money" (subtlety was not the strong point of the ladies' magazines) depicts Gertrude, the heroine, rueing the day she made her crass choice: "It is a terrible thing to live without love. . . . A woman who dares marry for aught but the purest affection, calls down the just judgments of heaven upon her head."[105]

The corollary to marriage, with or without true love, was motherhood, which added another dimension to her usefulness and her prestige. It also anchored her even more firmly to the home. "My Friend," wrote Mrs. Sigourney, "If in becoming a mother, you have reached the climax of your happiness, you have also taken a higher place in the scale of being . . . you have gained an increase of power."[106] The Rev. J. N. Danforth pleaded in *The Ladies' Casket,* "Oh, mother, acquit thyself well in thy humble sphere, for thou mayest affect the world."[107] A true woman naturally loved her children; to suggest otherwise was monstrous.[108]

America depended upon her mothers to raise up a whole generation of Christian statesmen who could say "all that I am I owe to my angel mother."[109] The mothers must do the inculcating of virtue since the fathers, alas, were too busy chasing the dollar. Or as *The Ladies' Companion* put it more effusively, the father "weary with the heat and burden of life's summer day, or trampling with unwilling foot the decaying leaves of life's autumn, has forgotten the sympathies of life's joyous springtime. . . . The acquisition of wealth, the advancement of his children in worldly honor—these are his self-imposed tasks." It was his wife who formed "the infant mind as yet untainted by contact with evil . . . like wax beneath the plastic hand of the mother."[110]

The Ladies' Wreath offered a fifty-dollar prize to the woman who submitted the most convincing essay on "How May An American Woman Best Show Her Patriotism." The winner was Miss Elizabeth Wetherell who provided herself with a husband in her answer. The wife in the essay of course asked her husband's opinion. He tried a few jokes first—"Call her eldest son George Washington," "Don't speak French, speak American"—but then got down to telling her in sober prize-winning truth what women could do for their country. Voting was no asset, since that would result only in "a vast increase of confusion and expense without in the smallest degree affecting the result." Besides, continued this oracle, "looking down at their child," if "we were to go a step further and let the children vote, their first act would be to vote their mothers at home." There is no comment on this devastating male logic and he continues: "Most women would follow the lead of their fathers and husbands," and the few who would "fly off on a tangent from the circle of home influence would cancel each other out."

The wife responds dutifully: "I see all that. I never understood so well before." Encouraged by her quick womanly perception, the master of the house resolves the question—an American woman best shows her patriotism by staying at home, where she brings her influence to bear "upon the right side for the country's weal." That woman will instinctively choose the side of right he has no doubt. Besides her "natural refinement and closeness to God" she has the "blessed advantage of a quiet life" while man is exposed to conflict and evil. She stays home with "her Bible and a well-balanced mind" and raises her sons to be good Americans. The judges rejoiced in this conclusion and paid the prize money cheerfully, remarking "they deemed it cheap at the price."[111]

If any woman asked for greater scope for her gifts the magazines were sharply critical. Such women were tampering with society, undermining civilization. Mary Wollstonecraft, Frances Wright and Harriet Martineau were condemned in the strongest possible language—they were read out of the sex. "They are only semi-women, mental hermaphrodites." The Rev. Harrington knew the women of America could not possibly approve of such perversions and went to some wives and mothers to ask if they did want a "wider sphere of interest" as these nonwomen claimed. The answer was reassuring. " 'NO!' they cried simultaneously, 'Let the men take care of politics, *we will take care of the children!*' " Again female discontent resulted only from a lack of understanding: women were not subservient, they were rather "chosen vessels." Looked at in this light the conclusion was inescapable: "Noble, sublime is the task of the American mother."[112]

"Women's Rights" meant one thing to reformers, but quite another to the True Woman. She knew her rights,

> The right to love whom others scorn,
> The right to comfort and to mourn,
> The right to shed new joy on earth,
> The right to feel the soul's high worth . . .

Such women's rights, and God will bless
And crown their champions with success.[113]

The American woman had her choice—she could define her rights in the way of the women's magazines and insure them by the practice of the requisite virtues, or she could go outside the home, seeking other rewards than love. It was a decision on which, she was told, everything in her world depended. "Yours it is to determine," the Rev. Mr. Stearns solemnly warned from the pulpit, "whether the beautiful order of society . . . shall continue as it has been" or whether "society shall break up and become a chaos of disjointed and unsightly elements."[114] If she chose to listen to other voices than those of her proper mentors, sought other rooms than those of her home, she lost both her happiness and her power—"that almost magic power, which, in her proper sphere, she now wields over the destinies of the world."[115]

But even while the women's magazines and related literature encouraged this ideal of the perfect woman, forces were at work in the nineteenth century which impelled woman herself to change, to play a more creative role in society. The movements for social reform, westward migration, missionary activity, utopian communities, industrialism, the Civil War—all called forth responses from woman which differed from those she was trained to believe were hers by nature and divine decree. The very perfection of True Womanhood, moreover, carried within itself the seeds of its own destruction. For if woman was so very little less than the angels, she should surely take a more active part in running the world, especially since men were making such a hash of things.

Real women often felt they did not live up to the ideal of True Womanhood: some of them blamed themselves, some challenged the standard, some tried to keep the virtues and enlarge the scope of womanhood.[116] Somehow through this mixture of challenge and acceptance, of change and continuity, the True Woman evolved into the New Woman—a transformation as startling in its way as the abolition of slavery or the coming of the machine age. And yet the stereotype, the "mystique" if you will, of what woman was and ought to be persisted, bringing guilt and confusion in the midst of opportunity.[117]

The women's magazines and related literature had feared this very dislocation of values and blurring of roles. By careful manipulation and interpretation they sought to convince woman that she had the best of both worlds—power and virtue—and that a stable order of society depended upon her maintaining her traditional place in it.

To that end she was identified with everything that was beautiful and holy.

"Who Can Find a Valiant Woman?" was asked frequently from the pulpit and the editorial pages. There was only one place to look for her—at home. Clearly and confidently these authorities proclaimed the True Woman of the nineteenth century to be the Valiant Woman of the Bible, in whom the heart of her husband rejoiced and whose price was above rubies.

Notes

1   Authors who addressed themselves to the subject of women in the mid-nineteenth century used this phrase as frequently as writers on religion mentioned God. Neither group felt it necessary to define their favorite terms; they simply assumed—with some justification—that readers would intuitively understand exactly what they meant. Frequently what people of one era take for granted is most striking and revealing to the student from another. In a sense this analysis of the ideal woman of the mid-neneteenth century is an examination of what writers of that period actually meant when they used so confidently the vague phrase True Womanhood.

2   The conclusions reached in this article are based on a survey of almost all of the women's magazines published for less than three years; all the gift books cited in Ralph Thompson, *American Literary Annuals and Gift Books, 1825–1865* (New York, 1936) deposited in the Library of Congress, the New York Public Library, the New York Historical Society, Columbia University Special Collections, Library of the City College of the University of New York, Pennsylvania Historical Society, Massachusetts Historical Society, Boston Public Library, Fruitlands Museum Library, the Smithsonian Institution and the Wisconsin Historical Society; hundreds of religious tracts and sermons in the American Unitarian Society and the Galatea Collection of the Boston Public Library; and the large collection of nineteenth-century cookbooks in the New York Public Library and the Academy of Medicine of New York. Corroborative evidence not cited in this article was found in women's diaries, memoirs, autobiographies and personal papers, as well as in all the novels by women which sold over 75,000 copies during this period, as cited in Frank Luthor Mott, *Golden Multitudes: The Story of Best Sellers in the United States* (New York, 1947) and H. R. Brown, *The Sentimental Novel in America, 1789–1860* (Durham, N. C., 1940). This latter information also indicated the effect of the cult of True Womanhood on those most directly concerned.

3   As in "The Bachelor's Dream," in *The Lady's Gift: Souvenir for All Seasons* (Nashua, N. H., 1849), p. 37.

4   *The Young Ladies' Class Book: A Selection of Lessons for Reading in Prose and Verse*, ed. Ebenezer Bailey, Principal of Young Ladies' High School, Boston (Boston, 1831), p. 168.

5   A Lady of Philadelphia, *The World Enlightened, Improved, and Harmonized by* WOMAN! ! ! A lecture, delivered in the City of New York, before the Young Ladies' Society for Mutual Improvement, on the following question, proposed by the society, with the offer of $100 for the best lecture that should be read before them on the subject proposed;—What is the power and influence of woman in moulding the manners, morals and habits of civil society? (Philadelphia, 1840), p. 1.

6   *The Young Lady's Book: A Manual of Elegant Recreations, Exercises, and Pursuits* (Boston, 1830), p. 29.

7   *Woman As She Was, Is, and Should Be* (New York, 1849), p. 206.

8   "The Triumph of the Spiritual Over the Sensual: An Allegory," in *Ladies' Companion: A Monthly Magazine Embracing Every Department of Literature, Embellished With Original Engravings and Music,* XVII (New York) (1842), 67.

9   *Lecture on Some of the Distinctive Characteristics of the Female,* delivered before the class of the Jefferson Medical College, Jan. 1847 (Philadelphia, 1847), p. 13.

10   "Female Education," *Ladies' Repository and Gatherings of the West: A Monthly Periodical Devoted to Literature and Religion,* I (Cincinnati), 12.

11   *Woman, in Her Social and Domestic Character* (Boston, 1842), pp. 41-42.

12   *Second Annual Report of the Young Ladies' Literary and Missionary Association of the Philadelphia Collegiate Institution* (Philadelphia, 1840), pp. 20, 26.

13   *Mt. Holyoke Female Seminary: Female Education. Tendencies of the Principles Embraced, and the System Adopted in the Mt. Holyoke Female Seminary* (Boston, 1839), p. 3.

14   *Prospectus of the Young Ladies' Seminary at Bordentown, New Jersey* (Bordentown, 1836), p. 7.

15   *Catalogue of the Young Ladies' Seminary in Keene, New Hampshire* (n.p., 1832), p. 20.

16   "Report to the College of Teachers, Cincinnati, October, 1840" in *Ladies' Repository,* I (1841), 50.

17   *Woman's Record: or Sketches of All Distinguished Women from 'The Beginning' Till A. D. 1850* (New York, 1853), pp. 665, 669.

18   "Female Irreligion," *Ladies' Companion,* XIII (May-Oct. 1840), 111.

19   *The Lady's Book of Flowers and Poetry,* ed. Lucy Hooper (New York, 1842), has a "Floral Dictionary" giving the symbolic meaning of floral tributes.

20   See, for example, Nathaniel Hawthorne, *The Blithedale Romance* (Boston, 1852), p. 71, in which Zenobia says: "How can she be happy, after discovering that fate has assigned her but one single event, which she must contrive to make the substance of her whole life? A man has his choice of innumerable events."

21   Mary R. Beard, *Woman As Force in History* (New York, 1946) makes this point at some length. According to common law, a woman had no legal existence once she was married and therefore could not manage property, sue in court, etc. In the 1840s and 1850s laws were passed in several states to remedy this condition.

22   *Excellency of the Female Character Vindicated: Being an Investigation Relative to the Cause and Effects on the Enroachments of Men Upon the Rights of Women, and the Too Frequent Degradation and Consequent Misfortunes of The Fair Sex* (New York, 1807), pp. 277, 278.

23   By a Lady (Eliza Ware Rotch Farrar), *The Young Lady's Friend* (Boston, 1837), p. 293.

24 *Girlhood and Womanhood: or, Sketches of My Schoolmates* (Boston, 1844), p. 140.

25 Emily Chubbuck, *Alderbrook* (Boston, 1847), 2nd. ed., II, 121, 127.

26 *Woman and Her Era* (New York, 1864), p. 95.

27 "The Two Lovers of Sicily," *The Lady's Amaranth: A Journal of Tales, Essays, Excerpts—Historical and Biographical Sketches, Poetry and Literature in General* (Philadelphia), II (Jan. 1839), 17.

28 *The Young Man's Guide* (Boston, 1833), pp. 229, 231.

29 *Female Influence: and the True Christian Mode of Its Exercise; a Discourse Delivered in the First Presbyterian Church in Newburyport, July 30, 1837* (Newburyport, 1837), p. 18.

30 W. Tolles, "Woman The Creature of God and the Manufacturer of Society," *Ladies' Wreath* (New York), III (1852), 205.

31 Prof. William M. Heim, "The Bloomer Dress," *Ladies' Wreath*, III (1852), 247.

32 *The Young Lady's Offering: or Gems of Prose and Poetry* (Boston, 1853), p. 283. The American girl, whose innocence was often connected with ignorance, was the spiritual ancestress of the Henry James heroine. Daisy Miller, like Lucy Dutton, saw innocence lead to tragedy.

33 *The Mother's Book* (Boston, 1831), pp. 151,152.

34 Mrs. L. H. Sigourney, *Whisper to a Bride* (Hartford, 1851), in which Mrs. Sigourney's approach is summed up in this quotation: "Home! Blessed bride, thou art about to enter this sanctuary, and to become a priestess at its altar!," p. 44.

35 S. R. R., "Female Charms," *Godey's Magazine and Lady's Book* (Philadelphia), XXXIII (1846), 52.

36 Charles Elliot, "Arguing With Females," *Ladies' Repository,* I (1841), 25.

37 *Ladies' Companion,* VIII (Jan. 1838), 147.

38 *The Young Lady's Book* (New York, 1830), American edition, p. 28. (This is a different book than the one of the same title and date of publication cited in note 6.)

39 *Sphere and Duties of Woman* (5th ed., Baltimore, 1854), p. 47.

40 *Woman,* p. 15.

41 *Letters to Young Ladies* (Hartford, 1835), p. 179.

42 *Lecture,* p. 17.

43 *The Young Lady's Friend,* p. 313.

44 Maria J. McIntosh, *Woman in America: Her Work and Her Reward* (New York, 1850), p. 25.

45 *Poems and a Memoir of the Life of Mrs. Felicia Hemans* (London, 1860), p. 16.

46 Letter "To an Unrecognized Poetess, June, 1846" (Sara Jane Clarke), *Greenwood Leaves* (2nd ed.; Boston, 1850), p. 311.

47 "The Sculptor's Assistant: Ann Flaxman," in *Women of Worth: A Book for Girls* (New York, 1860), p. 263.

48 Mrs. Clarissa Packard (Mrs. Caroline Howard Gilman), *Recollections of a Housekeeper* (New York, 1834), p. 122.

49 *Recollections of a Southern Matron* (New York, 1838), pp. 256, 257.

50 *The Lady's Token: or Gift of Friendship,* ed. Colesworth Pinckney (Nashua, N. H., 1848), p. 119.

51 Harvey Newcomb, *Young Lady's Guide to the Harmonious Development of Christian Character* (Boston, 1846), p. 10.

52 "Rules for Conjugal and Domestic Happiness," *Mother's Assistant and Young Lady's Friend,* III (Boston), (April 1843), 115.

53 *Letters to Mothers* (Hartford, 1838), p. 199. In the diaries and letters of women who lived during this period the death of a child seemed consistently to be the hardest thing for them to bear and to occasion more anguish and rebellion, as well as eventual submission, than any other event in their lives.

54 "A Submissive Mother," *The Ladies' Parlor Companion: A Collection of Scattered Fragments and Literary Gems* (New York, 1852), p. 358.

55 "Woman," *Godey's Lady's Book,* II (Aug. 1831), 110.

56 *Sphere and Duties of Woman,* p. 172.

57 Ralph Waldo Emerson, "Woman," *Complete Writings of Ralph Waldo Emerson* (New York, 1875), p. 1180.

58 As in Donald Fraser, *The Mental Flower Garden* (New York, 1857). Perhaps the most famous exponent of this theory is Edgar Allan Poe who affirms in "The Philosophy of Composition" that "the death of a beautiful woman is unquestionably the most poetical topic in the world. . . ."

59 "Domestic and Social Claims on Woman," *Mother's Magazine,* VI (1846), 21.

60 *Woman,* p. 173.

61 *The Young Ladies' Class Book,* p. 166.

62 T. S. Arthur, *The Lady at Home: or, Leaves from the Every-Day Book of an American Woman* (Philadelphia, 1847), pp. 177, 178.

63 Caspar Morris, *Margaret Mercer* (Boston, 1840), quoted in *Woman's Record,* p. 425.

64 These particular titles come from: *The Young Ladies' Oasis: or Gems of Prose and Poetry,* ed. N. L. Ferguson (Lowell, 1851), pp. 14, 16; *The Genteel School Reader* (Philadelphia, 1849), p. 271; and *Magnolia,* I (1842), 4. A popular poem in book form, published in England, expressed very fully this concept of woman as comforter:

Coventry Patmore, *The Angel in the Home* (Boston, 1856 and 1857). Patmore expressed his devotion to True Womanhood in such lines as:

> The gentle wife, who decks his board
> And makes his day to have no night,
> Whose wishes wait upon her Lord,
> Who finds her own in his delight. (p. 94)

65 The women's magazines carried on a crusade against tight lacing and regretted, rather than encouraged, the prevalent ill health of the American woman. See, for example, *An American Mother, Hints and Sketches* (New York, 1839), pp. 28 ff. for an essay on the need for a healthy mind in a healthy body in order to better be a good example for children.

66 The best single collection of nineteenth-century cookbooks is in the Academy of Medicine of New York Library, although some of the most interesting cures were in hand-written cookbooks found among the papers of women who lived during the period.

67 Sarah Josepha Hale, *The Ladies' New Book of Cookery: A Practical System for Private Families in Town and Country* (5th ed.; New York, 1852), p. 409. Similar evidence on the importance of nursing skills to every female is found in such books of advice as William A. Alcott, *The Young Housekeeper* (Boston, 1838), in which, along with a plea for apples and cold baths, Alcott says "Every female should be trained to the angelic art of managing properly the sick," p. 47.

68 *The Young Lady's Friend,* pp. 75-77, 79.

69 "A Tender Wife," *Godey's,* II (July 1831), 28.

70 "MY WIFE! A Whisper," *Godey's,* II (Oct. 1831), 231.

71 *Letters to Young Ladies,* p. 27. The greatest exponent of the mental and moral joys of housekeeping was the *Lady's Annual Register and Housewife's Memorandum Book* (Boston, 1838), which gave practical advice on ironing, hair curling, budgeting and marketing, and turning cuffs—all activities which contributed to the "beauty of usefulness" and "joy of accomplishment" which a woman desired (I, 23).

72 *The Young Lady's Friend,* p. 230.

73 "Learning vs. Housewifery," *Godey's,* X (Aug. 1839), 95.

74 *Letters to Young Ladies,* p. 25. W. Thayer, *Life at the Fireside* (Boston, 1857), has an idyllic picture of the woman of the house mending her children's garments, the grandmother knitting and the little girl taking her first stitches, all in the light of the domestic hearth.

75 "The Mirror's Advice," *Young Maiden's Mirror* (Boston, 1858), p. 263.

76 Mrs. L. Maria Child, *The Girl's Own Book* (New York, 1833).

77 P. 44.

78 T. S. Arthur, *Advice to Young Ladies* (Boston, 1850), p. 45.

79　R. C. Waterston, *Thoughts on Moral and Spiritual Culture* (Boston, 1842), p. 101. Newcomb's *Young Lady's Guide* also advised religious biography as the best reading for women (p. 111).

80　*Godey's*, I (1828), 1. (Repeated often in *Godey's* editorials.)

81　*The Lily of the Valley*, n. v. (1851), p. 2.

82　For example, "The Fatalist," *Godey's*, IV (Jan. 1834), 10, in which Somers Dudley has Catherine reading these dangerous books until life becomes "a bewildered dream. . . . O passion, what a shocking perverter of reason thou art!"

83　Review of *Society in America* (New York, 1837) in *American Quarterly Review* (Philadelphia), XXII (Sept. 1837), 38.

84　"A Finished Education," *Ladies' Museum* (Providence), I (1825), 42.

85　Helen Irving, "Literary Women," *Ladies' Wreath*, III (1850), 93.

86　"Women of Genius," *Ladies' Companion*, XI (1839), 89.

87　"Intellect vs. Affection in Woman," *Godey's*, XVI (1846), 86.

88　"The Only Daughter," *Godey's*, X (Mar. 1839), 122.

89　*The Annual Catalogue of the Officers and Pupils of the Young Ladies' Seminary and Collegiate Institute* (Monroe City, 1855), pp. 18, 19.

90　*Chronicles of a Pioneer School* from 1792 to 1833: Being the History of Miss Sarah Pierce and Her Litchfield School, Compiled by Emily Noyes Vanderpoel; ed. Elizabeth C. Barney Buel (Cambridge, 1903), p. 74.

91　*Mt. Holyoke Female Seminary*, p. 13.

92　*The American Frugal Housewife* (New York, 1838), p. 111.

93　"Female Influence," in *The Ladies' Pearl and Literary Gleaner: A Collection of Tales, Sketches, Essays, Anecdotes, and Historical Incidents* (Lowell), I (1841), 10.

94　Mrs. S. T. Martyn, "The Wife," *Ladies' Wreath*, II (1848-49), 171.

95　*The Young Ladies' Oasis*, p. 26.

96　"On Marriage," *Ladies' Repository*, I (1841), 133; "Old Maids," *Ladies' Literary Cabinet* (Newburyport), II (1822) (Microfilm), 141; "Matrimony," *Godey's*, II (Sept. 1831), 174; and "Married or Single," *Peterson's Magazine* (Philadelphia) IX (1859), 36, all express the belief that while marriage is desirable for a woman it is not essential. This attempt to reclaim the status of the unmarried woman is an example of the kind of mild crusade which the women's magazines sometimes carried on. Other examples were their strictures against an overly genteel education and against the affectation and aggravation of ill health. In this sense the magazines were truly conservative, for they did not oppose all change but only that which did violence to some cherished tradition. The reforms they advocated would, if put into effect, make woman even more the perfect female, and enhance the ideal of True Womanhood.

97　*Girlhood and Womanhood*, p. 100. Mrs. Graves tells the stories in the book in the person of an "Old Maid" and her conclusions are that "single life has its happiness too" for the single woman "can enjoy all the pleasures of maternity without its pains and trials" (p. 140). In another one of her books, *Woman in America* (New York, 1843), Mrs. Graves speaks out even more strongly in favor of "single blessedness" rather than "a loveless or unhappy marriage" (p. 130).

98   A very unusual story is Lela Linwood, "A Chapter in the History of a Free Heart," *Ladies' Wreath*, III (1853), 349. The heroine, Grace Arland, is "sublime" and dwells "in perfect light while we others struggle yet with the shadows." She refuses marriage and her friends regret this but are told her heart "is rejoicing in its *freedom.*" The story ends with the plaintive refrain:

> But is it not a happy thing,
> All fetterless and free,
> Like any wild bird, on the wing,
> To carol merrily?

But even in this tale the unusual, almost unearthly rarity of Grace's genius is stressed; she is not offered as an example to more mortal beings.

99   Horace Greeley even went so far as to apply this remedy to the "dissatisfactions" of Margaret Fuller. In his autobiography, *Recollections of a Busy Life* (New York, 1868) he says that "noble and great as she was, a good husband and two or three bouncing babies would have emancipated her from a deal of cant and nonsense" (p. 178).

100   *Sphere and Duties of Woman*, p. 64.

101   *A Sermon: Preached March 13, 1808, for the Benefit of the Society Instituted in the City of New-York, For the Relief of Poor Widows with Small Children* (New York, 1808), pp. 13, 14.

102   *Lady's Magazine and Museum: A Family Journal* (London) IV (Jan. 1831), 6. This magazine is included partly because its editorials proclaimed it "of interest to the English speaking lady at home and abroad" and partly because it shows that the preoccupation with True Womanhood was by no means confined to the United States.

103   *Sphere and Duties of Woman*, p. 102

104   "Matrimony," *Lady's Amaranth*, II (Dec. 1839), 271.

105   Elizabeth Doten, "Marrying for Money," *The Lily of the Valley*, n. v. (1857), p. 112.

106   *Letters to Mothers*, p. 9.

107   "Maternal Relation," *Ladies' Casket* (New York, 1850?), p. 85. The importance of the mother's role was emphasized abroad as well as in America. *Godey's* recommended the book by the French author Aimeé-Martin on the education of mothers to "be read five times," in the original if possible (XIII, Dec. 1842, 201). In this book the highest ideals of True Womanhood are upheld. For example: "Jeunes filles, jeunes épouses, tendres mères, c'est dans votre âme bien plus que dans les lois du législateur que reposent aujourd'hui l'avenir de l'Europe et les destinées du genre humain," L. Aimée-Martin, *De l'Education des Meres de famille ou De la civilisation du genre humain par les femmes* (Bruxelles, 1857), II, 527.

The Cult of True Womanhood 249

108   *Maternal Association of the Amity Baptist Church:* Annual Report (New York, 1847), p. 2: "Suffer the little children to come unto me and forbid them not, is and must ever be a sacred commandment to the Christian woman."

109   For example, Daniel Webster, "The Influence of Woman," in *The Young Ladies' Reader* (Philadelphia, 1851), p. 310.

110   Mrs. Emma C. Embury, "Female Education," *Ladies' Companion,* VIII (Jan. 1838), 18. Mrs. Embury stressed the fact that the American woman was not the "mere plaything of passion" but was in strict training to be "the mother of statesmen."

111   "How May An American Woman Best Show Her Patriotism?" *Ladies' Wreath,* III (1851), 313. Elizabeth Wetherell was the pen name of Susan Warner, author of *The Wide Wide World* and *Queechy.*

112   Henry F. Harrington, "Female Education," *Ladies' Companion,* IX (1838), 293, and "Influence of Woman—Past and Present," *Ladies' Companion,* XIII (1840), 245.

113   Mrs. E. Little, "What Are the Rights of Women?" *Ladies' Wreath,* II (1848-49), 133.

114   *Female Influence,* p. 18.

115   *Ibid.,* p. 23.

116   Even the women reformers were prone to use domestic images, i.e., "sweep Uncle Sam's kitchen clean," and "tidy up our country's house."

117   The "Animus and Anima" of Jung amounts almost to a catalogue of the nineteenth-century masculine and female traits, and the female hysterics whom Freud saw had much of the same training as the nineteenth-century American woman. Betty Friedan, *The Feminine Mystique* (New York, 1963), challenges the whole concept of True Womanhood as it hampers the "fulfillment" of the twentieth-century woman.

Just how frail the cult of "true womanhood" was is seen in O'Neill's discussion of divorce in the Progressive Era. Divorce might be thought of as a good indicator of women's status, since it obviously involves a return to single status of women whose potential as marriage candidates is to some extent reduced, if only because of age. In a time when women were totally subservient economically to men, the divorce rate would out of necessity be low, but what the increase in divorce in the second half of the nineteenth century meant was that women were becoming more and more independent and capable of standing on their own feet when a marriage failed. O'Neill quotes George Howard to the effect that these increases did not reflect any rending of the nation's moral fiber; instead they reflected a new and perhaps better conception of what marriage should and could be, and a willingness to disengage when an existing relationship failed to meet this standard. What should be kept in mind here is that the new standard recognized that women had rights and needs of their own, and while it did not at all grant them equality with men, it at least gave them the means to sever an unsatisfying relationship.

WILLIAM L. O'NEILL

13 Divorce in the Progressive Era

During the Progressive years the divorce rate, which had been rising steadily since the Civil War, attained critical dimensions. Consequently, Americans of this period took a graver view of the problem than any subsequent generation. Their varied responses proved to be decisive as far as the future of divorce itself was concerned, and they illuminate aspects of the Progressive Era which have received little attention from historians.

The precipitate growth of the divorce rate can be easily demonstrated. In 1880 there was one divorce for every twenty-one marriages; in 1900 there was one divorce for every twelve marriages; in 1909 the ratio dropped to one in ten, and by 1916 it stood at one in nine.[1] Naturally this dramatic increase in the divorce rate stimulated public alarm.

In 1881 the New England Divorce Reform League was established to conduct research on family problems, educate the public and lobby for more effective legislative curbs on divorce.[2] Under the leadership of Samuel Dike, a Congregational minister, the league enjoyed a long and useful life, but Dike's reluctance to advance legislative solutions to the divorce problem failed to deter others from resorting to politics.

Efforts to arrest the spread of divorce by legal means took two forms. State campaigns were waged to amend local divorce laws, and repeated attempts were made to achieve uniform marriage and divorce laws either through a constitutional amendment or through the voluntary enactment of uniform codes by the several states.[3] Typical of the many local fights to alter state divorce laws was the successful battle in 1893 to end South Dakota's status as a divorce colony. After their admission to the Union in 1889 North and South Dakota retained Dakota Territory's generous ninety-day residence requirement. Sioux City, largest and most accessible town in the two states, soon developed a substantial divorce trade and gained national fame as a divorce colony. The resulting notoriety provoked local resentment which was mobilized by the return from Japan of the popular Episcopal Bishop William Hobart Hare, who in 1893 led Protestants, Catholics and Populists in an attack on the ninety-day residence requirement. The state legislature was successfully petitioned to extend the residence requirement to six months and the migratory divorce trade was diverted to North Dakota.[4]

The South Dakota campaign conformed to what was already an established pattern. It was led by conservative clergymen, supported by women's groups, and met little apparent opposition. Although these local campaigns did not succeed anywhere in abolishing divorce, they were part of a widespread tendency toward stricter divorce legislation.[5] When such local crusades failed, it was usually because of public apathy, sometimes coupled with undercover resistance from commercial and legal interests which profited from the divorce trade.

Serious attempts to secure uniform marriage and divorce legislation through a constitutional amendment began in 1892 when James Kyle, the Populist Senator from South Dakota, introduced a joint resolution which read in full: "The Congress shall have the exclusive power to regulate marriage and divorce in the several states, Territories, and the District of Columbia."[6] Senator Kyle's resolution died in committee as did all later resolutions, presumably because of a disinclination on the part of Congress to increase the power of the Federal government at the expense of the states.[7]

More popular, if equally unsuccessful, was the movement to secure voluntary uniformity through the drafting of model statutes which were to be enacted by the states. The most persistent of the organizations dedicated to this goal was the National Conference of Commissioners on Uniform State Laws, which met annually in connection with the American Bar Association. It was established by the Bar Association in 1889 to frame model codes on a wide range of subjects. The Commissioners were usually appointed by their state governors, and over the years drafted seven model statutes concerning marriage and divorce.[8] However, few of the states demonstrated an interest in these models, and by 1916 the Commissioners were forced to admit that their approach had been a failure.

If the experience of the National Conference of Commissioners on Uniform State Laws to 1906 had not been conclusive, the fate of the National Divorce Congress in that year was. A national meeting to draft uniform legislation had been talked about for years on the grounds that it would attract sufficient attention to succeed where the more diffident Commissioners had failed. In 1906 President Roosevelt was persuaded to request a new census study of marriage and divorce, and the interest aroused by this led Governor Pennypacker of Pennsylvania to call a national conference to draft model uniform legislation on these subjects. The Congress met twice, once in Washington to appoint committees, and again in Philadelphia to ratify the proposed statutes. The first meeting was attended by delegates from 42 of the 45 states and consisted largely of clergymen and lawyers, many of the latter having also been members of the NCCUSL. Despite the widespread approval which met their efforts, few states adopted their model statutes.[9]

The antidivorce forces were also active within the established Protestant churches. During the Progressive Era repeated efforts were made in almost all the great Protestant denominations to stiffen their positions on divorce. The Episcopal church, traditionally more hostile to divorce than most Protestant bodies, was in the van of this movement, thanks principally to William Croswell Doane, Bishop of Albany, New York. Doane was perhaps the most vocal and consistent enemy of divorce in the whole country. He favored prohibiting divorce altogether, and his activities within the Episcopal church were directed at the canon which allowed the innocent party in an adultery suit to remarry. This canon was only slightly less severe than the refusal of the Roman Catholic church to allow any divorced person to remarry, but it seemed dangerously lax to Doane and he regularly introduced an amendment which would have denied the sacraments to all divorced persons without exception.

In 1898 the House of Bishops, usually more conservative than the lower House, which included laymen, at the policy-making Triennial Convention, rejected Doane's amendment 31 to 24.[10] In 1901 his amendment was defeated by a narrower margin, but in 1904 it passed the House of Bishops only to fail in the House of Deputies, whose members felt that it was too far removed from the spirit of the country.[11] Thereafter enthusiasm within the Episcopal church for the Doane amendment declined, and while it was reintroduced at later conventions, it failed to pass even in the House of Bishops. Similar efforts were made in the other Protestant denominations with what proved to be an equal lack of success.[12]

American attitudes toward marriage and divorce during the Progressive years must be seen in terms of the widespread fear of divorce demonstrated by these examples. It is not too much to say that there was a national crisis generated by divorce. It was a crisis to begin with because people believed it was. As Daniel Bell has demonstrated in his *The End of Ideology,* it is not necessary for activities seen to be antisocial actually to increase in order to create a crisis atmosphere— it is enough if people simply believe that such activities are increasing.[13]

An even better example perhaps was the white slave panic of 1912–13. If anything, prostitution was declining, but irrespective of the facts, widespread public alarm over this presumed social evil was triggered by local investigations and newspaper publicity.[14]

However, divorce actually was increasing by leaps and bounds. When one marriage in twelve ended in divorce, there were legitimate grounds for concern. These were crucial years for divorce, finally, because the Progressive period was the last time when public opinion could reasonably have been expected to support genuinely repressive action. With the 1920s and the advent of the revolution in morals the opportunity to abolish or seriously restrict divorce was lost forever. Some of the antidivorce leaders sensed that time was running out for them, and this awareness gave their strictures an urgent tone which became more shrill with the years.

Although divorce had political, psychological and other dimensions, the increase of divorce was usually seen as a moral and social problem.[15] It is difficult, if indeed not actually pointless, to try to determine which of these two aspects alarmed critics of divorce the most. The enemies of divorce invariably regarded it as both immoral and antisocial. Since most opponents of divorce were either clergymen or strongly religious people, it seems fair to assume that the moral side of the divorce question was what first engaged their attention, but having once declared divorce to be immoral, there is little more one can say in that direction, and most of the serious attacks on divorce emphasized its antisocial character.[16]

The attack on divorce hinged on the common belief that divorce destroyed the family, which was the foundation of society and civilization. Theodore Schmauk, editor of the *Lutheran Church Review*, President of the Lutheran General Council and a leading theologian, characterized the family as "the great and fundamental institution in social life."[17] *The Catholic World* in an attack on H. G. Wells' view of divorce felt that it had demolished his position when it observed that Wells failed to see that the family "was the cradle of civil society."[18] Lyman Abbott, an influential Progressive editor and associate of Theodore Roosevelt, once charged a prominent divorcee with being "the worst type of anarchist" because divorce, like anarchy, threatened to destroy society altogether.[19] President Roosevelt, in addressing Congress on the need for uniform legislation, described marriage as being "at the very foundation of our social organization. . . ."[20] Marriage and the family are, of course, quite different institutions, but the critics of divorce did not usually distinguish between them.

Felix Adler took this contention a step further when he insisted that divorce menaced "the physical and spiritual existence of the human race. . . ."[21] Adler was in some ways a surprising figure to find on this side of the divorce question. The founder of Ethical Culture and a leading advocate of liberal religion, he consistently attacked dogma and orthodoxy and supported a wide variety of social reforms.[22] He had earlier supported divorce, but by 1915 had changed his mind and accepted the point, usually advanced by the theologically orthodox, that divorce had to be suppressed as a matter of social survival. His conversion showed how this argument operated independently of its conservative religious base, and helps to explain why some enemies of divorce attached such importance to their campaign. One could hardly play for higher stakes.

A related theme which engaged the attention of divorce critics was the role of woman. It was generally believed that the family was woman's special responsibility and its protection her primary concern. Moreover women were thought to be more active than men in securing divorces (and they probably were since about two-thirds of all divorces were awarded to women). *The North American Review* reflected this point of view when it entitled one of its divorce symposiums, "Are Women to Blame?"[23] The *Review*'s female panelists charged women with responsibility for the divorce rate, and accused them of being spoiled, romantic, impatient, jealous of men and usurpers of the male's time-honored functions. Many of these women were successful writers, as was Anna B. Rogers, a popular essayist, who repeated the same charges in her book, *Why American Marriages Fail,* nineteen years later.[24]

While the critics of divorce, especially the men, were inclined to argue that women were really happier when they stayed at home and held the family together, the more tough-minded accepted the fact that the woman's traditional role was often painful and difficult.[25] Few had a clearer picture of what was involved than the respected novelist Margaret Deland. Mrs. Deland was a warm supporter of many Progressive causes and a woman with courage enough to defend the rights of unwed mothers in Victorian Boston. But she believed that civilization "rests on the permanence of marriage."[26] For this reason women dared not turn to divorce, for it would mean the end of everything. "If we let the flame of idealism be quenched in the darkness of the senses," she cried, "our civilization must go upon the rocks."[27] Even adultery was no excuse for giving up the fight, she continued, because men were instinctively promiscuous and their lapses from grace had to be tolerated for the sake of the greater good.

Implicit in these arguments was the belief that the individual was less important than the group. Most opponents of divorce agreed that divorce was part of an unwholesome tendency toward a "dangerous individualism." Margaret Deland bewailed the absence of team-play among women and Professor Lawton called frankly for the "suppression of the individual in favor of the community."[28] Samuel Dike in his Cook Lecture attributed divorce to the rising tide of individualism menacing all progressive societies, while Felix Adler as early as 1890 was tracing the whole ugly business back to Rousseau's "false democratic ideals."[29] Although, as we shall see, most leading sociologists believed in divorce, Charles A. Ellwood did not. This future president of the American Sociological Society, despite his Progressive sympathies, also attributed divorce to excessive individualism.[30] Francis Peabody, an eminent theologian and student of the Higher Criticism, believed that the family's major enemies were scientific socialism and "the reactionary force of self-interested individualism. . . ."[31]

The opponents of divorce were more varied and had much more to say than I have been able to indicate, but the foregoing gives at least some idea of who they were and what they thought. The defenders of divorce, by way of contrast, were fewer in number and easier to locate. Opinion against divorce was so widespread and diffuse that it cannot be attributed to a handful of groups, but the sentiment favoring divorce was largely confined to sociologists, liberal clergymen and feminists. The defenders of divorce, like its enemies, viewed the problem primarily in moral and social terms. But unlike the critics of divorce, its supporters, who were with few exceptions liberals, were much more interested in the morality of divorce and more inclined to see its moral and social dimensions as too interrelated for separate discussion and analysis.

The case for divorce gained initial momentum in the 1880s and 1890s when a trickle of protest against Victorian marriage began to make itself heard. The plays of Henrik Ibsen, especially *A Doll's House* (1879) and *Ghosts* (1881), were affecting English audiences in the late 1880s and American opinion somewhat later. By the 1890s a number of Englishmen were attacking marriage and the views of Mona Caird and Grant Allen became well known in the United States through their own writings, and through the publicity given their ideas by the American press. Mona Caird was a feminist whose essays appeared for the most part in high-quality limited circulation periodicals. Her most controversial proposal was an attempt to substitute for divorce short-term marriage contracts whose expiration would leave both parties free to separate or to negotiate a new contract.[32]

Grant Allen's best-known statement on the question was a sensational novel boosting feminism and free love entitled *The Woman Who Did*.[33] Allen was really calling for an end to marriage altogether, but his polemics against the institution supported divorce as much as free love. Within a few years the radical attack on marriage enlisted such big guns as H. G. Wells, who in a characteristically exuberant preview of the future in 1901 announced that monogamy was dissolving and sexual standards relaxing to the point where in a hundred years the present moral code "would remain nominally operative in sentiment and practice, while being practically disregarded. . . ."[34] Marriage was also under fire from the new moralists like the mystical Edward Carpenter, Havelock Ellis and his wife Edith, and the South African feminist Olive Schreiner, among others.[35]

The effect of this stream of marriage propaganda was to invigorate and inspire those Americans who believed in the right to divorce. Few respectable Americans were prepared to go as far as new moralists like Wells and Carpenter, but a substantial number of liberals were beginning to feel that traditional marriage was needlessly tyrannical and repressive, that it discriminated against women, and that divorce was not only an escape hatch for abused women, but offered real opportunities for a reform of the whole marriage system. At the bottom of most, if not all, of this sentiment was the feminist impulse, for most divorce liberals were acutely conscious of the usefulness of divorce as an instrument for the emancipation of women.

Unlike the new moralists whose feminism was concerned with freeing women for a fuller sex life, the American feminist was inclined to defend divorce because it freed women from sex. Benjamin O. Flower, who edited the populistic *Arena,* called for easier divorce laws as a way of protecting women from the excessive sexual appetites of their husbands. He argued that the common prostitute was "far freer than the wife who is nightly the victim of the unholy passion of her master. . . ."[36] By 1914 this argument had become so familiar that it was thought fit for the respectable readers of the cautious *Good Housekeeping* magazine. In that year Jesse Lynch Williams, feminist and playwright, asked rhetorically, "is allowing herself to be owned body and soul by a man she loathes doing right?" before going on to delicately suggest "that seems rather like a dishonorable institution more ancient than marriage."[37]

Many feminists contended that not only did traditional marriage make women the sexual victims of their husbands, but it also exaggerated the importance of sex by denying women the chance to develop their other traits of character through work and education, and by forcing them to compete in the marriage market largely on the basis of their sexual attractions. The most desirable women had the best marital opportunities and so, through a kind of natural selection, sexuality prospered at the expense of other attributes. Divorce, along with expanded opportunities for education and employment, was a way of combatting this pernicious tendency.[38]

If the impulse to defend divorce came first from feminists who agreed with Elizabeth Cady Stanton on the need for a "larger freedom in the marriage relation," social scientists performed a crucial service in coping with the public's fear of the social consequences of divorce.[39] The first man of stature to defend divorce was Carrol Wright, U.S. Commissioner of Labor Statistics and a self-trained social scientist, who at the national Unitarian convention in 1891 boldly declared himself for liberal divorce laws. A few years later he wrote:

> The pressure for divorce finds its impetus outside of laws, outside of our institutions, outside of our theology; it springs from the rebellion of the human heart against that slavery which binds in the cruelest bonds human beings who have by their haste, their want of wisdom, or the

intervention of friends, missed the divine purpose as well as the civil purpose of marriage.[40]

But it was not until 1904 that a leading professionally trained social scientist joined the fight. In his massive *A History of Matrimonial Institutions* and subsequent writings George E. Howard, an eminent historian and sociologist, tried to show how the divorce rate was the product of forces which were dramatically improving American society.[41] He argued that industrialization, urbanization and the other pressures which were breaking up the old patriarchal family produced not only more divorces, but a new kind of marriage marked by higher spiritual standards and greater freedom. Closing with the problem of individualism which so alarmed the enemies of divorce, he declared that the growing power of the state was tending to make the individual and not the family the functional unit of society and that this process not only freed the individual from familial authoritarianism but elevated the family by abolishing its coercive power and transforming it into a "spiritual and psychic association of parent and child based on persuasion."[42]

Within a few years Wright and Howard were joined by a host of social scientists including most of the leading men in the field.[43] The weight of sociological opinion was solidly on the side of divorce by 1908 when the American Sociological Society devoted its third annual meeting to the family.[44] President William G. Sumner, the crusty, aging president of the society who had done so much to establish sociology as an academic discipline, opened the proceedings by observing gloomily that "the family has to a great extent lost its position as a conservative institution and has become a field for social change."[45] The program of the convention confirmed Sumner's fears for virtually every paper described the changes affecting the family, called for more changes, or did both. Charlotte P. Gilman read a paper summarizing her *Women and Economics,* and a group of papers dealt with the damage inflicted on the family by urban, industrial life.[46]

The high point of the meeting was George Howard's "Is the Freer Granting of Divorce an Evil?" Howard repeated his now familiar views and touched off a controversy which showed the drift of professional opinion.[47] He was attacked by Samuel Dike, who insisted that divorce was produced by a dangerous individualism and the decline of ideals, and by Walter George Smith. Smith was a prominent Catholic lawyer who had advocated stricter divorce laws for many years and was a leader in the campaign for uniform divorce legislation. His criticisms stressed divorce's incompatibility with orthodox religion and he accused Howard of condoning a social revolution that destroyed the divinely constituted order of things. Nothing, he declared, could alter the fact of feminine inferiority. Howard replied that marriage was a purely social institution "to be freely dealt with by men according to human needs."[48]

Despite this unusually spirited clash, Smith and his friends were making an illusory show of strength. The moralistic flavor of their language, so different in tone from Howard's, revealed their professional isolation. Theirs was the faintly anachronistic rhetoric of a discredited tradition of social criticism. The opponents of Howard's position were, moreover, all laymen with the exception of President Sumner and Albion Small, while on his side were ranged most of the speakers, including E. A. Ross, James Lichtenberger and other leading scientists. As a profession then, sociology was committed to a positive view of divorce at a time when virtually every other organized group in the country was opposed to it. But although heavily outnumbered, the sociologists were the only people who could claim to speak on the problem with expert authority, and in the Progressive Era expertise was coming to be highly valued. As experts, the social scientists conferred respectability on the cause of free divorce at the same time as they did much to allay public anxiety over its effects.

A final problem that remained for the divorce liberals was finding some way to weaken the general conviction that divorce was forbidden by the Bible, and to diminish the impact of the clergy's opposition to divorce. It was here that the handful of liberal ministers who supported divorce performed a signal, and indeed indispensable, service. Simply by saying that divorce was a morally acceptable device, the liberal ministers endowed it with a certain degree of legitimacy. If supporting divorce with their moral prestige was the more important function performed by the liberal ministers, some went beyond this and effectively disputed the traditional charge that the Bible specifically prohibited divorce.

One of the most impressive statements of the liberal position was delivered by William G. Ballentine, classicist, Bible scholar, onetime president of Oberlin College and for twenty years editor of the *Bibliotheca Sacra*. Ballentine argued that "even if all thoughtful Christian men were today united in a resolute purpose of conformity to the letter of Scripture the path of duty would be far from plain."[49] He pointed out that a Biblical injunction against divorce cited by Bishop Doane in a recent magazine article appeared in the same passage as the admonition to resist evil. How, he asked, were Christians to know which commandment to obey and which to ignore? Ballentine described the life of Jesus as a struggle against Talmudic literalism:

During His whole life, He fought against the tyranny of mere words, and for the lordship of the present living spiritual man. In his discourse He suggested great truths by parables, by questions, by metaphors, by paradoxes, by hyperboles, by every device that could elude the semblance of fixed judicial formulas. It is the irony of history that such language should be seized upon for statute law.[50]

Other scholars, theologians and Higher Critics attacked the presumed Biblical sanctions against divorce in different ways, but the effect of their work was to undercut the general belief that the Bible clearly forbade divorce.[51]

On a more popular level the Rev. Minot J. Savage declared that as love was the essence of marriage two people who no longer loved each other had every reason to get divorced.[52] This same conviction informed the writings of John H. Holmes, a great civil libertarian and advocate of liberal Christianity, who believed that the passing of love destroyed marriage in fact if not in name.[53]

Gradually the climate of opinion began to change. As noted earlier there was a substantial organized opposition to divorce during the Progressive period, but despite local victories, the movement to retard divorce by legal and political means was resoundingly unsuccessful. There were other signs which demonstrated that attitudes were being modified. Samuel Dike died in 1913 and his League expired shortly thereafter. It was essentially a one-man operation, but it was supported by the enemies of divorce, whose financial contributions had declined sharply even before his death, to the point where receipts after 1910 were about half of what they had been in the 1890s.[54] The Committee on the Family which was routinely formed by the Federal Council of Churches in 1911 was singularly inactive, and in 1919 it was dropped altogether.[55]

At the same time the solid wall of opposition to divorce maintained by the nation's press was repeatedly breached. Before 1900 no important American magazine defended the right to divorce except the radical *Arena*. Articles favorable to divorce were very rare in the general press. After about 1900, however, a few bold magazines like the *Independent* endorsed the right of divorce editorially, and many more began to print occasional articles defending divorce. The *North American Review*, which was more interested in the problem than any other major periodical, began the new century with a rousing attack on the opponents of divorce by the aging but still magnificent Elizabeth Cady Stanton.[56] Other magazines, too numerous to mention, also began to print articles favoring divorce. Even the uncompromisingly hostile *Outlook* unbent to this extent, and in 1910 it conceded editorially that there were times when divorce was permissible.[57] This shift influenced popular as well as serious magazines. In 1910 the slick monthly *World's Work* announced that "The True View of Increasing Divorce" was that the divorce rate was not alarming, and that divorces should not be subject to excessive restrictions.[58]

Obviously the changes in public opinion which these articles represented did not constitute a general recognition of the desirability of divorce. Although a few journals accepted the liberal argument that divorce was a therapeutic social mechanism, most did not. In many cases nothing more was involved than the admission that there were probably two sides to the question. This of itself, however, was a form of moral relativism on the issue which would have been unthinkable in the 1890s. This new tolerance of divorce coincided with the eruption of a number of curious phenomena like the dance craze and the white slave panic which marked the onset of the revolution in morals.[59]

Divorce was a part of the complex transformation of moral values and sexual customs which was to help give the 1920s their bizarre flavor. It was not only the most visible result of this vast social upheaval, but in many ways it was the most compatible with traditional modes of thought. It was, on the whole, an orderly, public and institutionalized process which took due account of the formal difference between right and wrong, guilt and innocence. It had the blessings of the highest sociological authorities, and it was recommended by many feminists as a cure for the brutalizing sexual indignities known to occur in some marriages. Conservatives could, therefore, more easily resign themselves to divorce than to other, more extravagant, demonstrations of the changing moral order.

Although divorce has today assumed proportions undreamed of in the Progressive Era, the nature of the American response to mass divorce was determined at that time. Between 1905, when the magnitude of divorce as a social problem had become fully apparent, and 1917, when the movement to limit or direct the spread of divorce had clearly failed, something of importance for American social history had occurred. This was the recognition by moral conservatives that they could not prevent the revolution in morals represented by mass divorce. Their failure of morale in the immediate prewar period paved the way for spectacular changes which took place after the war.

Notes

1 The definitive statistical study is Paul H. Jacobson, *American Marriage and Divorce* (New York, 1959). Two great government reports contain the raw materials —they are U. S. Bureau of Labor, *Marriage and Divorce 1867–1887* (1889), and the later more comprehensive U. S. Bureau of the Census, *Marriage and Divorce 1867–*

1906 (1909). Interesting contemporary analyses are contained in E. A. Ross, *Changing America* (New York, 1912) and William B. Bailey, *Modern Social Conditions* (New York, 1906).

2   Its origins are described in an untitled autobiographical manuscript by Samuel Warren Dike in the Dike Papers, Library of Congress.

3   The legal and political history of divorce is described very fully in Nelson Manfred Blake, *The Road to Reno* (New York, 1962).

4   See M. A. DeWolfe Howe, *The Life and Labors of Bishop Hare* (New York, 1912), *passim;* Blake, "Divorce in South Dakota," *Nation,* IX (January 26, 1893), 61.

5   National League for the Preservation of the Family, *Some Fundamentals of the Divorce Question* (Boston, 1909). A pamphlet written by Samuel Dike and published by his organization, which had undergone two changes of name since its founding, deals with these changes at some length. They involved extending the time required to obtain divorces, and limiting the causes for which they could be granted.

6   U. S. Congressional Record, 52 Cong., 1st Sess. (February 3, 1892), p. 791.

7   See Senator Shortridge's candid remarks to this effect during hearings on a similar resolution years later. *Senate Judiciary Committee,* "Hearings on S. J. Res. 31" (November 1, 1921), *passim.*

8   "Secretary's Memorandum," *Proceedings of the 26th Annual Meeting of the NCCUSL* (1916).

9   See Blake, 140–45, and *Proceedings of the Adjourned Meeting of the National Congress on Uniform Divorce Laws* (Harrisburg, Pa., 1907).

10   "The Canon on Marriage and Divorce," *Public Opinion,* October 27, 1898.

11   "Remarriage After Divorce," *Outlook,* October 22, 1904.

12   The positions of the principal denominations on divorce and the efforts to change them are summarized in James P. Lichtenberger, *Divorce: A Study in Social Causation* (New York, 1909), chap. vii.

13   Daniel Bell, "The Myth of Crime Waves" (New York, 1961), pp. 151–74.

14   Roy Lubove, "The Progressives and the Prostitute," *The Historian,* XXIV (May 1962), 308–29.

15   Generalizations of this sort which depend upon a close acquaintance with the popular literature are notoriously hard to document. My own conclusions are derived from an examination of almost everything dealing with marriage and divorce published either in book form or in more than thirty leading periodicals from 1889 through 1919. For details see my unpublished "The Divorce Crisis of the Progressive Era" (Doctor's dissertation, Berkeley, Calif., 1963).

16   By dismissing the moral side of the opposition to divorce so casually I do not mean to imply that it was not important, but only that it was unremarkable and required no detailed analysis. Divorce was considered immoral because it was forbidden by the New Testament, and because it encouraged lust. Naturally the clergymen who opposed divorce supported themselves with Scriptural citations. One of the most

elaborate efforts to relate divorce to licentiousness was Samuel Dike's first major address on the subject, reprinted in *Christ and Modern Thought: The Boston Monday Lectures 1880–81,* ed. Joseph Cook (Boston, 1882).

17 "The Right to Be Divorced," *Lutheran Church Review,* XXVIII (October 1909), 661.

18 W. E. Campbell, "Wells, the Family, and the Church," *Catholic World,* XCI (July 1910), 483.

19 "The Worst Anarchism," *Outlook,* August 11, 1906, p. 826.

20 Bureau of the Census, *Marriage and Divorce 1867–1906,* p. 4.

21 *Marriage and Divorce* (New York, 1915), p. 15.

22 Henry Neumann, *Spokesmen for Ethical Religion* (Boston, 1951), deals with Adler's career at some length.

23 Rebecca Harding Davis, Rose Terry Cooke, Marion Harland, Catherine Owen, Amelia E. Barr, *North American Review,* CXLVIII (May 1889).

24 Boston, 1909.

25 Among the frequent male efforts to sentimentalize over the role and nature of woman were Lyman Abbott, *Christianity and Social Problems* (Boston, 1896), and Robert Lawton, *The Making of a Home* (Boston, 1914).

26 "The Change in the Feminine Ideal," *Atlantic Monthly,* CV (March 1910), 295; see also her interesting autobiography *Golden Yesterdays* (New York, 1940).

27 *Ibid.,* p. 297.

28 *The Making of a Home,* p. 594.

29 "The Ethics of Divorce," *Ethical Record,* II (April 1890), 207.

30 *Sociology and Modern Social Problems* (New York, 1913).

31 *Jesus Christ and the Social Question* (New York, 1903), p. 145.

32 *The Morality of Marriage and Other Essays on the Status and Destiny of Women,* London, 1897. A collection of articles which had previously appeared in the *North American Review,* the *Fortnightly Review,* the *Westminster Review* and the *Nineteenth Century.* Typical of the American press's treatment of her ideas are "The Millenium of Marriage—Mona Caird's Views," *Current Literature,* XVI (July 1894), reprinted from the *Boston Herald.* "The Practice of Marriage," *Current Literature,* XVIII (October 1895), reprinted from the *Saturday Review.*

33 Boston, 1895.

34 "Anticipations; An Experiment in Prophecy—II," *North American Review,* CLXXIII (July 1901), 73–74.

35 Carpenter, *Love's Coming of Age* (New York, 1911). *Little Essays of Love and Virtue* (New York, 1921), summarized the ideas Havelock Ellis had been advocating for years and the *New Horizon in Love and Life* (London, 1921), contains the thoughts of his wife, who died in 1916. Schreiner, *Woman and Labor* (New York, 1911).

36 "Prostitution Within the Marriage Bond," *Arena,* XIII (June 1895), 68.

37 "The New Marriage," *Good Housekeeping,* LII (February 1914), 184.

38 Charlotte Perkins Gilman, *Women and Economics* (Boston, 1898), was an especially influential exposition of this point of view. For other information on this remarkable woman's life and work see Carl N. Degler's appreciative article, "Charlotte Perkins Gilman on the Theory and Practice of Feminism," *American Quarterly,* VIII (Spring 1956). See also Rheta Childe Dorr, *What Eight Million Women Want* (Boston, 1910), and C. Gasquoine Hartley, *The Truth About Women* (London, 1914).

39 "Divorce vs. Domestic Warfare," *Arena,* I (April 1890), 568. Alone of the great feminist leaders, Mrs. Stanton was a lifelong supporter of divorce, and in her later years it became one of her major interests. In this respect she was hardly a typical feminist, for while most divorce liberals were also feminists, they remained very much a minority within the women's movement.

40 *Outline of Practical Sociology* (New York, 1900), p. 176.

41 Chicago, 1904.

42 "Social Control and the Function of the Family," Congress of Arts and Sciences, *Proceedings,* VII (St. Louis, 1904), 701. This abbreviated summary may not bring out the markedly utopian flavor which permeated discussions on the family by liberal sociologists and feminists during the Progressive period. Indeed, they entertained hopes for the future of the family which seem fantastically imaginative by the standards of our own more somberly clinical age. This visionary strain in Progressive social thought has been underestimated by historians in recent years, especially by Richard Hofstadter, whose influential *The Age of Reform* (New York, 1955), ignores the role played by feminism and the new morality in shaping the Progressive mood.

43 So many statements were made on marriage and divorce by sociologists during these years that I can list only a few of them here. Walter F. Willcox, *The Divorce Problem* (New York, 1891), was a seminal monograph that laid the statistical base for most later studies of divorce, but which was not well known outside of the profession and did not have the impact of other works which were more widely publicized. Elsie Clews Parsons, *The Family* (New York, 1906), caused a minor sensation by calling for trial marriages. Mrs. Parsons was a student of Franz Boas and the most radical of the academicians who dealt with the problem. Arthur W. Calhoun, *A Social History of the American Family, From the Civil War* (Cleveland, 1919), Vol. III, was written from an avowedly socialist point of view and is still the only comprehensive work on the history of the American family.

44 *Papers and Proceedings of the American Sociological Society,* III (Chicago, 1909).

45 *Ibid.,* p. 15.

46 "How Home Conditions React Upon the Family," *Papers . . . of American Sociological Society,* pp. 16–29. Margaret F. Byington, "The Family in a Typical Mill Town," pp. 73–84. Edward T. Devine, "Results of the Pittsburgh Survey," pp. 85–92; Charles R. Henderson, "Are Modern Industry and City Life Unfavorable to the Family?" pp. 93–105, among others.

47 *Papers . . . of American Sociological Society,* pp. 150–60.

48 *Ibid.,* p. 180.

49 "The Hyperbolic Teachings of Jesus," *North American Review*, CLXXIX (September 1904), 403.

50 *Ibid.*, p. 447.

51 E.g., Ernest D. Burton, "The Biblical Teachings Concerning Divorce," *Biblical World*, XXIX (February and March 1907). Norman Jones, "Marriage and Divorce: The Letter of the Law," *North American Review*, CLXXXI (October 1905). Thomas S. Potwin, "Should Marriage Be Indissoluble?" *New Englander and Yale Review*, LVI (January 1892).

52 *Men and Women* (Boston, 1902).

53 *Marriage and Divorce* (New York, 1913).

54 *Annual Reports* of the National League for the Protection of the Family.

55 *Annual Reports* of the Executive Committee of the Federal Council of Churches of Christ in America.

56 "Are Homogenous Divorce Laws in all the States Desirable?" *North American Review*, CLXX (March 1900).

57 E. R. Stevens, "Divorce in America: The Problem," *Outlook*, June 1, 1907; "Just Grounds for Divorce," November 23, 1910.

58 *World's Work*, XIX (January 1910).

59 Henry F. May, *The End of American Innocence* (New York, 1959), II, Part IV, 333, 343–44.

Richard Jensen, the author of the final piece in this section, found himself in the enviable position of having available to him what amounted to survey data of an historical nature. Early in the century a compiler of a directory of prominent women hit upon the idea of asking those whose names were to be included how they felt about the suffrage movement. Since this was before women had the vote, the responses are very important, especially since Jensen also had at his disposal a considerable amount of information about these women which he could treat as independent variables. Yet, despite this brief moment in historical paradise, the results are somewhat disappointing to Jensen. None of the usual predictors of attitude such as education, religion, class, and family size appears to account for much of the revealed variation. What does emerge is that those who supported suffrage were also involved in other political and social movements. Perhaps the problem lies in the population studied, since by definition these were all eminent women; the range of variation which may have been apparent in the whole female population is not evident. Still, this material provides an important beginning to the further understanding of the suffrage movement and women activists.

RICHARD JENSEN

14 *Family, Career, and Reform: Women Leaders of the Progressive Era*

American historiography has ignored women. The reason is not a lack of data or suitable topics or trained scholars, but rather a failure of the historians' imagination—an inability to conceptualize the ways in which women are important. The historian covering political, military, diplomatic, or economic topics sees only men, and, on a deeper level, only forces, ideas, and movements pertaining to men. Even social historians have largely ignored women, save in accounts of changing standards of morality (in which the double standard forces some consideration of women) or in the analysis of demographic trends (where it is standard practice to compute female rather than male fertility).

Most of the recent work on women has concentrated on their role in reform movements—concerning equal rights, temperance, abolition, child labor, and the like. The best books focus on women in the Progressive Era, usually viewing the equal suffrage movement as another phase of progressivism itself.[1] These studies trail off after 1920, either because the woman's movement lost its dramatic quality, or because women themselves became more withdrawn—a trend calling for more sophisticated psycho-history and family studies than have yet been undertaken.

Historians of women's movements have followed standard models of political and ideological historiography. Although open to the use of social and psychological approaches, they have neither the data nor the technique to analyze which women supported, ignored, or opposed various causes. One purpose of this paper is to show how computerized collective biography can point the way to answering the deeper questions of who supported the equal rights and other movements, and why those supporters were so motivated.[2]

The study of women as individuals is at a lower stage of historiographical development than the study of organizations and movements. Recently Radcliffe sponsored a companion to the *Dictionary of American Biography,* which displayed the old biases by including 200 men for every woman. However, biographies of some outstanding female reformers and artists, usually written by other women, do exist. And *Notable American Women 1607–1950,* with its 1359 entries ranging from Lizzie Borden to Jane Addams, marks a major breakthrough in the field. The introductory essay by Janet James, while only thirty-four pages long, represents the first systematic effort to discuss the role of prominent women in American history, all three and a half centuries of it. The editors admit that neither they nor the several contributors could find an over-arching interpretive framework for their compilation. Less grandly, but more to our point, they found it difficult to interpret the women's lives one by one and place each in a satisfactory context. "Motivation was often obscure or complex," the editors lament, citing a woman's upbringing and environment, her family's attitudes, her responsibilities as wife and mother, changes in economic status, and, ultimately, "the vagaries of pure chance" as the determining factors in producing noteworthy careers.[3]

The purpose of this paper is not to castigate historians for their neglect of the roles and motivations of women but rather to report new findings on the interaction of environment, life-cycle, and attitudinal and behavioral patterns displayed by a very large number of locally or nationally prominent women in art, education, society, clubs, and the professions.

Like most historical research, this paper deals with elites. However, it does not select an arbitrary handful of "representative" individuals and infer from their lives what the lives of other women must have been like. Rather, we study 9,000 women and look for subtle patterns with statistical techniques. The vast majority of middle- and working-class women are not treated here, and our findings must not be extrapolated to them. Instead, consider how privileged women of the late nineteenth and early twentieth centuries structured their lives in a rapidly changing society.

The dilemma of women in a world run by men is how to balance the roles of motherhood, career, and social concern. Writing during a time when feminism was in retreat, a Vassar alumna, class of 1913, recalled the liberated spirit of her undergraduate days.

> Twenty years ago we all believed in the economic independence of women. Domesticity was regarded with impatience. When we planned what we should do with our lives, we thought of some money-making occupation, preferably in a field in which women were unwelcome. We all expected to have careers, and we all hoped to be distinguished as the leading woman in this or the first woman in that. It was part of the doctrine that we should marry and have children, but that these incidents should not stand in the way of our work. Marriage does not interfere with a man's work. A woman, too, should have both a rich personal life and a useful public career.[4]

On the basis of such texts historians have begun to examine the values and beliefs of American women. The puzzle is how closely such views fitted the actual values as expressed by behavior. If social history is to become credible, it must be grounded in evidence more valid and representative than fugitive wit.

The data for this study comes from 9,000 autobiographical questionnaires assembled by a pioneer editor of who's who directories who systematically sought out women recognized by their peers as "nationally, sectionally, or locally prominent." A random sample of 879 women was chosen; their entries were coded into forty variables;

and SPSS (statistical package for the social sciences) programs were used to cross-tabulate the results.[5]

A full spectrum of ages and life patterns for upper- and upper-middle-class women is represented. According to their primary careers, 21 percent of the women were professionals (doctors, social workers, suffrage leaders, missionaries, among others); 16 percent were artists or writers; 17 percent were educators; 13 percent were middle-class clubwomen; and 33 percent were upper-class socialites. Unlike most who's whos, which concentrate on older notables, our source included a large proportion of younger women: 13 percent were 34 or younger in 1914; 31 percent were 35–44; 29 percent were 45–54; 18 percent were 55–64; and 10 percent were 65 and over. Although two-thirds of the women had been married (68 percent, including 7 percent who were widowed or had married twice), they produced only half the children necessary to reproduce their generation.

Geographically, the women parallel the locations of contemporary male leaders. Nearly half had been born in the Northeast (48 percent), and the same proportion lived there. Although a third (32 percent) had been born in the Midwest, only a fourth (25 percent) still lived there. Many moved westward (3 percent born there, and 11 percent living there), while one in seven was southern (13 percent born in the South, 14 percent living there). These totals mask a high rate of interregional mobility—35 percent changed regions, fewer than a fourth spent their entire lives in one state, and about half reported living in four or more different places. Naturally, the group was well educated (21 percent with college degrees, and another 23 percent with postgraduate work, not to mention 20 percent who had attended but not completed college) and urban (57 percent lived in or near a metropolis of 100,000 population in 1910, and another 13 percent lived in cities of 20,000 to 100,000).

The women in our study comprised most of the local, state, and national women's leaders of the day. They were keenly interested in public affairs, and in the suffrage movement especially. One in four actively promoted equal suffrage, usually as a member of a club specifically organized for that purpose. Another 30 percent declared in favor of equal suffrage when asked by the editor, while 8 percent were opposed and a handful (1.5 percent) were actively opposed to equal suffrage. (Curiously, some of those opposed mentioned that they voted anyway.) No renegade ex-suffragists appeared in the sample. Although few were partisan,[6] 55 percent indicated some interest in civic affairs and current events, 62 percent engaged in humanitarian work, and 30 percent were active in church societies (another 42 percent were church members—usually Episcopalians, Presbyterians, and Congregationalists). The women's club movement (including here the DAR, alumnae groups, equal suffrage clubs, literary and social organizations, and anything that seemed eligible for the General Federation of Woman's Clubs) enlisted three-fourths of the group, and three out of four members in turn held leadership posts at one time or another. The women had seen something of the world (25 percent, at least, had traveled to Europe) and were eager to express themselves (38 percent had published some of their writing).

Analytically, the basic question of this paper is not how many women were active in this or that, but which of them were? Table 1 shows the correlates of prosuffrage attitudes. Six strong correlations

Table 1. Correlates of Suffrage Support*

Strong		Moderate		Weak	
WCTU membership	+.69	Private practice or business	+.29	Teaching experience	+.13
Interest in current events	.55	National recognition	.22	Level of education	.12
Membership in Professional or National organization	.39	Listed in *Notable Am. Women*	.20	Degree of long distance mobility	.11
Active in Woman's club	.39	Alumnae, sorority member	.20	Number of places lived	.10
Humanitarian interests	.39	Can vote in home state	.16	Size of home city	.08
		Ever published	.17	Level of literary interest	.07
		Outdoor enthusiast	.15	Level of religious activity	.05
				Age at marriage**	.04
				Number of children**	.00
				Size of birthplace	−.02
				Displays interest in geneology	−.03
				Rated as upper class socialite	−.06

*Value of gamma used, since dependent and independent variables are both ordered categorically. Gamma ranges from +1 to −1 with positive values indicating that support for suffrage was associated with high levels of variable listed.
**Married women only.

Family, Career, and Reform

are apparent. Suffragism was positively associated with temperance, current-events interest, public lecturing (which involved college professors, ministers, and literary lecturers as well as stump speakers), membership in a professional or national organization, activism in women's clubs, and humanitarian concern. Seven correlations of moderate strength link suffragism to business experience (usually by physicians), national or historical recognition, alumnae club or sorority affiliation, publication, the person's current legal voting rights, and her enthusiasm for the outdoors. The weak correlations show that suffragism was not directly linked to the basic demographic, educational, and life-cycle variables, at least not in monotonic fashion. The use of multivariate methods, however, will enable us to glean some important patterns from the weak list.

The best predictors of suffragism were public activities, listed in the first column of table 1. Temperance work, specifically WCTU (Women's Christian Temperance Union) membership was surprisingly uncommon (noted for only 6 percent), but more often than anything else it was associated with devotion to equality. The WCTU members were older women who could remember the exciting crusades of the 1870s and 1880s and who never discarded their moralistic fervor despite the cold-blooded professionalism of the now dominant Anti-Saloon League (which very few mentioned). They knew that they had a duty to reform society, and they demanded the vote to do it—64 percent were suffrage activists and/or leaders. Women's clubs likewise afforded an arena for demanding the ballot, and humanitarians thought they would be more effective if they could vote directly for reforms and reformers of their own choosing.[7]

The moderate correlations show a systematic prosuffrage bias among women with national recognition, female writers, outdoors women—perhaps with an interest in conservation, and women who already enjoyed either a full vote (as in much of the West), or a vote in local or school elections (as in much of the Midwest and part of the Northeast). These moderate correlations do not directly indicate much about suffragism, and it would be wrong to base conclusions on them. However, they do serve to point the way to further inquiry.

Most disappointing are the weak correlations between suffragism and the basic life-cycle variables—age, education, mobility, region, religion, family size, and class. These are precisely the factors a historian would like to use to explain attitudes, but seemingly they explain nothing at all. Deeper probing shows that the reason for the low correlations was the diversity of the women. When career types are suitably categorized, the key life-cycle variables are indeed correlated with suffragism, though not necessarily in the expected way. It is only the mistake of thinking of women leaders as a homogeneous group, which most historians make, that provokes initial disappointment when weak global patterns appear.

A major correlate of suffragism which cannot be neatly summarized by gamma coefficients or the like is career. Professional women frequently were suffrage leaders—43 percent of the physicians, 40 percent of the social workers, and 64 percent of the "agitators and lawyers." By contrast, fewer than 20 percent of the journalists, secondary-school teachers, college teachers, and authors joined equal suffrage clubs, and only 6 percent of the librarians did so. Women who were primarily upper-class socialites were the largest group on the low end of the suffrage scale. Table 2 ranks each primary career by an attitudinal "suffragism index," which can range from $+2$ to -2; the overall mean was $+.66$.

With the striking exception of the apathetic librarians, it appears that women who held responsible positions in competition with men were more prosuffrage, while those with basically private lives were less supportive.[8] This generalization would be highly significant, if accurate, but it hinges on the assumption that professional women, school administrators, researchers, professors, journalists, and performing artists did, in fact, compete directly with men on male terms in the early twentieth century. A careful review of the individual cases and the biographies in *Notable American Women* suggests, however, that they did not really compete with men but rather found female niches in male-dominated fields. The women lawyers, for example, rarely practiced day-to-day law but used their legal training to serve other causes. Mary Bryan, one of the two or three best-known women

Table 2. Suffragism Index by Primary Career* (sample size in parentheses)

Above Mean		Below Mean	
+1.59	Agitators and lawyers (29)	+.63	Middle-class clubwomen (117)
1.17	Government employees,	.63	Journalists (16)
	social workers (30)	.55	Authors (75)
1.16	Doctors (56)	.54	Public-school teachers (24)
1.08	College administrators (13)	.52	Upper-class socialites (287)
.92	Public-school administrators (12)	.48	Studio artists (23)
.82	Missionaries, ministers (17)	.46	Art educators (13)
.82	Businessmen, farmers (17)	.42	Private-school teachers (36)
.75	Performing artists (16)	.30	Decorators, illustrators (10)
.69	Scientific reseachers (16)	.06	Librarians (17)
.68	College professors (47)		

*The suffragism index equals $2x$ suffrage workers $+$ $1x$ prosuffrage $+$ $1x$ pro-limited suffrage $-$ $1x$ against suffrage $-$ $2x$ actively against suffrage, all divided by the total number of women in the category, including those with no opinion.

in the sample, took a law degree and was admitted to the bar "in order to be more companionable to Mr. Bryan . . . but shortly after, he entered politics and she did not pursue the subject further."[9] Likewise, female physicians usually held staff hospital posts or specialized in the health of women and children. Other women held designated female roles—sopranos, deans of women, heads of home economic departments, and the like. Perhaps only those thoroughly cowed librarians had to outqualify men for their jobs. Active suffragism may then have been a reaction to sexual stereotyping rather than a manifestation of de facto equality in the job market. Unfortunately, the brief autobiographies do not yield enough data about individual career patterns to resolve the point. What we need is a systematic analysis of sex differentiation and discrimination in high-status occupations in the early twentieth century, and at this stage only individual biographies specifically addressed to the problem could provide clues. We thus have a case of a significant statistical generalization that requires traditional biographical studies for corroboration.

A more subtle approach to the relationships among career, family, and reform requires more careful generalizations about career types than can be gotten from differentiated occupational titles. The problem can be resolved (not necessarily optimally) by a two-dimensional scheme in which the first dimension is the primary career group (professions, education, etc.) and the second dimension incorporates the secondary career types that have been recorded for most of the women. A person with no secondary occupation is included in the first column of table 3; if her secondary career is in the same group as her primary career, she is included in the second column; if in a different group (except upper class), in the third column; and if it is upper-class socialite, in the fourth column. Table 3 gives the suffragism index for each of the sixteen career types that result from this reclassification.

Table 3. Suffragism Index by Primary and Secondary Career Types*

Primary Group	Secondary Career			
	None	Same Group as Primary	Different Group	Upper-class Socialite
Professional	+.88	+1.43	+1.05	+.90
Education	.36	.63	.59	.83
Arts-Writing	.33	.41	.74	.72
Upper-class socialite	.44		.68	
Middle-class clubwoman	.54		.90	

*Number of cases, by row: 34, 44, 63, 40/ 45, 24, 41, 40/36, 39, 39, 29/ 194, 0, 93, 0/ 86, 0, 31, 0, Σ = 878. Inexplicably, one person slipped through our recording scheme.

Richard Jensen   274

Within each primary grouping (row), the narrow-interest women without secondary careers (first column) were less supportive of suffrage than women with broader interests. Career specialization inhibited suffragism. In the case of socialites (row 4), the stay-at-homes were low on suffragism, not only in contrast to socialites with a secondary career (column 3), but also in contrast to career women who additionally played the role of socialite (column 4). However, the lowest scores occurred among career women in education and art/-writing with little outside interest. Even controlling for suffrage opinion, the undiversified artists and educators scored lowest on interest in current affairs, but here they were joined by educator/upper-class socialites.

Using the same career typology, it is possible to study the relationships between career and family. Table 4 shows the proportion of women in each group who were married by the time of the survey; table 5 shows the proportion of the wives who became mothers; and table 6 shows the proportion of all women who were mothers in 1913. Of course, some of the younger women later married and became mothers. The younger ages predominated among the women without secondary careers (column 1), the Education-Same, and the Professional-Upper Class groupings.

Table 5 shows that half to two-thirds of the wives became mothers, except for teachers (22 percent), clubwomen, and socialites (80 percent, 76 percent). Since the likelihood of motherhood was fairly constant (we cannot tell whether this was a social or a biological

Table 4. Family Status by Primary-Secondary Career Type: Proportion Married*

Primary Group	None	Secondary Career Same	Different	Upper class
Professional	29%	54%	57%	65%
Education	20	12	17	55
Arts-Writing	58	56	54	76
Upper class	93	—	88	—
Middle class	95	—	90	—

*Number of cases: same as Table 3.

Table 5. Family Status by Primary-Secondary Career Type: Proportion of Wives Who Are Mothers*

Professional	50	46	56	58
Education	22	67	43	68
Arts-Writing	43	54	48	68
Upper class	80	—	65	—
Middle class	76	—	61	—

*Number of cases, by row: 10, 24, 36, 26/ 9, 3, 7, 22/ 21, 22, 21, 22/ 180, 0, 82, 0/ 82, 0, 28, 0.

Family, Career, and Reform

phenomenon), career women who did not want to be saddled with children simply avoided marriage.[10] In any case, career women seldom were mothers—and educators rarely were, as table 6 shows. Career women who were mothers typically developed upper-class affiliations (DAR, Episcopalian church work, country club membership, etc.), as the fourth column of table 6 suggests.[11] Artists and, especially, writers (row 3) were less handicapped by family responsibility than other careerists and therefore were more willing to marry. Notice that there is little evidence of a motherhood ethic—or feminine mystique—in these tables. Socialites and clubwomen were the only groups with a majority of mothers, and even then a large proportion were childless.

Table 6. Family Status by Primary-Secondary Career Type: Proportion of Total Who Are Mothers*

Professional	15	25	32	38
Education	4	8	7	38
Arts-Writing	25	31	26	52
Upper class	74	—	57	—
Middle class	72	—	55	—

*Number of cases: same as Table 3.

Not only was motherhood not obligatory, it was distinctly unpopular among career women. It does not follow, however, that mothers were in the clutches of a feminine mystique that confined them to family duties and occasional social events. On the contrary, mothers were *more* interested in humanitarian and civic causes, and in equal suffrage, than were childless wives. Indeed, mothers of two children were actually stronger suffragists than single women! Table 7 gives the suffragism index for each family type, controlling for age. Mothers of two children emerge as the most prosuffrage group, followed by single women, childless wives, mothers of one child, and mothers of large families. The most valid results are in the second column, where only women with completed families are included. In that case, childless wives drop below all categories of mothers except those with five or more children. The liberated woman of 1913 was not an unsexed spinster trying to outscore men; rather she was the mother of one or two children.

There is a puzzling curvilinear pattern in table 7—why should a second baby increase suffragism and a third one diminish that spirit? A clue comes from the age pattern: within each family type, the older women are stronger for equality than the younger ones—another surprising finding, at least in contrast to the women's liberation move-

Table 7. Suffragism Index by Family Size, Controlling Age

Number of Children	44 Years & Younger*	45 Years & Older	All
Single	+.64	+.83	+.74
None	.65	.57	.61
One	.57	.62	.59
Two	.65	.91	.79
Three or four	.44	.68	.60
Five or more	.67**	.52	.49
Total	.61	.71	.66

*Includes 60 women, mostly single, for whom age could not be estimated.
**Only 6 cases; other cells represent 25 or more cases.

ment of today's younger women.[12] Perhaps women developed specific interests by virtue of their children's needs, and these interests changed as the children progressed through school and finally left home. There is nothing daring in that hypothesis—except that our evidence shows that these special interests were in suffrage, humanitarianism, and civic activism. Suffrage leaders of the day kept telling mothers that they ought to become interested in public matters to protect their homes and children; historians have known about that argument for some time. The new result here is that such rhetoric was not mere exhortation; it was the normal state of affairs among leading women, and the rhetoric was designed to convince the next lower tier of middle-class women to adopt those behavior patterns. Children made women leaders more concerned about the state of society and encouraged them to take positive steps to improve it. Having three or more children probably represented not antifeminism but merely a personal ideal family size. Note that women with five or more children actually displayed a stronger interest in humanitarian concerns than the average (68 percent versus 62 percent for other women), as well as in temperance (11 percent versus 6 percent), religious activism (46 percent versus 30 percent), and current events (65 percent versus 54 percent), not to mention genealogy (35 percent versus 25 percent). However, they scored no higher on women's club work (evidence of being tied down at home?). Mothers of three or four children were slightly less activist than mothers of five or more, though they did give more support to equal suffrage.

Mothers showed distinctly higher levels of interest in current events, women's clubs, church work, and humanitarianism than did childless wives. The latter concerned themselves more with amateur art, drama, literature, and foreign travel.[13] In sum, mothers would strive for civic uplift and a better environment for their children; childless wives sought culture and personal refinement.

Historians should pay more heed to the exhortations to women to assert themselves in civic affairs and claims that women really could have a decisive impact upon public life. The millenium, it is true, did not arrive with the nineteenth amendment, and that failure has blinded historians to the actual accomplishments of women. By 1900 many states were allowing women to vote in school and municipal elections; by 1913, 70 percent of our woman leaders had that right. Although state and national political contests hinged on questions like the tariff, currency, railroad rates, utility regulation, and, above all, party loyalty—matters in which women were not usually involved— municipal and school elections were usually nonpartisan, nonideological, and of far more direct concern to women, especially mothers. Together with prohibition, school policy was a topic uncontaminated by national political factors—and one that even opponents of equal suffrage admitted was related to the woman's "proper" sphere. Much further research is called for, but it can be argued that mothers, and women leaders generally, were *more* interested in school questions than their overly partisan husbands.[14] Except for taxation, transit, and utility policies, women of the class with which we are dealing probably had a stronger concern than their husbands for municipal problems like sanitation, public health, juvenile supervision, prostitution, child welfare, charities, pure milk, pure food, settlement work, beautification, and recreation.[15] Indeed, they probably were the opinion leaders within the home on these matters. In that case, it must have been especially galling to be denied equal suffrage with their less-competent husbands! Mary Beard clearly observed this phenomenon at the time.

> Middle- and upper-class women, having more leisure than middle- and upper-class men, have had greater opportunity for social observation and the cultivation of social sympathies. . . . It is these women therefore who have seen, felt, experimented, learned, agitated, constructed, advised, and pressed upon the municipal authorities the need of public prevention of the ills from which the people suffer.[16]

Suffragism was not merely the hobbyhorse of career women frustrated by male chauvinism, nor was a career the only way a woman could influence society.

The map of suffragism, civic activism, and family structure obtained by statistical profiles does not, and cannot, by itself provide a theoretical explanation for patterns of behavior. Theory must be grounded in more intensive biographical studies of individual women

—but semi-intellectual histories of "attitudes" expressed in popular writings are not likely to generate theoretical leads. Aggregate statistical patterns provide the basic factual context that theory must set out to explain. And theory must be tested against the statistical patterns of choice of real people, operating in the real world, with their real lives at stake.[17]

Perhaps the most striking result of this analysis is not so much the delineation of previously unknown specific behavioral patterns of prominent women as the demonstration that quantification can be used to untangle, and even measure, the various environmental, familial, and attitudinal forces that intertwined in the life of each woman to produce her distinct life pattern. Direct reportorial evidence on why this or that famous woman did this or that is valuable when used with great caution, but it cannot be relied upon totally any more than the attitudinal patterns deduced from the actions of fictional characters. Certainly the contributors to *Notable American Women* discovered that. Contemporary observers, after all, reported rumors, half-truths, and misperceptions just as convincingly as they recounted genuine insights. And for many of their insights they relied on a sort of crude or intuitive correlational analysis that the historian can make for a larger and more representative population more systematically and reliably. Similar quantitative approaches can be applied to other sources (Gallup polls, for example) to recapture a vastly more complete and accurate picture of the great totality of American womanhood. The historian, if his data is rich enough, can be a better observer of the past than any contemporary.

Notes

1   Notably Aileen Kraditor, *Ideas of the Woman Suffrage Movement, 1890–1920* (New York, 1965); William O'Neill, *Everyone Was Brave* (Chicago, 1971); and David Morgan, *Suffragists and Democrats* (East Lansing, 1972). Of the more general studies, note should be made of Anne Scott, *The Southern Lady: From Pedestal to Politics, 1830–1930* (Chicago, 1970), and William Chafe, *The American Woman: Her Changing Social, Economic, and Political Roles, 1920–1970* (New York, 1972).

2   The methods of multivariate collective biography, together with an application to prominent men of the early twentieth century, are discussed in Richard Jensen, "Quantitative Collective Biography," in Robert Swierenga, ed., *Quantification in American History* (New York, 1970), pp. 389–405.

3   Edward James and Janet James, eds, *Notable American Women, 1607–1950* (Cambridge, 1971), vol. 1 p. xii.

4   Harriet Bradley Fitt, "In Praise of Domesticity," in Herbert Mills, ed., *College Women and the Social Sciences* (New York, 1934), p. 266. Mrs. Fitt held a Ph.D. in economics.

5   Richard Jensen and Barbara Campbell, "How to Handle a Liberated Woman," *Historical Methods Newsletter* 5 (1972): 109–13 provides the full coding scheme and marginal totals. John William Leonard, *Woman's Who's Who in America . . . 1914–1915* (New York: 1914) provides all the data.

6   Republicans numbered 6 percent, Democrats 4 percent, and third parties— Progressive, Socialist, and Prohibitionist—8 percent.

7   Hidden by the simple correlations was a U-shaped pattern, in which opponents were also more interested in humanitarian and civic matters than were the women with no opinion on suffrage.

8   Journalists seem to be the chief exception, but when we add in those women with a secondary career in each field, the journalists and public-school teachers climb above the new mean ($+.71$), while missionaries, performing artists, and scientists slip below it; authors rise to the mean, and librarians go up slightly.

9   Leonard, *Woman's Who's Who*, p. 140.

10   Until 1913, in New York City and presumably elsewhere, pregnant public-school teachers were fired. Whether this happened to married college and private-school teachers as well is not known. Compare June Sklar, "Childless Women," *Population Index* 37 (1971): 194–95, and Thomas Woody, *A History of Women's Education in the United States* (New York, 1929), 1:505–18. On the general question of marriage and fertility among educated women, see Woody, 2:203–10, and G. Stanley Hall, *Adolescence* (New York, 1904), 2: 590–612.

11   Most mothers completed their families by age 30 or 35, which was usually before the great growth of woman's clubs in the late 1890s and early 1900s. Club activism was not likely to have inhibited motherhood for this population, therefore.

12   An apparent exception is row 2. However, when young wives without children age, some of them become mothers and move into lower rows, leaving in row 2 an antimotherhood residue that is less prosuffrage than the average mother. The new mothers in row 3 may carry with them for a while the weaker suffrage index of childless wives, thus producing a smaller difference across columns in row 3.

13   This pattern holds controlling for suffrage attitude. Among all 118 married women over 45 with no opinion on suffrage, the gamma correlation between number of children and clubwork was $+.33$; and churchwork, $+.28$; and humanitarianism, $+.27$; and current-events interest, $+.16$; and community art or drama, $-.12$; and literary clubs, $-.33$. The difference of proportions when comparing motherhood with each activity in a 2x2 table was about two-thirds of the corresponding gamma value.

14   See *Report of the Commissioner of Education for . . . 1893–94* (Washington, 1896), 2: 1416–19, and Woody, *Women's Education*, 2: 441–44.

15   See Mary Beard, *Women's Work in Municipalities* (New York, 1915), and David Thelen, *The New Citizenship: Origins of Progressivism in Wisconsin 1885–1900* (Columbia, 1972), pp. 86–99.

16   Beard, *Woman's Work*, p. 221–22.

17   Other dimensions of family and reform include regionalism and urbanism. Preliminary results indicate that they do not significantly affect the patterns reported here among career, family, and reform.

Richard Jensen   280

PART IV

Sex:
Behavior and Ideology

Edmund Morgan's classic article on Puritan sexuality is the only selection included in this volume that was published prior to the 1960s; to that extent it might be thought of as an example of the "old" social history of the family. Old or new, this is a fine piece of scholarship, and it raises serious questions about stereotypes of Puritan sexual attitudes and behavior. Obviously, an important distinction has to be made between the realistic, though by no means permissive, stance taken on these matters by the Puritans and the prudery and downright repressiveness we encounter during the mid-nineteenth century, if only in public statements and law. It is unfortunate that these two distinct periods in the history of America's sexual customs are often lumped together and spoken of as if they were of the same cloth, when in fact they are very different.

EDMUND S. MORGAN

15 The Puritans and Sex

Henry Adams once observed that Americans have "ostentatiously ignored" sex. He could think of only two American writers who touched upon the subject with any degree of boldness—Walt Whitman and Bret Harte. Since the time when Adams made this penetrating observation, American writers have been making up for lost time in a way that would make Bret Harte, if not Whitman, blush. And yet there is still more truth than falsehood in Adams's statement. Americans, by comparison with Europeans or Asiatics, are squeamish when confronted with the facts of life. My purpose is not to account for this squeamishness, but simply to point out that the Puritans, those bogeymen of the modern intellectual, are not responsible for it.

At the outset, consider the Puritans' attitude toward marriage and the role of sex in marriage. The popular assumption might be that the Puritans frowned on marriage and tried to hush up the physical aspect of it as much as possible, but listen to what they themselves had to say. Samuel Willard, minister of the Old South Church in the latter part of the seventeenth century and author of the most complete textbook of Puritan divinity, more than once expressed his horror at "that Popish conceit of the Excellency of Virginity."[1] Another minister, John Cotton, wrote that

> Women are Creatures without which there is no comfortable Living for man: it is true of them what is wont to be said of Governments, *That bad ones are better than none:* They are a sort of Blasphemers then who dispise and decry them, and call them *a necessary Evil,* for they are *a necessary Good.*[2]

These sentiments did not arise from an interpretation of marriage as a spiritual partnership, in which sexual intercourse was a minor or incidental matter. Cotton gave his opinion of "Platonic love" when he recalled the case of

> one who immediately upon marriage, without ever approaching the *Nuptial Bed,* indented with the *Bride,* that by mutual consent they might both live such a life, and according did sequestring themselves according to the custom of those times, from the rest of mankind, and afterwards from one another too, in their retired Cells, giving themselves up to a Contemplative life; and this is recorded as an instance of no little or ordinary Vertue; but I must be pardoned in it, if I can account it no other than an effort of blind zeal, for they are the dictates of a blind mind they follow therein, and not of that Holy Spirit, which saith *It is not good that man should be alone.*[3]

Here is as healthy an attitude as one could hope to find anywhere. Cotton certainly cannot be accused of ignoring human nature. Nor was he an isolated example among the Puritans. Another minister stated plainly that "the Use of the Marriage Bed" is "founded in mans Nature," and that consequently any withdrawal from sexual intercourse upon the part of husband or wife "Denies all reliefe in Wedlock unto Human necessity: and sends it for supply vnto Beastiality when God gives not the gift of Continency."[4] In other words, sexual intercourse was a human necessity and marriage the only proper supply for it. These were the views of the New England clergy, the acknowledged leaders of the community, the most Puritanical of the Puritans. As proof that their congregations concurred with them, one may cite the case in which the members of the First Church of Boston expelled James Mattock because, among other offenses, "he denied Coniugall fellowship vnto his wife for the space of 2 years together vpon pretense of taking Revenge upon himself for his abusing of her before marryage."[5] So strongly did the Puritans insist upon the sexual character of marriage that one New Englander considered himself slandered when it was reported, "that he Brock his deceased wife's hart with Greife, that he wold be absent from her 3 weeks together when he was at home, and wold never come nere her, and such Like."[6]

There was just one limitation which the Puritans placed upon sexual relations in marriage: sex must not interfere with religion. Man's chief end was to glorify God, and all earthly delights must promote that end, not hinder it. Love for a wife was carried too far when it led a man to neglect his God:

> . . . sometimes a man hath a good affection to Religion, but the love of his wife carries him away, a man may bee so transported to his wife, that hee dare not bee forward in Religion, lest hee displease his wife, and so the wife, lest shee displease her husband, and this is an inordinate love, when it exceeds measure.[7]

Sexual pleasures, in this respect, were treated like other kinds of pleasure. On a day of fast, when all comforts were supposed to be foregone in behalf of religious contemplation, not only were tasty food and drink to be abandoned but sexual intercourse, too. On other occasions, when food, drink, and recreation were allowable, sexual intercourse was allowable too, though of course only between persons who were married to each other. The Puritans were not ascetics; they never wished to prevent the enjoyment of earthly delights. They merely demanded that the pleasures of the flesh be subordinated to the greater glory of God: husband and wife must not become "so transported with affection, that they look at no higher end than marriage it self." "Let such as have wives," said the ministers, "look at them not for their own ends, but to be fitted for Gods service, and bring them nearer to God."[8]

Toward sexual intercourse outside marriage the Puritans were as frankly hostile as they were favorable to it in marriage. They passed laws to punish adultery with death, and fornication with whipping.

Edmund S. Morgan   284

Yet they had no misconceptions as to the capacity of human beings to obey such laws. Although the laws were commands of God, it was only natural—since the fall of Adam—for human beings to break them. Breaches must be punished lest the community suffer the wrath of God, but no offense, sexual or otherwise, could be occasion for surprise or for hushed tones of voice. How calmly the inhabitants of seventeenth-century New England could contemplate rape or attempted rape is evident in the following testimony offered before the Middlesex County Court of Massachusetts:

> The examination of Edward Wire taken the 7th of october and alsoe Zachery Johnson. who sayeth that Edward Wires mayd being sent into the towne about busenes meeting with a man that dogd hir from about Joseph Kettles house to goody marches. She came into William Johnsones and desired Zachery Johnson to goe home with her for that the man dogd hir. accordingly he went with her and being then as far as Samuell Phips his house the man over tooke them. which man caled himselfe by the name of peter grant would have led the mayd but she oposed itt three times: and coming to Edward Wires house the said grant would have kist hir but she refused itt: wire being at prayer grant dragd the mayd between the said wiers and Nathanill frothinghams house. hee then flung the mayd downe in the streete and got atop hir; Johnson seeing it hee caled vppon the fellow to be sivill and not abuse the mayd then Edward wire came forth and ran to the said grant and took hold of him asking him what he did to his mayd, the said grant asked whether she was his wife for he did nothing to his wife: the said grant swearing he would be the death of the said wire. when he came of the mayd; he swore he would bring ten men to pul down his house and soe ran away and they followed him as far as good[y] phipses house where they mett with John Terry and George Chin with clubs in there hands and soe they went away together. Zachy Johnson going to Constable Heamans, and wire going home. there came John Terry to his house to ask for beer and grant was in the streete but afterward departed into the towne, both Johnson and Wire both aferme that when grant was vppon the mayd she cryed out severall times.
>
> Deborah hadlocke being examined sayth that she mett with the man that cals himselfe peeter grant about good prichards that he dogd hir and followed hir to hir masters and there threw hir downe and lay vppon hir but had not the use of hir body but swore several othes that he would ly with hir and gett hir with child before she got home.
>
> Grant being present denys all saying he was drunk and did not know what he did.[9]

The Puritans became inured to sexual offenses, because there were so many. The impression which one gets from reading the records of seventeenth-century New England courts is that illicit sexual intercourse was fairly common. The testimony given in cases of fornication and adultery—by far the most numerous class of criminal cases in the records—suggests that many of the early New Englanders possessed a high degree of virility and very few inhibitions. Besides the case of Peter Grant, take the testimony of Elizabeth Knight about the manner of Richard Nevars's advances toward her:

> The last publique day of Thanksgiving (in the year 1674) in the evening as I was milking Richard Nevars came to me, and offered me abuse in putting his hand, under my coates, but I turning aside with much adoe, saved my self, and when I was settled to milking he agen took me by the shoulder and pulled me backward almost, but I clapped one hand on the ground and held fast the cows teatt with the other hand, and cryed out, and then came to mee Jonathan Abbot one of my Masters Servants, whome the said Never asked wherefore he came, the said Abbot said to look after you, what you doe unto the Maid, but the said Never bid Abbot goe about his businesse but I bade the lad to stay.[10]

One reason for the abundance of sexual offenses was the number of men in the colonies who were unable to gratify their sexual desires in marriage.[11] Many of the first settlers had wives in England. They had come to the new world to make a fortune, expecting either to bring their families after them or to return to England with some of the riches of America. Although these men left their wives behind, they brought their sexual appetites with them; and in spite of laws which required them to return to their families, they continued to stay, and more continued to arrive, as indictments against them throughout the seventeenth century clearly indicate.

Servants formed another group of men, and of women too, who could not ordinarily find supply for human necessity within the bounds of marriage. Most servants lived in the homes of their masters and could not marry without their consent, a consent which was not likely to be given unless the prospective husband or wife also belonged to the master's household. This situation will be better understood if it is recalled that most servants at this time were engaged by contract for a stated period. They were, in the language of the time, "covenant servants," who had agreed to stay with their masters for a number of years in return for a specified recompense, such as transportation to New England or education in some trade (the latter, of course, were known more specifically as apprentices). Even hired servants who worked for wages were usually single, for as soon as a man had enough money to buy or build a house of his own and to get married, he would set up in farming or trade for himself. It must be emphasized, however, that anyone who was not in business for himself was necessarily a servant. The economic organization of seventeenth-century New England had no place for the independent proletarian workman with a family of his own. All production was carried on in the household by the master of the family and his servants, so that most men were either servants or masters of servants; and the former, of course, were more numerous than the latter. Probably most of the inhabitants of Puritan New England could remember a time when they had been servants.

Theoretically no servant had a right to a private life. His time, day or night, belonged to his master, and both religion and law required that he obey his master scrupulously.[12] But neither religion nor law could restrain the sexual impulses of youth, and if those impulses could not be expressed in marriage, they had to be given vent outside marriage. Servants had little difficulty in finding the occasions. Though they might be kept at work all day, it was easy enough to slip away at night. Once out of the house, there were several ways of meeting with a maid. The simplest way was to go to her bedchamber, if she was so fortunate as to have a private one of her own. Thus Jock, Mr. Solomon Phipps's Negro man, confessed in court

> that on the sixteenth day of May 1682, in the morning, betweene 2 and one of the clock, he did force open the back doores of the House of Laurence Hammond in Charlestowne, and came in to the House, and went up into the garret to Marie the Negro.
>
> He doth likewise acknowledge that one night the last week he forced into the House the same way, and went up to the Negro Woman Marie and that the like he hath done at severall other times before.[13]

Joshua Fletcher took a more romantic way of visiting his lady:

> Joshua Fletcher . . . doth confesse and acknowledge that three severall nights, after bedtime, he went into Mr Fiskes Dwelling house at Chelmsford, at an open window by a ladder that he brought with him. the said windo opening into a chamber, whose was the lodging place of Gresill Juell servant to mr. Fiske. and there he kept company with the said mayd. she sometimes having her cloathes on, and one time he found her in her bed.[14]

Sometimes a maidservant might entertain callers in the parlor while the family were sleeping upstairs. John Knight described what was perhaps a common experience for masters. The crying of his child awakened him in the middle of the night, and he called to his maid, one Sarah Crouch, who was supposed to be sleeping with the child. Receiving no answer, he arose and went downe the stayres, and at the stair foot, the latch of doore was pulled in. I called severall times and at the last said if shee would not open the dore, I would breake it open, and when she opened the doore shee was all undressed and Sarah Largin with her undressed, also the said Sarah went out of doores and Dropped some of her clothes as shee went out. I enquired of Sarah Crouch what men they were, which was with them. Shee made mee no answer for some space of time, but at last shee told me Peeter Brigs was with them, I asked her whether Thomas Jones was not there, but shee would give mee no answer.[15]

In the temperate climate of New England it was not always necessary to seek out a maid at her home. Rachel Smith was seduced in an open field "about nine of the clock at night, being darke, neither moone nor starrs shineing." She was walking through the field when she met a man who

asked her where shee lived, and what her name was and shee told him. and then shee asked his name, and he told her Saijing that he was old Good-man Shepards man. Also shee saith he gave her strong liquors, and told her that it was not the first time he had been with maydes after his master was in bed.[16]

Sometimes, of course, it was not necessary for a servant to go outside his master's house in order to satisfy his sexual urges. Many cases of fornication are on record between servants living in the same house. Even where servants had no private bedroom, even where the whole family slept in a single room, it was not impossible to make love. In fact many love affairs must have had their consummation upon a bed in which other people were sleeping. Take for example the case of Sarah Lepingwell. When Sarah was brought into court for having an illegitimate child, she related that one night when her master's brother, Thomas Hawes, was visiting the family, she went to bed early. Later, after Hawes had gone to bed, he called to her to get him a pipe of tobacco. After refusing for some time,

at the last I arose and did lite his pipe and cam and lay doune one my one bead and smoaked about half the pip and siting vp in my bead to giue him his pip my bead being a trundell bead at the sid of his bead he reached beyond the pip and Cauth me by the wrist and pulled me on the side of his bead but I biding him let me goe he bid me hold my peas the folks wold here me and if it be replyed come why did you not call out I Ansar I was posesed with fear of my mastar least my master shold think I did it only to bring a scandall on his brothar and thinking thay wold all beare witnes agaynst me but the thing is true that he did then begete me with child at that tim and the Child is Thomas Hauses and noe mans but his.

In his defense Hawes offered the testimony of another man who was sleeping "on the same side of the bed," but the jury nevertheless accepted Sarah's story.[17]

The fact that Sarah was intimidated by her master's brother suggests that maidservants may have been subject to sexual abuse by their masters. The records show that sometimes masters did take advantage of their position to force unwanted attentions upon their female servants. The case of Elizabeth Dickerman is a good example. She complained to the Middlesex County Court,

> against her master John Harris senior for profiring abus to her by way of forsing her to be naught with him: . . . he has tould her that if she tould her dame: what cariag he did show to her shee had as good be hanged and shee replyed then shee would run away and he sayd run the way is before you: . . . she says if she should liwe ther shee shall be in fear of her lif.[18]

The court accepted Elizabeth's complaint and ordered her master to be whipped twenty stripes.

So numerous did cases of fornication and adultery become in seventeenth-century New England that the problem of caring for the children of extra-marital unions was a serious one. The Puritans solved it, but in such a way as to increase rather than decrease the temptation to sin. In 1668 the General Court of Massachusetts ordered:

> that where any man is legally convicted to be the Father of a Bastard childe, he shall be at the care and charge to maintain and bring up the same, by such assistance of the Mother as nature requireth, and as the Court from time to time (according to circumstances) shall see meet to Order: and in case the Father of a Bastard, by confession or other manifest proof, upon trial of the case, do not appear to the Courts satisfaction, then the Man charged by the Woman to be the Father, shee holding constant in it, (especially being put upon the real discovery of the truth of it in the time of her Travail) shall be the reputed Father, and accordingly be liable to the charge of maintenance as aforesaid (though not to other punishment) notwithstanding his denial, unless the circumstances of the case and pleas be such, on the behalf of the man charged, as that the Court that have the cognizance thereon shall see reason to acquit him, and otherwise dispose of the Childe and education thereof.[19]

As a result of this law a girl could give way to temptation without the fear of having to care for an illegitimate child by herself. Furthermore, she could, by a little simple lying, spare her lover the expense of supporting the child. When Elizabeth Wells bore a child, less than a year after this statute was passed, she laid it to James Tufts, her master's son. Goodman Tufts affirmed that Andrew Robinson, servant to Goodman Dexter, was the real father, and he brought the following testimony as evidence:

> Wee Elizabeth Jefts aged 15 ears and Mary tufts aged 14 ears doe testyfie that their being one at our hous sumtime the last winter who sayed that thear was a new law made concerning bastards that If aney man wear aqused with a bastard and the woman which had aqused him did stand vnto it in her labor that he should bee the reputed father of it and should mayntaine it Elizabeth Wells hearing of the sayd law she sayed vnto vs that If shee should bee with Child shee would bee sure to lay it vn to won who was rich enough abell to mayntayne it wheather it wear his or no and shee farder sayed Elizabeth Jefts would not you doe so likewise If it weare your case and I sayed no by no means for right must tacke place: and the sayd Elizabeth wells sayed If it wear my Caus I think I should doe so.[20]

A tragic unsigned letter that somehow found its way into the files of the Middlesex County Court gives more direct evidence of the practice which Elizabeth Wells professed:

> der loue i remember my loue to you hoping your welfar and i hop to imbras the but now i rit to you to let you nowe that i am a child by you and i wil ether kil it or lay it to an other and you shal have no blame at al for I haue had many children and none have none of them. . . . [i.e., none of their fathers is supporting any of them.][21]

In face of the wholesale violation of the sexual codes to which all these cases give testimony, the Puritans could not maintain the severe penalties which their laws provided. Although cases of adultery occurred every year, the death penalty is not known to have been applied more than three times. The usual punishment was a whipping or a fine, or both, and perhaps a branding, combined with a symbolical execution in the form of standing on the gallows for an hour with a rope about the neck. Fornication met with a lighter whipping or a lighter fine, while rape was treated in the same way as adultery. Though the Puritans established a code of laws which demanded perfection—which demanded, in other words, strict obedience to the will of God, they nevertheless knew that frail human beings could never live up to the code. When fornication, adultery, rape, or even buggery and sodomy appeared, they were not surprised, nor were they so severe with the offenders as their codes of law would lead one to believe. Sodomy, to be sure, they usually punished with death; but rape, adultery, and fornication they regarded as pardonable human weaknesses, all the more likely to appear in a religious community, where the normal course of sin was stopped by wholesome laws. Governor Bradford, in recounting the details of an epidemic of sexual misdemeanors in Plymouth, wrote resignedly:

> it may be in this case as it is with waters when their streames are stopped or damned up, when they gett passage they flow with more violence, and make more noys and disturbance, then when they are suffered to rune quietly in their owne chanels. So wickednes being here more stopped by strict laws, and the same more nerly looked unto, so as it cannot rune in a comone road of liberty as it would, and is inclined, it searches every wher, and at last breaks out wher it getts vente.[22]

The estimate of human capacities here expressed led the Puritans not only to deal leniently with sexual offenses but also to take every precaution to prevent such offenses, rather than wait for the necessity of punishment. One precaution was to see that children got married as soon as possible. The wrong way to promote virtue, the Puritans thought, was to "ensnare" children in vows of virginity, as the Catholics did. As a result of such vows, children, "not being able to contain," would be guilty of "unnatural pollutions, and other filthy practices in secret: and too oft of horrid Murthers of the fruit of their bodies," said Thomas Cobbett.[23] The way to avoid fornication and perversion was for parents to provide suitable husbands and wives for their children:

> Lot was to blame that looked not out seasonably for some fit matches for his two daughters, which had formerly minded marriage (witness the contract between them and two men in *Sodom,* called therfore for his Sons in Law, which had married his daughters, Gen. 19. 14.) for they seeing no man like to come into them in a conjugall way . . . then they plotted that incestuous course, whereby their Father was so highly dishonoured. . . .[24]

As marriage was the way to prevent fornication, successful marriage was the way to prevent adultery. The Puritans did not wait for adultery to appear; instead, they took every means possible to make husbands and wives live together and respect each other. If a husband deserted his wife and remained within the jurisdiction of a Puritan government, he was promptly sent back to her. Where the wife had been left in England, the offense did not always come to light until the wayward husband had committed fornication or bigamy, and of course there must have been many offenses which never came to light. But where both husband and wife lived in New England, neither had much chance of leaving the other without being returned by order of the county court at its next sitting. When John Smith of Medfield left his wife and went to live with Patience Rawlins, he was sent home poorer by ten pounds and richer by thirty stripes. Similarly Mary Drury, who deserted her husband on the pretense that he was impotent, failed to convince the court that he actually was so, and had to return to him as well as to pay a fine of five pounds. The wife of Phillip Pointing received lighter treatment: when the court thought that she had overstayed her leave in Boston, they simply ordered her "to depart the Towne and goe to Tanton to her husband." The courts, moreover, were not satisfied with mere cohabitation; they insisted that it be peaceful cohabitation. Husbands and wives were forbidden by law to strike one another, and the law was enforced on numerous occasions. But the courts did not stop there. Henry Flood was required to give bond for good behavior because he had abused his wife simply by "ill words calling her whore and cursing of her." The wife of Christopher Collins was presented for railing at her husband and calling him "Gurley gutted divill." Apparently in this case the court thought that Mistress Collins was right, for although the fact was proved by two witnesses, she was discharged. On another occasion the court favored the husband: Jacob Pudeator, fined for striking and kicking his wife, had the sentence moderated when the court was informed that she was a woman "of great provocation."[25]

Wherever there was strong suspicion that an illicit relation might arise between two persons, the authorities removed the temptation by forbidding the two to come together. As early as November, 1630, the Court of Assistants of Massachusetts prohibited a Mr. Clark from "cohabitacion and frequent keepeing company with Mrs. Freeman, vnder paine of such punishment as the Court shall thinke meete to inflict." Mr. Clark and Mrs. Freeman were both bound "in XX£ apeece that Mr. Clearke shall make his personall appearance att the nexte Court to be holden in March nexte, and in the meane tyme to carry himselfe in good behaviour towards all people and espetially towards Mrs. Freeman, concerneing whome there is stronge suspicion of incontinency." Forty-five years later the Suffolk County Court took the same kind of measure to protect the husbands of Dorchester from the temptations offered by the daughter of Robert Spurr. Spurr was presented by the grand jury

> for entertaining persons at his house at unseasonable times both by day and night to the greife of theire wives and Relations &c The Court having heard what was alleaged and testified against him do Sentence him to bee admonish't and to pay Fees of Court and charge him upon his perill not to entertain any married men to keepe company with his daughter especially James Minott and Joseph Belcher.

Edmund S. Morgan   *292*

In like manner Walter Hickson was forbidden to keep company with Mary Bedwell, "And if at any time hereafter hee bee taken in company of the saide Mary Bedwell without other company to bee forthwith apprehended by the Constable and to be whip't with ten stripes." Elizabeth Wheeler and Joanna Peirce were admonished "for theire disorderly carriage in the house of Thomas Watts being married women and founde sitting in other mens Laps with theire Armes about theire Necks." How little confidence the Puritans had in human nature is even more clearly displayed by another case, in which Edmond Maddock and his wife were brought to court "to answere to all such matters as shalbe objected against them concerning Haarkwoody and Ezekiell Euerells being at their house at unseasonable tyme of the night and her being up with them after her husband was gone to bed." Haarkwoody and Everell had been found "by the Constable Henry Bridghame about tenn of the Clock at night sitting by the fyre at the house of Edmond Maddocks with his wyfe a suspicious weoman her husband being on sleepe [*sic*] on the bedd." A similar distrust of human ability to resist temptation is evident in the following order of the Connecticut Particular Court:

> James Hallett is to returne from the Correction house to his master Barclyt, who is to keepe him to hard labor, and course dyet during the pleasure of the Court provided that Barclet is first to remove his daughter from his family, before the sayd James enter therein.

These precautions, as we have already seen, did not eliminate fornication, adultery, or other sexual offenses, but they doubtless reduced the number from what it would otherwise have been.[26]

In sum, the Puritan attitude toward sex, though directed by a belief in absolute, God-given moral values, never neglected human nature. The rules of conduct which the Puritans regarded as divinely ordained had been formulated for men, not for angels and not for beasts. God had created mankind in two sexes; He had ordained marriage as desirable for all, and sexual intercourse as essential to marriage. On the other hand, He had forbidden sexual intercourse outside of marriage. These were the moral principles which the Puritans sought to enforce in New England. But in their enforcement they took cognizance of human nature. They knew well enough that human beings since the fall of Adam were incapable of obeying perfectly the laws of God. Consequently, in the endeavor to enforce those laws they treated offenders with patience and understanding, and concentrated their efforts on prevention more than on punishment. The result was not a society in which most of us would care to live, for the methods of prevention often caused serious interference with personal liberty. It must nevertheless be admitted that in matters of sex the Puritans showed none of the blind zeal or narrow-minded bigotry which is too often supposed to have been characteristic of them. The more one learns about these people, the less do they appear to have resembled the sad and sour portraits which their modern critics have drawn of them.

Notes

1 Samuel Willard, *A Compleat Body of Divinity* (Boston, 1726), 125 and 608–613.

2 John Cotton, *A Meet Help* (Boston, 1699), 14–15.

3 *A Meet Help,* 16.

4 Edward Taylor, Commonplace Book (manuscript in the library of the Massachusetts Historical Society).

5 Records of the First Church in Boston (manuscript copy in the library of the Massachusetts Historical Society), 12.

6 Middlesex County Court Files, folder 42.

7 John Cotton, *A Practical Commentary . . . upon the First Epistle Generall of John* (London, 1656), 126.

8 *A Practical Commentary,* 126.

9 Middlesex Files, folder 48.

10 Middlesex Files, folder 71.

11 Another reason was suggested by Charles Francis Adams in his scholarly article, "Some Phases of Sexual Morality and Church Discipline in Colonial New England," *Proceedings* of the Massachusetts Historical Society, XXVI, 477–516.

12 On the position of servants in early New England see *More Books,* XVII (September, 1942), 311–328.

13 Middlesex Files, folder 99.

14 Middlesex Files, folder 47.

15 Middlesex Files, folder 52.

16 Middlesex Files, folder 44.

17 Middlesex Files, folder 47.

18 Middlesex Files, folder 94.

19 William H. Whitmore, editor, *The Colonial Laws of Massachusetts. Reprinted from the Edition of 1660* (Boston, 1889), 257.

20 Middlesex Files, folder 52.

21 Middlesex Files, folder 30.

22 William Bradford, *History of Plymouth Plantation* (Boston, 1912), n, 309.

23 Thomas Cobbett, *A Fruitfull and Usefull Discourse touching the Homour due from Children to Parents and the Duty of Parents towards their Children* (London, 1656), 174.

24 Cobbett, 177.

25 Samuel E. Morison and Zechariah Chafee, editors, *Records of the Suffolk County Court,* 1671–1680, *Publications* of the Colonial Society of Massachusetts, XXIX and XXX, 121, 410, 524, 837–841, and 1158; George F. Dow, editor, *Records and Files of the Quarterly Courts of Essex County, Massachusetts* (Salem, 1911–1921), I, 274; and V, 377.

26 *Records of the Suffolk County Court,* 442–443 and 676; John Noble, editor, *Records of the Court of Assistants of the Colony of Massachusetts Bay* (Boston, 1901–1928), II, 8; *Records of the Particular Court of Connecticut, Collections* of the Connecticut Historical Society, XXII, 20; and a photostat in the library of the Massachusetts Historical Society, dated March 29, 1653.

The significance of Edward Shorter's article on illegitimacy in modern Europe lies not only in the important data he provides showing the rise in out-of-wedlock births from the middle of the eighteenth century to the middle of the nineteenth century but also in the interpretation that he brings to them. He argues that this escalation in rates reflects a fundamental change in orientation toward sexuality. He describes this change as a shift from "manipulative sexuality" to "expressive sexuality," which must be understood in terms of broader social processes, namely, the growth of the market economy and industrialization. It should be apparent from this selection that no matter how "good" certain data are, they take on meaning only when they are seen in terms of a theoretical perspective bolstered by alternative sources of evidence.

EDWARD SHORTER

16 *Illegitimacy, Sexual Revolution, and Social Change in Modern Europe*

Sexuality in traditional society may be thought of as a great iceberg, frozen by the command of custom, by the need of the surrounding community for stability at the cost of individuality, and by the dismal grind of daily life. Its thawing in England and Western

Europe occurred roughly between the middle of the eighteenth and the end of the nineteenth centuries, when a revolution in eroticism took place, specifically among the lower classes, in the direction of libertine sexual behavior. One by one, great chunks—such as premarital sexuality, extra- and intra-marital sexual styles, and the realm of the choice of partners—began falling away from the mass and melting into the swift streams of modern sexuality.

This article considers the crumbling of only a small chunk of the ice: premarital sexuality among young people, studied from the evidence of illegitimacy. However, in other realms of sexuality, a liberalization was simultaneously in progress. There is evidence that masturbation was increasing in those years. The first transvestite appears in Berlin police blotters in 1823. Prostitution in Paris tripled in the first half of the nineteenth century. And, between 1830 and 1855, reported rapes in France and England climbed by over 50 per cent.[1] It is not the concern of this paper, however, to pin down qualitatively these other developments. This is a task reserved for future research based upon a content analysis of pornographic literature and a statistical study of the dossiers of sexual offenders in France and Germany.

What is meant by "liberalization" or "sexual revolution"? With these terms I wish to indicate a change in either, or both, the quantity and quality of sexual activity. Quantity refers to how often people have intercourse and with whom—premarital, extramarital, and marital. By quality I mean to locate the style of activity upon a spectrum running from genital to "polymorphous" sexuality: A genital orientation is the concentration of libidinal gratifications in the genitals alone; polymorphous is the discovery of other areas of the body to be erogenous zones. Liberalization will thus be understood as an increase in the quantity of sexual activity or a shift on the quality spectrum from genital to polymorphous gratification.[2]

Premarital adolescent sexuality, basically a "quantitative" subject, is the easiest portion of the sexual revolution to deal with because reliable statistics pertaining to the behavior of common people may be found and correlated with other indicators of social and economic transformation. Before 1825 data on illegitimacy were accurately preserved in parish registers throughout Europe. And nineteenth-century government statisticians meticulously noted in their annual reports not only the movement of the population, but also the number of illegitimate children born in the various districts of their lands. New insights into the intimate realms of popular life may be gained from these statistics.

Starting around the mid-eighteenth century a dramatic increase in the percentage of illegitimate births commenced all over Europe;[3]

illegitimacy further accelerated around the time of the French Revolution, and continued to increase until approximately the mid-nineteenth century. This illegitimacy explosion clearly indicates that a greater number of young people—adults in their early twenties, to go by the statistics on the age of women at the birth of their first illegitimate child—were engaging in premarital sex more often than before.[4] There were slip-ups, and the birth of illegitimate children resulted.

The alternate constructions one might place upon the statistical increase in illegitimacy are, in my view, incorrect. It is impossible to dismiss such a rise as a result of improved procedures for reporting illegitimate births. By all accounts, few bastard children slipped through the net of the baptismal register. In the 1700s, some village pastors of stern morality were inclined to enter all children conceived premaritally as illegitimate, whether born in wedlock or not. To the extent that this practice was abandoned the real proportions of the increase would be masked, but in no event enhanced.[5]

It is also untenable to argue that the illegitimacy explosion stemmed from a "compositional" effect: that, for whatever reason, late in the 1700s more unmarried young women were around than ever before, and so these unmarried women just naturally produced more bastards. To be sure, the percentage of single women in the population did increase all over the continent, but the mentalities of these women, as well as their proportion in the population, were shifting, for the rise in illegitimate fertility, measured by the number of illegitimate births per 1,000 single women, shows that they were behaving more "immorally" than in the past.[6] We are unquestionably confronting a genuine change in popular sexual behavior, not a statistical artifact.

Nor should the illegitimacy explosion be dismissed as the sudden lengthening of the gap between conception and marriage, and as nothing more than that. Some might argue that an increase in illegitimacy was a sign not of changing mentalities but merely of a pregnant girl's increasing difficulty in forcing her seducer to marry her. Or increasing illegitimacy may have stemmed from a couple's greater willingness to see their first child born out of wedlock. Both arguments account for rising illegitimacy in terms of technical shifts in courtship practices, ignoring changes in attitudes toward sexuality among young people as a whole. Neither argument would demand that the percentage of young people sleeping together before the sealing of a formal engagement had increased.

One piece of evidence forces us to reject both of these arguments: the number of children born within eight months of their parents' marriage. In virtually every community we know about, pre-nuptial conceptions rose along with illegitimate births. This indicator is charted, where available, in the Appendix. The simultaneous up-ward march of illegitimacy and prenuptial pregnancy means that the rise in illegitimacy itself was *not* merely the result of increasing delay in marriage, with the level of intercourse remaining stable. Rather, if both bastardy and prebridal pregnancy rose, there is an almost com-plete certainty that the total volume of premarital intercourse was rising.[7] This demonstrates that engaged couples were copulating before marriage more often than before, and that many more casual sexual alliances were being constituted than in the past.

Finally, we should inspect the rough outlines of traditional sexu-ality. By "traditional" I refer to European rural and small-town society between 1500 and 1700. It was a period of cultural homogeneity in which all popular strata behaved more or less the same, having similar social and sexual values, the same concepts of authority and hierarchy, and an identical appreciation of custom and tradition in their primary social goal, the maintenance of static community life. We have numer-ous testimonies to the quality of peasant and burgher sex life, but almost none to that of the lower classes (domestic servants, laborers, journeymen, and the industrious poor). But I think it is safe to assume that the comportment of the two strata was similar. Möller has por-trayed sex life among the *Kleinbürgertum* in the 1700s: man on top, no foreplay, quick ejaculation, and indifference to partner's orgasm. The gamut seems paper-thin, and the more exotic perversities which de-lighted the upper classes were doubtless unheard of and unimagined in provincial backwaters. More importantly, people were either chaste before marriage, or began sleeping together only after the engage-ment was sealed.[8] This is the situation from which the great liberaliza-tion emerged.

A Typology of Illegitimacy

In order to understand why an increasing number of illegimate children were born, two questions must be asked: (1) Why did the level of intercourse outside of marriage rise, thereby increasing the incidence of premarital conceptions? (2) Why did a greater percent-age of conceptions fail to lead to marriage—why did more of this increased sexual activity result specifically in illegitimacy? To answer the first question one must distinguish, in a general way, among the reasons for having sex; to answer the second requires an understand-ing of the social situation in which a couple found themselves—for the stability and durability of their own relationship, and the firmness of their integration into the social order about them, would determine whether they would marry before the child was born.

The reader must be warned of the speculative character of my answers to these two questions. The explanations of shifts in sexual mentalities and the typologies of interpersonal relationships from one period to the next are preliminary efforts to make sense of badly fragmented and scattered information on intimate life. The arguments that follow thus are not to be understood as hard statements of fact, but rather as informed guesses about the likely course of events. Only the hope of spurring further research justifies this kind of speculative enterprise, for we are unable to determine what kinds of evidence to seek out until we have arguments that specify exactly what is to be sought.

As a first imprudent step, let us assume that people have intercourse for one of two reasons. They may wish to use their sexuality as a tool for achieving some ulterior external objective, such as obtaining a suitable marriage partner and setting up a home, or avoiding trouble with a superior. If they have such motives in mind as they climb into bed, they are using sex in a *manipulative* fashion. Alternatively, they may be intent upon developing their personalities as fully as possible, upon acquiring self-insight and self-awareness, and, accordingly, think of sex an an integral component of their humanity. For such people, sex is a way of expressing the wish to be free, for the egoism of unconstrained sexuality is a direct assault upon the inhibiting community authority structures about them. I call this *expressive* sexuality. This level of intercourse is higher than that for the manipulative variety because self-expression is an ongoing objective, whereas once the object is attained to which manipulative sexuality was employed, the person may lapse into the unerotic torpor society has ordained as proper. Expressiveness means a lot of sex; manipulativeness means little.

But what about the sex drive? It is always with us, a dark motor of human biology moving men and women to intercourse in all times and all places. Yet its position in the hierarchy of *conscious* needs and impulses is by no means constant, but is rather a function of social and cultural variables which changes from one time and place to another. Gagnon and Simon have shown for twentieth-century America that social structure and cultural stances interpose themselves between the steady thrust of the libido and the act of intercourse.[9] My point is that such factors constituted "reasons for intercourse" in nineteenth-century Europe as well. Specifically, there are two: the conscious wish to use sex as a means of manipulating other people to perform non-sexual acts, and the conscious wish to use sex as a spotlight in the introspective search for identity. Changes in these reasons for intercourse suggest that the history of the sexual revolution in Europe may be written as the transformation of lower-class eroticism from manipulation to expression.[10]

But if the social order about the expressive couple remains the same, they will doubtless get married and appear in the records of the statisticians only as contributors to the legitimate birth rate. In order to see why the child whom they conceive is born a bastard, we must look at the stability of their relationship. Instability may result when one of the partners in a relationship (normally the male) is using his social or economic authority to exploit the other sexually (usually the female). In such a case, marriage is unlikely to follow pregnancy. The likelihood of a subsequent marriage is also reduced when the partners are caught up in a society undergoing rapid flux, so that either the establishment of a family household is impossible, or the male can easily escape the consequences of impregnation by fleeing. The notion of stability in the social situation of the couple therefore incorporates several possibilities.

These two variables—the nature of sexuality (expressive vs. manipulative) and the nature of the couple's social situation (stable vs. unstable)—are strategic in accounting for the illegitimacy explosion in Europe. Because each has its own history (although both must be considered together) we may construct a table which cross-classifies and derives four different situations resulting in the birth of an illegitimate child:

Table 1. The Types of Illegitimacy

	Expressive sexuality	Manipulative sexuality
Stable social situation	True love	Peasant-bundling
Unstable social situation	Hit-and-run	Master-servant exploitation

"Peasant-bundling" illegitimacy lies at the intersection of instrumental sexuality and a stable social situation: persons with things on their mind other than sex whose cohabitation is sanctioned by custom. "Master-servant exploitation" denotes the coercion of women into bed by men who use their power as employers or social superiors to wrest sexual favors from them. Less than rape, the woman consents to being exploited in order to exist in peace wth her superiors. There is little question of marriage when pregnancy ensues, a sign of the instability inherent both in the relationship and in the society which permits this kind of illicit exercise of authority. "Hit-and-run" illegitimacy identifies temporary liaisons where the partners articulate romantic sentiments and substantial ego awareness, and thereby are sexually expressive, yet are not inclined to remain together after a conception has taken place, or are prohibited by the force of events from doing so. Finally, in "true love" illegitimacy the psychological orientation of the partners is roughly the same as with the hit-and-run situation (although the couple may come more quickly to think of itself as a domestic unit), yet both their intent and their social environment conspire to permit a swift subsequent wedding and the establishment of a household. The child is technically illegitimate, but, like the offspring of peasant bundlers, is soon enmeshed in orderly family life. Children born of master-servant and of hit-and-run unions are more enduringly illegitimate.

All four types of illegitimacy were present in European society at all stages of historical development, but, in some epochs, some types were more prevalent than others. The explosion of bastardy may be written as the supplanting of peasant-bundling and master-servant exploitation by hit-and-run and true-love illegitimacy as the predominant types. This transition came about because popular premarital sexuality shifted from manipulative to expressive, thus elevating the number of conceptions, and because inconstancy crept into the couples' intentions toward each other, and instability into the structure of the social order in which they found themselves. The result was to make more premarital conceptions into illegitimate births.

These four types represent, in fact, four distinct historical stages in the unfolding of illegitimacy, one giving way to the next in a neat chronological progression.

Stage I Peasant-bundling was the paramount form of illegitimacy in Europe before the eighteenth century. England and Europe had always known some bastardy, on the order of 1 or 2 percent of all births, and most parish registers turned up an isolated illegitimate child or two in the course of a decade. But these children, when not the offspring of the poor servant girl raped by the village half-wit, stemmed normally from engaged peasant couples who commenced sleeping together before marriage, as was customary, yet delayed the marriage too long. Social authorities in these village and small-town communities put enormous pressure upon hesitant males to wed their swollen fiancées, being persuasive only because the seducer had been, and would continue to be, resident locally and dependent upon the good will of his social betters.

I have not seen data on the legitimation of illegitimate children before 1800, so the characterization cannot be made exactly. Yet excellent information on prenuptial conception and illegitimacy convince me that this portrait must be essentially accurate.[11]

Stage II Master-servant exploitation became an even brighter thread in illegitimacy as the seventeenth century gave way to the eighteenth. Manipulativeness continued paramount in lower-class eroticism; the change seems to have been that people in positions of influence and authority were able, as they had not been before, to take advantage of their exalted stations. We must keep in mind that these little dramas of exploitation happened mostly within the context of lower-class life. At that humble level, the authority of the oldest journeyman of the master tanner, for example, may have been minimal in absolute terms, yet to the girl who swept out the shop it must have appeared commanding. The abuse of social and economic power to sexual ends doubtless was more difficult in the good old days, with the rest of the community watching vigilantly for disfunctions in the smooth mechanisms of prerogatives and obligations,[12] but the stirrings of social change weakened traditional control over such goings on.

Among the evidence for this characterization is Solé's work on the city of Grenoble in the late seventeenth century. He noted that around half of the illegitimate births (illegitimacy was around 3 percent of all births) were the work of men who held the mothers of the bastards in some kind of thralldom, as masters of domestic servants or employers of female wage labor. And many of the cases of "rapt" coming before the judiciary of Angoulême in 1643–44 involved the master's sexual violation of the servant. "The most common case is that of the farmers *(laboureurs à boeufs)* or village officials who, upon becoming widowers, take as servants a young girl from the parish. They speak to her vaguely of marriage, then when a birth approaches chase her from the house. . . ."[13] In the early 1700s, the illegitimacy ratio in numerous urban communities had just begun to rise, as may be seen from the Appendix, whereas that in small rural communities continued at an infinitesimal level, a statistical demonstration of a rise in Stage II illegitimacy. But a detailed study of fathership in parish register data is needed to confirm our picture of master-servant exploitation.

A number of large-scale social changes intervened between Stages II and III, running roughly from 1750, which had the end effect of giving lower-class people a new conception of self and thus an expressive notion of sexuality. The fabric of lower-class life was thus shaken in a way that substantially decreased a pregnant girl's chances of getting married.

Stage III Hit-and-run illegitimacy typified a period when young people swooned romantically through a social landscape of disorder and flux. There was much intercourse, but people were stepping out of their old places en route to new ones, and temporary cohabitations often failed to turn into permanent concubinages. This combination of circumstances raised illegitimacy to historic heights, for the years 1790–1860 were, in virtually every society or community we know about, the peak period of illegitimacy. The graphs in the Appendix reveal this conclusion unmistakably.

Time-series data on legitimation demonstrate that only a quarter to a third of all illegitimate children were subsequently legitimated by the *inter*marriage of their parents.[14] The other two-thirds either died, typically a consequence of indifferent care and the lack of a secure home, or remained unlegitimated—by definition outside of a glowing familial hearth. Some mothers eventually found husbands other than the fathers of their children; their bastards would then be raised in a domestic atmosphere, but rarely would their new stepfathers adopt them.[15] Legitimation statistics point to an unsettledness in the sexual relations between men and women, hence the sobriquet "hit-and-run."

Stage IV From about 1875, the reintegration of the lower classes into the structure of civil society appears to have removed the transient quality from romantic relationships, leaving their expressive nature unimpaired. Stable communities developed in the sprawling worker quarters of industrial cities; a cohesive lower-class subculture with distinctive values and symbols became elaborated in distinction to the bourgeois society. Outside society accepted placidly the idea of early worker marriage, and, within premarital liaisons themselves, thoughts of subsequent marriage were present at the beginning.[16]

During this stage illegitimacy ratios declined somewhat from their Stage III heights, although they did not return to the low levels of traditional society. And legitimation rates rose steadily during the last third of the century, a sign that couples who coalesced briefly for intercourse were staying together with connubial intent. The modern pattern of cohabitation is between social and economic equals, not between unequals, as in Stage II. The only survey I have been able to find of illegitimate fatherhood late in the century demonstrates that the seducers came from similar social stations as the seduced, which implies a growth of romantic, expressive sexuality in place of the manipulative, instrumental sort.[17]

These portraits of the four stages are meant as ideal types suggesting the sequence of events most places would experience. I do not intend to argue that the infinitely disparate cities and regions of Western Europe marched in lockstep, for the timing of each of these stages would vary from one place to another, depending on events. But the illegitimacy explosion sooner or later came to Breslau and Liverpool, to the Scottish lowlands and the Zurich highlands. Exactly when depended upon the pace of modernization.

Social Change and the Wish to Be Free

What touched off the wish to be free—the great drift toward individual innovation and autonomy at the cost of community custom and hierarchy—is one of the most vexing problems of modern scholarship, and a solution to it does not lie within the scope of this paper. Weinstein and Platt state that at the psychoanalytic level, the separation of home and workplace was responsible, for as the father exchanged his continuing presence within the family circle for workday employment outside, certain emotional connections caused sons to rebel against their fathers' authority. With fathers no longer emotionally nurturant, male children no longer had to obey them.[18] Classical sociology provides other answers: Marx with his insistence upon the capitalist economy as the generator of proletarian rebellion, de Tocqueville with his assertion that equality had proven too much of a good thing. The matter is still unclarified, and my puzzlement is as great as anyone's. But the pattern of takeoff in illegitimacy ratios, and the correlates of illegitimacy with other socioeconomic variables, suggest a partial answer to the question.

It is in the area of changes which enhanced the individual's sense of self and which correspondingly broke down allegiances to custom and to the community that we must seek the motor of the wish to be free. At many levels of social relations and of psychodynamics, sexual freedom threatens the maintenance of community life because of the radical privatism and "egoism" it instills in individuals. (The classic European tradition of conservatism was intensely aware of the nature of this threat, and often damned libertine sexual behavior as "Egoismus.") Following accepted practice in the study of modernization, I shall call those areas of the economy and society effecting such changes in individual mentalities the "modern" sector. A case can be made that exposure to the modern sector at least sensitizes the population to the values of individual self-development and precipitates a readiness to experiment with new life styles and personality configurations, which then leads to action, *should all other things be equal.*

Most corrosive of the traditional communitarian order was the modern marketplace economy. This insight into the individualizing impact of capitalism upon the *local* arena is almost as old as the free marketplace itself, and Nisbet, Polanyi, and Wolf have recently reminded us of it again.[19] The notion of the individual as an isolated actor in the economy hell-bent upon maximizing his own profit was the diametric opposite of concepts binding together the traditional local corporation, be it a small-town guild or open-field village. The reality, of course, was quite different from the classical *laissez-faire* model, yet it is likely that the concept was constantly in the thoughts of those involved in wage negotiations, for example, or those who offered their services in a competitive labor market. To be sure, Western Europe had known *export* capitalism, the fabrication of goods for non-local sale, since the Middle Ages, but free markets within the *local* economy date from the eighteenth century in France and England, and from the early nineteenth in Germany.[20]

In the context of sexual history, however, a free economy meant something a little more precise than the general exchange of goods and services regulated only by the price mechanism. In the countryside it meant agricultural capitalism and the rationalization of husbandry. The laborers and live-in hired hands who worked for improving farmers all over Europe were highly prone to illegitimacy. This is no less true of such English areas of agricultural modernization as Norfolk, Surrey, and Sussex, as it is of French departments—the Somme, the Eure, and the Pas-de-Calais—employing numerous rural wage laborers. In Germany, the great farms of Mecklenburg and Niederbayern employed workers among whom illegitimacy flourished.[21] Parish data from the late eighteenth century are still not abundant enough to tell if the accumulation of an agricultural proletariat produced a corresponding initial increase in bastardy, but I suspect that this finding will turn up in the work that E. A. Wrigley and Louis Henry are now directing for England and France.

In towns, a free market economy meant capitalism in the form of factory industry. A distinctive feature of factory worker life in the 1800s was staggering rates of illegitimacy. In France, local studies of industrial towns have established that female factory workers were substantially over-represented among unwed mothers in proportion to the population. In Dresden and Munich, an illegitimate child often accompanied worker parents to the altar.[22] Yet these are only examples; the systematic statistical analysis required to demonstrate such hypotheses is inordinately difficult to obtain because: (1) as noted, we simply do not know about the development of illegitimacy over time in a sufficient number of municipalities to permit us to isolate the impact of factory industrialization; and (2) what appears to be the effect of factory industry may, in fact, be the effect of residence in a city.

The fact that the single group most prone to illegitimacy was urban domestic servants gives pause to attaching too much importance to factories and to the modern economy.[23] I have argued elsewhere that urbanity itself constitutes an important independent variable in accounting for the distribution of illegitimacy, but I was unable then, and still cannot now, fit the impact of the city into a neat theoretical structure. We can see the city accelerating illegitimacy by reducing the chances that an impregnation will eventuate in marriage. But does urban residence by itself shift lower-class mentalities from manipulativeness to expressiveness? What difference the city makes is one of the big questions in modern social sciences, and another unresolved puzzle in this paper.

Among the empirical evidence I can offer on this subject is that illegitimacy began to turn upward in the cities first, spreading to the villages only later. In every city in England and the continent for which data are available, the upsurge in illegitimacy commenced around 1750 or before, as may be seen from the Appendix. Second, except in England cities had much higher illegitimacy ratios than surrounding rural areas. Yet such illegitimacy may have been solely due to the fact that there were more single women in the cities than in the countryside. And, because of all of these urban maidservants, seamstresses, and the like, a higher proportion of all urban births were illegitimate than in the countryside. But that does not mean that the typical urban girl would be more likely than the typical country girl to behave immorally and produce illegitimate children. Maybe no differences existed in the morality of young women in the city and the country. Further research will clarify this question.[24]

English cities are a puzzling case apart, for their illegitimacy *ratios* were often beneath those of the surrounding countryside. In London, for example, illegitimacy in 1859 was an unbelievably low 4 per cent of all births. (In Vienna in 1864, illegitimate births exceeded the legitimate.) Either something about English cities, such as their great prostitution, made them remarkably different from their continental counterparts, or many births were not being registered as bastards (something that could easily have happened in English vital statistics registration).[25]

The final sensitizing variable crucial in value change appears to be exposure to primary education. Formal education, if only of a rudimentary sort, is calculated precisely to give the individual a sense of self by teaching logical thought. Learning to read requires the acquisition of linear logic, which mode of thought then surely spreads to other intellectual processes and levels of perception, to say nothing of the logical capacities instilled by other kinds of formal education.

Logic and rationality are just other words for ego control, the psycho-structural state of mind when expressive sexuality flows. It is surely significant that the illegitimacy explosion coincided closely in time with the spread of primary education, and in space with the diffusion of literacy among the population.[26]

To review a provisional reconstruction of the psychodynamics of the sexual revolution: It appears that liberal sexual attitudes probably flowered from heightened ego awareness and from weakened superego controls. Traditional European society internalized anti-sexual values which commanded repression. But, when new values began to replace old ones, the superego restrictions on gratification gave way to the demands of the ego for individual self-fulfillment, and it was but a short logical step to see sexual fulfillment as integral to this larger personality objective. I do not mean that people became "sexualized" human beings; instead they became pluralized, seeing sex as an intrinsic part of their humanity. This makes the sexual revolution an integrated movement of self-awareness, not a turbulent unleashing of carnality. If my argument is correct, behind this wish to be free lay the market economy, evoking ego orientation from those caught up in it, and primary education, stressing logical thought and control of the external world.

Social Changes Decrease the Likelihood that Conception Leads to Marriage

Let us imagine a young girl has just told her suitor that she is pregnant. He has three possible responses, in the event that he does not wish to propose marriage in short order:

(1) "I love you but we can't get married until I inherit the shoe shop at age 42."
(2) "I love you but the authorities won't let us get married because they're afraid we might go on welfare."
(3) "So long, honey."

Which of these responses hundreds of thousands of young men selected is the key to the second strategic variable in accounting for illegitimacy: the chances of conception resulting in marriage before the child was born. The response was determined by the presence or absence of three principal social conditions, and our understanding of the sources of illegitimacy will be incomplete without a quick glance at them.

Response (1), the need to delay marriage until the man could establish an independent livelihood, was doubtless spoken most often in areas of lagging artisanal economy and impartible agricultural inheritance, late in the eighteenth and early in the nineteenth centuries.

Age-old custom in Europe stipulated that the ability to support a family was a precondition of marriage, and, customarily, young men would not take brides until a master craftsman's license was in the offing or until the parents declared themselves ready to abandon farming and let the son take over the big house. In the 1700s, however, population grew so rapidly that the vacant positions which would allow for economic independence were soon filled up. Though other jobs entailing economic dependence were always available (witness the howls over a shortage of rural wage laborers), these positions were not thought suitable for establishing a "bürgerliche Existenz." A hesitancy to subdivide the fields and the stranglehold of the guilds upon the expansion of the artisanal sector saw to it that these economic backwaters did not expand with the growth of population. Hence there were rising ages at marriage and cries of "overpopulation"— and illegitimacy.

This model of population growth, rising ages at marriage, and illegitimacy works best for the areas of Europe not permeated by cottage industry. Where the domestic system was found, people married earlier, yet *also* produced more illegitimate children. (I do not wish to argue a direct positive correlation between age at marriage and illegitimacy. Too many other variables intervened: such as strength of familial controls and the mentalities of the population.) But in a cottage industrial area the delay in marriage was more likely due to abandonment of the mother by her seducer (response 3), rather than to a need for patience arising from economic exigencies (response 1).[27]

Response (2) is a special Central European variant of response (1), for in most German-speaking areas from Austria to Pomerania legal restrictions on marriage were reinforced in the nineteenth century. These laws were the bureaucratic elaboration of traditional community bars upon the marriage of the indigent, and were promulgated in the first half of the century at the behest of municipal governments. Town councils all over Germany feared that permitting the lower classes to marry freely would result in the swamping of local poor-relief funds by the children of the poor. Had things been as before, with no value changes underway among the lower classes, this calculation might have proved rewarding. Yet the lower classes had by now (as we have seen) abandoned their traditional chastity before marriage, and proceeded to saddle these anxious municipalities with hordes of illegitimate children. This is why Central European illegitimacy ratios in the first two-thirds of the century were so strikingly high. In the late 1860s these laws were repealed, and, in the space of a year or two, illegitimacy ratios all over Germany sagged.[28]

It must be borne in mind that these laws were not responsible for the initial take off of illegitimacy, postdating that explosion by several decades. Other factors were behind the central European illegitimacy as well, for even in the absence of such legislation several German states experienced the highest incidence of bastardy on the continent.

Under different circumstances than in responses (1) and (2), the man might refuse to marry the girl altogether (response 3), and, after obliging her by "recognizing" the child at its birth, he would disassociate himself entirely from his foundering family.[29] Chronologically, the period of most frequent absconding was the first half of the nineteenth century (when the other two responses were also most often heard), yet refusals to stay by the fallen woman probably happened most in the modern sector—family industry and the city—rather than in the small towns of traditional society. All statistics point to the city as a place where conception out of wedlock meant abandonment by one's lover, as seen by the numbers of foundlings, of single women in lying-in hospitals (a sign, in the eyes of some, that the unwed mother was alone), and of single women on relief. In Austria, a negative correlation turns up in communes larger than 2,000 between the percentage of bastard children legitimated and the size of place, indicating the relative impermanence of sexual liaisons in the metropolis. Some of this dismal showing of urban places was due to the pregnant country girls who would come to the city to bear their illegitimate children, and then return home. But, even after they have been discounted, the mid-nineteenth century city remained a place of dislocation.[30]

Illegitimacy reached its absolute height during the first half of the nineteenth century simply because these three kinds of responses to the announcement of a pregnancy happened to coincide. Illegitimacy declined when such social conditions ceased to obtain.

Sexual Behavior and Family Patterns

At the end, we must resolve a paradox which has emerged from the uneven distribution among the social classes of the contagion of libertine sexual behavior. The middle classes, as the lower, were exposed to marketplace mentalities and education, yet their sexual attitudes throughout the 1800s remained defiantly puritanical; indeed, the evidence of Victorianism would have it that the more one were educated, the more prudish and moralistic one became.[31] How ironical that those middle-class types who preached the gospel of autonomy—liberalism, *laissez-faire* capitalism, and universal suffrage—were the most repressive people sexually. In class terms, they were the movers and doers, the *bourgeoisie d'affaires.* Yet those who favored economic collectivism and political community were the most liberated sexually, with a high degree of personal control and autonomy. In class terms, they comprised the proletariat.[32]

If the argument about exposure to modernity and education is correct, one would expect the middle classes, rather than the lower classes, to have been in the vanguard of the sexual revolution. Other variables must have intervened to leap the gap between thinking about "the real me" and actually climbing into bed for intercourse. That is where the family enters. The lower classes were able to respond to the priming of the pump only because the family ceased for them to be an agency of social control. To go by existing evidence, it was the middle-class family which maintained the restrictive sexual taboos of traditional society, and which continued to demand chastity before marriage throughout the 1800s. For the family, sexuality and marriage went hand-in-hand. Intercourse before marriage would harm the family by (1) sullying the daughter and ruining her prospects of an advantageous marriage, and (2) threatening the continuation of the family name and property from generation to generation.

But even beyond this calculus of familial interest, the concept of *Ehrbarkeit* has always been a lynch pin in the ideology of the petty-bourgeois family. The quickest way to make oneself dishonorable was by sexual transgression. This notion of honor had disseminated from the master craftsmen of the guild system to all bourgeois family circles, but lower-class persons by definition were not master artisans, and, although formerly they had been willing respectfully to look on as the burghers exhorted one another to be honorable, for them this social ideology had become meaningless by the nineteenth century.[33]

One might plausibly argue that in the course of the eighteenth century population growth decapitated the authority of the lower-class family by creating so many children that parents had nothing to pass on to their extra-numerous offspring, and hence no control over their behavior. And cottage industry created alternate sources of employment to enable children to escape the authority of the family by physically removing themselves or otherwise acquiring economic independence. Once children decided to exchange the old internalized values of abstinence for new ones of self-fulfillment, parents were powerless to stop them. The petty-bourgeois family did not undergo this fate because it managed to control its fertility[34] and to preserve the sense of family tradition which said that children would follow in the footsteps of the father. To be sure, young men of middle-class origin responded to a new *Zeitgeist* of gratification by sleeping with prostitutes; but these liaisons posed no threat to the family. What we know about middle-class daughters suggests that they stayed pure before marriage. Thus the authority of the middle-class family over its offspring remained inviolate, and, as a result, middle-class youth, however sensitized by change, did not actually break out of the web of familial custom and control. But the youth of the lower classes did, which resolves the apparent paradox. Thus in a long chain of argumentation we get from rising illegitimacy to the emergence of class differences in family structure. The chain has a number of linkages, the solidity of which may be verified by the test of quantitative data. These may be time-series data relating the change from year to year in some possible causative factor, such as an increase in literacy, to some such index of sexual behavior as prenuptial conceptions. Or the testing may be done with "ecological" data, using census information to spot a statistical relationship between the number of factory workers in an area and the number of young people living away from home, or the number of illegitimate children in the population. I have tried to cast the argument of this paper to permit precisely this kind of verification with statistical procedures.

If the propositions presented here about sexual behavior, family structure, and social change are correct, we may expect future work to turn up the following kinds of regularities:

1. If the proposition is true that illegitimacy stemmed from a change in mentalities (rather than from some purely "compositional" effect, such as an increase in the number of single women), we should expect to find the incidence of shotgun weddings increasing in the same places and at the same times as illegitimacy. This simultaneity would indicate that the percentage of all young people practicing premarital intercourse was climbing, ruling out explanations of bastardy which fixed solely upon courtship practices.

2. If the proposition is right that exposure to primary education effected a liberalization of sexual values, we should expect parish register data to point to a higher level of illegitimacy among young women with some rudiments of education than among those without. If the hypothesis is accurate that involvement in marketplace situations brought about libertine sexual behavior, we should expect female servants within the rationalized sector of capitalist agriculture to evidence higher illegitimacy rates than servants on traditional seigneurial estates.

3. If the proposition is true that the passage from Stage III illegitimacy (hit-and-run) to Stage IV (true love) came in consequence of greater residential stability, we should expect strong areal correlations between territorial mobility and illegitimacy, taken district by district. Likewise, the notion of a transition from Stage II illegitimacy (master-servant exploitation) to the subsequent romantic-love stages

may be critically inspected through parish register data: Did a tendency emerge over the years for premarital lovers to come from the same social class?

If all of the correlations turn out in the predicted direction, we may smile and use our footing on this tiny base of confidence for better leverage on other vexing questions. If the correlations turn out to be zero, or, worse yet, the reverse of what the argument had anticipated, we shall have to return to the drawing board.

Yet this is an agenda for the future. As a starting point in the unraveling of European sexual history this paper has attempted: (1) to verify with exact quantitative data the existence of a late eighteenth-century revolution in premarital sexual behavior, and (2) to speculate, with arguments about social change and psychodynamics at many removes from the actual data, why this revolution took place. Future work will doubtless modify substantially the speculative elements of this argument. Future work will probably not, however, dispute that there is something to be explained. The evidence of illegitimacy and of prebridal pregnancy point inescapably to a drastic change in the sexual experience of the European lower classes in the course of modernization.

Appendix: A Note on the Measurement of Illegitimacy
To avoid confusion in the terminology of measurement, I refer to the percentage of illegitimate births among all births (illegitimate births/100 total births) as the illegitimacy *ratio;* and to the number of illegitimate births per 1,000 unmarried women in the population of childbearing age as the illegitimacy *rate.* The latter measure is clearly preferable to the former as an indicator of relative illegitimacy because the ratio is dependent upon the number of legitimate births. If, for example, the number of legitimate births in a place dropped, the illegitimacy ratio would appear to rise, for fewer legitimate births in the denominator would make the illegitimate births in the numerator appear more important, even though, in fact, illegitimacy had not changed at all. Another peril one encounters in using the ratio is the possibility that differences from one place to another (or one time to another) in illegitimacy may be solely attributable to differences in the distribution of single women from one place or time to another. If there are more single women in a town, more illegitimacy may be found there, all else being equal. Yet the single women in a town with a high illegitimacy ratio may not be more immoral, or find themselves abandoned at the altar more often, than the women in another town with a lower illegitimacy ratio. The illegitimacy rate would indicate that both towns were the same.

Experienced researchers, such as the INED scholars in France, are generally convinced of the accuracy, or at least of the constancy over time, in the biases of parish register data. The only major collapse of illegitimacy reporting of which I am aware came with English civil registration of births in 1838. The Act (Statute 6 and 7 Will. IV, cap. 86) made no mention of illegitimacy, and statisticians were able to determine if a child were a bastard only if the space for the father's name were left blank. Needless to say, an unwed mother could easily invent something, or take the name of her suitor, if the man were agreeable, and no one would be the wiser. See Lumley, "Observations upon the Statistics of Illegitimacy," esp. 220–221; *Sixth Annual Report of the Registrar General of Births, Deaths, and Marriages in England* (London, 1845), xxx–xxxix. Some deficiencies also crop up in seventeenth-century English parish register data, and it is possible that an apparent early seventeenth-century peak in illegitimacy may be an artifact caused by a late seventeenth-century tendency not to register the children of common-law unions as illegitimate. I have this information from E. A. Wrigley, who says that of the genuineness of the eighteenth-century explosion there can be no doubt. For an instance of the registration of legitimate but prenuptially conceived children as *illegitimate,* see Julius Gmelin, "Bevölkerungsbewegung im Hällischen seit Mitte des 16. Jahrhunderts," *Allgemeines Statistisches Archiv,* VI (1) (1902), 248.

Hélin noted some improvement in the accuracy of illegitimacy statistics in Liège, nonetheless attributing the great rise in bastardy there to a "relâchement de contraintes sociales devenues traditionnelles depuis la Contre Réforme" (209–210). Although I am suspicious of Hélin's explanation, I think the data he reports are of excellent quality. Etienne Hélin, *La démographie de Liège aux XVIIe et XVIIIe siècles* (Brussels, 1963).

Time Series on the Legitimation of Illegitimate Children
I have been able to obtain only two time series on legitimation: statistics for the city of Paris and for the Kingdom of Belgium. The figures represent the total number of children legitimated in a given bloc of years per 100 illegitimate children born in that time, not the illegitimate children born in a given period who were subsequently legitimated.Sources for Paris: *Recherches statistiques sur la Ville de Paris et la département de la Seine* (Paris, 1826), tables 23 and 24. *Annuaire statistique de la Ville de Paris,* yearly after 1880. Sources for Belgium: *Annuaire statistique de la Belgique et du Congo Belge,* XXXIV (1903), 109–111, and XLIV (1913), 129–131.

Paris		Belgium	
Percent legitimated		Percent legitimated	
1822	7.2	1851–60	34.7
1881–84	18.6	1861–70	38.7
1885–89	20.1	1871–80	43.1
1890–94	23.2	1881–90	46.9
1895–99	25.6	1891–1900	57.5
1900–04	27.1	1901–10	65.2
1905–09	31.3	1911–13	61.1
1910–14	35.3		

The standard treatments of legitimation are Moriz Ertle, "Uneheliche Geburt und Legitimation. Ein Beitrag zur Beurtheilung der 'unehelichen Geburtenziffer.' " *Statistische Monatschrift* (Austria), XIII (1887), 393–438, which reviews available statistics throughout Europe; Seutemann, "Die Legitimationen unehelicher Kinder," 13–68. Analysis of Swiss conditions may be found in yearly volumes of the *Zeitschrift für Schweizerische Statistik,* for example, XLIV (1908), 168–173, and XLIX (1913), 122–128, which yield a short time series. France is discussed in Legoyt, "Les Naissances naturelles," 71–72. Three studies trace legitimation among cohorts of illegitimate births after allowing for mortality: Eugen Würzburger, "Zur Statistik der Legitimationen unehelicher Kinder," *Jahrbücher für Nationalökonomie und Statistik,* XVIII (1899), 94–98; Othmar Spann, "Die Legitimation der unehelichen Kinder in Österreich unter Berücksichtigung der Sterblichkeit nach Gebieten," *Statistische Monatschrift,* XIV (1909), 129–138; "Legitimirung unehelicher Kinder," *Statistisches Jahrbuch der Stadt Berlin,* XXII (1895), 55–57.

Notes

Edward Shorter is Associate Professor of History at the University of Toronto. He is the author of *The Historian and the Computer* (Englewood Cliffs, N. J., 1971) and is working on the large-scale transformation in popular patterns of family life and intimate relationships in modern Europe.

An earlier version of this paper was presented at the 1970 annual meeting of the American Historical Association. The Institute for Advanced Study gave the author the time to write it, and John Gillis, Joan Scott, Charles Tilly, Fred Weinstein, and E. A. Wrigley were kind enough to read it critically.

1 E. H. Hare, "Masturbatory Insanity: The History of an Idea," *Journal of Mental Science,* CVIII (1962), 12 (Hare's explanation for the phenomenon—a sexual outlet imposed by Puritan restrictions on intercourse—strikes me as unlikely); Hans Haustein, "Transvestitismus und Staat am Ende des 18. und im 19. Jahrhundert," *Zeitschrift für Sexualwissenschaft,* XV (1928–29), 116–126 (the man had begun wearing women's clothes in 1797); A.-J.-B. Parent-Duchâtelet, *De la Prostitution dans la ville de Paris* (Paris, 1857), I, 32, 36; Alexander von Öttingen, *Die Moralstatistik in ihrer Bedeutung für eine Socialethik* (Erlangen, 1882; 3rd ed.), 235.

2   This definition permits us to utilize the distinctions Herbert Marcuse first elaborated in *Eros and Civilization: A Philosophical Inquiry into Freud* (Boston, 1955). Paul Robinson has recently reviewed the question in *The Freudian Left: Wilhelm Reich, Gaza Roheim and Herbert Marcuse* (New York, 1969).

3   See the note on the measurement of illegitimacy in the Appendix.

4   Louis Henry agrees that illegitimacy data are a valid indicator of premarital sexual morality. "L'apport des témoignages et de la statistique," in Institut national d'études démographiques (INED), *La prévention des naissances dans la famille: ses origines dans les temps modernes* (Paris, 1960), 368. When we speak of a sexual revolution, we are not talking primarily of teenagers, as may be seen from data on unwed mothers' ages presented by P. E. H. Hair, "Bridal Pregnancy in Earlier Rural England Further Examined," *Population Studies*, XXIV (1970), 65; and by Alain Lottin, "Naissances illégitimes et filles-mères à Lille au XVIIIe siècle," *Revue d'histoire moderne et contemporaine*, XVII (1970), 306. The average age of unwed mothers probably decreased somewhat in the course of the sexual revolution; on nineteenth-century Sweden, see Gustav Sundbärg, *Bevölkerungsstatistik Schwedens, 1750–1900: Einige Hauptresultate* (Stockholm, 1923; 2nd ed.), 126, table 46.

5   See the note on the measurement of illegitimacy in the Appendix.

6   In few places are time series data available on the number of single unmarried women in the population, the standard denominator for the illegitimate fertility rate. Eighteenth-century Swedish data, presented in the Appendix, show that illegitimate fertility was rising at the same time as the illegitimacy ratio, and shorter series found elsewhere confirm this trend. For a sophisticated measurement of illegitimacy, see Joginder Kumar, "Demographic Analysis of Data on Illegitimate Births," *Social Biology*, XVI (1969), 92–107.

7   The certainty is not quite total because a rise in both of these indicators could be due to a drop in infanticide and abortion, or to an increase in fecundity. Yet there is no evidence that the first two lessened at all, to say nothing of decreasing on a scale sufficient to cause the illegitimacy explosion. Nor is there evidence of a change in fecundity.

8   An extensive popular literature on peasant sex practices exists for the nineteenth and twentieth centuries, of which Grassl's "Bäuerliche Liebe," *Zeitschrift für Sexualwissenschaft*, XIII (1926–27), 369–380 is typical. The only scholarly works I have been able to rely on for this picture of premodern sexuality are K. Rob. V. Wikman, *Die Einleitung der Ehe: Eine vergleichend ethno-soziologische Untersuchung über die Vorstufe der Ehe in den Sitten des Schwedischen Volkstums* (Turkü [Finland], 1937), 350–355; Helmut Möller, *Die kleinbürgerliche Familie im 18. Jahrhundert: Verhalten und Gruppenkultur* (Berlin, 1969), 282–301; Peter Laslett, *The World We Have Lost* (New York, 1965), 128–149.

9   They summarize their thinking in "Psychosexual Development," reprinted in John Gagnon and William Simon (eds.), *The Sexual Scene* (Chicago, 1970), 23–41.

10   A case study linking romantic love and self-awareness in the eighteenth century is Rudolf Braun, *Industrialisierung und Volksleben: Die Veränderungen der Lebensformen in einem ländlichen Industriegebiet vor 1800 (Zürcher Oberland)* (Erlenbach-Zurich, 1960), 65–72. On the eighteenth-century diffusion of romantic love, see also Jean-Louis Flandrin, "Contraception, mariage et relations amoureuses dans l'Occident

chrétien," *Annales,* XXIV (1969), 1370–1390; Philippe Ariès, "Interprétation pour une histoire des mentalités," in *Prévention des naissances,* 311–327, esp. 323.

11   The standard work on bundling *(Kiltgang, Freirei)* is Wikman, *Die Einleitung der Ehe.* Parish register investigations now in progress have turned up in most places lots of premarital conceptions among traditional peasant populations. In addition to the graphs in the Appendix, see E. A. Wrigley, *Population and History* (New York, 1969), 88 (a third of all first children in Colyton were baptized within eight months of marriage); P. E. H. Hair, "Bridal Pregnancy in Rural England in Earlier Centuries," *Population Studies,* XX (1966–67), 233–243; Michael Drake, *Population and Society in Norway, 1735–1865* (Cambridge, 1969), 138–144 (especially good on the stability of sexual relations among the cottager class); J.-C. Giacchetti and M. Tyvaert, "Argenteuil (1740–1790)," *Annales de Démographie Historique, 1969,* 40–61. The last say that even where illegitimacy was 1 percent, 11 percent of all first births were premaritally conceived. Intercourse during engagement was not everywhere the rule in traditional peasant society, as is pointed out in Emmanuel Le Roy Ladurie, *Les Paysans de Languedoc* (Paris, 1966), 644. See also Patrice Robert, "Rumont (1720–1790)," *Annales de Démographie Historique, 1969,* 32–40. Oscar Helmuth Werner, *The Unmarried Mother in German Literature with Special Reference to the Period 1770–1800* (New York, 1917), describes the violence of the traditional response to libertine behavior.

12   Chaunu has speculated that in open-field communities, where communal interaction was frequent and controls omnipresent, illegitimacy came from premarital intercourse among youths of the same age. In "bocage" communities, where relative isolation weakened social controls upon the superordinates, illegitimacy came from the masters' sexual exploitation of servants. Open-field morality was, however, more strict. See Pierre Chaunu, *La civilisation de l'Europe classique* (Paris, 1970), 196–197.

13   Yves-Marie Bercé, "Aspects de la criminalité au XVIIe siècle," *Revue historique,* CCXXXIX (1968), 33–42; Angoulême evidence, 38; Jacques Solé, "Passion charnelle et société urbaine d'Ancien régime: Amour vénal, amour libre et amour fou à Grenoble au milieu du règne de Louis XIV," *Villes de l'Europe méditerranéenne et de l'Europe occidentale du Moyen Age au XIXe siècle: Actes du Colloque de Nice (27–28 Mars 1969)* (Paris, 1970), IX-X (1969), 211–232. In the Norman village of Troarn, Michel Bouvet identified master-servant exploitation as a common source of illegitimacy during the 1700s. "Troarn: Etude de démographie historique (XVIIe–XVIIIe siècles)," *Cahiers des Annales de Normandie,* VI (1968), 53.

14   See the time series on the legitimation of children in the Appendix.

15   In Frankfurt am Main around 1900, only one-fifth of the illegitimate children whose mothers had married another man were actually adopted by their stepfathers *(Namensgebung).* Othmar Spann, *Untersuchungen über die uneheliche Bevölkerung in Frankfurt am Main* (Dresden, 1905), 26.

16   The resiliency of social networks in lower-class neighborhoods around this time has not been a subject of monographic investigation. One occasionally finds in the secondary literature relevant observations, such as Michel Collinet's view that the skilled workers of Paris become "sedentary" after the turn of the twentieth century *(L'Ouvrier francais: Essai sur la condition ouvrière [1900–1950] [Paris, 1951], 114).*

Social Change in Modern Europe

17 Theodor Geiger, "Zur Statistik der Unehelichen," *Allgemeines Statistisches Archiv*, XI (1918–19), 212–220. Geiger presents some Norwegian data (1897–98) which show that in 76 per cent of the illegitimate births, both parents were from the same social class; in a further 18 per cent of the cases, a lower-class female had slept with a middle-class male; in a final 7 per cent, a middle-class woman and a lower-class man (216–218).

18 I have borrowed the phrase from the title of the book by Fred Weinstein and Gerald M. Platt, *The Wish to be Free: Society, Psyche, and Value Change* (Berkeley, 1969). Although I think that the overall argument in Weinstein and Platt is substantially correct, I disagree with their views on the timing of the development of autonomy: (1) The search for autonomy from the family (not just from politics) probably began late in the 1700s, not in the late 1800s, when Freud was writing; (2) Weinstein and Platt argue that women were to acquire a sense of autonomy only in the 1900s, whereas men had liberated themselves from their fathers' authority much earlier. My view is that the shift from manipulative to expressive sexuality happened as much (if not more) among women as among men, and that it occurred late in the 1700s.

19 Robert Nisbet, *Community and Power* (formerly *The Quest for Community*) (New York, 1962), *passim;* Karl Polanyi, *The Great Transformation* (New York, 1944), Chs. 1–4; Eric R. Wolf, *Peasant Wars of the Twentieth Century* (New York, 1969), 276–302.

20 On England see E. A. Wrigley, "A Simple Model of London's Importance in Changing English Society and Economy, 1650–1750," *Past and Present*, XXXVII (1967), 44–70; on France, Louise A. Tilly, "The History of the Grain Riot as a Form of Political Conflict in France," *The Journal of Interdisciplinary History*, II (1971), 23–57. On Germany, Gustav Schmoller, "Die Epochen der Getreidehandelsverfassung und -politik," *Schmollers Jahrbuch*, XX (1896), 695–744, as well as his *Zur Geschichte der deutschen Kleingewerbe* (Halle, 1870) for local markets in non-agricultural goods.

21 A glance at maps of illegitimacy in any of these countries shows that counties, departments, or *Regierungsbezirke* with a high concentration of landownership in the hands of a few have, by and large, high levels of bastardy. I examined the statistical relationship betwen engrossment and illegitimacy in Bavaria in "Sexual Change and Illegitimacy: The European Experience," in Robert Bezucha (ed.), *New Directions in European Social History* (forthcoming).

22 Jules Michelet suggested that factory workers sought out sex as a compensation for the ghastliness of shop floor life. Cited in Georges Duveau, *La Vie ouvrière en France sous le Second Empire* (Paris, 1946), 423. See Ernest Bertrand, "Essai sur la moralité des classes ouvrières dans leur vie privée," *Journal de la Société de Statistique de Paris*, XIII (1872), 86–95 for occupations of illegitimate mothers in Châlons-sur-Marne, Troyes, and Reims.

23 Othmar Spann was preoccupied with this problem. See his "Die geschlechtlichsittlichen Verhältnisse in Dienstboten- und Arbeiterinnenstande, gemessen an der Erscheinung der unehelichen Geburten," *Zeitschrift für Socialwissenschaft*, VII (1904), 287–303, and his *Uneheliche Bevölkerung*, 170–171. Illegitimacy rates of factory women and domestic servants in Berlin in 1907 were twice as high as for those groups in Prussia as the whole (measured as the number of illegitimate births per

1,000 single women of childbearing age), even though overall illegitimate fertility in Berlin was only fractionally higher than in Prussia as a whole. L. Berger, "Untersuchungen über den Zusammenhang zwischen Beruf und Fruchtbarkeit unter besonderer Berücksichtigung des Königreichs Preussen," *Zeitschrift des königlich preussischen statistischen Landesamts*, LII (1912), 231–232. I am grateful to John Knodel for calling this article to my attention.

Robert Michels wrote about illegitimacy among "isolated" groups within the population, such as urban domestics and seamstresses, in *Sittlichkeit in Ziffern? Kritik der Moralstatistik* (Munich, 1928), 172–180. Abel Châtelain has been working on the entire question of maidservant migration. "Migrations et domesticité feminine urbaine en France, XVIIIe siècle-XXe siècle," *Revue d'histoire économique et sociale*, XLIV (1969), 506–528.

24 The urban-rural distinction is standard in illegitimacy discussions, and the interested reader may consult A. Legoyt, "Les Naissances naturelles," *Journal de la Société de Statistique de Paris*, VIII (1867), 62–77; Karl Seutemann, "Die Legitimationen unehelicher Kinder nach dem Berufe und der Berufsstellung der Eltern in Oesterreich," *Statistische Monatschrift*, V (1900), 13–68; Öttingen, *Moralstatistik*, and other works cited in the Appendix. Some, such as Möller in *Kleinbürgerliche Familie*, say the bigger the city, the greater the illegitimacy (289). F. G. Dreyfus talks of an urban "masse de population flottante, très mal enracinée et intégrée," *Sociétés et mentalités à Mayence dans la seconde moitié du XVIIIe siècle* (Paris, 1968), 254.

25 The English statistical service thought prostitution a likely explanation of low urban illegitimacy. Anon., "Illegitimacy in England and Wales, 1879," *Journal of the Statistical Society*, XLIV (1881), 397.

26 W. G. Lumley, "Observations upon the Statistics of Illegitimacy," *Journal of the Statistical Society of London*, XXV (1862), 219–274, raises the possibility of a positive correlation among bastardy and the level of education in Scotland, although he is uncertain about England (234, 260). There are strong theoretical reasons for suspecting a causal relationship between illegitimacy and primary education, but no evidence is available in published sources to permit verification. I am reluctant to put much faith in correlations among census data because so many other factors among a literate population could account for illegitimacy. The case history method seems most promising for checking this linkage in my model.

27 For population dynamics in a society with ossified guilds and nonpartible farms, I have drawn on the case most familiar to me: the state of Bavaria. See Edward Shorter, "Social Policy and Social Change in Bavaria, 1800–1860" unpub. Ph.D. thesis (Harvard, 1968). On long-term trends in the distribution of property in rural areas, see Günther Franz, *Geschichte des deutschen Bauernstandes vom frühen Mittelalter bis zum 19. Jahrhundert* (Stuttgart, 1970), 210–227.

28 On these marriage and settlement laws, see Karl Braun, "Das Zwangs-Zölibat für Mittellose in Deutschland," *Vierteljahrschrift für Volkswirtschaft und Kulturgeschichte*, XX (1867), 1480; Eduard Schübler, *Die Gesetze über Niederlassung und Verehelichung in den verschiedenen deutschen Staaten* (Stuttgart, 1855); John Knodel, "Law, Marriage and Illegitimacy in Nineteenth-Century Germany," *Population Studies*, XX (1966–67), 279–294; Mack Walker, "Home Towns and State Administrators; South German Politics, 1815–30," *Political Science Quarterly*, LXXXII (1967), 35–60. Illegitimacy *rates*, however, were much less affected by the abolition of marriage laws.

29   Recognition in French and Belgian law meant that the father conceded to the child some inheritance rights and support obligations, but this did not constitute either a legitimation or an adoption of the bastard. In Paris during 1880–84, more children were recognized (20.5 per cent) than legitimated (18.6 per cent), a sign of great instability in relationships between the sexes. Keep in mind that some of those recognized also turn up in the legitimation statistics, which means that we cannot add the two figures together to determine the total proportion of illegitimate children brought into the charmed circle of family life.

30   Seutemann, "Legitimation unehelicher Kinder," 42, for Austrian urban legitimation. The Dresden illegitimacy ratio in 1873–79 was around 20 percent with non-local mothers included, 16 percent with them excluded, indicating that urban ratios were high for reasons other than the "fleeing pregnant peasant" effect. Öttingen, *Moralstatistik,* 317.
A sad little literature on child mortality, foundlings, and unwed mothers on relief shows in a way that most cold demographic statistics do not the human cost of illegitimacy. The historian must span a long emotional distance between all of this expressive sexuality and the thousands of small tragedies behind the astonishingly high rate of illegitimate infant mortality. See William Acton, "Observations on Illegitimacy in the London Parish of St. Marylebone, St. Pancras . . . during the Year 1857," *Journal of the Statistical Society of London,* XXII (1859), 491–505; Ed. Ducpetiaux, "Du sort des· enfants trouvés et abandonnés en Belgique," *Bulletin de la Commission Centrale de Statistique* (of Belgium), I (1843), 207–271; René Lafabrègue, "Des enfants trouvés à Paris," *Annales de démographie internationale,* II (1878), 226–299; Othmar Spann, "Die Lage und das Schicksal der unehelichen Kinder," *Mutterschutz. Zeitschrift zur Reform der Sexuellen Ethik,* III (1907), 345–358; H. Neumann, "Die jugendlichen Berliner unehelicher Herkunft," *Jährbucher für Nationalökonomie und Statistik,* VIII (1894), 536–549.

31   See Steven Marcus, *The Other Victorians: A Study of Sexuality and Pornography in Mid-Nineteenth-Century England* (New York, 1966).

32   This paradox was pointed out to me by Fred Weinstein.

33   For this discussion of the traditional petty-bourgeois family, I rely on Möller, *Kleinbürgerliche Familie.*

34   There is now a mass of evidence, both literary and statistical, that middle-class French families had consciously adopted family limitation by about 1775. See *Prévention des naissances;* on birth control, see the most recent in a chain of local studies, Marcel Lachiver, *La Population de Meulan du XVIIe au XIXe siècle (vers 1600–1870)* (Paris, 1969), 210. The question is still unclarified for Germany.

For a decade now sociologists have been speaking about a revolution in American sexual behavior that supposedly occurred in the 1920s. This misconception stems largely from the findings of the Kinsey group, though notions of the disruptive effects of World War I on American life are also a contributing factor. Smith's interpretation of the facts stands in marked contrast to this point of view, since he seems to feel that the take-off point for the changes we have been seeing in this area throughout the twentieth century probably occurred in the second half of the nineteenth century. However, he also goes beyond this and shows that American sexual behavior has followed a cyclical pattern, with the eighteenth and the twentieth centuries being periods during which premarital sex—in the case of the eighteenth century, as indicated by bridal pregnancy—was not uncommon, though, to be sure, the meaning and context of premarital sex in the eighteenth century was different from today. The author draws upon a variety of sources to fill out his picture of American sexual attitudes and behavior, and he presents us with an excellent discussion of some of the methodological problems one encounters in trying to work with historical data.

DANIEL SCOTT SMITH

17 *The Dating of the American Sexual Revolution: Evidence and Interpretation*

Prevailing views of current patterns and recent changes in sexual behavior have been limited by the absence and neglect of systematic historical comparison. The very notion of a "sexual revolution," defined here narrowly as a substantial sustained increase in nonmarital coitus and broadly as a qualitatively more positive evaluation of sex as a human activity, implicitly embodies an attempt at historical periodization. Unfortunately, our understanding of the prerevolutionary phase of the history of sexual behavior rests mainly on ignorance. Sociologists typically place the significant beginnings of a sexual revolution for white American women during the 1920s.[1] Most historians, on the other hand, locate these important changes in values and behavior some ten to twenty years earlier.[2] Other scholars have hinted at cyclical patterns, a constant ongoing revolution since the eighteenth century, or even historical stability in rates of premarital intercourse.[3] Since the attempt to gather historical data about American sexual behavior and attitudes has only recently begun, the overall trends necessarily remain uncertain and confused. What is presently known about the history of sexual attitudes is confined to what may be called "respectable" ideology—extracted from marriage manuals, magazines, novels, and medical literature. What little is available about sexual behavior is concerned with some of the obvious though not inevitable consequences of nonmarital sexual activity—illegitimacy and premarital (or bridal) pregnancy.

This article will be limited to a comparison of the premarital pregnancy indices with other measures of sexual change during the last century in order to specify the dimensions of the complex process commonly labeled the "sexual revolution." Since the last one hundred years are not the most dramatic in the history of American premarital pregnancy, defining the trend is relatively more difficult than for the previous two centuries. The proportion of women pregnant at marriage has varied cyclically, with peaks in the late eighteenth century and in recent years and troughs in the mid-seventeenth and mid-nineteenth centuries (Table 1).[4] Such a long cycle is also apparent in Western European illegitimacy and premarital pregnancy data; however, the major downturn in European nonmarital pregnancy rates came some fifty years or more after the American decline of the early nineteenth century.[5] Since World War II, both illegitimacy and premarital pregnancy have increased significantly in England and Australia as well as in the United States.[6] In order to draw precise inferences about premarital behavior from these data, the alternative possibilities—contraception, fecundability, spontaneous and induced abortion—must be estimated. The biological determinants probably vary within too narrow limits to explain the trends; the social variables appear to be positively correlated over time. For example, illegitimacy, premarital pregnancy, contraceptive use, and perhaps induced abortion have all increased since World War II. Since little is

Daniel Scott Smith

Table 1. Long-Term Historical Variation in White American Premarital Pregnancy

Period	Percentage of first births within nine months of marriage		Description of sample
	Marriages	Areas	
Before 1701[a]	11.1%	9.9%	1,113 marriages in nine areas (8 in New England)
1701–1760[a]	23.3	19.4	1,311 marriages in nine areas (6 in New England)
1761–1800[a]	33.7	34.0	1,011 marriages in six areas (5 in New England)
1801–1840[a]	25.1	28.3	573 marriages in two areas (1 in New England)
1841–1880[a]	15.5	16.9	555 marriages in two areas (both in New England)
1960–1964[b]	22.5		
1964–1966[c]	19.5		

[a]Daniel Scott Smith and Michael S. Hindus, "Premarital Pregnancy in America, 1640–1966: An Overview and Interpretation". (Paper presented at the annual meeting of the American Historical Association, New York City, December 1971).

[b]Wilson H. Grabill and Maria Davidson, "Marriage, Fertility and Childspacing: June 1965," U.S. Bureau of the Census, Current Population Reports, series p-20, no. 186 (Washington, 1969), table 17, p. 39. This measure includes births from eight months and zero days to nine months and thirty days after marriage but excludes those born before marriage; the denominator includes all births within forty-eight months of marriage.

[c]U.S. Department of Health, Education and Welfare, Public Health Service, "Interval between first marriage and legitimate first birth, United States, 1964–66," *Monthly Vital Statistics Report* 18, no. 12 (March 27, 1970): 2, table 2. Proportion of first births under eight months of marriage.

known about the variation in these alternative possibilities for more distant periods, they cannot be definitely excluded.[7]

Relevant information for the study of sexual change during the last century includes data on premarital pregnancy incidence from surveys and the matching of birth and marriage records; illegitimacy for the last half century; premarital coitus for selected samples of twentieth-century women; "respectable" sexual attitudes and values; and other indicators of sociofamilial change such as the divorce rate. By itself, any of the above five sources gives an inadequate and misleading picture of the timing of changes in sexual behavior; considered together, they present a coherent and plausible pattern.

Premarital Pregnancy
SURVEY DATA

In 1959 and 1965 the Current Population Survey (CPS) of the Census Bureau asked national samples of American women the month and year of their first marriage and of the birth of their first child.

Between 7 and 9 percent of white women marrying in pre-World War II cohorts had their first child before eight months of marriage; between 10 and 14 percent of white first births born within forty-eight months of marriage came within the first eight months of marriage (Table 2). During 1940–44 and 1960–64 both measures doubled, increasing to 20.5 percent and 25.0 percent respectively for the first half of the 1960s. Some 19.5 percent of a national sample of white mothers of legitimate first children born in 1964–66 reported that they had been married less than eight months.[8] These data, considered alone, suggest that premarital sexual behavior or the outcomes of premarital intercourse have changed significantly only during the last twenty years.[9]

RECORD MATCHING DATA

This clear picture of a post-World War II sexual revolution becomes questionable when local studies of the interval between marriage and first birth are compared to the CPS national samples. No trend is apparent from the first decade of the twentieth century to the early 1960s (Table 3). Using a long interval, ranging from 251 to 265 days, or allocating uncertain cases by birth weight, between 17 and 30 percent of first births occurring in the same geographical location as the marriage were conceived before marriage in these twentieth-century samples. In the most recent data, the record-matching method produces a figure comparable to the CPS surveys. The 18.8 percent figure for Wood County, Ohio, for 1957–62 and the 19-20 percent indicated for Detroit couples in the early 1960s are sufficiently close to the national survey of mothers of 1964–66 legitimate first births (19.5 percent) to be considered identical.[10] For the pre-1940 samples, record matching consistently produces a higher incidence than the retrospective CPS cohorts surveyed in 1959.

At first glance one might dismiss the narrow, unrepresentative local samples, such as the Mormon Utah study, as reflecting special circumstances. Since a substantial proportion of marriages cannot be linked to a first birth because of such factors as geographically exogamous marriage, migration of the couple after marriage but before childbearing, and infertility of the couple, record matching provides an index but perhaps not a precise measure of the absolute level of premarital pregnancy. For assessing trends the key issue is the stability of the ratio of migratory pregnant couples to those who migrate nine or more months after marriage but before they have their first child. Since it seems unlikely that social censure of the premaritally pregnant has increased during the twentieth century, the record-matching index

Table 2. CPS Premarital Pregnancy Rates for Twentieth-Century White Marriage Cohorts

	|	Number of first births within a specified time per 1,000 marriages[a]								
Marriage cohorts	Before marriage		Six months		Seven months		Eight months		Nine months	
	1959	1964	1959	1965	1959	1965	1959	1965	1959	1964
1900–1909	n.a.		45		57		74		133	
1910–1919	n.a.		55		69		89		139	
1920–1924	n.a.		48		59		83		127	
1925–1929	n.a.		44		56		81		122	
1930–1934	n.a.		54		69		90		123	
1935–1939	n.a.		51		68		86		118	
1940–1944	n.a.	22	44	55	61	66	80	87	114	122
1945–1949	n.a.	23	57	63	77	83	103	108	156	165
1950–1954	n.a.	25	71	77	96	104	119	130	175	186
1955–1959	n.a.	37	85b	112	127b	147	160b	183	223b	248
1960–1964		36		129		168b		205b		261b

[a]Based on a question asking for calendar month and year of first marriage and birth. Hence, those born six months after marriage fall in the range from five months and zero days to six months and thirty-one days.
bRate adjusted for part of marriage cohort that has not reached stated interval.

Sources: 1959 survey: Wilson H. Grabill and Robert Parke, "Marriage, Fertility and Childspacing: August 1959," U.S. Bureau of the Census, Current Population Reports, series P-20, no. 108 (Washington, D.C., 1961): 38, table 17.

1965 survey: Wilson H. Grabill and Maria Davidson, "Marriage, Fertility and Childspacing: June 1965," U.S. Bureau of the Census, Current Population Reports, series P-20, no. 186 (Washington D.C., 1969): 39, table 17.

Table 3.Comparison of CPS and Record-Matching Data on Premarital Pregnancy

Marriage cohort	Percent within six months*		Percent within seven months*		Percent within 196 days*	
	1959 survey	1965 survey	1959 survey	1965 survey	Record-matching studies	
1900–09	5.8%		7.4%		1905–07[a]	11.9%
					1913–15[a]	14.8
1910–19	7.3		9.2		1919–21[b]	11.9
					1918–22[c]	10.9
1920–24	6.7		8.3		1921–23[a]	9.6
1925–29	6.4		8.1		1929–31[b]	8.0
1930–34	8.1		10.4		1929–31[a]	14.8
1935–39	7.7		10.3		1928–32[c]	14.1
					1939–41[a]	4.5
1940–44	6.3	7.7%	78.8	9.3%	1939–41[b]	9.8
1945–49	7.4	8.0	10.0	10.6	1939–42[c]	6.9
1950–54	9.0	9.6	12.1	13.0	1949–51[a]	5.3
1955–59		13.5		17.7		
1960–64		15.7		20.4	1957–62[d]	9.3

*In order to provide comparability with the measured used in record-matching studies percentages are based on first births occurring within 48 months of marriage.

[a] *Utah County, Utah:* Harold T. Christensen, "Child-Spacing Analysis via Record Linkage," *Marriage and Family Living* 35 (1963): 275.

[b] *Tippecanoe County, Indiana:* Ibid., p. 275.

[c] *Defiance County, Ohio:* Ibid., p. 275.

[d] *Wood County, Ohio:* Samuel H. Lowrie, "Early Marriage, Premarital Pregnancy and Associated Factors," *Journal of Marriage and the Family* 27 (1965): 50.

Sources: *CPS surveys.* See notes for table 2.

of premarital pregnancy should exhibit an upward movement similar to the CPS trend.

The reliability of the CPS curve as an index of change depends on the absence of an age bias in response to the survey. The women surveyed in 1959 who were first married before 1940 were all over forty; their answers may reflect to some extent their current attitudes, expecially with regard to the premarital sexual behavior of their daughters, and not their actual experience several decades earlier.[11] If sexual attitudes have actually become progressively more liberal in recent years, younger women should be less concerned than their elders with suppressing the fact of a premarital conception. Supporting this hypothesis of increasing honesty about the subject is the higher reported incidence (0.7 percent, 0.5 percent, 1.1 percent and 2.3 percent for the 1940–44, 1945–49, 1950–54 and 1955–59 marriage cohorts) of children born within eight months of marriage in the 1965 survey as compared to the group sampled in 1959 (see Table

Daniel Scott Smith

2). Thus, it is quite likely that the upward trend since 1945 in the CPS premarital pregnancy curve is exaggerated. Nevertheless, the upsurge is not entirely a statistical mirage. Since premarital pregnancy and early marriage are related, the decline in the age at first marriage between 1940 and 1960 implies an increasing number of brides pregnant at marriage. Since World War II, women marrying at age twenty-two or over have been only three-fourths as likely to have a birth within seven months of marriage as those women marrying under that age.[12] Without any increase in age-specific premarital pregnancy rates, the overall proportion of women pregnant at marriage would increase somewhat. The shape of the national trend for the first forty years of the twentieth century is not necessarily flat. In Australia, for example, just over 30 percent of women married in 1911 were pregnant at marriage; by 1942 a mere 11.7 percent were, while in 1965, 23.6 percent of all brides were pregnant.[13]

Illegitimacy

Further evidence of a substantial increase in white premarital sexual activity since 1940 is found in the striking rise in illegitimacy, i.e., the conception and birth of children outside marriage. Following two decades of stability, the white illegitimacy rate leaped 250 percent between 1940 and 1967 (Table 4). The general increase in illegitimacy for women of all ages reflects mainly an increase in the incidence of premarital coitus. If the CPS post-1940 trend in premarital pregnancy is biased upward, then a decreasing proportion of white nonmarital pregnancies are now being terminated within marriage.[14] This relative shift from bridal pregnancy to illegitimacy is also appar-

Table 4. Age-Specific Illegitimacy Rates for White American Women (births per 1,000 of unmarried women)

Year	15–44	15–19	20–24	25–29	30–34	35–39	40–44
			Age of women				
1940	3.6	3.3	5.7	4.0	2.5	1.7	0.7
1950	6.1	5.1	10.0	8.7	5.9	3.2	0.9
1960	9.2	6.6	18.2	18.2	10.8	3.9	
1965	11.6	7.9	22.1	24.3	16.6	4.9	
1967	12.5	9.0	23.1	22.7	14.0	4.7	
Increase 1940–67	247%	273%	305%	467%	460%	292%	

Sources: U.S. Department of Health, Education and Welfare, Public Health Service, Vital and Health Statistics, series 21, no. 15, "Trends in Illegitimacy, United States, 1940–1965" (Washington, D.C., 1968), p. 4, table B; Vital and Health Statistics, series 21, no. 19, "Natality Statistics Analysis, United States, 1965–1967," (Rockville, Maryland, 1970), p. 33, table 23.

ent in national data for England and Australia.[15] Consistent with this development is the reported lesser emotional commitment required for coitus by modern college coeds.[16] The qualitative context as well as the quantitative incidence of premarital sexual activity has been modified since World War II.

Premarital Coitus

The behavioral evidence for the dating of the sexual revolution in the 1920s consists of surveys of the premarital coital experience of selected groups of American women. Although sociologists allow for an important liberalization of attitudes and an increase in noncoital sexual activity such as petting, they have cautiously concluded that between the 1920s and the early 1960s no marked increase in premarital coitus occurred. With evidence indicating a jump in the level of premarital intercourse during the late 1960s, a new phase of the sexual revolution is apparently now in progress.[17] While the increase in illegitimacy and premarital pregnancy in the late 1940s and 1950s may cast some doubt on the timing of this second take-off, the dating of the first phase relies on the small minority of women who attended college. Between two-thirds and three-fourths of the women in the three most important historical studies of premarital coitus had some college experience, while only 10.2 percent and 13.1 percent of native-born women born, respectively, between 1891 and 1900 and between 1901 and 1910 went beyond high school. While nearly half of all native-born white women terminated their formal education before the ninth grade, a mere 2.3 percent to 4.5 percent in the three studies had less than a high school education.[18] For this college-educated minority, the sexual revolution may have originated in the 1920s or, as the Terman sample suggests, during the preceeding decade (Table 5).[19] Furthermore, it is not clear *which* college-educated women appear in these studies; it is possible that the older women interviewed by Kinsey and associates were drawn more heavily from religious groups instead of universities and clubs.[20]

Since late nineteenth- and early twentieth-century premarital pregnancy ratios are very close to the reported pre-1900 levels of premarital coitus, a downward bias of the pre-1900 reported intercourse incidence is likely. While 7 percent of the Davis sample, 13 percent of the pre-1890 and 26 percent of the 1890–99 birth cohorts in the Terman study, and 27 percent of the pre-1900 Kinsey birth cohort had premarital intercourse, 16 percent of first births were conceived before marriage in Hingham, Mass. (1861–80), 19 percent in Lexington, Mass. (1885–95), 20 percent (1905–07) and 29 percent (1913–15) in Utah County, Utah, and 20 percent in Tippecanoe

Daniel Scott Smith   328

Table 5. Incidence of Premarital Coitus for White American Women: The Sexual Revolution of the 1920s?

Authors of study	Birth dates of women in study	Percent with premarital coitus
Davis[a]	before 1900	7.2%
Terman[b]	before 1890	13.5%
	1890–1899	26.0
	1900–1909	48.8
	1910–later	68.3
Kinsey et al.[c]	before 1900	26.6
	1900–1909	51.3
	1910–1919	56.1
	1920–1929	51.2

[a]Katherine B. Davis, *Factors in the Sex Lives of Twenty-Two Hundred* (New York, 1929), p. 19.

[b]Lewis M. Terman, *Pyshcological Factors in Marital Happiness* (New York, 1938), p. 321.

[c]Ira L. Reiss, "Standards of Sexual Behavior," in Albert Ellis and Albert Abarbanel, *The Encyclopedia of Sexual Behavior* (New York, 1961), 2: 999. Calculated from unpublished data from the Institute for Sex Research.

County, Indiana (1919–21).[21] As every school girl should know, intercourse is a necessary though not sufficient prerequisite to pregnancy. The absence of a larger differential between premaritally conceived first births and the incidence of premarital coitus suggests that the timing of the first phase of the sexual revolution varied for different social strata in the white population. College-educated women, largely of middle- and upper-middle-class backgrounds, maintained conservative sexual standards longer than the remainder of the population. The premarital pregnancy ratio in Hingham increased from 8.5 percent (1841–60) to 16.0 percent (1861–80), and in Lexington the comparable index jumped from 3.6 percent (1854–66) to 19.3 percent (1885–95). For the general population of women, important changes in premarital sexual behavior already were under way during the late nineteenth century.

Very recent data from the first national probability sample of the incidence of teenage premarital coitus helps define more precisely the magnitude of change in sexual behavior since the 1940s. Today's teenagers from 15 to 19 are at least twice as likely to have had coital experience as the Kinsey women born during the 1920s. Two-fifths of single white nineteen-year-old women have experienced coitus while only 23 percent in the 1910–19 and 21 percent in the 1920–29 Kinsey birth cohorts had such experience by the age of twenty.[22] It is possible that this doubling of teenage coital incidence rates merely represents a lowering of the age of sexual participation, which may be attributed to the declining age at menarche and earlier socio-sexual maturity.[23] The incidence figures for sixteen- and eighteen-year-olds in the recent survey are only slightly above the Kinsey figures for women marrying between sixteen and twenty (17.5 percent and 33.5 percent versus 15 percent and 30 percent, respectively).[24] However, the illegitimacy rate has increased more for women between twenty-five and thirty-four than for those between fifteen and twenty-four (bottom row of Table 4), and the concentration of premarital pregnancy among younger women has not increased between 1945–49 and 1960–64.[25] While the Kinsey sample is not a representative benchmark, the apparent increase in teenage premarital coitus is consistent with the other indicators of change in sexual behavior. Finally, of course, this focus on the significance of the past decade or so as a period of comparatively rapid sexual change does not contradict the obvious manifestations of changing social attitudes and increasing *public* interest concerning sexuality.

Attitudes

Since sexual standards are largely maintained by the family, the most impenetrable social institution, the connection between shifts in behavior and public attitudinal change is not automatic or inevitable, especially in the short run. However, the investigation of ideal sexual standards does supplement the tentative conclusions with regard to behavior. Following a more general trend in American historiography that focuses on the internal dissolution of Victorian bourgeois culture, the emergence of new, more liberal sexual attitudes is now being dated before the First World War.[26] The origins of these changes, like the increase in premarital pregnancy in the two Massachusetts towns with available data, lie in the last decades of the nineteenth century. By 1900 the ideal conception of woman as frail, dependent, and virtuous was being challenged by a small but vocal group of feminists.[27] By the beginning of World War I the "newness" of non-Victorian attitudes was wearing off.[28] Articles on birth control, prostitution, divorce, and sexual morals between 1910 and 1914 were more numerous than articles indexed by the *Reader's Guide* for either 1919–24 or 1925–28. [29] During the last two decades of the nineteenth century authors of marriage manuals for middle-class educated readers were beginning to endorse pleasure as a positive aspect of marital sexuality; during the first two decades of this century this shift continued but was not complete until the 1920s.[30]

The movement for legal sexual repression associated with the work of Anthony Comstock and state anticontraception laws during the last third of the nineteenth century is consistent with the hypothe-

Daniel Scott Smith   *330*

sis that the Victorian moral order was already in crisis before 1900.[31] By the end of the century the conservative defenders of premarital continence were becoming more defensive and frenetic. During the early twentieth century their efforts met with both ridicule and support.[32] If public opinion and individual internalization of morality were operative, official repression of deviant sexual activity would have been superfluous and unnecessary. The official response to what was considered sexual deviancy resulted from an objective increase in "deviant" behavior.

Divorce

Changes in attitudes and behavior must be considered simultaneously to ascertain if *significant* change is occurring. In as sensitive an area as sexual behavior before marriage, considerable divergence is to be expected. Hence, information on another aspect of family change is quite relevant to this discussion of the dating of the sexual revolution. The conceptual rationale for divorce as an integral part of a marriage system based on affection was established in the late nineteenth century.[33] Since divorce is an indicator of the social meaning of marriage, time-series data on the divorce rate provide a suggestive supplement to this periodization of sexual change. The number of divorces per 1,000 existing marriages increased 102 percent between 1860–64 and 1880–84, 79 percent between 1880–84 and 1900–04, 71 percent between 1900–04 and 1920–24, and 43 percent between 1920–24 and 1940–44. However, the absolute increases were greatest during the twentieth century with upward increments of 1.2, 1.9, 3.0, and 3.1 per 1,000 existing marriages, respectively, for the above periods.[34] Although the absolute change increases, the rate of change declines over time. A parallel conclusion with regard to changes in the incidence of premarital sexual behavior seems plausible for the period between the Civil War and World War I.

Concluding Scenario of the "Sexual Revolution"

Clearly more research is needed on both behavior and attitudes before firm conclusions can be drawn about the history of American sexuality and the dating of the sexual revolution. Considerable and surprising variation is obvious, particularly in the premarital pregnancy boom of the eighteenth century and the bust of the nineteenth. For the sexual revolution since the Victorian nadir, the following conclusions may be tentatively advanced:

(1) The "revolutionary" character of the sexual revolution can easily be overstated. The trend toward increasing nonmarital sexual intercourse has been ongoing for nearly a century from a level which

was not fully restrictive. Even in respectable sexual ideology, mid-nineteenth-century women were not typically considered to be asensual.[35] Two-thirds of all women in the most conservative pre-1900 birth cohort in the Kinsey study experienced orgasm during the first year of marriage, compared to 78 percent of those born in the 1920s.[36] Clearly there was an increase, but equally clearly "sexlessness" was nowhere near being a majority experience for American women before the sexual revolution began. The qualitative meaning of the sexual revolution in behavior is not promiscuity; for the great majority of American women, premarital sexual permissiveness is intimately related to affection, mutuality, and a positive choice for a close interpersonal relationship. Half of the sexually experienced teenagers surveyed by Zelnik and Kantner said they intended to marry their lovers.[37] A substantial minority are pregnant at marriage but only a tiny fraction bear an illegitimate child.

(2) Change in sexual behavior has probably not been linear and continuous. Little or no change in premarital pregnancy, illegitimacy, or premarital coitus occurred between the 1920s and the 1940s. Both quantitatively and qualitatively, the most significant phase of the sexual revolution has occurred during the last two decades.

(3) The timing of the first wave of the sexual revolution has probably varied markedly for different groups in the white population. If one particular period can be labeled the "origins," the last third of the nineteenth century probably encompassed a larger proportion of the population than either the 1920s or the decade before World War I. During the late nineteenth century the intellectual basis for a more positive evaluation of human sexuality was established. The first three decades of this century may be characterized as an era in which the behavior of the educated minority of women converged upon the behavior of the less-educated majority. During the same three decades the sexual attitudes of the younger educated strata were significantly liberalized. Then from the 1920s to the 1950s the higher level of premarital coitus was increasingly supported by a further democratization of this more tolerant ideology. When this convergence of attitudes and behavior neared completion during the 1950s, the stage was set for the most recent transformation in both behavior and attitudes.

Notes
    1   Ira L. Reiss, "The Sexual Renaissance: A Summary and Analysis," *Journal of Social Issues* 22, no. 2 (1966): 123–37. Erwin O. Smigel and Rita Seiden, "The Decline and Fall of the Double Standard," *The Annals of the American Academy of Political and Social Science* 376 (1969): 6–17.

Daniel Scott Smith

2 James R. McGovern, "The American Woman's Pre-World War I Freedom in Manners and Morals," *Journal of American History* 55, no. 2 (1968): 315–33. David M. Kennedy, *Birth Control in America: The Career of Margaret Sanger* (New Haven, 1970). William L. O'Neill, *Divorce in the Progressive Era* (New Haven, 1967). Nathan G. Hale, Jr., *Freud and the Americans: The Beginnings of Psychoanalysis in the United States, 1876–1917* (New York, 1971).

3 For an implied cyclical view, see Robert R. Bell, *Premarital Sex in a Changing Society,* (Englewood Cliffs, N.J., 1966), pp. 17–40; and Paul Woodring, "Some Thoughts on the Sexual Revolution," in Gerald D. Winter and Eugene M. Nuss, *The Young Adult: Identity and Awareness* (Glenview, Ill., 1969), pp. 116–19. Winter and Nuss claim in their introduction to the Woodring essay that "it would appear that America has been the scene of a continuous sexual revolution from at least as early as the beginning of the eighteenth century." More commonly, evidence of high levels of premarital sexual activity in the distant past has been used to conclude that little change has occurred in the course of American history. For this inference, see Thomas P. Monahan, "Premarital Pregnancy in the United States: A Critical Review and Some New Findings," *Eugenics Quarterly* 7, no. 3 (1960): 133–47; and Ira L. Reiss, *Premarital Sexual Standards in America* (New York, 1960), p. 132.

4 A speculative explanation and more detailed examination of this long cycle is provided in Daniel Scott Smith and Michael S. Hindus, "Premarital Pregnancy in America, 1640–1966: An Overview and Interpretation" (paper presented at the annual meeting of the American Historical Association, December 1971).

5 Edward Shorter, "Illegitimacy, Sexual Revolution and Social Change in Modern Europe," *Journal of Interdisciplinary History* 2, no. 2, (1971): 237–72. P. E. H. Hair, "Bridal pregnancy in rural England in earlier centuries," *Population Studies* 20 (1966): 233–43 and "Bridal pregnancy in earlier England further examined," *Population Studies* 24 (1970): 59–70. Edward Shorter, John Knodel, and Etienne van de Walle, "The Decline of Non-Marital Fertility in Europe, 1880–1940," *Population Studies* 24 (1971), 375–93.

6 Phillips Cutright, "Illegitimacy: Myths, Causes and Cures," *Family Planning Perspectives* 3, no. 1 (1971): 26. Shirley M. Hartley, "The Amazing Rise of Illegitimacy in Great Britain, *Social Forces* 44, no. 4 (1966): 533–45. K. G. Basavarajappa, "Pre-marital Pregnancies and Ex-Nuptial Births in Australia, 1911–66," *Australian and New Zealand Journal of Sociology* 4, no. 2 (1968): 126–45.

7 On the alternative possibilities, see Kingsley Davis and Judith Blake, "Social Structure and Fertility: An Analytic Framework," *Economic Development and Cultural Change* 4, no. 3 (1956): 211–35, and Cutright, "Illegitimacy," pp. 26–28.

8 U.S. Department of Health, Education, and Welfare, Public Health Service, "Interval between first Marriage and Legitimate first Birth, United States, 1964–66," *Monthly Vital Statistics Report* 18, no. 12, supplement (March 27, 1970): 2, table 2.

9 In an important analysis of the components of the increase in teenage illegitimacy, Phillips Cutright allocates 77 percent of the white increase in premarital pregnancy and illegitimacy to higher rates of premarital intercourse and 23 percent to improved fecundity and health. "The Teenage Sexual Revolution and the Myth of an Abstinent Past," *Family Planning Perspectives* 4, no. 1 (1972), table 3, col. 6.

10 Samuel H. Lowrie, "Early Marriage, Premarital Pregnancy and Associated

Factors," *Journal of Marriage and the Family* 27 (1965): 50. Lolagene C. Coombs, Ronald Freedman, Judith Friedman, and William F. Pratt, "Premarital Pregnancy and Status before and after Marriage," *American Journal of Sociology* 75, no. 5 (1970): 804.

11   Reiss has found that the social roles associated with age are important determinants of attitudes toward premarital sexual permissiveness. Some 21 percent of persons between 21 and 34, 20 percent of those 35–49, but only 13 percent of persons over 50 expressed "highly permissive" views on the subject. Similarly, people with teenage children were less permissive than those with preteenagers or no children. Reiss, *The Social Context of Premarital Sexual Permissiveness* (New York, 1967), pp. 141–43.

12   Wilson H. Grabill and Maria Davidson, "Marriage, Fertility and Child-spacing: June 1965," U.S. Bureau of the Census, *Current Population Reports,* series P-20, no. 186 (Washington, 1969), p. 47, table 21.

13   Basavarajappa, "Pre-marital Pregnancies," p. 143, table A.

14   Accepting the accuracy of the CPS premarital pregnancy series, Reynolds Farley and Albert I. Hermalin have calculated that 55 percent, 63 percent, and 60 percent, of the offspring of all white first premarital pregnancies were born after marriage in the 1940–49, 1950–59, and 1960–64 marriage cohorts. See "Family Stability: A Comparison of Trends between Blacks and Whites," *American Sociological Review* 36, no. 1 (1971): 12–13.

15   Hartley, "The Amazing Rise," p. 540, table 3. Basavarajappa, "Pre-marital Pregnancies," p. 141.

16   Compared to 1958 the percentages of coeds having intercourse in 1968 in a "dating" situation has increased from 10 percent to 23 percent, in a "going steady" context from 15 percent to 28 percent, but in an "engagement" relationship the rise has only been from 31 percent to 39 percent. Furthermore, the proportion feeling they "went too far" has been cut in half in all three contexts. Robert R. Bell and Jay B. Chaskes, "Premarital Sexual Experience among Coeds, 1958–1968," *Journal of Marriage and the Family* 23, no. 1 (1970): 83. For a general review of recent events, see Kenneth L. Cannon and Richard Long, "Premarital Sexual Behavior in the Sixties," *Journal of Marriage and the Family* 53, no. 1 (1971): 36–49.

17   Reiss, "The Sexual Renaissance," p. 127.

18   Lewis M. Terman, *Psychological Factors in Marital Happiness* (New York, 1938), p. 43. Katherine B. Davis. *Factors in the Sex Life of Twenty-Two Hundred American Women* (New York, 1929), p. 3. Paul H. Gebhard, Wardell B. Pomeroy, Clyde E. Martin, and Cornelia V. Christenson, *Pregnancy, Birth and Abortion,* (New York, 1958), p. 24. Data for native-born white women from Wilson H. Grabill, Clyde V. Kiser, and Pascal K. Whelpton, *The Fertility of American Women* (New York, 1958), p. 191.

19   Coital incidence and educational level are not related in the Kinsey sample, once age at marriage is controlled. However, there are only 97 single women over twenty with less than a high-school education. Alfred C. Kinsey, Wardell B. Pomeroy, Clyde E. Martin, and Paul H. Gebhard, *Sexual Behavior in the Human Female,* (New York, 1965), p. 333, table 75.

20   How Kinsey prodigiously collected his sexual histories is related by Wardell

B. Pomeroy, *Dr. Kinsey and the Institute for Sex Research* (New York, 1972), pp. 106–37, 369–71; and Cornelia V. Christenson, *Kinsey: A Biography* (Bloomington, Ind., 1971), pp. 103–10, 134–35. On the inadequacies and the considerable relative merits of the Kinsey population, see the analysis of the male volume by William C. Cochran, Frederick Mosteller, and John W. Tukey, *Statistical Problems of the Kinsey Report* (Washington, 1954), pp. 21–29, 44–65.

21   Smith and Hindus, "Premarital Pregnancy," pp. 55–56, 67. A measure of 8 1/2 months was used for the Massachusetts towns and 251 days for the samples in Table 3.

22   Report on the study undertaken by Melvin Zelnik and John F. Kantner for the Commission on Population Growth and the American Future, *New York Times*, May 10, 1972, p. 9.

23   Cutright, "The Teenage Sexual Revolution," pp. 25–26. J. M. Tanner, "Earlier Maturation in Man," *Scientific American* 218, no. 1 (1968): 24–27.

24   *New York Times*, May 10, 1972, p. 9. Kinsey *et al.*, p. 337, table 79.

25   Grabill and Davidson, "Marriage, Fertility and Childspacing: June 1965," p. 47, table 21.

26   The pioneering revisionist study is Henry F. May, *The End of American Innocence: A Study of the First Years of our Time, 1912–1917* (New York, 1959), esp. pp. 334–47.

27   Kennedy, *Birth Control in America*, pp. 53–63.

28   Ibid., p. 71

29   McGovern, "American Woman's Pre-World War I Freedom," p. 316.

30   Michael Gordon, "From an Unfortunate Necessity to a Cult of Mutual Orgasm: Sex in American Marital Education Literature, 1830–1940," in James Henslin, ed., *Studies in the Sociology of Sex* (New York, 1971), pp. 53–77.

31   Carol Flora Brooks, "The Early History of the Anti-Contraceptive Laws in Massachusetts and Connecticut," *American Quarterly* 18 (1966): 3–23. Robert Bremner, ed., *Traps for the Young by Anthony Comstock* (Cambridge, 1967), pp. vii-xxxi.

32   Hale, *Freud and the Americans*, p. 26. Bremner, *Traps for the Young*, pp. xxix-xxxi and cartoons following p. 130.

33   O'Neill, *Divorce in the Progressive Era*, pp. 89–167.

34   Paul H. Jacobson, *American Marriage and Divorce* (New York, 1959), estimated rates on p. 90, table 42.

35   Gordon, "Sex in American Marital Education Literature," pp. 53–77.

36   Kinsey *et al.*, p. 403, table 104.

37   *New York Times*, May 10, 1972, p. 9.

This article, by Barker-Benfield, represents a tradition in historiography not found elsewhere in this volume, namely, what we might speak of as critical or radical history. In it, the author attempts to look at nineteenth-century attitudes toward male and female sexuality in terms of larger currents present in the society. His interpretation of the growth of gynecological surgery as a response of men to their anxieties about their own sexuality, but more importantly to their anxieties over female sexuality, is provocative, particularly given current concern on the part of women with control over their own bodies. While some may take issue with Barker-Benfield's interpretation, he nonetheless forces us to consider issues which should not be ignored.

BEN BARKER-BENFIELD

18 *The Spermatic Economy: A Nineteenth-Century View of Sexuality*

In nineteenth-century America, the world outside the home was regarded by men as "a vast wilderness."[1] They were "naked and alone surrounded by savages";[2] their lives were consumed in "a rage of competitive battle."[3] Democratic leveling in the New World, the

336

disintegration of class stability and of transgenerational family crafts-manship exposed all men to a perplexing choice of identities that they experienced as relentless pressure. Freedom of this kind proved a mortal burden. Potentially everyone could make it; but in effect al-most no one could distinguish himself from the ruck of atoms all pressing in the same direction.[4] A man was forced to face this hostile world of relentless competition because he was born with a penis: "the whirl and contact with the world . . . is the inheritance of our sex."[5]

Woman's role as wife and mother was geared to this necessary strife among men. In addition to showing her menfolk a perpetually cheerful smile, a wife was deemed to impart morality to her husband and sons. But morality derived from woman-in-her-world was irrele-vant to the life-style to which men were addicted.[6] In fact, women themselves were felt to be a persistently explosive threat to the sur-vival and prosperity of men.

Hence the well-known and otherwise perplexing coexistence of an ideology[7] of male self-sufficiency with that of woman's moral power over men's lives.[8] Placing her on a pedestal symbolized the circumscription in such rhetoric. And from the early 1830's, a son could turn to a stream of self-help expertise from clergymen and assorted medical practitioners, the sheer numbers of whom, together with the numbers of books they sold, bear out the assumption Alexis de Tocqueville made of the irrelevance to men of the mother's educa-tional function.[9] These advice manuals competed with the mother for the allegiance of the son old enough to read: they competed both in authority and in their assumption of the ideal of self-sufficiency. In addition, such experts as Amariah Brigham (1798–1849) and Isaac Ray (1807–1881) carried their challenge to the mother's putative authority in early childbearing. They urged the development of a "bodily constitution possessing extraordinary powers of endurance" to prepare the sons for confrontation with the withering blast of competitive, vicissitudinous democracy.[10] They were also concerned to check the dangerous development of the intellect of girls. Female education was, in the last resort, dispensable since girls should be designed only for robust motherhood.[11]

The Reverend John Todd (1800–1873), author of *The Student's Manual,* was among those offering a young man a program for suc-cess. His views of male psychology were typical of all kinds of nine-teenth-century American writers from Emerson and Thoreau to John C. Calhoun and Ik Marvell as well as Brigham, Ray, and a host of other doctors including J. Marion Sims and Augustus Kinsley Gard-ner.

After brief and divisive ministries in Groton, Massachusetts,

Northampton, and Philadelphia, Todd settled in Pittsfield in 1842 until his death and held powerful and ecclesiastical sway over his part of Massachusetts. Todd was the subject of Melville's short satire "The Lightning-Rod Man."[12] Melville's attack was based on Todd's role as behavioral stylist for hundreds of thousands, if not millions, of young men. A prolific writer, Todd came to see *The Student's Manual* as his most important work, although he did not see the irony of the book's title; it focused, in the final analysis, on masturbation. Within two years after its publication in 1835 the *Manual* had gone into seven editions; in the twenty-fourth edition of 1854 Todd pointed out that there had "never been less than one edition yearly published in this country." It remained as popular throughout the nineteenth century. Young men came to Todd to acknowledge, "I owe most or all of what I am to your pen."[13]

Paradoxically, Todd told young men how to become self-made. Self-making was the product of will and energy. Energy was one of the most frequent and most characteristic terms associated with male activity in this period (along with its synonyms: vigor, vitality, vital powers, and vital forces). Todd's books constantly break down into rules for the generation, hoarding, and miserly expenditure of "that moving active spirit."[14] Men "are naturally and practically indolent and . . . need powerful stimulants and heavy pressure to awaken their powers and call forth exertions."[15] Dr. Ray said that "most men go through life with a large amount of latent power underdeveloped, and utterly unable to concentrate their energies on any particular point." Men needed a "course of suitable discipline,"[16] in addition to the useful "rivalry" and the "pressure" of frightening competition, which Todd asserted "we cannot get at home."[17] Men needed competition in developing a psychic system to defend themselves against the competition which made the system necessary, and so on.

The courses of discipline advocated by Amariah Brigham, Isaac Ray, and John Todd reflected two conventional assumptions about man's being. First was the somatic basis of the mind: the intellect depended on the material body for "vigor and power."[18] Properly developed, the mind itself could stimulate the body's resources: "mental excitement increases the flow of blood to the brain," the organ that "manifested" mind.[19] But too much exercise, too large a flow, could "enfeeble or derange the mind."[20] The second assumption was that the underlying model for the operation of the whole man, psychological and physiological, was economic.[21] Americans shared this convention with Europeans, some of whom Brigham cited. It was, he said, a "fundamental law of the distribution of vital powers . . . that when they are increased in one part, they are diminished in all the rest of the living economy . . . to increase the powers of one organ it is absolutely necessary that they should be diminished in all the others."[22] This law underlay Todd's and Ray's recommendations for the arousing and channeling of energies from latency and waste into self-education, railroading, business—in short, into the "majesty and destiny of Manhood. . . . "[23]

So men were committed to goals that they believed necessarily drove some of them insane. American doctors accepted the dicta of the French psychiatrist, Jean-Dominique Esquirol, that insanity was a disease of civilization, and that the number of the insane was in proportion to civilization's progress. Since America was regarded as the most advanced country, doctors found there the highest incidence of insanity: conditions thought to derange the mind were the unchecked nature of democratic ambitions; a lifetime's enervation by perplexing choice; and the chronic uncertainty of the modern economy. All were pressures experienced most directly by males.[24] Concentration of energies was the inevitable characteristic of the Faustian figures of nineteenth-century literature, from Melville's Ahab to Bradley Headstone in Dickens' *Our Mutual Friend.* In each case, fixity of purpose was described in the specific terms of the contemporary psychological definition of "monomania," the too successful concentration of energies on one "mad mark."[25]

Todd's young man had to be constantly on the watch for opportunities to incorporate energy and at the same time to prevent loss of his energy to others. A chapter in *The Student's Manual* is arranged according to the metaphor of thieves who steal time: for example the thieves of sloth and sleep. All of one's experiences were reified and quantified into a drum-tight economic system in which every gain was someone's loss, every loss someone else's gain. This seems to have been a projection of the intra-personal "law of animal economy" on to inter-personal relations.

Todd represented the assimilation of resources to oneself as a specific physical process: the incorporation of material that could be converted into "mental powers." "We want to have the mind continually expanding and creating new thoughts or at least feeding itself on manly thoughts. The food is to the blood, which circulates through your veins, what reading is to the mind."[26] Todd's image for the working of the male body under the stimulus of a properly resolute will was that of a "fountain"[27] of "unequaled . . . inconquerable energy" that showed itself best in the "pure" achievements of railroad building and the related extractive industries out West—logging and mining.[28] Hanging on the walls of Todd's study in Pittsfield, where he turned his energy into successful tracts about turning energy, was a phallic arsenal of guns, spears, fishing rods, tools, canes and clubs. In the midst of all stood a covered, five-foot-three-inch high, indoor fountain, self-contained and ever replenished, furnishing the "waters of life." Todd proudly explained "I have only to touch a little brass cock" for the waters to "leap up" and generate "pearls dropping into a well, "golden balls falling into cups of silver."[29] A young man, he said, should regard books as "fountains"' from which he should draw "gold dust," converting his reading into an inner and permanent "fountain." "What you read today, will so be gone—expended or forgotten, and the mind must be continually filled up with new streams of knowledge. . . . It is the hand of the diligent which maketh rich."[30]

That reference to "hand" (where "eye" or "mind" would have seemed more appropriate) brings to mind the constant temptation faced by the young male reader to masturbate. Part of man's difficulty in self-government was his sexual eruptibility. Experts like Dr. Edward Jarvis emphasized that men were naturally appetitive beings who could break out from the social control that, they said, democracy had placed in individual and putatively autonomous hands. One manifestation of this lack of sexual control in men, uniquely recorded in American asylums, was masturbation.[31] The facility with which Todd attacked masturbation was analogous to the facility with which a young male reader found himself masturbating. Todd's work is pervaded with masturbation phobia, explicit and implicit. In the course of willing his energies into the proper channels to replenish or increase his "fountain," a young man was inevitably beset with the temptation to masturbate. The hoarding and concentration of energy—ultimately, of sexual energy—in an obsessively self-sufficient system that was preoccupied with masturbation (i.e., with avoiding it) was very much like the contemporary definition of the autonomous, secretive, addictive habit such a system was designed to avoid.[32] And, in fact, the treatment of masturbation, the absorption of a young man's energies in constructive male tasks, was the same as the course a normal non- (or undiscovered) masturbator would take. An article in the *New Orleans Medical and Surgical Journal* of 1855 described a "young man of fine physical development who wrote good verses and practiced masturbation to excess. [He] asked for medical advice . . . [and] was persuaded to try severe manual labor, he cleared six acres of heavily timbered beech and sugar tree bottoms—was cured and rose to distinction in civil life."[33] Todd's masturbator exactly reversed this productive relation with his surroundings. Instead of feeding one's blood with resources, the masturbator found "vipers" feeding on his own "life's blood."[34] The masturbator's "fountain" became "corrupted," the "ship" of his self-sufficient being having a "worm hole" in it.[35] Clearly there was a proportionate relationship between positive and negative male behaviors. Masturbation was the most thoroughly appropriate sin for a society preoccupied with the autonomous accumulation of male energies (and monomania perhaps the most appropriate and extreme form of its "lunacy").[35]

The discharge of sperm, it was generally believed, "obliterated", "prostrated", and "blotted out" all of "the energies of the system." Instead of "concentrating" those energies onto the nonsexual end of success, the masturbator concentrated what was left of them onto his penis and testicles. "All the remaining energies of animal life seem to be concentrated in these organs, and all the remaining power to gratification left is in the exercise of this . . . loathsome and beastly habit." That the ejaculation of sperm then diminished and exhausted all of the rest of the body's energy suggests that, somehow, in its focussing on the genital organs the previously undefined energy was transformed into sperm.[36]

The significance attached to the ejaculation of sperm reflected an amalgam of popular ideas. Widespread in the eighteenth and nineteenth centuries was the belief in pangenesis—each part of the body contributed a fraction of itself to the sperm by way of the blood. The belief that sperm represented its bearer was probably intensified by Lamarck's elaboration in 1802 of the theory of the hereditability of acquired characteristics, a notion held both popularly and by such luminaries as Charles Lyell, Herbert Spencer, and Charles Darwin.[37] The American sex expert, Dr. Gardner, said in 1872, that sperm was "the concentrated powers of man's perfected being . . . " "Sperm is the purest extract of the blood and according to the expression of Feruel, *totus homo semen est.*"[38]

After midcentury, beliefs about sperm and the body's economy were influenced by the increasingly mechanistic, materialistic views associated with Hermann von Helmholtz's "conservation of force." But views of the body as an economic system, or a system of energies held in equilibrium by reason, "the balance wheel of the mind", were already traditional in the early part of the century. In fact, the application of "conservation of force" to human physiology looked back to Benjamin Rush, for example, with his vascular theory, and forward to Freud via his teachers Brucke, Meynert, and Breuer. American acceptance of Freudian theory, particularly the economy of the libido and sublimation, was governed to a large extent by the way in which they coincided with widespread indigenous views of a very similar kind.[39]

While the system was economic ("the spermatic economy" of the title of this essay), and "spermatic plethora" was, therefore, of some slight concern, that could be dealt with easily by pursuing a normal path of nonsexual activity.[40] The deeper anxiety was spermatic *loss,* with its concomitant losses of will and order. Such a belief made *any* uncontrolled expenditure of sperm potentially dangerous. To its remarks on masturbation, an article signed "W" (Samuel Woodward?) in the *Boston Medical and Surgical Journal* of 1835 added the warning that nature "designs that this drain upon the system [i.e. ejaculation of sperm in copulation] should be reserved to mature age and even then that it should be made but sparingly. . . . Sturdy manhood . . . loses its energy and bends under the too frequent expenditure of this important secretion: and so age or condition will protect a man from the dangers of unlimited indulgence, [even] legally and naturally exercised."[41] Expenditure was the term for which "spend" (i.e., reach orgasm) was the nickname (used, for example in *Moby Dick* and the anonymous *My Secret Life*). Pangenesis and Lamarckism were expressed in the belief that "runts," feeble infants, and girls would be produced by debilitated sperm, old man's prostrated sperm, businessman's tired sperm, masturbator's exhausted, debaucher's exceeded, contraceptor's impeded, coward's unpatriotic, and newlywed's green, sperm.[42]

In his book, *Conjugal Sins* (1870), Dr. A. K. Gardner (1822–1876) laid out elaborate conditions and precautions for productive non-damaging procreation which reflected the specific stresses and strains of the nineteenth-century American male world and the law of animal economy. *Conjugal Sins* sold 30,000 copies in its first six years[43] and the preface to the ninth edition of 1923 claimed an increasing demand. If one followed its rules to the letter, in the normal run of things one could only copulate at high noon on Sundays. Failure to follow these rules would result in "nervous exhaustion."[44] One only survived if very lucky.

Physicians intervened in the marriage relationship to tell husband and wife that their joint concern was to keep the male's sperm souped up to a particular level of richness. The idea was to use neither more nor less sperm than was necessary for the production of a baby and for the preservation of the richness of sperm at the next copulation. At the same time, very significant concern was given to the appeasing of woman's coital appetite, which demanded the infusion of sperm.[45]

Perhaps the most famous American gynecologist of the nineteenth century, J. Marion Sims (1813–1883), was led to quantify sperm. "I do not know that anyone has thought of measuring the quantity of semen, ejected in the act of copulation. . . . I was induced on several occasions to remove semen with a syringe and to measure it subsequently, and I found that ordinarily there was about a drachm and ten minims."[46] Someone else had followed the logic of the translation of the body's economy into measure, this time of fiscal currency. He was the anonymous English author of *My Secret Life,* who said that on several occasions he stuffed money into a woman's vagina, to have her excrete it into a chamber pot for quantification.[47] Dr. Gardner called sperm "Danaean shower," that is, a shower of procreative gold.[48] The inter-penetrative confusion of sexual and economic terms represented the two overriding preoccupations of nineteenth-century Western man, sex and money, which were rapidly becoming the only measures of his identity.[49] They also seemed to promise certain kinds of immortality. The ambiguity of the value of sperm in the author of *My Secret Life's* account also was true of American ideology. Masturbation was "pollution," a "stain," its vehicle a "curse . . . hang[ing] upon a man." Gardner's Danaean shower, a "life-giving emanation" under some conditions, was "unclean excretion" under others.[50]

The notion of concentrating the body's energies, whether on the genitals or on success, suggests how energies were something a man deployed from a pre-existing form. In 1870, Dr. J. H. Walters used the word "organization" for such deployment. "In 1850, while yet an under-graduate student of medicine, I could not accept the doctrines of life, at that time generally received and taught. Those doctrines uniformly started with the assumption of some peculiar vital force or forces, either as existing independently of the matter of the organism, or as properties originally 'stamped' upon matters capable of assimilation, and which become phenomenal by the act of organization. How different soever might be the fancies as to the nature and origin of this peculiar force, it was assumed to account for those phenomena which are peculiar to living organisms, such as the development of special forms, nutrition, reproduction, etc.; and also to account for phenomena, it was assumed allowable to endow it with any imaginable property to meet every emergency, such as the capacity of being dormant or depressed on the one hand, or of being excited or stimulated on the other." Among the medical students vulnerable to such generally taught doctrine were Brigham (whose book appeared in Boston just three years before Todd's *Student Manual* in Northhampton), Eli Todd and Samuel Woodward (both acknowledged by Todd to have influenced his views on masturbation), and Isaac Ray.[51]

According to Ray, everyone had a "given amount of original endowment," but he needed a course of suitable discipline to bring it to focus. Such discipline was the willing of Walter's "organization." Todd's work was meant to supply the pattern for such organization. The two concentrations to which Todd addressed himself most insistently, reading and masturbation, occurred as alternatives to one another. The advance of one was at the expense of the other. If the young man followed Todd's advice, he would be able to "call forth the highest efforts of the whole man, body and soul, in enterprise that will do good to men" and over-ridingly, in attaining his own worldly success. One slip of imagination while reading would lead him to the perversion of his energies in masturbation. In short, sublimation, or something very like it was a general belief long before Freud formulated and refined it. One of the most concise expressions of the pre-Freudian form (which I shall call "proto-sublimation") was Thoreau's in 1854: "the generative which when we are loose, dissipates and makes us unclean, when we are continent invigorates and inspires us." This was Dr. Gardner's version in 1872: the sexual "passion may be restrained within proper limitations. He who indulges in lascivious thoughts may stimulate himself to frenzy; but if his mind were under proper control he would find other employment for it, and his body, obedient to its potent sway, would not become master of the man."[52]

Man's command of the unrefined, passionate part of himself formed the model for his conquest of nature. The Faustian idea of assimilating nature's resources to male powers was again a familiar theme in nineteenth-century history, in Europe as well as in America. It was essentially Marx's and Freud's depiction of bourgeois activity, and it was John C. Calhoun's Kantian vision of the progress of Western man. Almost exactly a century before Freud's formulation of the creation of civilization as the work of male psychical energy, economically withdrawn from women for that purpose, Tocqueville pointed out that American democracy had been first in developing the post-industrial revolution's alignments of work and sex.[53] The barrier between the sexes inside the home extended to a barrier between the homosexual world of work and the (divided) heterosexual life in the family. American men uniquely took "constant care" in maintaining "two clear and distinct lines of action for the sexes." Men were the "head" of the body politic, women its "heart."[54]

Todd said the prayers at the union of the first transcontinental railroad at Promontory Point in 1869. For him this union was "a marriage, consummated under the bright sun."[55] It was sublimation, or "sanctification," according to Todd's own sexual psychology; an all-male equivalent of sexual intercourse, the energies invested in a "work so great it made all other works of this kind seem small and insignificant." Male heroes in the creation of American civilization were, in Todd's view, "taking the materialism of earth, and sanctifying it and making it not merely harmonize with but be a carrier of spiritual things."[56] Todd received one of the rings commemorating the union, made from the gold of the final spike. Its inscription, "The Mountain Wedding, May 10th, 1869,"[57] is evidence of the general assumption of the sexual meaning of ostensibly nonsexual events.

Mining was a second epitome of this proto-sublimation of natural resources, turning them into uncontaminated treasures. Todd's idea of "perfect democracy" was the California mining camps, "perfect" because they were free of women.[58] Melville similarly presented a microcosm of America without women, the *Pequod,* but with a different evaluation of it—its mission was self-destructive. The only man who survived had chosen to withdraw his allegiance from Ahab, and place his "conceit of attainable felicity" in "the wife, the hearth, the bed."[59] But even the men who stayed within settlement could relegate women to the edges of the day, and identify their all-male work world with the Western ideals they created and bought.[60]

At the same time, men like Todd characterized the earth that they worked and exploited as female: "man can turn the coarse of the pit into the hair-spring of the watch, or be able to take Nature in her wild state and turn her wastes into gardens of beauty."[61] This was a view of nature described for example by Henry Nash Smith in *Virgin Land,* and apostrophized as sexual in Smith's account of Thomas Hart Benton, one of Todd's idols.[62] Precious metals "laid away in the dark" of the continent's womb had awaited their transfiguration at the hands of man as an expression of his "power . . . to multiply the anthems of heaven to all eternity."[63] Woman's corresponding activity, confined to her own body, was gestation and birth. "If she must go down almost to the grave in a pilgrimage [i.e., gestation] she brings up priceless jewels in which the heart may rejoice to all eternity."[64] Man's infinitely greater work somehow duplicated woman's reproductive power. The meaning becomes clearest in Todd's image for wresting value from reading, the mind's life's blood. It occurs in his discussion of the temptation to masturbate: one had to find the valuable bits in Byron, Todd said, without being seduced into masturbation. "There are beautiful pearls in the slimy bottom of the ocean, but they are found only here and there, and would you dive after them if there were many probabilities that you would stick and die in the mud in which they were imbedded, or if not, that you certainly shorten and embitter life in the process of diving and obtaining them?"[65] Being lured into masturbation was like being trapped and drowned in the slimy, dirty and dangerous bottom. Yet such a plunge into the depths was a necessary part of proto-sublimation, that is, the discovery, awakening and conversion of sexual power. And, again, masturbation was in a contemporary sense simulative of addictive, excessive intercourse which functioned as a drain on the economic system.

Diving for pearls was equivalent to mining for gold and precious stones, Todd's metaphor for all male progress. Dying or sticking in mud doubly evoked the dangers of sexual intercourse: in the first place by way of Todd's deliberate image for masturbation, simulative of copulation; and in the second by way of Todd's often-expressed account of diving for value (or male consummation under the sun) as man's sexless substitute for sexual relations. Both elements were expressions of anxiety over the self-sufficient, "non-sticking" utilization of sexual energy, of which an underlying meaning was the fear of finding oneself held under, being absorbed by a vagina. The image of not getting out of the depths into which one plunged also conjured up the fear of not passing through the dangers of being born, of not being distinguished from woman, from the mass. Woman, Todd said elsewhere, could "lay the foundation of many suns" (for example, George Washington or Napoleon), or she could decide that a "new star" be "quenched shortly and lost in darkness and forgetfulness."[66] Todd eventually came to cope with woman's obliterative power by demanding that she be confined and controlled in the only kind of production he could not duplicate. The common images for the issue of woman's and the continent's body—in this case, precious minerals —linked them together as areas viewed by men as exploitable in the same way, and as expressions of man's mastery over his own resources. Todd also gave vent to the fantasy of doing without muddy woman altogether, in his construction of a fountain self-sufficiently, inexhaustibly "dropping pearls,' and in his social ideal, the mining camp.

These assumptions about male activity and its relation to nature were interpenetrative with assumptions about woman and men's relations with her. (I should note that the women with whom this paper is concerned were those whose lives first reflected the effects of the industrial revolution in America through the historically unique role of the non-working wife, the new trendsetting "women of the future" whom both Tocqueville and the experts took for "all women.")[67] Throughout the century men held some notion of woman as being of both body and mind, although the significance they attached to each greatly varied. In 1832 Brigham articulated anxiety about the social effects of the education of women, on their health, on their offspring, and on the future of society, but, like Todd in the same period, he concentrated on programs for the support and development of the *male* physique and intellect.[68] It was a typical belief that even if women could not govern feeling and affection by their weaker intellects, they did have an innate appetitivelessness that allowed them greater "self-control" than men. At the same time "all the various and manifold derangements of the reproductive system, peculiar to females, add to the causes of insanity." It would seem difficult to separate the idea of woman's sexual self-control from this domination of her mind by her sexual organs. The division between woman's relative immunity to "sensuality," and her essential liability to her sexual organs was a version of the well-known two views of woman as sexless and entirely sensual, which represented perhaps men's wish for woman's sexlessness, and the fear out of which that wish originated.[69]

The circumstances that drove *men* to insanity were assumed to be givens of their society and of their sexual role within it. The characteristic disorder of boom and slump was, as Tocqueville put it, an "endemic disease" of the democratic "temperament."[70] The corollary of accepting such conclusions about men was to direct social/medical/-psychological expertise at that area of society that was not held by men to be so inalienable as the nature of their own existences, and, consequently was controllable; that is, to direct it at women. And a step beyond that was to concentrate it on that part of woman that made her specially liable to insanity, her sexual organs.

The growing number of workless women and alarm over the possibility that their life style might become a widespread trend,[71] together with the growing strength of the woman's rights movement intensified male anxieties. As the century wore on it was a function of those anxieties that the medically materialistic therapy of gynecological surgery got under way. The significance men attached to the body part of woman increased in proportion to their devaluation of her mind. Dr. Charles Meigs advised his gynecological pupils in 1848 (the year of the first Woman's Rights Convention at Seneca Falls) that their studies necessarily should include woman's psychology, since her generative organs exercised a "strange" influence over her heart, mind and soul. By 1871, Dr. Horatio Storer represented the general belief quite bluntly. "Woman was what she is [sic] in health, in character, in her charms, alike of body, mind and soul because of her womb alone."[72]

For gynecological purposes women became creatures entirely of body, a conviction expressed by a multitude of euphemisms. Woman's only function was to bear children. After menopause a woman was, in Gardner's words, "degraded to the level of a being who has no further duty to perform in this world."[73] Among the elements in this exclusion of women from the male world of work, rationalized by her psychological unfitness for it, was the fear of doubling the already severe competition that men faced. At the same time, both Todd and Gardner occasionally expressed simply jealousy at the escape of women from that harsh world, even though men demanded it.[74]

Gynecologists' labeling of sexual organs revealed the significance of that familiar synecdoche "the sex." Throughout J. Marion Sims' *Clinical Notes on Uterine Surgery* (1866) the vagina has a "mouth," the womb a "neck" and a "throat," and he compared the cervix to "the tonsils."[75] A woman's reproductive tract stood for her total identity as a man's face stood for his. The only criterion a reasonable man needed to have in selecting a wife was her capacity to bear children. Woman was simply a "natal mechanism," her menses "mechanical action."[76] Sims also advocated a "mechanical view" of sexual intercourse.[77] According to Gardner, frigidity "may or not accompany the act [of coitus]; the result is as independent of sensation"[78] in either case. Mechanically, of course, men had to put up with orgasm; not so women. Sims described the enjoyment of sex as "mere animal sensuality."[79] Doctors' adherence to the notion of the irrelevance of woman's pleasure in copulation and to the idea of her natural frigidity reflected and reinforced the general social belief that "sensuality is unusual in the sex."[80] The phenomenon of vaginismus (a condition where a woman's genitals frigidified or became so painful on being touched that they were impenetrable) was simply a more thoroughgoing version of James Fenimore Cooper's "shrinking delicacy."[81] Defining the absence of sexual desire in woman as normal, doctors came to see its presence as disease, for which some of them tested by manipulating clitoris or breasts.[82] Sexual appetite was a male quality (to be properly channelled of course). If a woman showed it, she resembled a man.

The paradox of confining a woman's identity to the distinction of her sexual organs while at the same time claiming she was sexless should be apparent. Sexless woman was a sexual definition. Men's fantastic and unappeasable demands that women not be what they were rested on what they could not avoid perceiving women to be. So Gardner's assertion that "woman when she has her period takes the greatest care to conceal it from all eyes," above all those of her husband, was a wish that she conform more nearly to the healthy norm of sexlessness. Gardner said woman considered menstruation "a blot or infirmity."[83] That is, an intrinsic part of her being was a temporary, even curable, anomaly. Menstruation, like woman's sexual desire was a powerful reminder of woman's "animal" nature, a manifestation of "notorious appetite." Woman's menstrual blood was corrupt and virulent, imperiling an unwitting penis with "disease," "excoriations" and "blenorrhagias."[84] Not only was sex dangerous for men, it was dirty, "bestial" and "brutish." Sims, an internationally known gynecologist, hated to examine a woman's pelvic organs; Gardner found no "scenes . . . more appalling than [those] in the obstetric chamber. . . ."[85]

Above all, woman's latent boundlessness posed a threat to male energies, and through them, to civilization. A woman was a sperm absorber, "a drag on the energy, spirits and resolution of her partner."[86] Moreover, the repression of woman's sexual feelings represented sexual and social order generally. It demonstrated to man his subordination of his own dangerous but necessary sexual eruptibility. Desirous woman represented man's loss of control over himself. All women were potentially antagonistic to the fundamental value scheme of society. Female masturbation was universally attacked on the grounds that it raised woman to a state of sexual craving, that is, it made her a threat to men.[87] Even critics of gynecological-surgical excesses reserved the right to castrate "nymphomaniacs."[88] During the earlier phase of masturbation phobia (before the decade preceding the Civil War), the emphasis had been on how masturbation affected *male* health and energy, with no suggestion that masturbation addicted men to heterosexual craving. After mid-century, men became increasingly anxious about female masturbation, and developed several drastic techniques to deal with it. Assertion of woman's natural sexlessness was the wishful thinking of men scared spermless, as it were, by woman's potential appetite. "To the man there is a limitation of physical capability which no stimulants from without or within can goad to excess. The erethism [i.e., sexual appetite] of woman has no boundary."[89] Stirred by an unwary bridegroom, allowed to masturbate, or placed in contact with a dance partner at the time of her menstruation, a woman became a vast impending menace: all body, when aroused she became all appetite.[90]

Consistent with the increasing projection of masturbation phobia on to women was the increasing projection on to her of both sexual explosiveness and of the spermatic economy.[91] J. A. Jackson's 1896 article describing the "torture" to a man of the thought of the loss of semen, and the identical anxiety by the anonymous quantifier of nocturnal emissions in 1904 were evidence of the continuation of the spermatic economy tradition (on which projection depended).[92] A. J. Himel's unacknowledged quotation in 1907 of Oliver Wendell Holmes' characterization of hysterical woman was a reminder that the fear of sperm absorbent woman also continued: "A woman of flesh and blood and with infinite variety will, like a vampire drain a man, *nolens volens,* of his life's blood." Himel generalized Holmes' characterization to all women.[93] The inference was that only a woman without flesh and without the blood that correspond to the blood of the man she was draining would not so debilitate a man. It would seem that part of the fear men had of copulating with a woman at the time of menstruation was that she would be more likely at that time to regain from man's life blood what she was losing. (And on the projective side, her loss of blood would remind him of his.) Man's absence of will in this fantasy of Himel's and the inevitability of woman's absorption of man (since all women were of flesh and blood) suggests, too, another aspect of nineteenth-century male psychology generally —a yearning to escape the necessity of facing manhood's relentless destiny, and making woman responsible for the escape.[94]

The connection between contemporary beliefs about the position and function of women and disease and treatment is suggested by the ambiguous term "disorder," used to denote both physical/psychical malfunctions, and social trespasses of a sexual and political kind. Gardner associated his patients, the new, workless women, with the whole range of subversive feminism—Bloomer wearers to women's righters, women doctors and midwives.[95] Todd linked his 1867 attack against contraception and abortion (for which he made women almost entirely responsible) with his attack on women's rights published in the same year. He detected among "the other sex [woman] . . . a widespread uneasiness, a discontentment with woman's lot, impatient of its burdens, rebellious against its sufferings, [with] an undefined hope of emancipation . . . by some great revolution . . . propagating theories, weak, foolish and criminal." The logic of describing woman's independence as "revolutionary" and "criminal" is obvious. Woman was "the sex," her highest and single function, reproduction: therefore contraception and abortion were rebellion against social order. Conversely, any demand for social or political rights on the part of a being construed as entirely as body was a sexual rebellion. Abortion, according to Todd, was "a direct war against human society, . . . [and] against the family order. . . ."[96] Gardner wrote *Conjugal Sins* to "Arrest the Rapid Extinction of the American People." Rebellious women threatened the United States with disintegration on the scale of the fall of the Roman Empire.[97]

Todd put such feelings into another historical context. The French Revolution had unleashed, he said, an infidel, fiendish, "voluptuous" and depraved experiment that threatened to dissolve ordered, God-fearing, American society. Revolutionaries had sunk so far as to ordain "the worship of a vile woman." Such "political vandals" still threatened to dismantle the family, the basic unit of order, and "substitute the vagrancy of desire, the rage of lust, and the solicitude [sic; solitude?], and disease and desolation which follow the footsteps of unregulated nature exhausted by success."[98] Within the obvious fear of a leveled, disordered society were anxieties about isolation and the waste of undisciplined sexual energy, to both of which Todd's behavioral manuals contributed. Gardner's conceptions of the breaking down of the barriers of reason and morality and the abandonment of sexuality to "the hazards of free will," his personification of the will as a ruler with "potent sway" over the body so that it would "not become master of the man"[99] reflected a similar apprehension of a social struggle between hierarchy and anarchy, which, as I have suggested, was a projection of the individual's attempt to discipline and utilize his own bodily powers.

The metaphor of the body-politic linked man's view of the state to his most personal and indestructible source of identity, his body. The rational achievement of civilization seemed to rest on the subordination of the dark passions. Western man's apprehensions of a conflict between order and enthusiasm, reason and passion, head and heart, had been increasing in the period between the Reformation and the eighteenth century Enlightenment. The Revolutions cut off the head, or at least seemed to bring it closer to the passions, to the genitals. And revolutionary rhetoric promised further leveling. Freud neatly represented what I would regard as a characteristically post-Revolutionary apprehension of the association between head and heart, and order and anarchy: "Civilization behaves towards sexuality as a people or a stratum of its population does which has subjected another one to its exploitation. Fear of a revolt by the suppressed elements drives it to stricter precautionary measures."[100] Freud's previous definition of civilization as male activity clearly put women into the subordinated stratum, just as Marx did. Marx's consideration of the bourgeois' exploitation of "his" wife makes that quite clear. The bourgeoisie was male.[101]

The absence in America of counter traditions of class and other established psychic benchmarks posed more immediate problems for social and individual identity than was the case in the more slowly leveled Europe.[102] (Americans were also denied the modern form of that ethnic identity, nationalism, on which the evolving mass societies in Europe could rely after the French Revolution.) Tocqueville's account of intrafamilial democracy in the relations between fathers and sons was interlocked with the effacement of what he called "class identity."[103] He observed that "hardly anything but money" remained to leveled society as a source of distinction, of identity.[104] He defined that "hardly anything" by suggesting that men fell back on body: as they "relinquish more and more the peculiar opinions and feelings of a caste, a profession, or a family, they simultaneously arrive at something nearer to the constitution of man, which is everywhere the same."[105] America was the freest field for the fulfillment of this tendency. White men constituted themselves the headship of American society on the basis of physiology (namely skin color and genital organs), and charted their superiority according to the differences in

beings regarded as naturally lower on the great chain of being—closer to the animal, to dark passions, appetite. That, I think, is the explanation for Todd's reiterated use of the term "emancipation" in 1867 to label the goals of turbulent, revolutionary women. It followed by four years Lincoln's "Emancipation Proclamation."

Sexual identity was the persistent and explicit concern of all kinds of nineteenth-century literature, delineating "a gospel of real manhood and real womanhood."[106] Men's insistence on inexorable difference and separation seems to have indicated an anxiety that such distinctions would not be sustained. Men asseverated the exclusion of women from the arena of individuation-by-success within which men felt themselves so threatened already. A concern for identity based on body provided the authority for the claims by doctors to be social engineers. The reiterated fantasy that independent women could only become men similarly reflected the precarious, solipsistic vulnerability of sexual identity—that any challenge from a different group could only mean that they wanted to become you; that is, they wanted to remove your mark of distinction, your difference from them.

The need to control women in America intensified according to the stresses and strains of the social breakdown described, for example, by the modern historian, Robert Wiebe, in his account of the "search for order," 1877–1920.[107] In 1867 Todd turned his attention to the sexual transgressions of Anglo-Saxon women, who were aborting and contracepting, denying existence to governors, generals, lawyers, and judges of "our race," to the advantage of alien and "sexually potent" immigrants.[108] Todd's "watchful eye," and that of the native physician, observed that "while our foreign population have large families our own native American families are running out, and at this rate must entirely run out."[109] Todd repeated this fear again and again, as he watched the back-door threat to the long-term and representatively racist, Messianic vision of Anglo-Saxon energies reaching to China.[110] Like Todd, Gardner associated the "flood" of dirty, sexually vicious immigrants with the threat from rebellious women who were, he said, "a tide of error, sin and misery with which the community is being overwhelmed by unholy practices [sic]," flooding up from the lower depths to convert good, holy and productive sexuality into "bestiality."[111]

The coterminous rise of eugenics and of drastic gynecology[112] were aspects of a renewed and more desperate attempt to control and shape procreative powers as if the American body politic were literally a body. Gardner declared that the "well-being of society demands that means shall be adopted to separate its good elements from the bad." In the future, he said, medical science would enable American men "to separate the pure from the impure."[113] He advocated the execution of all criminals, and would have Anglo-Saxon parents reproduce on stock breeding and stock raising principles.[114] Restored to the pedestal, women would preserve "the blood of strong races in our veins," produce sons of a new "national physique," and thus "repulse the invaders" (whom Gardner called "dirty" and "effete") all of which would lead in his view to an advance in human rights.[115] One of the most frequent and putatively irrefutable rationales for the castration of women defined as somehow disorderly was that they would cease to contribute to the degeneracy of the American body politic.[116]

Gardner's assertion that it was a "crime" for women to be sick[117] in light of his world-view and of his commitment to the control of women, suggests the historical significance of the phenomenal pre-eminence of American gynecological surgery in nineteenth-century medical history.[118] It was an expression of the hypostasis of sexual identity. The gynecologists' underlying aims cannot be separated from the society in which they moved: these aims were retaliation against and control of women, and the assumption of as much of their reproductive power as possible,[119] all part and parcel of the projective meaning of the subordination of "the sex."

Late in the 1860's gynecologists began to practice surgical treatment of the psychological disorders of woman, identifying her sexual organs with her whole being. While hideous, Abraham Jacobi's recommendation in 1875 for the creation of a sore on the penis for the discouragement of masturbation in boy children[120] fell far short of the drastic surgery performed on girls' and women's genitals.[121] Clitoridectomy was performed for indications of masturbation and the duplicity associated with it, always with the idea of re-establishing order, regaining control. The British gynecologist who re-invented[122] clitoridectomy in 1858 was expelled from the London Obstetrical Society almost immediately after the published results of his clitoridectomies in 1866, and the operation was not performed in England thereafter.[123] But clitoridectomy was performed in the United States from 1867 (or earlier) until at least 1904, and perhaps until 1925.[124] Circumcision of females co-existed with clitoridectomy in the 1890's, and was widely advocated in response to what was gauged to be a growing incidence of masturbation and other dangerously unappeasable irritations of the clitoris. The operation removed a piece of skin, the "hood" above the clitoris.[125] Circumcision of both girls and adult women continued to be performed in the United States at least until 1937, its fundamental rationale the curbing of woman's masturbation and the unappeasable erethism induced by unsatisfactory intercourse.[126]

The difference in the recognition accorded clitoridectomy in England and America, and the length of time between the acceptance of contraception in each country,[127] were perhaps measures of the difference in attitudes toward women, and in the difference in pressures felt by men; so, too, the respective acceptance and elimination of the midwife. She was given governmental recognition and institutional status early in the twentieth century in England, where obstetrics is today the domain of women. American gynecologists reached the climax of their hundred years' war against midwives in the first two decades of the twentieth century, implementing a legislative and propaganda campaign, the latter to persuade women that "normal" pregnancy and parturition were the exception, and childbirth a "wound" that only the expertise of males could master. Midwives were finally driven out before World War II, and in 1968, 99 per cent of all pregnant women were delivered by men.[128]

A third surgical treatment of women's psychology was female castration, invented by Robert Battey of Rome, Georgia, in 1872.[129] Battey called it "normal ovariotomy" because this excision of the ovaries was indicated by non-ovarian conditions—neurosis, insanity, abnormal menstruation and practically anything untoward in female behavior. Among the indications were troublesomeness, eating like a ploughman, masturbation, attempted suicide, erotic tendencies, persecution mania, simple "cussedness," and dysmenorrhoea (painful menstruation, long held to be one consequence of masturbation). Most apparent in the enormous variety of symptoms doctors took to indicate castration was a strong current of sexual appetitiveness on the part of women. That is, castratable women evinced a quality held to be characteristic of men.[130]

Female castration was a very much more widespread and frequently performed operation in America than clitoridectomy. Women were castrated from New York to New Orleans, Youngs Crossroads in South Carolina to Ottumwa and Keokuk in Iowa, from Philadelphia to Portland, Oregon, from Boston to Los Angeles and San Francisco. Battey performed the first female castration in 1872 and the record continued until at least 1921. Infinitely more operations were performed than were written up and published. By the early 1890's female castration had reached the proportions of an "epidemic," a "rage," a "thriving industry,"[131] and continued to be performed in spite of the opposition that had begun in the early 1890's. A major part of the opposition was based on the rise of "conservative ovarian surgery," which itself came under fire for puncturing, burning, resecting and otherwise tampering with ovaries, and therefore can be placed in the same context with the operation it was largely introduced to replace.[132] Indeed, female castration gave way to further drastic gynecological surgery including salpingectomy (extirpation of the Fallopian tubes), hysterectomy, and the transplanting of ovaries. (The latter operation depended on the availability of "normal ovaries," that is, on Battey's operation and was initially performed, to a considerable extent, to solve the problems created by Battey's operation.[133] So gynecological transplanters were part of a cycle perpetuated by gynecologists who created and cured "their" own symptoms.) Doctors competed with each other in the number of ovaries they extirpated, and handed them around at medical society meetings on plates like trophies.[134] It was estimated in 1906 that for every one of the one hundred and fifty thousand doctors in the U.S. there was one sterilized woman; and "some of this large number [of doctors] have openly boasted . . . that they have removed from fifteen hundred to two thousand ovaries."[135]

In addition to the sheer volume, duration, and geographical spread of female castration, and the meanings of physicians' rhetoric explaining, advocating and justifying it, a salient feature of the operation was the early recognition of its failure to cure (indeed, of its tendency to exaggerate previous symptoms and to drive women insane). Battey quite soon tried to modify his initial assertion that the removal of normal, healthy ovaries for insanity was justified by arguing that *after* the operations had been performed the ovaries were always found to be diseased or abnormal.[136] That ground also crumbled as other gynecologists slowly came to realize that a *normal* ovary could be encysted, inflamed, enlarged, prolapsed and anteflexed, all of which had been regarded as indications of abnormalcy and disease.[137] In any case, Battey and other proponents of wholesale female castration continued to extirpate healthy ovaries for non-ovarian indications.

Gynecologists treated their patients as if they were rebels or criminals. Defending the continued performance of demonstratedly useless castration, and suggesting that the operation would be effective if it included extirpation of the womb thus made useless, Dr. Arnold Praeger stated in 1895 that the "principles of surgery . . . resemble justice."[138] Dr. David Gilliam making a plea in 1896 for the "More General Adoption of Oophorectomy" applied the lesson of the beneficial effects of the castration of animals to the castration of women. "Why do we alter our colts and calves? Not that we expect to abate strength or endurance, nor yet to render them less intelligent; but that we may make them tractable and trustworthy, that we may convert them into faithful, well disposed servants." Bulls, and men, he said, were naturally and should remain belligerent. Like the other gynecologists, he integrated his surgical vision with the spermatic economy, of which his statement was even more concise than Thoreau's. "It is the equity of nature; procreative power and mental energy are inverse." But an emasculated creature's remaining sexual passion was "tempered with prudence and tame besides the fierce energy of untethered masculinity." Castrated women became "tractable, orderly, industrious and cleanly." A wife should be a faithful servant, as tractable and undemanding as a castrated animal.[139] In short, Gilliam justified female castration as a way of returning women to that ideally repressed and circumscribed self of Tocqueville's account and Todd's and Gardner's dreams. Many of the patients for whom doctor and husband claimed a cure had exhibited symptoms of unmanageableness at home, and were deemed "cured" when they were restored to their husband's management after castration.

Gynecologists' authority in matters pertaining to control of woman's disorders was much harder to dispute than husbands'. So it may well be that disorderly women were handed over to the gynecologist for castration by husbands unable to enforce their minimum identity guarantee. Women by and large shared men's beliefs about roles and social order; if such beliefs drove them inevitably to disorder, they went to the proper authorities. Many of the case reports describe husband and friends pressuring the woman to obtain freedom from "disorder," much as Tocqueville described the young woman pressured toward the yoke of marriage.[140]

Castrated patients were rich enough to afford a gynecologist, and all seem to have been non-workers, home-bodies; a high proportion was addicted to morphine or brandy, and quite a few were bedridden.[141] They seem to have been those women left workless by the change in work patterns accelerated by the industrial revolution, and re-enslaved as possessions.[142] Moreover, the ascription by these women of their disorder (that is, of social displacement, and a lack of a sense of personal value and identity) to their sex organs reflected the male assumption that their identity must somehow reside in "the sex." One critic of wholesale castration, Dr. Ely Van de Warker, realized that the doctor's clamor about the ovaries had a "sociological reflex." "So constantly," he pointed out in 1906, "have they been held up before her as the one evil spot in her anatomy that she has grown to look with suspicion on her own organs."[143] Women pleaded with the gynecologist for castration, "fully convinced that all their grief emanates from their pelvis . . . this idea fostered and augmented by their friends."[144] Some gynecologists eventually realized that some patients came to them for the same reasons that others went to faith cures and Christian Science.[145] In short, this enormous phenomenon was symbiotic between patient and doctor, reflecting and refracting the largest contours of social beliefs and expectations.[146]

The meaning that both patients and doctors attached to sickness and cure, disorder and order, suggest that the variety of symptoms focussed on woman's sex organs can be explained as a language of anxiety shaped by a language of conformity. In W. P. Manton's phrase, castratable women were mentally alienated.[147] But all women were supposed to be "alien" from the democratic norm. It was male. The doctors' own sexual values condemned them to sustain the disease of being female. Just as men confined women to the "butterfly" existence that made them sick,[148] and more demanding, more in need of more confinement (to bed, or to asylum or to both), so doctors created specific symptoms they attempted to cure, their therapy expressing the same social assumptions of a male identity that made it necessary to exclude and subordinate women, make them sick, and so on. Castration itself destroyed woman's one remaining thread of identity, her hope for children. Her symptoms intensified and men became still more desperate. But by the same standard of social beliefs generating disease, castration could and did work, although much less frequently than it proved iatrogenic.[149]

Impregnation could be as much a way of controlling woman as castration. Hence the paradox of the co-existence of castration and the inducing of fertility as areas of gynecological experiment, and the paradox of the general anxiety about the increasing sterility of Anglo-Saxon women, even as the jeremiahs castrated some of them.[150] Gynecologists were in a better position than Todd to attempt procreation without diving into dangerous woman: for years Sims experimented in the impregnation of supposedly sterile women with a mechanical penis, and claimed some success.[151] Driving out midwives was an assertion of control at the end of gestation; and like Todd, Gardner compared the delivery of children to the mining of California gold.[152] The work of Gardner and Sims reveals the persistent desire to master the process of copulation, gestation and delivery, while other male experts tried to pre-empt mother's power in childbearing. "From the foundation of the world man has been born of woman; and notwithstanding that his inventive genius has discovered steam . . . and harnessed him to his chariot, and sent lightning to do his bidding over the almost boundless extent of the world; yet we cannot hope that any change may be effected in this particular."[153] The complaint betrays the wish. To sever dependence on women for reproduction would be a feat surpassing the harnessing of steam and electricity, and would enable man to escape the deadly danger with which, like Todd, Gardner associated woman's reproductive power.[154]

The Spermatic Economy   *357*

Furthermore, Gardner and Sims (and the castrators generally) identified the mastery of woman's body both with man's encroachment on and utilization of nature's body. Sims' invention of his speculum for the examination of woman's reproductive tract enabled him to see "everything as no man had ever seen before. . . . I felt like an explorer in medicine who first views a new and important territory."[155] Battey, too, was depicted as a "pioneer" travelling "in paths hitherto untrod."[156] Gardner associated his sexual energies with the mechanized steam power of the new "iron horse," and represented the male sexual organ as a "railroad train" that could easily be thrown from its track by woman's rebellious contraception.[157] Just as a woman's body was a source of babes of gold who were to constitute the pure spermatic power of the new nation, so too "the mountains and forests" of the West were "vast reservoirs of health and strength" from which "we may annually recruit our exhausted energies at every fresh contact with our worthy mother earth." This assimilation of natural resources had a corresponding excretive dimension: The West was waiting to "draw off, through the mighty sluices of our continental railway lines" a "superabundance of poverty," which otherwise "stagnates into cesspools of abomination . . . which breed plagues and pestilence."[158] Gardner, then, shared Todd's alimentary view of the use of resources, ingesting and excreting apt metaphors for the ambiguous evaluation of sperm, and for the fantasy of self-sufficiency.[159] Gynecologists saw themselves as being in a special position to mediate man's interaction with nature, of which woman was at once part and representative. Male energy was the icon to which man's vision of his relations with women, his appropriation of her power and that of nature, was captive. This accumulation of power, representing the three conquests of self, woman and nature, betrayed in its own terms the fantasy of self-reproduction, the climax of male claims to self-making.

It would be misleading to end a sketch of nineteenth-century male anxieties about themselves and women on a note of assertion, that is, to suggest that men were unambiguous even in their fantasies. So I will conclude with some suggestions about the psychic ambiguities in men, warning the reader that the following remarks are the tip of an iceberg to be more fully uncovered with the publication of *The Horrors of the Half-Known Life.* The assertion of mastery over reproduction, and over the disorders of women had a self-destructive side. In the first place, such efforts were the displacement of anxieties over the inescapable anarchy of American malehood, intensified by the subversiveness of indolent women, which itself was the function of the displacement of the responsibility of male order on to women. The need for control could not be satisfied. Gynecological disciplines manifested the same "mad impatience" Tocqueville had perceived in democratic men generally, and their methods drove women to more sickness, demanding further gynecological disciplines, and so on.

Secondly, the gynecologists' "performances" of operations, their piling up of records, and their repeated attempts to innovate and prove priority in innovations (which they termed "conceptions," "bantlings" and "babies")[160] were held up to other *men's* eyes for judgment. So surgeons claimed to be self-made successes in virtue of the invention of an original operation (or operative technique); they then presented themselves for judgment at the hands of other surgeons. Accounts of this process (of which the cutting of a woman's body was a phase) were shot through with exactly the same legal metaphors the surgeons applied in their judgment of women.

The second installment of Battey's account of his first female castration illustrates this ambiguous process, that is, one both assertive and submissive towards other men. First Batty repeated his claim to be a Daniel Boone of the human dimension of virgin land—i.e., the female body—"carving out for myself a new pathway through consecrated ground [that phrase evoking the burial of dead bodies], upon which the foot of man has not dared willingly to tread." He then gave a more complicated picture of his psychic state at the time of his conception. "However pure may have been the motives actuating me, however cogent may have appeared, to my own mind, the reasons which have impelled me—I must of necessity stand before the bar of the medical world, and submit myself to its just judgment. It becomes me, too, to appear before you, my brothers and my peers, to answer for myself."[161] Robert Morris, a circumcisor and a castrator of females, and a transplanter of ovaries, warned that patients "must be classified carefully if physicians are not to be subjected to the humiliation of doing unnecessary and harmful surgery."[162] An over-riding concern in his assertively autonomous performances was what other experts thought of the individual gynecologist. The process expressed the same circular world-view to which Todd's work testifies in behalf of men generally. Men defended themselves against a general, democratic hostility which was intensified by each individual's defense against it.

In 1901, A. Palmer Dudley (Professor of Gynecology, Harlem Post-Graduate Medical School and Hospital, and Dartmouth Medical College, New York City) expressed a similar apprehension to that of Robert Morris. Analysis of his words suggest how he confused his judgment of woman's genitals with his fear of being judged himself, and how that confusion reflected his uncertainty about his own sexual identity. He told his colleagues that "a man is put to the test at the operating table."[163] The gynecologist was reduced to his manhood; his physiological identity seemed to be at issue as well as his professional identity. If he was successful he might be handing "his" ovaries around on a plate as part of his success, his affirmation of his professional identity and his manhood. What was important was not her, but himself. Her body furnished the material for his identity: in fact, he proved his manhood to other men by appropriating that part of her body that characterized her as female. Her body stood for his. I have mentioned men's fear of becoming not-men, of becoming women. Yet here Dudley used woman's body for his manhood. Such a process of assimilation was the counterpart of the other sexually confused fantasy, that of "mannish" woman's righters (characterized as such by doctors like Gardner), of the "phallic" heroines of the popular literature cited by Henry Nash Smith.[164] Dudley's patient's complaint was sexual disorder; given the limited number of slots in the sexual order, the sexually disordered woman was construed to be a man. If a woman deviated from the contemporary standard of womanhood, she became a man. If a man deviated from the contemporary standard of manhood, he became a woman. So it may be that what was being put to the test was the ambiguity of Dudley's sexual identity. Robert Edes suggested in 1896 that gynecological surgery was performed to relieve the surgeon of the anxieties women occasioned him, rather than relieve her of her own sickness. "I have heard an eminent surgeon offer a vivid description of his sufferings from the importunities of a patient whom he had skillfully relieved of her ovaries but not of her sufferings say: 'I told her at last that she had better try Christian Science.' "[165] But relief was hard to come by, when, in the final analysis, it depended on other men, all of whom suffered from the same unresolvable tensions Dudley did, and all of whom were burdened by the pressure to depend for judgment on no one at all, to be self-sufficient. Neither success nor failure could protect a man from such pressure.

So on the one side, there was a powerful undercurrent of desire of gynecologists to reproduce themselves to the extent of designating female castration as reproduction. According to his and his contemporaries' metaphor, Battey's normal ovariotomy was his own baby. One irony in this psychic circle was that the removal of woman's ovaries made a castrated woman more like a man insofar as she did not menstruate or give birth; conversely it made men like the "sexless" kind of woman the pedestal rhetoric idealized. This latter irony represents the other side of castration's meaning, in its projective dimension —that men desired to be beyond the anxiety and responsibility to which they were committed by the existence of their penes and testicles, a desire in the work of both Gardner and Todd, as well as the castrating gynecologists. The following quotation is from an article in which Arnold Praeger was defending a gynecology he assumed to be synonymous with female castration. He said that opponents of castration implied that "gynecology is a sort of illegitimate appendage of medicine, which should be choked and strangled out of existence as a monster which has suddenly arisen to unsex and destroy lovely woman."[166] Most immediately, the image compared gynecological surgery to the diseased ovary it demanded to destroy. Both sides of the self-reproductive fantasy invoked a projective and introjective hall of mirrors which stood for the profound ambiguities of only negatively knowing who one was. Praeger's mixed metaphor conveys both the ambition of giving legitimate birth, and the ambition to experience the existence represented by the castrated, ornamental woman, free even of childbearing. The "natural" source of generation, the ovary, was monstrous.

Dudley's and Praeger's confusions reflected the ambiguities in being male that I have indicated in the earlier parts of this paper. Men maintained a rigid sex line yet felt it could dissolve at the drop of a hat; men wanted the competition they simultaneously dreaded; they were told by experts how not to rely on experts, in other words, to be self-sufficient; they accepted a model for behavior—obsessive energization—that they believed ran them into the danger of having their sanity destroyed (and, in fact, it was this particular psychic circularity men dealt with by projecting their incipient insanity on to women). Further circularities were these: the terms of anti-masturbation tracts would themselves cause men to masturbate; men depended on the control and use of energy they also felt to be uncontrollable; they depended on copulation to implement their social vision, yet believed they ran dreadful risks (of debilitation, disease and death) in sexual intercourse. Men claimed to control reproduction when they were dependent on women for it; they saw women as entirely sex organs even as they claimed she was sexless. Furthermore, those views of women must have been as susceptible to her human reality as the definitions of blacks as property or animals were susceptible to their human reality (in spite of attempts of both women and blacks to fulfill white men's expectations of them). Gynecologists reflected such circularities: they attempted artificial insemination of woman, and they castrated her—both actions were intended to assume power over reproduction. By the late 1890's, they were transplanting ovaries to cure woman of castration, thereby relieving themselves of their own sufferings.

Notes

1 John Todd, *The Student's Manual* (Northampton: Hopkins, Bridgman, 1835), pp. 326–27.

2 Ibid., p. 372.

3 George Rogers Taylor, *The Transportation Revolution* (New York: Harper and Row, 1968), pp. 22, 153.

4 Alexis de Tocqueville, *Democracy in America,* 2 vols. (New York: Vintage Books, 1945 [1st ed., Paris, 1835, 1840]) 2: bks. 2 and 3; see, too, Alexander Mitscherlich, *Society Without the Father,* trans. E. Mosbacher (New York: Harcourt, Brace and World, 1969); Dr. Edward Jarvis, "On the Supposed Increase of Insanity," *American Journal of Insanity,* 8 (April, 1952): 360–64.

5 John Todd, *The Young Man, Hints Addressed to the Young Men of the United States* (Northamptom: Hopkins, Bridgman, 1856 [1st ed., 1844]), p. 113.

6 Donald B. Meyer, *The Positive Thinkers* (Garden City: Doubleday, 1965), pp. 55–56.

7 I use the word in one of the ways in which Erik Erikson defines it: "The tendency at a given time to make facts amenable to ideas, and ideas to facts, in order to create a world image convincing enough to support the collective and individual sense of identity" (*Young Man Luther* [New York: W. W. Norton and Co., 1962], p. 22). It should be obvious that there was more to the ideology of nineteenth-century American males than "self-making."

8 For examples of the rhetoric see James Fenimore Cooper, *Notions of the Americans,* 2 vols. (London: Henry Colburn, 1828), 1: 140–42.

9 For Tocqueville's logic here, see pt. 1 of my recent book *The Horrors of the Half-Known Life* (New York: Harper Torchbooks, 1972).

10 Isaac Ray, *Mental Hygiene* (reprint edition, New York: Hafner Publishing Co., 1968 [1st ed., 1865]), p. 58; Amariah Brigham, *Remarks on the Influence of Mental Cultivation and Mental Excitement upon Mental Health* (Boston: Marsh Capen and Lyon, 1833 [1st ed. 1832]), p. 16.

11 Brigham, *Remarks,* preface, pp. 81–82, 84; Ray, *Mental Hygiene,* p. 54.

12 See Egbert S. Oliver, "Explanatory Notes" to Melville, *Piazza Tales* (New York: Hendricks House, 1962), pp. 238–41; and see too Benfield, *The Horrors.*

13 John Todd, *The Story of His Life, Told Mainly by Himself,* comp. and ed. Jonathan Edwards Todd (New York: Harper and Brothers, 1876), p. 461, Dr. Augustus Kinsley Gardner said he and "thousands" were decisively influenced by *The Student's Manual,* particularly by the chapter on masturbation, "so potent to rob man of the high prerogatives of manhood. . . ." (*Conjugal Sins* [New York: J. S. Redfield, 1870], pp. 69–70).

14 Todd, *Life,* p. 280.

15 Todd, *Student's Manual,* p. 125. "We consist of two parts; the one inert, passive, utterly incapable of directing itself, barely ministerial to the other, moved, animated by it" (p. 176).

Ben Barker-Benfield   *362*

16   Ray, *Mental Hygiene,* p. 205. Ray saw this power being wasted on a national scale: "The amount of mental power which has . . . been destroyed is infinitely greater . . . than that which has been suffered to work out its destined purpose" (p. 53). This view may be compared to Freud's apprehension of one of civilization's sources of discontent, that " a piece of unconquerable nature may lay behind—this time a piece of our own psychical constitution" (*Civilization and Its Discontents,* trans. James Strachey [New York: W. W. Norton and Co., 1962], p. 33).

17   Todd, *Student's Manual,* p. 284.

18   Brigham, *Remarks,* pp. ix–x, 15, 36.

19   Ibid., p. 15.

20   Ibid., p. 36.

21   This medical/psychological idea pervaded nineteenth-century literature with powerful undertones of "the spermatic economy." One example was the best seller in 1850: Ik Marvell [pseud.], *Reveries of a Bachelor* (New York: Charles Scribner, 1859 [1st ed., 1850]), pp. 31, 96, 133.

22   Brigham, *Remarks,* pp. 45–46.

23   Todd, *The Young Man,* p. 43.

24   Edward Jarvis, "On the Supposed Increase of Insanity," *American Journal of Insanity,* 8 (1852): 349, 354–55; Ray, *Mental Hygiene,* pp. 228–29, 284; Norman Dain, *Concepts of Insanity* (New Brunswick: Rutgers University Press, 1964), pp. 89, 212, n. 9. Ray was explicit about this necessity for men to run the danger of going mad. "I do not suppose that insanity inducing excitement can be banished from every sphere of human activity, or that such a result would be desirable, if it could. It has its uses, and within certain limits it furnishes indispensable aid in realizing the purposes and aspirations of men" (*Mental Hygiene,* p. 191).

25   Herman Melville, *Moby Dick* (New York: Harper and Brothers, 1851), ch. XLI; Charles Dickens, *Our Mutual Friend* (London: Chapman and Hall), chs. XXXII, XLIV.

26   Todd, *Student's Manual,* pp. 375–76.

27   Todd, *Life,* p. 451.

28   John Todd, *The Sunset Land* (Boston: Lee and Shepard, 1871), pp. 226–33, 84–85.

29   Todd, *Life,* pp. 438, 429–31.

30   John Todd, *The Daughter at School* (Northamptom: Bridgman and Childs, 1868 [1st ed., 1853]), p. 110; idem, *Student's Manual,* p. 165.

31   Edward Jarvis, "Of the Comparative Liability of Males and Females to Insanity, and their Comparative Curability and Mortality When Insane," *American Journal of Insanity,* 7 (1850): 158.

32   This is an argument I spell out in *The Horrors* (and one that Melville suggests in "The Lightning-Rod Man"). The characteristics of the masturbatory habit can be picked up from almost any case history, with which medical journals are replete, especially in the period c. 1830–1910. Three articles, published in the same year as

The Student's Manual, give the idea. All are by 'W' and in the *Boston Medical and Surgical Journal:* "Remarks on Masturbation," 12, no. 6 (March, 1835): 94–97; "Insanity, Produced by Masturbation," 12, no 7 (March, 1835): pp. 109–11 and "Effects of Masturbation, with Cases," 12, no. 9 (April, 1835): 138–41. It should be noted that the cases discussed at that early stage of the modern history of American masturbation phobia were all male. See, too, Ray, *Mental Hygiene,* 274–77.

33   Anon., "Legislative Control of Prostitution," *New Orleans Medical and Surgical Journal,* 11 (March, 1855): 704.

34   Todd, *Student's Manual,* p. 209.

35   Todd, *The Young Man,* pp. 139–40. Compare Kai Erikson's account of the relations between deviant and normal behavior in *Wayward Puritans* (New York: John Wiley, 1966), pp. 19–21.

36   "W", "Insanity," p. 109.

37   Conway Zirkle, "The Early History of the Inheritance of Acquired Characters and of Pangenesis," *Transactions of the American Philosophical Society,* 35, pt. 2, (1946): pp. 141, 146. The history of ideas about sperm is complicated, and can be approached by way of Elizabeth Gasking, *Investigations of Generation, 1651–1828* (London: Hutchinson, 1967). See too, B. Seeman, *The River of Life* (New York: Norton, 1961), pp. 26, 27, 31. Another tradition informing attitudes towards "healthy" human reproduction in nineteenth-century America was eighteenth-century English stockbreeding, transmitted by way of the French physiocrats by Thomas Jefferson, and applied by him to human beings. Jefferson, *Notes on Virginia* (New York: Harper Torchbooks, 1964). p. 133. The physiocrat to whom Jefferson was particularly indebted was D'Aubenton, as his frequent references attest (*Notes,* pp. 39, 44, 47, 48, 49, 53, 54).

38   Augustus Kinsley Gardner, *Our Children* (Hartford: Belknap ánd Bliss, 1872), pp. 51, 162–63.

39   John Bowlby, *Attachment* (New York: Basic Books, 1969), pp. 14–15; "W", "Insanity", p. 110; idem, "Remarks," p. 95; R. H. Shryock, *Medicine in America,* (Baltimore: Johns Hopkins U. Press, 1966), p. 239; John Burnham, "Psychoanalysis and American Medicine: 1894–1918," *Psychological Issues* 5, no. 4 (1967): *passim.*

40   Gardner, *Conjugal Sins,* ch. IV.

41   "W", "Remarks," p. 96; see, too, Gardner, *Conjugal Sins,* pp. 174–75, 190, 193.

42   Augustus Kinsley Gardner, *Our Children* (Hartford: Belknap and Bliss, 1872), pp. 39–40, 323; idem, *Conjugal Sins,* pp. 174–75, 190–93, 83–84, 88, 78, 81.
Spermatic waste, the associated disease of "spermatorrhoea," the idea of the economic use of sperm/energy, and its relation to a wider social context, are discussed in chapter 20 of Wayland Young's insightful *Eros Denied* (New York: Grove Press, 1964). Gardner quotes extensively from what he cites as "M. Lallemand. A practical treatise on the causes, symptoms and treatment of Spermatorrhoea, Philadelphia, 1853"(*Conjugal Sins,* pp. 81–82). Young's book describes the essential elements of a "spermatic economy" for nineteenth-century England; Michael Bliss has recorded the identical phenomenon in Canadian history in "Pure Books on Avoided Subjects;

Pre-Freudian Sexual Ideas in Canada," Read to the Canadian Historical Association, June 4, 1970.

43 *Ladies' Home Journal,* February 27, 1865.

44 Gardner, *Conjugal Sins,* pp. 141–42.

45 J. Marion Sims, *Clinical Notes on Uterine Surgery* (New York: William Wood, 1866), p. 373; Gardner, *Conjugal Sins,* passim, esp. pp. 101–02.

46 Sims, *Clinical Notes,* p. 373.

47 Anon., *My Secret Life,* abr. ed. (New York: Grove Press, 1966 [1st private printing, c. 1890]), pp. 525–57; the book describes a lifetime of sexual activity or fantasy stretching over decades prior to its first printing.
Another figure, this time an anonymous American, was also driven to quantify sperm. From 1895 to 1903 he calculated that he averaged 3.43 nocturnal emissions each month. Since he was a bachelor and did not masturbate, he felt this was an accurate measure of permissible expenditures, and while 3.43 would vary for different men, it did represent the physiological limit that should be a warning to both "unmarried masturbator and married incontinent." His article is complete with statistics and a graph. "Nocturnal Emissions," *American Journal of Psychology,* 15 (January, 1904): 104–07.

48 Augustus Kinsley Gardner, *The Causes and Curative Treatment of Sterility* (New York: DeWitt and Davenport, 1856), p. 9.

49 The evidence is overwhelming. I shall discuss sex in this context later; for money as one remaining source of identity, see Tocqueville, *Democracy,* 2, bk. 2, ch. 17: "When the reverence that belonged to what is old has vanished, birth, condition, and profession no longer distinguish men, or scarcely distinguish them; hardly anything but money remains to create strongly marked differences between them and to raise some of them above the common level. The distinction originating in wealth is increased by the disappearance or diminution of all other distinctions. Among aristocratic nations money reaches only to a few points in the vast circle of man's desires; in democracies it seems to lead to all."

50 Todd, *Student's Manual,* p. 147; Gardner, *Sterility,* p. 28; idem, *Conjugal Sins,* p. 50.

51 J. H. Walters, "Report on the Doctrine of Force, Physical and Vital," *Transactions of the American Medical Association,* 21 (1870): 273; Todd's acknowledgement of Eli Todd—a distant relative—and Samuel Woodward, is included in a footnote to his discussion of masturbation in *Student's Manual,* p. 148: this discussion was in Latin, and a translation is appended to G. J. Barker-Benfield, "The Horrors of the Half-Known Life: Aspects of the Exploitation of Women by Men," (Unpublished doctoral dissertation, University of California, Los Angeles, 1968).

52 Ray, *Mental Hygiene,* p. 205; Todd, *Student's Manual,* pp. 375–76 (for a full account of the meaning of reading in the ideology of self-making and masturbation-phobia, see chapters 14 and 15 of Benfield, *The Horrors*); Henry David Thoreau, *Walden* (New York: New American Library edition, 1960), p. 149; Gardner, *Conjugal Sins,* p. 182. Gardner re-states such proto-sublimation in the special context of democratic anxiety described by Tocqueville, Todd (and Jarvis, see note 4 above). "In American life . . . [there] are few whose minds are sufficiently freed from the cares

The Spermatic Economy   *365*

and anxieties of life, from the necessity of earning a livelihood, with the consequent employment of time and the fatigues of body and brain. The physical energies are too completely used up by these necessities to allow for much excess in pleasure, save at such infrequent intervals as to be comparatively harmless" (p. 85).

53   Freud, *Civilization and Its Discontents,* pp. 50–57; Tocqueville, *Democracy,* vol. 2, bk. 3, ch. 12.

54   Ibid.; John Todd, *Woman's Rights* (Boston: Lee and Shepard, 1867), pp. 26–27.

55   Todd, *Sunset Land,* p. 245.

56   Ibid., p. 26.

57   Ibid., p. 245.

58   Ibid., pp. 226–33.

59   Melville, *Moby Dick,* ch. XCIV.

60   Arthur Moore, *The Frontier Mind* (New York: McGraw-Hill, 1963), p. 127; R. M. Dorson, *Jonathan Draws the Long Bow* (Cambridge, Mass.: Harvard University Press, 1946), pp. 14–15; Henry Nash Smith, *Virgin Land* (New York: Vintage Books, 1950), bk. 2.

61   Todd, *Sunset Land,* pp. 66–67.

62   Smith, *Virgin Land,* p. 35; Todd, *Sunset Land,* pp. 28, 241. This is how William Hall described the observation of the advance of the railroad, in a speech to the 1847 Railroad Convention in Chicago: "They saw him pluck out forests, tear up and fling aside the seated hills, and with the rejoicing sound of progress in his train, made way into the body of the continent, with the step of a bridegroom going to his chambers or a prince to occupy his throne" ("Speech of William M. Hall of New York in favor of a National Railroad to the Pacific at the Chicago Convention, July 7, 1847," [New York: The Day Book Female Type Setting Establishment, 1853], p. 5).

63   Todd, *Sunset Land,* pp. 74–75.

64   Todd, *Daughter at School,* p. 214.

65   Todd, *Student's Manual,* p. 150.

66   Todd, *Daughter at School,* pp. 208–09.

67   Meyer, *Positive Thinkers,* p. 48.

68   See note 11 above.

69   Jarvis, "Comparative Liability," pp. 154–55, 158.

70   Tocqueville, *Democracy,* 2, bk. 2, ch. 19.

71   For evidence of male concern about women's new life style, see Anon., *Employment of Females as Practitioners in Midwifery* (Boston: Cummings and Hillard, 1820), pp. 14–15, 22; Cooper, *Notions,* 1: 252–53; A. K. Gardner, "The Physical Decline of American Women," *The Knickerbocker,* 55, no. 1 (January, 1860): 37–52;

Marvin Meyers, *The Jacksonian Persuasion* (New York: Vintage Books, 1960), pp. 129-31.

72   Charles D. Meigs, *Woman: Her Diseases and Remedies* (Philadelphia: Blanchard and Lea, 1852 [1st ed., 1848]), p. 54; Horatio Robinson Storer, *The Causation, Course and Treatment of Reflex Insanity in Women* (Boston: Lee and Shepard, 1871), p. 79.

73   Gardner, *Conjugal Sins,* p. 150.

74   Todd, *Woman's Rights,* pp. 18, 37; Gardner, *Our Children,* p. 180; see Benfield, "Horrors," pp. 409-11, 574-76 for elucidation.

75   Sims, *Clinical Notes.* "I have seen the inside of an immense number of vaginas, and I never saw two that were in all particulars exactly alike. They are as different from each other as our faces and noses" (p. 18).

76   Gardner, *Our Children,* p. 19; idem; *Conjugal Sins,* p. 143.

77   Sims, *Clinical Notes,* p. 360

78   Gardner, *Sterility,* p. 111; see, too, p. 49.

79   Sims, *Clinical Notes,* p. 360.

80   Gardner, *Sterility,* p. 111.

81   Cooper, *Notions,* 2:263.

82   For examples of the assumption of "positive amorous signs" as disorder, or symptoms of disorder, see B. Sherwood-Dunn, "Conservation of the Ovary: Discussion," *Transactions of the American Association of Obstetricians and Gynecologists,* 10 (1897): 219, 220, 223; George J. Englemann, "Cliterodectomy" [sic], *The American Practitioner,* 25 (1882): 3, 5; Anon., "Transactions of the Woman's Hospital Society," *American Journal of Obstetrics and Gynecology,* 43 (1901): 721; A. J. Bloch, "Sexual Perversion in the Female," *New Orleans Medical and Surgical Journal,* 22, no. 1 (July, 1894): 7.

83   Gardner, *Conjugal Sins,* p. 147; see, too, Meigs, *Woman,* p. 432.

84   Gardner, *Conjugal Sins,* pp. 17, 145-46.

85   J. Marion Sims, *The Story of My Life,* comp. and ed. H. Marion Sims (New York: D. Appleton, 1885), p. 231; A. K. Gardner, "Treatise on Uterine Haemorrhage," *American Medical Monthly* (June, 1855): 1.

86   Gardner, "Physical Decline," p. 37.

87   Engelmann, "Cliterodectomy," p. 3, passim; E. H. Pratt, "Circumcision of Girls," *Journal of Orificial Surgery,* 6, no. 9 (March, 1898): 390; Anon., "Transactions of the Woman's Hospital Society" (1901): 721-22; Wallace C. Abbott, "The Importance of Circumcision of the Female," *The Medical Council,* 9 (December, 1904): 437-39.

88   Archibald Church, "Removal of Ovaries and Tubes in the Insane and Neurotic," *American Journal of Obstetrics and the Diseases of Women and Children,* 28 (1893): 494-95; ibid., "Discussion," p. 573.

The Spermatic Economy

89   Gardner, *Conjugal Sins,* p. 81.

90   Ibid., pp. 72, 78; idem, *Our Children,* pp. 200–01.

91   This is a point *The Horrors* sets out in detail.

92   J. A. Jackson, "Hygiene of Adolescence," *Transactions of the Wisconsin State Medical Society,* 30 (1896): 288; the nocturnal emissions article is cited in note 47 above.

93   A. J. Himel, "Some Minor Studies in Psychology, with Special Reference to Masturbation," *New Orleans Medical and Surgical Journal,* 70 (1907): 442; Holmes is quoted in Ilza Veith, *Hysteria: The History of a Disease* (Chicago: University of Chicago Press, Phoenix Books, 1970), p. 216.

94   See below; see also, Benfield, *The Horrors.*

95   Gardner, "Physical Decline," p. 49; A. K. Gardner, *History of the Art of Midwifery* (New York: Stringer and Townshend, 1852), p. 4.

96   John Todd, *Serpents in the Dove's Nest* (Boston: Lee and Shephard, 1867), pp. 12, 25.

97   Gardner, *Conjugal Sins,* dedication, p. 195. Gardner maintained that subversely sick women should turn their warlike hostility against themselves in the interests of their subordination, and "not only assert their independence, but vindicate their claim to equality, not with chalk powder and balls . . . but by actual attainments over self-degeneracy" (p. 52).

98   Todd, *Young Man,* p. 278. For an account of earlier fears of the same stripe, see Sidney Mead, *The Lively Experiment: The Shaping of Christianity in America* (New York: Harper and Row, 1963), ch. III.

99   Gardner, *Conjugal Sins,* p. 64. These remarks about the body politic have been influenced considerably by Winthrop Jordan, *White Over Black* (Baltimore: Pelican Books, 1969).

100   Freud, *Civilization and its Discontents,* p. 51.

101   Karl Marx and Friedrich Engels, *Manifesto of the Communist Party* (New York: International Publishers, 1948 [1st ed., 1848]), p. 27.

102   See, for example, Louis Hartz, *The Liberal Tradition in America* (New York: Harcourt Brace and World, 1955), pp. 3, 50–64; Leslie Fiedler, *Love and Death in the American Novel* (New York: Stein and Day, 1966 [1st ed., 1960]), p. 76; Jack P. Greene, "Political Mimesis," *The American Historical Review,* 75 (December, 1969): 337–60. The well-known crowings of Daniel Boorstin and lament of Henry James are symptoms of the same phenomenon.

103   Tocqueville, *Democracy,* 2: bk. 2, ch. 2; bk. 3, ch.17.

104   Ibid.

105   Ibid.

106   Evert A. and George L. Duyckinch, 2 vols., *Cyclopoedia of American Literature* (Philadelphia: William Rutter, 1880), 1: iii.

Ben Barker-Benfield   368

107 Robert Wiebe, *The Search for Order* (New York: Hill and Wang, 1967), pp. xiii, 1, 5–6, 8.

108 Ibid., p. 52; Todd, *Serpents,* p. 21.

109 Todd, *Serpents,* p. 16.

110 See Benfield, "Horrors," pt. III, ch. 2.

111 Gardner, *Conjugal Sins,* pp. 8, 203.

112 Mark Haller, *Eugenics: Hereditarian Attitudes in American Thought* (New Brunswick: Rutgers University Press, 1963); John Higham, *Strangers in the Land* (New York: Atheneum Publishers, 1968), pp. 150–53. For the rise of drastic surgery see below.

113 Gardner, *Old Wine,* p. 223; Gardner, "Thoughts on Health," *Frank Leslie's Illustrated Newspaper,* 34, no. 876 (July 13, 1872): 283.

114 Gardner, *Old Wine,* pp. 256–57; idem, *Our Children,* pp. 52–53 and passim; see also, idem, *Conjugal Sins,* p. 192.

115 Gardner, *Our Children,* pp. 36, 37, 40.

116 Sources for this are numerous: E.g., David T. Gilliam, "Oophorectomy for the Insanity and Epilepsy of the Female: A Plea for its More General Adoption," *Transactions of the American Association of Obstetricians and Gynecologists,* 9 (1896): 320–21; Todd, *Woman's Rights;* Gardner, *Conjugal Sins;* Gardner, "Physical Decline."

117 Gardner, *Our Children,* p. 60.

118 Benfield, *The Horrors,* pt. II; Sims, *Clinical Notes,* pp. 131–35; 206–07.

119 These conclusions and the following section of the paper reflect research into nineteenth-century medical journals which will be more elaborately documented in *The Horrors.*

120 Abraham Jacobi, "On Masturbation and Hysteria in Young Children," 2 pts., *American Journal of Obstetrics and Diseases of Women and Children,* 8 & 9 (1875, 1876), 9:603.

121 The gradual acceptance of the routine circumcision of male babies seems to have originated as an expression of masturbation phobia (removing the thrill of pulling back the foreskin to urinate or wash). It is a story I give briefly in *The Horrors.*

122 Pierre Lefort, "A Case of Excision of the Clitoris," *Medical Repository,* 4 (1818): 84–87.

123 "Meeting to Consider the Proposition of the Council for the Removal of Mr. I. B. Brown," *British Medical Journal,* 1 (April, 1867): 395–410; Lawson Tait, "Masturbation," *The Medical News,* 53, no. 1 (July 7, 1888): 3; René A. Spitz, "Authority and Masturbation," *Psychoanalytic Quarterly,* 21 (1952): 502.

124 For a chronological and analytical account of clitoridectomy in the United States, see Benfield, *The Horrors,* pt. V.

125   E.g., Robert Morris, "Circumcision in Girls," *International Journal of Surgery,* 25 (1912): 135–36.

126   Frank J. Iiams, "Female Circumcision," *Medical Record and Annals* (Houston, Texas) 31 (1937): 171–73; again, see Benfield, *The Horrors.* This operation was a favorite one of a battery of operations on the lower parts of the body, most frequently the female body, developed from the late 1880's under the auspices of the Orificial Surgery Society, but not in the least limited to "orificialists." These operations, including "the American operation" (removal of the last inch of the rectum), were performed for everything from measles to melancholia, in accordance with a "philosophy" that was nothing more or less than a monistic, monomaniac version of the spermatic economy projected onto women. This philosophy was elaborated into twenty-three rules to guarantee the unobstructed circulation of the bloodstream according to laws of "the waste and supply of the sympathetic nerve." The nerve's energy, and in consequence, the blood flow it supported could become congested in "sphincter openings" which then had to be snipped and trimmed to release the tensions, flush the capillaries and smooth the openings. B. E. Dawson, *Orificial Surgery, Its Philosophy, Application and Technique,* ed. Minnie Elder Dawson (Kansas City, Missouri: Western Baptist Publishing Co., 1925 [1st ed., 1912]), ch. 2, and passim.

127   Norman Himes suggests that contraception was widely accepted in England after the Bradlaugh case of 1879, and not accepted in the United States until after Jacobi's Presidential address to the A.M.A. in 1912, and Margaret Sanger's work in New York in the 1920's. *Medical History of Contraception* (New York: Schocken, 1970 [1st ed., 1936]), pp. 243, 311–15.

128   See Benfield, *The Horrors,* pt. II.

129   Robert Battey, "Normal Ovariotomy—Case," *Atlanta Medical and Surgical Journal,* 10 (1872): 321–39.

130   For an account of female castration, see Benfield, *The Horrors,* pt. V.

131   Church, "Removal—Discussion," p. 570; Howard A. Kelly, "Conservatism in Ovariotomy," *Journal of the American Medical Association,* 26 (1896): 251.

132   Ely Van de Warker, "The Fetich of the Ovary," *American Journal of Obstetrics and the Diseases of Women and Children,* 54 (July-December, 1906): 369.

133   E.g., Robert Morris, "A Cast of Heteroplastic Ovarian Grafting, Followed by Pregnancy, and the Delivery of a Living Child," *Medical Record,* 69 (1906): 697–98.

134   E.g., Kelly, "Conservatism," p. 251.

135   Van de Warker, "Fetich," p. 371.

136   Sims, "Normal Ovariotomy—Battey's Operation," *North Carolina Medical Journal,* 1 (1878): 26–29.

137   See Benfield, *The Horrors,* pt. II.

138   Arnold Praeger, "Is So-Called Conservatism in Gynecology Conducive to the Best Results to the Patient?" *Transactions of the American Association of Obstetricians and Gynecologists,* 8 (1895): 322.

139   Gilliam, "Oophorectomy," pp. 317–20.

140 Tocqueville, *Democracy*, vol. 2, bk. 3, ch. 10.

141 Benfield, *The Horrors*, pt. V.

142 Meyer, *Positive Thinkers*, pp. 52–54.

143 Van de Warker, "The Fetich," p. 372.

144 James W. Cokenower, "A Plea for the Conservative Operations on the Ovaries," *Transactions of the section on Obstetrics and Diseases of Women of the American Medical Association* (1904): 291.

145 Robert T. Edes, "Points in the Diagnosis and Treatment of Some Obscure Common Neuroses," *Journal of the American Medical Association*, 27 (1896): 1081; idem, "The relations of Pelvic and Nervous Diseases," *Journal of The American Medical Association*, 31 (1898): 1136.

146 Edes, "Points" and "Relations." Gardner expressed such a relation in 1870: "It has been a matter of common observation that the physical status of the women of Christendom has been gradually deteriorating . . . that a numerous class of specialists has arisen within a quarter of a century, devoting their whole energies to the investigation of these [women's] complaints, to the inventing of new instruments for the observation and diagnosis of these physical lesions . . . to remedy these diseases" (*Conjugal Sins*, pp. 13–14). Confusing cause with effect he said "nervous complications," masturbation, contraception and abortion created "hours of uselessness" and made "of life itself a burden which is worse than valueless" (*Conjugal Sins*, pp. 13–14).

147 W. P. Manton, "Mental Alienation in Women and Abdomino-Pelvic Disease," *Transactions of the Section on Obstetrics and Diseases of Women of the American Medical Association* (1909). This is an argument Donald Meyer makes in his account of the origins of Christian Science and other mind cures, *The Positive Thinkers*, pt. 1.

148 Ray, *Mental Hygiene*, pp. 216, 219. See, also, Jarvis, "Comparative Liability," pp. 150, 156.

149 Again, I must ask the reader to see part V of *The Horrors.*

150 George J. Engelmann, "The Increasing Sterility of American Women," *Transactions of the Section on the Diseases of Women of the American Medical Association* (1901): 271–95; William Goodell, *Lessons in Gynecology* (Philadelphia: D. G. Brinton, 1879), p. 176. See, too, John Higham, *Strangers in the Land* (New York: Atheneum, 1963), pp. 143, 146–48.

151 Sims, *Clinical Notes*, p. 369.

152 Gardner, *History of Midwifery*, p. 31.

153 Ibid.

154 Benfield, "The Horrors," pp. 534–36.

155 Sims, *Life*, p. 234.

156 E. P. Becton, "Batty [sic] and Batty's Operation," *Texas Courier-Record of Medicine*, 6 (1888–1889): 34.

157 Gardner, *Old Wine,* p. 309; idem, *Conjugal Sins,* p. 110. See Benfield, "The Horrors," pp. 509–17 for elucidation.

158 Gardner, *Our Children,* pp. 36, 53.

159 Gardner compared gestation to the eating and digesting process (*Old Wine,* pp. 291–92; *Our Children,* p. 56). See Benfield, "The Horrors," pt. IV, chs, 2, 9.

160 E.g., Battey, "Normal Ovariotomy," p. 324; Sims, *Life,* p. 346; Dawson, *Orificial Surgery,* p. 24.

161 Robert Battey, "Normal Ovariotomy," *Atlanta Medical and Surgical Journal,* 11 (1873): 1, 2.

162 Cokenower, "Plea"—"Discussion," p. 298.

163 A. Palmer Dudley, "Results of Ovarian Surgery," *Transaction of the Section on Obstetics and the Diseases of Women* (1901): 198.

164 Smith, *Virgin Land,* ch. X; the work of Todd and Gardner, and medical articles of the same period contain a like fantasy.

165 Edes, "Points," p. 1081.

166 Praeger, "So-Called Conservatism," p. 321.

Ben Barker-Benfield   372

PART V

Demographic Trends: Marriage, Birth, and Death

We begin this section on demographic patterns with a chapter from Grabill, Kiser, and Whelpton's important study, The Fertility of American Women. *Their research reveals that during the colonial and early federal periods birth rates were extremely high. In fact, women of completed fertility gave birth to an average of eight children, and the number of children living in a household in 1790 was three times greater than the number in 1950. Thus, while modernization may not have affected family form in the sense of a movement from extended to nuclear families, it is certainly associated with a reduction in childbearing and its concentration in a narrow span of years. However, the situation is more complex than this. In general, modernization is seen as being related to the "demographic transition," which involves declining mortality, brought about as a result of such things as improved sanitary conditions and vaccines, in settings where fertility is either increasing or remaining stable. Therefore, even though the birth rate, as the authors show, was declining in the nineteenth century, the population continued to grow—though, of course, migration was also a factor in this growth. Just how the decline in fertility during the nineteenth century was brought about is not as easily explained as Grabill, Kiser, and Whelpton suggest. Contraceptives were not well developed nor widely employed; possibly as much of the reduction was brought about through abstinence as it was through such methods as withdrawal.*

WILSON H. GRABILL, CLYDE V. KISER,
AND PASCAL K. WHELPTON

19 A Long View

The Colonial and Early Federal Periods

For more than two centuries, from the time of the first permanent settlements to the early decades of the nineteenth century, the fertility of the American people ranked among the world's highest. Estimates made by both contemporary and modern authorities, utilizing a variety of techniques and data, place the annual birth rate in the Colonial and early Federal periods at 50 to 57 births per 1,000 inhabitants. The women of completed fertility are variously estimated to have borne an average of eight children. According to Miller, the high American birth rate was sometimes cited for propaganda purposes before the Revolutionary War to indicate that it was only a question of time before the American population growth would shift the British Empire's balance of power westward.[1] Benjamin Franklin made this type of forecast himself.

CONTEMPORARY OBSERVATIONS

The contemporary explanation for America's high fertility is illustrated by the following quotations. In 1751, Benjamin Franklin wrote:

Tables of the proportion of Marriages to Births, of Deaths to Births, of Marriages to the number of inhabitants, &c., form'd on observations made upon the Bills of Mortality, Christenings, &c., of populous cities, will not suit countries; nor will tables form'd on observations made in full settled old countries, as *Europe,* suit new countries, as *America.*

2. For people increase in proportion to the number of marriages, and that is greater in proportion to the ease and convenience of supporting a family . . . which charges are greater in the cities, as Luxury is more common: many live single during life, and continue servants to families, journeymen to Trades, &c., hence cities do not by natural generation supply themselves with inhabitants; the deaths are more than the births.

4. In countries full settled, the case must be nearly the same; all Lands being occupied and improved to the heighth; those who cannot get land must labour for others that have it; when laborers are plenty, their wages will be low; by low wages a family is supported with difficulty; this difficulty deters many from marriage, who therefore long continue servants and single. Only as the Cities take supplies of people from the country, and thereby make a little more room in the country; Marriage is a little more encourag'd there, and the births exceed the deaths. . . .

7. Hence, marriages in *America* are more general and more generally early, than in *Europe.* And if it is reckoned there, that there is but one marriage per annum among one hundred persons, perhaps we may here reckon two; and if in *Europe* they have but four Births to a marriage (many of their marriages being late) we may here reckon eight, of which one half grow up, and our marriages are made, reckoning one with another at twenty years of age our people must be at least doubled every twenty years.[2]

Thomas Jefferson in a letter to Count de Montmorin, dated July 1787, said:

A century's experience has shown that we double our numbers every twenty or twenty-five years. No circumstances can be foreseen, at this moment, which will lessen our rate of multiplication for centuries to come.

The Chevalier Félix de Beaujour, a former French consular official in the United States declared in 1814:

Every thing in the United States favours the progress of population; the emigrations from Europe, the disasters of the European colonies, but, above all, the abundance of the means of subsistence. Marriages are there easier than in Europe, births more multiplied, and deaths relatively less frequent. It is calculated that out of sixty individuals, two are married annually, that one is born out of every twenty, and that the proportion of deaths is only one in forty. This last report, founded on careful observations, seems incredible in a country so recently cleared and naturally not healthy; but it is nonetheless true, because it accords with the number of births, which there is greater than in Europe. In the United States, more children are necessarily born than among us, because the inhabitants, in such an extent of country, finding the means of subsistence more abundant, marry at an earlier age. No human consideration there operates as a hindrance to reproduction, and the children swarm on the rich land in the same manner as do insects.[3]

TABLE 1.—ABSTRACT OF SAMUEL BLODGET'S ESTIMATES OF ANNUAL POPULATION INCREASE, BIRTHS, DEATHS, AND NET IMMIGRATION: 1790 TO 1805

[No correction has been made for errors in original table]

Year	Free persons	Slaves, increase yearly near 2 percent	Free blacks and persons of color	Annual migrations, free men and slaves	Births in each year, near 5 3/4 percent	Deaths in each year, near 2 1/2 percent	Total population, including Louisiana in the year 1804	Total increase each year, near 3 percent
1790	3,232,303	697,697	59,511	3,500	...	...	3,930,000	...
1791	3,333,761	714,139	63,500	4,000	215,900	101,000	4,047,900	117,900
1792	3,438,237	731,000	67,500	5,000	220,937	103,500	4,169,337	121,337
1793	3,446,417	748,000	71,600	3,600	227,680	107,100	4,294,417	125,180
1794	3,657,189	766,000	75,700	3,500	235,382	110,200	4,423,249	128,632
1795	3,771,946	784,000	79,800	3,900	242,197	113,400	4,555,946	132,697
1796	3,890,124	802,500	84,900	4,500	249,117	117,000	4,692,624	136,678
1797	4,012,902	820,500	89,900	3,500	257,516	120,300	4,833,402	140,776
1798	4,940,404	837,000	95,000	3,800	266,202	124,000	4,978,404	145,002
1799	4,273,756	854,000	100,600	4,000	273,334	128,000	5,127,756	149,352
1800	4,404,798	876,790	105,643	3,800	282,132	132,100	5,281,588	153,823
1801	4,544,300	898,300	110,800	4,000	290,712	136,200	5,440,100	158,512
1802	4,682,313	921,000	115,900	4,500	299,113	140,400	5,603,313	163,213
1803	4,727,412	944,000	121,900	3,900	308,749	144,550	5,771,412	168,099
1804	5,000,100	999,900	126,000	9,500	810,500	149,000	6,000,000	228,588
1805	5,156,000	1,024,900	131,000	...	321,000	153,000	6,180,000	180,000

Source: Samuel Blodget, *Economica, A Statistical Manual for the United States of America*, Washington, 1806, p. 58.

Beaujour's "observations" probably were based in part on esti-mates made by Samuel Blodget, which are reproduced in table 1 as an example of the work done in early times.[4]

Franklin's references to Europe seem to be based on an extensive investigation of parish records in several European countries by Süss-milch, a clergyman, who was much interested in population data and in the "laws" of population growth.[5] Franklin's remarks on urban and rural differences in marriages, etc., are evidently for Europe. Blod-get's later data indicate that American cities around 1800 had about two births for every death (table 2). The population of America increased by about 35 percent in most decades from 1660 to 1790 (table 3). This corresponds to a doubling of population every 23 years.

TABLE 2.—SAMUEL BLODGET'S VITAL RATES FOR VARIOUS LOCALITIES: CIRCA 1805

Area	Deaths per 100 births	Area	Population per death
Portsmouth, N. H........................	50	Portsmouth, N. H........................	48-49
Salem, Mass...........................	49-51	Salem, Mass...........................	48-49
Boston, Mass..........................	49-52	Boston, Mass..........................	47-49
Hartford, Conn........................	48-49	Philadelphia, Pa......................	44-50
Philadelphia, Pa......................	51-54	Baltimore, Md.........................	43-49
Baltimore, Md.........................	51-53	Washington, D. C......................	48-50
Washington, D. C......................	50-51	Norfolk, Va...........................	40-47
Norfolk, Va...........................	52-54	Charleston, S. C......................	35-40
Charleston, S. C......................	55-60	Healthiest parts of Georgia...........	45-50
Healthiest parts of South Carolina		New York State........................	44-50
and Georgia........................	45-49	Hartford, Conn........................	50-55
New York City.........................	51-53	Rhode Island..........................	50-56
		Low grounds south of 38° N. latitude...	34-39
Average for United States.............	49-51	Average for United States.............	39-41

Source: Samuel Blodget, *Economica, A Statistical Manual for the United States of America*, Washington, 1806, pp. 75 and 76.

TABLE 3.—ESTIMATED POPULATION DURING COLONIAL AND CONTINENTAL PERIODS: 1610 TO 1790

Year	Number	Decennial increase, percent	Year	Number	Decennial increase, percent
1790.........................	3,929,625	41.3	1690.........................	213,500	37.2
1780.........................	2,781,000	26.1	1680.........................	155,600	35.9
1770.........................	2,205,000	37.0	1670.........................	114,500	35.0
1760.........................	1,610,000	33.4	1660.........................	84,800	64.0
1750.........................	1,207,000	35.8	1650.........................	51,700	85.0
1740.........................	889,000	35.7	1640.........................	27,947	390.3
1730.........................	654,950	38.1	1630.........................	5,700	128.1
1720.........................	474,388	32.7	1620.........................	2,499	1,090.0
1710.........................	357,500	30.0	1610.........................	210	...
1700.........................	275,000	28.8			

Source: U. S. Bureau of the Census, *A Century of Population Growth in the United States, 1790-1900*, by W. S. Rossi-ter, pp. 9 and 10. Data based on estimates for separate Colonies made by a number of scholars who used tax lists, militia records, Colonial censuses, etc.

FERTILITY AND MIGRATION

Although Franklin and some of his contemporaries spoke of the high rate of population growth in the American Colonies, they gave relatively little attention to the role played by migration of population from abroad. Bountiful natural increase was regarded as the main source of future growth. A birth rate of about 55 and a population of about 1,207,000 in 1750 meant about 66,000 births per year at that time, compared with annual net immigration amounting to perhaps 4,000. It is likely that annual births exceeded annual net immigration shortly after the initial settlements were made in the seventeenth century and that the proportion of the population that was native increased rapidly.[6] The steady rate of decennial population increase after 1660, in contrast to an irregular flow of immigration, suggests that natural increase predominated in population growth. Various Colonial censuses show a fair balance of males and females in the population, probably from natural increase, whereas seventeenth century European data on emigration to the New World indicate that males much outnumbered females. Some examples of sex ratios from Colonial censuses are shown in the accompanying table:

	Males per 100 females		Males per 100 females
New Hampshire:		Connecticut:	
1767	107.4	1774	93.2
1773	103.0	New York:	
		1698	108.3
Massachusetts:		1703	101.2
1754	104.5	1731	[1]136.5
1764	90.3	1737	103.8
		1771	106.8
Maine:		New Jersey:	
1764	103.3	1726	111.4
		1737	119.0
Rhode Island:		1745	102.8
1774	96.6		

[1] The high ratio in New York in 1731 reflected the presence of English soldiers and Indian braves in two towns; the ratios were much smaller in other parts of New York.

In 1790, if not at a much earlier date, the proportion of the population that was American born was over 90 percent as determined by computation. Further evidence of the existence of a largely native population appears in the 1820 Census which counted only 53,687 "foreigners not naturalized" in the population of 9,638,453. (Over half of these "foreigners" were in the State of New York.)

Lest what has just been said lead to an underevaluation of the very important role played by immigration, mention is made of the

Grabill, Kiser, and Whelpton

Beards' estimate that between 1600 and 1700 about 750,000 persons journeyed from Europe to America to seek a new way of life.[7] Others have estimated that migration to the New World prior to the Revolutionary War exceeded 2,000,000. There are several difficulties in using such data. Many of the out-migrants from Europe died enroute; others went to places such as Canada, the Caribbean, and South America. Many who came to North America found conditions not to their liking and returned to Europe. The numerous male immigrants sometimes died without progeny and in that sense proved to have been only temporary additions to the population. There were enough immigrants of the family type to account for the much larger population growth in America than in Canada or in the French and Spanish colonies.

One theory for the high fertility in Colonial times is that the women had little to say in such matters. According to Willison, it was a man's world.[8] Governor Bradford is quoted as indignantly denying a libel that women in New Plymouth had any new rights or privileges: "Touching our governemente, you are quite mistaken if you think we admite weomen . . . to have to doe in the same, for they are excluded, as both reason and nature teacheth they should be." Willison says that more than one foreign visitor noted that the women of New England were all "pittifully Toothshaken" and apt to look much older than their years.

FERTILITY AND HOUSEHOLD SIZE

Although the women who reached the end of the childbearing ages had an average of about eight children ever born in Colonial and early Federal times, this did not necessarily mean that the average household was very large. In 1790, the average size of private households was 5.7 persons, or less than twice the size of households in 1950, 3.4 persons (table 4). In 1790, there was an average of 2.8 children (persons) under 16 years old per household, and in 1950 the average was 1.0 children of this age. The number of living children per household was thus about three times as large in 1790 as in 1950.

INFANT MORTALITY

What proportion of the high fertility in Colonial and early Federal times was offset by high mortality among the children? A very rough idea can be obtained thus: Tests indicate that a life table for England and Wales in 1838–54 may fit fairly well the mortality conditions in the United States around 1800.[9] According to this table, about 78 percent of the children born in a 5-year period would live to be enumerated at the end of the period as children under 5 years old in

TABLE 4.—PERCENT DISTRIBUTION OF HOUSEHOLDS, BY SIZE: 1790, 1900, AND 1950

Household size	Private households, 1790 (white and free colored)	Private households and quasi households, 1900	Occupied dwelling units, 1950	Household size	Private households, 1790 (white and free colored)	Private households and quasi households, 1900	Occupied dwelling units, 1950
Total........	100.0	100.0	100.0	7 persons............	11.2	7.7	2.7
1 person............	3.7	5.1	9.3	8 persons............	9.0	5.2	1.4
2 persons..........	7.8	15.0	28.1	9 persons............	6.5	3.2	0.8
3 persons..........	11.7	17.6	22.8	10 persons or more..	9.1	4.1	0.9
4 persons..........	13.8	16.9	18.4				
5 persons..........	13.9	14.2	10.4	Average number of persons............	5.7	4.6	3.4
6 persons..........	13.2	10.9	5.3				

Source: U. S. Bureau of the Census, *A Century of Population Growth in the United States, 1790-1900*, by W. S. Rossiter, p. 98; *1950 Census of Housing*, Vol. I, *General Characteristics*, Part 1, U. S. Summary, p. 8.

a census, and about 66 percent of newborn infants would live to the age of 20 years. Applied to a rapidly growing population having an age-sex distribution similar to the one existing in 1800, this mortality would result in as many annual reports of deaths at ages under 20 years as at all later ages. This agrees with the little information on ages that was available in bills of mortality of the type seen by Franklin when he assumed that half of the children "grew up."

A discussion of mortality is incomplete without some mention of early American life tables such as the Wigglesworth life table of 1789 for Massachusetts and New Hampshire combined. These life tables were based on deaths alone, without adequate allowances for the age distribution of the population at risk of dying, and they underestimated the expectation of life if they included too many infant deaths in relation to adult deaths. The expectation of life at birth in the Wigglesworth table was 36 years. The earliest American life tables that take specific account of the population at risk of dying are the Kennedy life tables for Massachusetts and Maryland in 1850. The registration data used were of questionable reliability, however, and for this reason the life tables are of value mainly for checking on the applicability of the English life tables. The Massachusetts life tables yield an expectation of life at birth of 38.3 years for males and 40.5 years for females; for Maryland the corresponding figures are 41.8 for males and 44.9 for females. It is possible that the death rates really were larger in more urban Massachusetts than in less urban Maryland and thus did not necessarily reflect a more nearly complete registration in Massachusetts. Around 1850 Massachusetts was host to many thousands of immigrants who fled a serious potato famine in Ireland. These immigrants were crowded into slum areas with poor sanitation facilities.

Grabill, Kiser, and Whelpton

Early censuses obtained little detail on the characteristics of Negroes, many of whom were slaves. It may be inferred, nonetheless, that the Negroes were quite fertile. Despite high mortality and no appreciable immigration after 1790, the Negro population increased at an average rate of about 2.5 percent per year between 1790 and 1870. Fertility data for rural-farm Negro women 70 to 74 years old in the 1910 Census indicate an average of seven to eight births in a lifetime. Most of these women were slaves during a major part of their childbearing years. The early available ratios of young children to Negro women are not impressively large, probably because of the effect of heavy infant mortality and also because of a large undercount of children. Negro fertility is discussed more thoroughly in the section on trends in the nineteenth century.

URBAN-RURAL DIFFERENTIALS

The subject of urban-rural differentials in fertility is of interest but not of great importance for America in the Colonial period because American cities were few and small. In 1750, the largest city in America (Boston) had only 15,731 inhabitants, Philadelphia and its suburbs had 13,400, New York had 13,300, and Newport had 6,000. As late as 1790 there were only 24 places in the United States with 2,500 inhabitants or more. Nationally, only 5 percent of the population resided in urban areas in 1790. The proportion ranged from none in a number of States to 13.1 percent in Massachusetts.

Table 5 presents a specially computed series of ratios of children under 16 to white women 16 years old and over, based on a series of early enumerations in the colony of New York. No other colony had as extensive a series of censuses. It may be noted from the figures in this table that the ratio of children to women declined appreciably as New York County (City) grew, but that between 1712 and 1786 the ratio remained nearly constant in the remainder of the colony. The population outside of New York County (City) was practically all rural. The data in table 5 indicate, therefore, that differential urban-rural fertility began in the colonies at a very early date. It is possible, as Franklin suggests, that at least some of the difference came from relatively more unmarried adults and a later marriage age in cities than on farms.

The Nineteenth Century

BIRTH STATISTICS

The New England States collected vital statistics long before the establishment of the Federal Government's Birth Registration Area in

TABLE 5.—TOTAL NUMBER OF INHABITANTS AND NUMBER OF CHILDREN UNDER 16 YEARS OLD PER 1,000 WHITE WOMEN 16 YEARS OLD AND OVER, FOR NEW YORK COUNTY AND THE REMAINDER OF THE COLONY OR STATE OF NEW YORK: 1703 TO 1786

[New York City, then at the southern tip of Manhattan Island, contained almost all of the population of New York County at each census]

Year	New York County		Remainder of the Colony or State of New York	
	Population	Children per 1,000 women	Population	Children per 1,000 women
1786..............................	23,614	1,278	215,283	1,998
1771..............................	21,863	1,279	146,154	1,886
1756..............................	13,046	1,260	83,544	2,022
1749..............................	13,294	1,441	60,054	2,025
1746..............................	11,717	1,426	¹49,872	2,179
1723..............................	7,248	1,564	33,316	1,968
1712²..............................	5,841	1,743	³13,563	2,057
1703..............................	4,375	1,906	16,290	2,446

[1] Albany County was excluded from the enumeration "because of the enemy."

[2] The returns of this census are deemed imperfect, "the people being deterred by a simple superstition, and observation that sickness followed upon the last numbering of the people."

[3] Kings and Richmond Counties are excluded because no age detail is available.

Source: Computed from data on early Colonial enumerations presented in U. S. Bureau of the Census, *A Century of Population Growth in the United States, 1790-1900*, by W. S. Rossiter.

1915. Annual reports on births have been issued in each State since the date specified: Massachusetts (1842), Connecticut (1848), Rhode Island (1853), Vermont (1857), New Hampshire (1880), and Maine (1892). Several States outside of New England, notably New York and Maryland, also have early data. In 1930, Spengler made a study of the New England data and also made estimates of annual numbers of native white and foreign-born white women of childbearing age for use in birth rates. His data, not corrected for underregistration (this was more serious in the early years), showed no consistent downward trend in the birth rate for native white women after about 1880. In Massachusetts, for example, there were around 77 reported births per 1,000 native white women 15 to 49 years old in 1853–60, 66 in 1880–90, and 62 in 1910–20. In Maine there were increases from about 70 in 1891–1900 to about 76 in 1910–20. In New England as a whole, the uncorrected birth rate for native white women increased from about 65 in 1891–95 to 71 in 1921–25. The uncorrected birth rate for the foreign born declined from 138 to 102 in the same period.[10] (New England had a less fertile population than the nation as a whole, as may be seen from data on ratios of young children to women in table 6.)

RATIOS OF CHILDREN UNDER 5 YEARS TO WOMEN 20 TO 44 YEARS OLD

In the absence of national birth statistics until the twentieth century, it is fortunate that we have decennial census data since 1790 on

Grabill, Kiser, and Whelpton 382

the population classified by age and sex. Ratios of young children to women of childbearing age, computed from such data, are fully as useful as birth rates for many purposes, although they must be used with due regard for their limitations. (See Appendix A.)

Because many of the children under 5 years old are past the first year of life, when most infant mortality occurs, the ratios of young children to women are often described as measures of effective fertility. Those who wish to allow for the factor of mortality may recall the rough estimate given in the section on infant mortality to the effect that about 78 percent of white infants around 1800 survived from birth to about the midpoint of the "under 5 years" age group. A relatively good estimate for white infants in 1901, based on Glover's life tables for the United States Death Registration Area, is 84 percent, and an excellent one for 1950, based on National Office of Vital Statistics' life tables, is 97 percent. Corresponding estimates for Negro infants are 72 percent in 1901 and 95 percent in 1950.

Variations in the age distributions of women may have an important effect on ratios of young children to women for small areas, but they are not of much consequence on a national basis. As tested by computations, standardization for age of woman would change the ratios of children under 5 years old to white women 20 to 44 years old by only 4 percent nationally in the long swing between the population of young average age in 1800 and the population of much older average age in 1950.

Variations in the census undercount of young children are discussed in Appendix A. In general, it should be noted that the undercount was greater than usual in 1850, 1870, and 1890. The quality of the count of young children was improved in 1900 when a check question on date of birth was asked. In other censuses the estimated undercount amounted to about 5 to 7 percent of white children and 10 to 15 percent of nonwhite children under 5 years old.

NINETEENTH-CENTURY DECLINES IN CURRENT FERTILITY

The data in table 6 shows clearly that ratios of young children to white women, and by inference white birth rates, declined from a very early date. The national decline began at least as early as 1810. The patterns of variation and trends by geographic divisions are discussed at some length in the chapter on geographical variations. As stated there, ratios of 1,300 to 1,400 probably were normal for long-settled areas before the Revolutionary War. Higher values occured in frontier areas, mainly from the selective migration of young married women. Selective migration had little or no effect on fertility ratios for the nation as a whole in the first half of the nineteenth century because

[In an attempt to improve the comparability of white and Negro ratios, all ratios have been adjusted for underenumeration of children, and all except those for whites in 1800 to 1820 have been standardized indirectly to the age distribution of women in the United States in 1930. The number of enumerated white children under 5 has been increased by 5 percent, and of Negro children by 13 percent, these being factors obtained from a study of data for 1925 to 1930]

Year	White										Negro, total
	United States	New England	Middle Atlantic	East North Central	West North Central	South Atlantic	East South Central	West South Central	Mountain	Pacific	
1800	1,342	1,164	1,334	1,918	(¹)	1,402	1,875	(¹)	(¹)	(¹)	(¹)
1810	1,358	1,111	1,365	1,777	1,915	1,382	1,794	1,446	(¹)	(¹)	(¹)
1820	1,295	980	1,244	1,683	1,768	1,330	1,708	1,483	(¹)	(¹)	(¹)
1830	1,145	826	1,044	1,473	1,685	1,189	1,530	1,369	(¹)	(¹)	(¹)
1840	1,085	770	951	1,280	1,446	1,162	1,424	1,310	(¹)	(¹)	(¹)
1850	892	636	776	1,037	1,122	957	1,115	1,061	875	896	1,087
1860	905	639	784	1,016	1,118	940	1,056	1,103	1,054	1,035	1,072
1870	814	564	702	892	1,012	833	922	953	982	916	997
1880	780	520	648	781	930	879	952	1,066	892	808	1,090
1890	685	456	563	668	797	802	873	994	770	600	930
1900	666	497	567	620	731	802	855	942	742	532	845
1910	631	505	554	576	650	780	836	861	680	478	736
1920	604	543	562	570	605	720	760	706	686	447	608
1930	506	467	447	482	520	618	680	586	582	357	554
1940	419	365	337	407	452	480	556	492	546	358	513
1950	587	552	507	586	642	601	666	644	699	576	706

¹ Data not available.

Source: U. S. Bureau of the Census, *Forecasts of the Population of the United States, 1945-1975*, by P. K. Whelpton, p. 16, and computations from *1950 Census of Population*, Vol. II, *Characteristics of the Population*, Parts 2-50, table 15.

immigration was small in relation to the size of the total population.[11] The ratio of children under 5 years old to 1,000 white women 20 to 44 years old declined 939 points between 1810 and 1940. About 29 percent of this decline occurred by 1840 and 74 percent occurred by 1900. The bulk of the decline in fertility as measured by ratios of young children to white women thus occurred in the nineteenth century, and a considerable amount occurred before the mid-century.

An important consideration is the extent to which fertility was adequate for maintenance of population. The ratios in table 6 may be compared with an intentionally too-large "replacement quota" for evidence that nineteenth century fertility was far above replacement needs in most parts of the country. A very high quota for permanent population replacement is 578 children under 5 years old per 1,000 women 20 to 44 years old. This is based on life tables for Negroes in the District of Columbia in 1910 plus age standardization to match the ratios in table 6. The mortality rates in the life tables that were used were high enough to yield a crude death rate of about 35 deaths per 1,000 persons if applied to the white population in 1800. (Blodget estimated a crude death rate of about 25 for around 1800.)

Grabill, Kiser, and Whelpton

A quota for 1940, based on United States life tables for 1939–41 is 440. This is too low for use with prior years when mortality was higher. However, it helps to indicate that national fertility fell below replacement needs by 1940. Low fertility did not pose a problem of potential population decline until the 1930s and then only because of a severe economic depression.

The decline in ratios of young children to women reflected a genuine demographic revolution, a growing disinclination of married couples to have many children. The revolution was related to the same forces that caused the development of modern society, the rapid advance in arts and science and the adoption of a rational approach in individual and family living. In America, fertility began to decline before there was any appreciable proportion of the population residing in urban areas. In New England, an early stronghold of industrialization, there was little increase before 1830 in the proportion of the population residing in urban areas (figure 1). Because the urban population comprised a very small part of the total population in the early years, it could not have been chiefly responsible for the early declines in fertility. Although few people lived in urban areas, New England did have a considerable nonfarm economy. The Census of

FIGURE 1.—RURAL AND URBAN POPULATION OF NEW ENGLAND: 1790 TO 1950

[Urban-rural classification by 1940 Census rules]

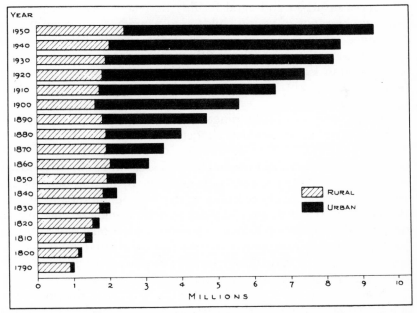

Source: *1950 Census of Population*, Vol. II, *Characteristics of the Population*, Part 1, U. S. Summary, p. 17.

1820 counted about 106,000 persons in New England as engaged in manufacturing and commerce, and 285,000 as engaged in agriculture.

URBAN AND RURAL DECLINES IN FERTILITY

Some demographers have stated a theory that the trend toward birth control began in urban areas and subsequently spread to the surrounding rural areas. The reference here is not to the age-old urban and rural differentials in fertility but to the progressively greater family limitations which accompanied the evolution of modern civilization. If it occurred, the spread of family limitation practices from urban to rural areas must have begun very early in the United States. The data in table 7 indicate that after 1810 the declines in fertility ratios of the rural population more than kept pace with those of the urban population.[12] Ratios of young children to white women declined very early in the rural population, and were already low in New England in 1800 as compared with other geographic divisions. Between 1810 and 1840, on a national basis, both the urban and rural ratios of children under 5 years old declined by about 200 children per 1,000 women; between 1840 and 1910, the decline amounted to about 230 in the urban population and 350 in the rural population; and between 1910 and 1940 the decline amounted to about 160 in the urban population and 230 in the rural population. Thus, absolute differences in urban and rural fertility narrowed over the years, as measured by ratios of young children to women. A different picture is obtained when one compares changes in relative proportions. In 1810, the urban ratio (900) was 68 percent as large as the rural ratio (1,329) and in 1940 the urban ratio (311) was 56 percent as large as the rural ratio (551). The pattern of change is shown graphically in figure 2.

In the early part of the nineteenth century, the national ratio of young children to women was almost equal in size to the rural ratio (figure 2 and table 7). This was because about 91 percent of the white women 20 to 44 years old resided in rural areas in 1810. In 1940 and 1950, only 37 percent resided in rural areas, by the old definition of urban-rural residence. (According to the new definition adopted for use in the 1950 Census, only 32 percent of the women resided in rural areas.) As the population became less rural, the national ratio of young children to women diverged in size from the rural ratio and approached the urban ratio. The national ratio therefore declined more than either of the component urban and rural ratios.

Some writers have speculated that the increase in the proportion of population residing in urban areas accounts for much of the decline in the nation's fertility. It is a fact that much of the population now

Grabill, Kiser, and Whelpton

386

[Ratios for 1800 to 1840 partly estimated from broad age groups. Urban-rural classification by 1940 Census rules]

Area	1950	1940	1930	1920	1910	1840	1830	1820	1810	1800
United States........	551	400	485	581	609	1,070	1,134	1,236	1,290	1,281
Urban.....................	479	311	388	471	469	701	708	831	900	845
Rural.....................	673	551	658	744	782	1,134	1,189	1,276	1,329	1,319
New England............	516	347	441	518	482	752	812	930	1,052	1,098
Urban.....................	486	321	417	500	468	592	614	764	845	827
Rural.....................	612	443	541	602	566	800	851	952	1,079	1,126
Middle Atlantic........	471	320	424	539	533	940	1,036	1,183	1,289	1,279
Urban.....................	432	286	386	501	495	711	722	842	924	852
Rural.....................	596	457	590	680	650	1,006	1,100	1,235	1,344	1,339
East North Central.....	552	388	458	548	555	1,270	1,467	1,608	1,702	1,840
Urban.....................	491	326	400	485	470	841	910	1,059	1,256	...
Rural.....................	679	533	605	668	672	1,291	1,484	1,616	1,706	1,840
West North Central.....	600	431	495	584	630	1,445	1,678	1,685	1,810	...
Urban.....................	514	324	365	416	426	705	1,181	...	...	...
Rural.....................	702	538	614	711	760	1,481	1,703	1,685	1,810	...
South Atlantic.........	572	464	593	694	760	1,140	1,174	1,280	1,325	1,345
Urban.....................	450	305	401	458	485	770	767	881	936	861
Rural.....................	677	596	744	851	894	1,185	1,209	1,310	1,347	1,365
East South Central.....	631	539	655	734	817	1,408	1,519	1,631	1,700	1,799
Urban.....................	494	333	414	441	469	859	863	1,089	1,348	...
Rural.....................	720	648	781	846	922	1,424	1,529	1,635	1,701	1,799
West South Central.....	607	474	584	686	845	1,297	1,359	1,418	1,383	...
Urban.....................	542	342	410	445	504	846	877	866	727	...
Rural.....................	703	591	723	823	977	1,495	1,463	1,522	1,557	...
Mountain...............	663	526	582	664	661	...	...	...	...	...
Urban.....................	584	404	428	470	466	...	...	...	...	...
Rural.....................	754	643	712	807	810	...	...	...	...	...
Pacific.................	539	339	360	425	460	...	...	...	...	...
Urban.....................	478	283	306	344	360	...	...	...	...	...
Rural.....................	652	466	507	603	640	...	...	...	...	...

Source: Computed from reports of censuses from 1800 to 1950, with corrections for clerical and printing errors in Censuses of 1800 to 1820.

resides in urban areas, where fertility normally is lower than in rural areas. However, the nation was so largely rural in much of the long period from 1810 to 1950 that declines in rural fertility had more effect on changes in national fertility than did the combined effects of (a) the increasing proportion of population residing in urban areas and (b) declines in urban fertility. This fact can be demonstrated by an indirect standardization technique, with results as shown in table 8.[13]

Comparisons for different periods of time than 1810 to 1940 would give different results from those in table 8. A progressively later starting date than 1810 would give progressively more weight to declines in urban fertility and less weight to the other two factors shown. The changing proportion of population residing in urban areas, measured separately from trends in urban fertility and rural fertility, thus would account for less than 20 percent of the changes in national fertility if a later starting date than 1810 were used. Urban

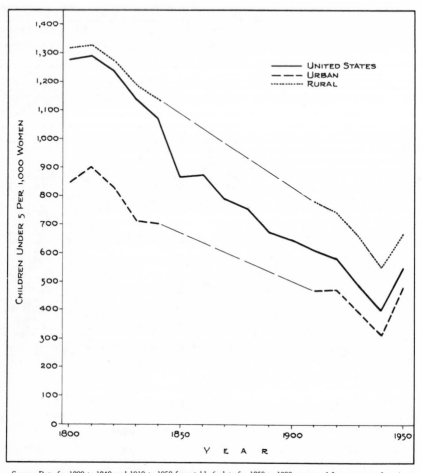

FIGURE 2.—NUMBER OF CHILDREN UNDER 5 YEARS OLD PER 1,000 WHITE WOMEN 20 TO 44
YEARS OLD, URBAN AND RURAL: 1800 TO 1950

[Urban-rural classification by 1940 Census rules]

Source: Data for 1800 to 1840 and 1910 to 1950 from table 6; data for 1850 to 1900 computed from reports of pertinent population censuses.

fertility became the most important component of national fertility after 1920.

NEGROES

Negroes have been enumerated by age in all censuses of the United States since 1820. The age intervals, such as 10 to 23 years, which were recorded for Negroes before 1850 obviously are not suitable for the computation of ratios of young children to women.

Grabill, Kiser, and Whelpton   388

TABLE **8.**—URBAN-RURAL COMPONENTS OF DECLINE IN NUMBER OF CHILDREN UNDER 5 YEARS OLD PER 1,000 WHITE WOMEN 20 TO 44 YEARS OLD, BY DIVISIONS: 1810 TO 1940

[Centralized averages]

Area	Absolute decline in children per 1,000 women	Percent distribution			
		Total	Decline due to--		
			Rural to urban shift of population	Decline in urban ratio	Decline in rural ratio
United States[1]..............	890	100.0	20.2	23.8	56.0
New England......................	705	100.0	17.0	33.5	49.5
Middle Atlantic..................	969	100.0	20.4	30.7	48.9
East North Central..............	1,314	100.0	17.3	25.1	57.6
West North Central[2]............	1,379	100.0	3.9	26.9	69.2
South Atlantic...................	861	100.0	16.3	18.6	65.1
East South Central..............	1,161	100.0	9.9	15.3	74.9
West South Central..............	909	100.0	15.4	14.4	70.2

[1] Includes the Mountain and Pacific Divisions in 1940 but not in 1810 when they were nonexistent.

[2] There was a nonexistent urban population in the West North Central Division in 1810 which of course had an indeterminate 0/0 ratio of children to women. It was necessary to assign some value to the ratio. The rural ratio was assigned.

Source: Computed from table 7.

However, it is possible to obtain some idea of trends in Negro fertility at early dates from other measures such as the proportion of young children in the population.

In 1820, 43.1 percent of the Negroes were children under 14 years old. Interpolation of other age detail results in an estimate that about 42.6 percent of the Negro population in 1850 were children under 14 years old. The nearly identical percentages under 14 in 1820 and 1850 indicate that little change probably occurred in the fertility of Negroes between 1820 and 1850. In 1830 and 1840, the age group "under 10" was listed in the census. More detailed data were obtained after 1840. This permits a comparison of the percentages that children under 10 years old comprised of the total nonwhite population:

1830	34.2
1840	33.2
1850	31.3
1860	30.5

These figures should be interpreted with caution because of a change in census procedures in 1850 which may have influenced the accuracy of age reporting. Comparisons between 1830 and 1840 and between 1850 and 1860 probably would not be affected, however. Both periods show declines of about 1 percentage point per decade in the proportion of young children in the population. It seems safe to say that there were no great changes in Negro fertility between 1830 and 1860 although a slight decline may have occurred.

Decennial rates of increase in the Negro population may also be used as indirect indicators of trends in Negro fertility but they are much rougher indicators than are data on the proportion of children in the population. They are of more value for showing that the fertility was ample for a considerable amount of population increase despite very high mortality. The intercensal increases were affected by varying degrees of completeness of the census enumerations. The first few enumerations probably were less complete than the later ones. It may be safe to assume that declines in rates of population increase among Negroes after 1810 did not come from any large increase in death rates. Importations of slaves were not an important factor, as these officially ceased in 1808.[14] The following data indicate some slowing down of the rate of population increase, and by inference a probable decline in fertility:

Period	Percent increase in Negro population
1790 to 1800	32.3
1800 to 1810	37.5
1810 to 1820	28.6
1820 to 1830	31.4
1830 to 1840	23.4
1840 to 1850	26.6
1850 to 1860	22.1

A series of ratios of children under 5 years old to women 20 to 44 years old was presented in table 6 and is repeated in the accompanying table for Negroes:

Year	Children under 5 per 1,000 Negro women 20 to 44 years old
1850	1,087
1860	1,072
1870	997
1880	1,090
1890	930
1900	845
1910	736
1920	608
1930	554
1940	513
1950	706

The series shows no large decline in the magnitude of ratios of young children to women among Negroes before 1880. The 1870 ratio may be disregarded because the quality of enumeration was not as good as usual.[15] A decline of more than 50 percent occurred in the ratios between 1880 and 1940, despite the offsetting effect of very large declines in infant mortality. (The proportion of Negro infants dying in the first year of life declined from 20 percent in 1910 to 7 percent in the period from 1939 to 1941 and 5 percent in 1950.)

DECLINES IN COMPLETED FERTILITY

The 1910 Census probably provides the best data available in this country on the fertility of women during the latter part of the nineteenth century. The women 45 to 74 years old in 1910 had most of their children in the nineteenth century. Comparisons of data on the number of children ever born for women in successive age groups provide a rough indication of secular trends in fertility. The qualification "rough" is used because it is not entirely satisfactory to relate total fertility over a lifetime to secular trends. Bias may result from differential mortality between women who have had many children and women who have had few, and from any tendency for under-reporting of children for old women. This bias may be negligible at ages up to 59 years and it may be as large as 10 percent or even more by age 70 to 74 years. (See Appendix A.) This should be kept in mind when data for aged women are compared. The bias means that, in general, the decline in fertility has been greater than is indicated by the data in tables 9 and 10.

Table 9 is for the total population of the United States. However, this table largely reflects white fertility because the white population comprises about nine-tenths of the total population. Other sections of this monograph show data for whites rather than for the total population, for reasons of convenience and precision of data. Separate data for the nonwhite population (97 percent Negro) are presented in table 10. The quality of census data and vital statistics for nonwhites has improved substantially since 1910 but is still below that for whites. Another reason for usually presenting separate data for whites is that there is more concern about fertility when it is low, and the whites thus far have more severely limited their fertility.

The data in table 9 for the Nation's total population show steady declines in completed fertility among the women in successive age cohorts, with the exception of the women 65 to 74 years old in rural-farm areas who were less fertile than the women in some of the subsequent cohorts. This exception can be traced to the South and it probably reflects adverse conditions during and after the War Between the States. The data for nonwhites in table 10 exhibit a similar pattern, except that at least three age cohorts of nonwhite women were adversely affected by conditions associated with the war and its aftermath. Perhaps the living conditions among the displaced ex-slaves were chaotic for many years.

The urban-rural classification in the tables reflects the residence of women in 1910 and may differ from the residence at the time most of the children were born. Only one-third of the Negro women lived on farms in 1910, although two-thirds lived in rural areas.

The white women 70 to 74 years old in the United States who had ever married had an average of 5.4 children ever born, compared with approximately 8 for Colonial times. This supports the preceding statement that a substantial amount of decline in fertility occurred prior to 1880. The Negro women probably had a much smaller decline, especially in rural-farm areas where the average in 1910 was still close to 8 children ever born. Nationally, the ever-married nonwhite women 70 to 74 years old in 1910 had an average of 6.9 children, compared with about 7.6 among nonwhite women in rural-farm areas. Although nonwhite women had more births, on the average, than the white women, this was nearly balanced by higher infant

TABLE 9.—NUMBER OF CHILDREN EVER BORN PER 1,000 WOMEN 45 TO 74 YEARS OLD, URBAN AND RURAL: 1910

Area and age of woman	Number of women	Percent ever married	Percent childless among ever married	Children ever born		
				Per 1,000 women	Per 1,000 women ever married·	Per 1,000 mothers
UNITED STATES						
45 to 49 years....................	2,088,000	91.0	9.5	4,295	4,744	5,241
50 to 54 years....................	1,790,000	91.6	8.9	4,529	4,972	5,459
55 to 59 years....................	1,302,000	92.8	8.3	4,816	5,218	5,692
60 to 64 years....................	1,090,000	92.7	8.2	4,847	5,266	5,734
65 to 69 years....................	819,000	93.5	7.9	4,982	5,364	5,822
70 to 74 years....................	554,000	93.5	7.7	5,001	5,395	5,845
URBAN						
45 to 49 years....................	1,088,000	88.8	11.7	3,615	4,098	4,639
50 to 54 years....................	889,000	89.5	10.6	3,901	4,385	4,905
55 to 64 years....................	1,139,000	91.3	9.4	4,316	4,758	5,250
65 to 74 years....................	630,000	92.8	8.6	4,639	5,036	5,511
RURAL NONFARM						
45 to 49 years....................	402,000	91.3	9.2	4,270	4,704	5,178
50 to 54 years....................	365,000	91.5	9.4	4,367	4,808	5,308
55 to 64 years....................	549,000	92.7	8.8	4,724	5,129	5,625
65 to 74 years....................	367,000	93.6	8.5	4,953	5,333	5,831
RURAL FARM						
45 to 49 years....................	598,000	94.9	6.0	5,553	5,869	6,244
50 to 54 years....................	536,000	95.1	6.0	5,686	5,996	6,377
55 to 64 years....................	705,000	95.0	6.1	5,752	6,080	6,472
65 to 74 years....................	376,000	94.6	5.7	5,632	5,994	6,359

Source: *1940 Census of Population, Differential Fertility, 1940 and 1910,* Fertility for States and Large Cities, table 4.

Grabill, Kiser, and Whelpton

Area and age of woman	Number of women	Percent ever married	Percent childless among ever married	Children ever born		
				Per 1,000 women	Per 1,000 women ever married	Per 1,000 mothers
UNITED STATES						
45 to 49 years......................	194,000	95.2	8.7	5,864	6,183	6,771
50 to 54 years......................	154,000	95.3	7.8	6,281	6,626	7,186
55 to 59 years......................	99,000	96.2	7.0	6,586	6,874	7,390
60 to 64 years......................	92,000	95.9	6.5	6,529	6,852	7,327
65 to 69 years......................	59,000	96.8	6.8	6,762	7,021	7,537
70 to 74 years......................	41,000	95.7	5.6	6,576	6,935	7,347
URBAN						
45 to 49 years......................	69,000	93.3	13.4	4,174	4,503	5,200
50 to 54 years......................	51,000	93.2	11.6	4,680	5,059	5,726
55 to 64 years......................	61,000	94.5	9.9	5,218	5,558	6,166
65 to 74 years......................	30,000	95.4	8.7	5,916	6,237	6,834
RURAL NONFARM						
45 to 49 years......................	45,000	94.7	8.0	5,849	6,208	6,747
50 to 54 years......................	38,000	95.1	7.8	6,183	6,541	7,095
55 to 64 years......................	52,000	95.5	7.0	6,553	6,908	7,431
65 to 74 years......................	30,000	96.0	6.8	6,607	6,932	7,436
RURAL FARM						
45 to 49 years......................	80,000	97.2	5.2	7,308	7,534	7,948
50 to 54 years......................	64,000	97.0	4.9	7,605	7,860	8,262
55 to 64 years......................	79,000	97.6	4.3	7,598	7,809	8,156
65 to 74 years......................	40,000	97.2	4.2	7,356	7,608	7,941

Source: Same as table 9.

mortality; in consequence, the effective fertility of nonwhites was not much different from that of whites, as noted earlier in terms of ratios of young children to women (table 6).

Quite small percentages of the nonwhite women 70 to 74 years old in 1910 who had ever married had never borne a child. The percentage was less than 5 in rural-farm areas and it was about 9 in urban areas. The fact that at one time the incidence of involuntary childlessness was low among nonwhites should be kept in mind when examining more modern data. As noted in some later sections, Negroes in recent years have had very high proportions of childlessness and, because of studies which show that Negroes practice contraception infrequently and inefficiently, much of the childlessness has been assumed to reflect involuntary causes.

The low percentages of childless women in 1910, among whites and nonwhites alike, are also in sharp contrast to indications in some modern local studies and to judgments by many physicians and demographers that at least 10 percent of women are involuntarily sterile.[16] The increase in involuntary sterility after 1910 may reflect more present-day postponement in childbearing, coupled with reduced fecundity as the women age. Thus, the 1910 data are useful for assessing the meaning of some more modern figures.

The data in tables 9 and 10 indicate that, in general, the trend toward fewer births per woman in the nineteenth century did not involve any sudden large increase in childlessness. The increase that occurred was gradual and accounted for only a part of the total decline in fertility. It is probable that the "psychological availability of contraception" came about in a gradual fashion as attitudes changed. That contraceptives and abortifacients were available is evident from newspaper advertisements between about 1820 and the passage of the Comstock Law in 1873.[17]

Notes

1 John C. Miller, *Origins of the American Revolution,* Little, Brown and Company, Boston, 1943, pp. 433-435.

2 Benjamin Franklin, "Observations Concerning The Increase of Mankind, The Peopling of Countries, &c.," *The Magazine of History, with Notes and Quotes,* Extra Number, No. 63, 1755.

3 Chevalier Félix de Beaujour, *Sketch of the United States of North America,* jointly published by several printing firms, London, 1814.

4 Blodget probably made his estimates somewhat as follows: He began with data from the first two censuses of the United States (1790 and 1800) and figured the average annual percent increase in population (3 percent). This percent was then applied in a chain computation to obtain annual population estimates and annual amounts of numerical increase. From custom house and port records, Blodget secured data on "passengers arriving," and allowed for Americans returning from abroad, aliens in transit to Canada or here temporarily, etc. Subtraction of the (net) migration from annual population increase gave annual natural increase. From bills of mortality for a few communities and rural areas, Blodget estimated the national death rate to be "near 2½ percent." The estimated numbers of deaths are uniformly 2½ percent of the total population. The births seem to be a residual estimate, obtained by adding deaths to the estimated annual natural increase. The birth estimates are the only component of population growth shown to the last digit.

5 Johann Peter Süssmilch, Die göttliche Ordnung in den Veränderungen des menschlichen Geschlechts, aus der Geburt, dem Tode und der Fortpflanzung desselben erwiesen, Berlin, 1741, and later editions. For an extended account in English, see Frederick S. Crum, "The Statistical Work of Süssmilch," *Quarterly Publications of the American Statistical Association,* Vol. VII, New Series, No. 55, September 1901.

6 Hypothetical computations can indicate something of the possibilities. One may assume, for illustrative purposes, (a) a constant flow of in-migration from year to year (the amount of immigration does not matter if one assumes an unchanging flow), (b) a sex ratio of 125 males per 100 females among the in-migrants, (c) an age distribution that places most of the immigrants within the young adult ages, (d) age-specific birth rates for women, of a level sufficient to yield a crude birth rate of 50 when applied to a population having an age-sex distribution similar to the one in

the general population in 1800, and (e) mortality according to English life tables for 1838–1854.

The results of the computation indicate that within 10 years the annual number of births would be more than twice the annual number of immigrants. Within 20 years there would be more native than European-born persons in the population. Thus, if the birth and death rates used were at all reasonable, there was a strong tendency for an early emergence of a large native population.

7　Charles A. and Mary R. Beard, *The Beards' Basic History of the United States,* Doubleday, Doran and Company, New York, 1944, p. 17.

8　George F. Willison, *Saints and Strangers,* Reynal and Hitchcock, New York, 1945, p. 385.

9　Glover's life tables for white persons in the Original Death Registration Area in 1901 would yield a crude death rate of about 16 if applied to a population having an age-sex distribution similar to that of the white population in 1800. Obviously, this level of mortality is much too low if Blodget's estimate of about 25 for this time is correct. A similar computation, using Glover's life tables for Negroes in the District of Columbia in 1901 as an example of very high mortality, would yield a crude death rate of about 37. Interpolation between these two tables may be performed to obtain mortality rates that would yield a crude death rate of about 25. The result is a life table with an expectation of life of about 42 years for females and 39 years for males, or a table that closely resembles one for England and Wales in 1838–1854.

10　Joseph J. Spengler, "The Fecundity of Native and Foreign-Born Women in New England," *Brookings Institution Pamphlet Series,* Vol. II, No. 1, June 30, 1930.

11　U.S. Bureau of the Census, *Historical Statistics of the United States: 1789–1945,* p. 34.

12　Censuses from 1800 to 1840 presented separate data on the population by age, sex, and color for various small areas. By adding the data for specific places fertility ratios were derived for the urban population and the rural population. Urban-rural data were directly available in the reports of the 1910 and later censuses. The data in table 7 differ from those in table 6 in that they have neither been standardized for age of woman nor adjusted for an undercount of young children.

13　In standardization to determine the relative importance of components of change in a rate, one has a choice of several methods which are each logical but which give different, rough indications of the relative importance. A direct method holds all components constant except the one being evaluated. An indirect or residual method holds constant only the component being evaluated. After all known components have been evaluated, both methods have left a small, unexplained residual which is often termed the "interaction component." In time series analysis involving only two dates like 1810 and 1940, the direct method works forward from 1810 and with the present data would emphasize the rural aspect, while the indirect method works backward from 1940 and would emphasize the urban aspect. The interaction component in the two methods turns out to be of identical magnitude but of opposite sign. An average of the two methods eliminates the interaction component, provides a centralized time reference, and avoids bias. Hence averages are shown in table 8.

14　For estimates of importations of slaves, see *Compendium of the Seventh Census, 1850,* page 83.

A Long View　　　　　　　　　　　　　　　　　　　　　　　　　　　　*395*

15   For evidence, see the reports of the 1880 Census.

16   For a general discussion and citations to some of the lengthy literature on this topic, see P. K. Whelpton and Clyde V. Kiser, "The Comparative Influence on Fertility of Contraception and Impairments of Fertility," *Social and Psychological Factors Affecting Fertility,* Vol. Two, pp. 303-357, the Milbank Memorial Fund, New York, 1950.

17   For examples, see the January 1861 issues of the *Cleveland Plain Dealer,* the *Boston Herald,* and the *Louisville Democrat.*

Daniel Smith's article, like the previous one, focuses largely on fertility, but it probes more deeply into the components of differential fertility in its intensive analysis of data from Hingham, Massachusetts, supplemented by other sources. Smith compares late eighteenth-century American net reproduction rates with those for Sweden during the same period, and in analyzing components he finds that actual marital fertility does not account for as much of the difference as we might have thought; mortality and variations in the number of women married make greater contributions to the higher American rates. Of the many important points made by Smith, perhaps none is more original than the one found in his discussion of the independent effect of the husband's age on the wife's fertility. Oddly enough, demographers sometimes seem to forget that sexual intercourse is at least a necessary condition for pregnancy. Smith's Hingham data seem to indicate that a woman marrying an older man had fewer children on the average than her counterpart who married a younger man, and this, Smith feels, is at least partially explainable in terms of differentials in coital frequency. The reader should not be put off by the technical nature of this contribution; it reveals a blend of demographic competence and historical knowledge not frequently encountered in the literature.

DANIEL SCOTT SMITH

20 The Demographic History of Colonial New England

The central fact of the demographic history of early North America is rapid growth. Both Canada and the white population of the English colonies experienced increases of 2½ percent per year during the eighteenth century. Seventeenth-century rates, beginning from a low base and more influenced by immigration, were even higher. In contrast, the expansion of population in early modern Europe rarely exceeded 1 percent per annum over an extended period.[1] Since Franklin and Malthus, interpretations of early American demography have centered on the high fertility associated with near universal marriage for women at a low average age. The extremely youthful population, high dependency ratio, and one of the largest mean census family sizes ever recorded all follow from the high level of fertility.[2]

Because the high growth and its explanation have been long recognized and virtually unquestioned, until recently very little scholarly research has focused on the estimation of the components of population increase or on the analysis of the socio-economic context of the colonial demographic experience. Interpretive consensus and an absence of reliable data have also hindered the construction of precise distinctions over time and space within the 150 years of colonial population history. By integrating knowledge of population trends on the colony-wide level with findings forthcoming from recent intensive demographic analyses of New England communities, generalizations are possible about three central issues: (1) the demographic sources of the higher colonial growth rate compared to a reliably documented European society; (2) decadal variation in the pattern of population growth, particularly the central role of lower fertility in the apparent pause in rapid growth around 1700; and (3) the determinants of the level of marital fertility, especially evidence for the conscious limitation of family size before the "demographic transition" of the first half of the nineteenth century.

A Comparative Perspective on New England Growth

Since the net reproduction rate (NRR) summarizes fertility, mortality, and marital patterns and is also algebraically related to the intrinsic growth rate of the population, it is a particularly useful measure for contrasting the demographic structures of two societies. Very simply the NRR is the ratio of the size of the female population one generation later to its size at a given point in time; mathematically it is related to the intrinsic growth rate (r) and the mean age of women at childbearing (T) by the expression, $NRR = Ee^{rT}$. Although data on immigration do not exist for the colonial period, the contribution of net migration to the region may be inferred from the difference between the crude and intrinsic growth rates. The crude growth rate can be calculated from two series of total population estimates at decadal intervals.[3] Although England would be the most relevant country for comparative purposes, Sweden is the only eighteenth-century European society for which the necessary parameters for the

TABLE 1

ANALYSIS OF THE COMPONENTS OF THE DIFFERENCE BETWEEN LATE EIGHTEENTH-CENTURY SWEDISH AND NEW ENGLAND FEMALE LEGITIMATE NET REPRODUCTION RATES

Component	ADJUSTED MODEL		RECORDED MODEL	
	Contribution to difference in NRR (1)	Percentage of total difference (2)	Contribution to difference in NRR (3)	Percentage of total difference (4)
(1) New England NRR	1.991		2.285	
(2) Lower New England mortality				
(a) Begin with Swedish GRR	0.140	15.2%	0.432	35.4%
(b) With marital structure	0.062	6.7	0.190	15.6
(c) With marital fertility	0.020	2.2	0.026	2.1
(d) Combination of (b) & (c)	0.006	0.6	0.001	0.1
(e) Begin with New England GRR	0.228	24.7	0.650	53.3
(3) Higher N.E. proportion married				
(a) New England mortality	0.535	58.0	0.668	54.8
(b) Swedish mortality	0.473	51.2	0.478	39.2
(c) Difference (a) − (b) = (2b)	0.062	6.7	0.190	15.6
(4) Higher N.E. marital fertility				
(a) New England mortality	0.178	19.3	0.093	7.6
(b) Swedish mortality	0.158	17.1	0.068	5.6
(c) Difference (a) − (b) = (2c)	0.020	2.2	0.026	2.1
(5) Interaction of proportions married and marital fertility				
(a) New England mortality	0.052	5.6	0.008	0.7
(b) Swedish mortality	0.046	5.0	0.006	0.5
(c) Difference (a) − (b) = (2d)	0.006	0.6	0.002	0.2
(6) Lower N.E. mean age at child-bearing (with Swedish NRR)	0.018	1.9	0.018	1.5
(7) Swedish NRR	1.068	100.0%	1.068	100.0%

TABLE 2

ESTIMATED TOTAL POPULATION AND DECADAL GROWTH RATES FOR NEW ENGLAND, 1650 TO 1790

Year	Estimated population in New England		Decadal growth rates		Percent change in succeeding decades	
	Rossiter (1)	Sutherland (2)	Rossiter (3)	Sutherland (4)	Rossiter (5)	Sutherland (6)
1650	21,800	22,832				
1660	36,800	33,136	68.8%	45.1%		
1670	45,500	51,896	23.6	56.6		
1680	61,000	68,462	34.1	31.9	+ 0.3%	− 4.0%
1690	82,000	86,961	34.4	27.0	− 5.1	−20.3
1700	106,000	92,763	29.3	6.7	−10.1	+17.4
1710	126,500	115,094	19.3	24.1	+ 1.2	+24.4
1720	152,500	170,893	20.5	48.5	+18.5	−21.3
1730	208,950	217,351	37.0	27.2	− 5.9	+ 6.1
1740	274,000	289,707	31.1	33.3	− 4.8	− 9.0
1750	346,000	360,009	26.3	24.3	+ 6.3	+ 0.6
1760	459,000	449,634	32.6	24.9	+ 1.2	+ 4.4
1770	614,000	581,308	33.8	29.3	−13.0	− 6.7
1780	742,000	712,959	20.8	22.6	+ 3.7	+ 7.0
1790	923,865	923,865	24.5	29.6		
Mean: 1670-80 to 1780-90			28.6%	27.4%		
Standard deviation			5.91	9.07		

Sources: W. S. Rossiter, A Century of Population Growth (New York: Johnson Reprint Corporation, 1966, orig. pub. 1909), pp. 9-10. U. S. Bureau of the Census, Historical Statistics of the United States, Colonial Times to 1957 (Washington, D.C.: GPO, 1960), Series Z1-19, p. 756.

Calculation:

(A) NRR = 1/2.05(TFR)(U')($1_T/1_0$), where 1/2.05 is the proportion of females among all births, TFR is the total fertility rate, U' is the correction factor for under-registration, and $1_T/1_0$ is the proportion of females surviving from birth to T, the mean age of women at childbirth.

(B) Total fertility rate, New England:

	15-19	20-24	25-29	30-34	35-39	40-44	45-49
(i) Pct. married, Conn., 1774[a]	.070	.545	.733	.816	.871	.840	.819
(ii) Hingham marital fertility, marriages of 1761-1780	.513	.454	.407	.320	.279	.138	.012
(iii) TFR = 5Σ(i)(ii) =	.036	.247	.298	.261	.235	.116	.009 = 6.01

(iv) GRR = (6.01)/2.05 = 2.93

(v) U' = (No. of births in reconstituted marriages, 1761-1780) + (No. of births necessary to raise infant mortality in first month to 60% of total)[b] + (No. of births omitted, estimated by unusual variance in birth intervals)[c]/(No. of births in reconstituted families) = (888 + 45 + 25.7)/(888) = 1.079.

(vi) Adjusted TFR = (6.01)(1.079) = 6.48; adjusted GRR = 3.16

(C) Total fertility rate, Sweden[d]:

	15-19	20-24	25-29	30-34	35-39	40-44	45-49
(i) Pct. married, 1800	.027	.194	.507	.675	.747	.767	.739
(ii) Marital fertility, 1776-1800	.522	.467	.387	.323	.229	.121	.029
(iii) TFR = 5Σ(i)(ii)	.014	.091	.194	.218	.167	.093	.021 = 3.99

(iv) GRR = (3.99)/(2.05) = 1.946

(D) Mortality, $1_T/1_0$, estimated by projecting $1_{20}/1_0$ for both sexes to age 30 for females by use of model life tables:

(i) Adjusted model: $1_{20}/1_0$ = 0.672; $1_{30}/1_0$ = 0.63 (Model West, Level 10).[e] Included as dying before age 20 are all recorded deaths (142) plus all children whose survival to maturity is unknown (101) plus additional deaths of children whose births were not recorded but whose existence was detected by large intervals between recorded births (25.7) and by the absence of deaths in the first month of life (45). This procedure yields a maximum estimate of mortality.

(ii) Recorded model: $1_{20}/1_0$ = 0.811; $1_{30}/1_0$ = 0.78 (Model West, Level 15).[e] Included as dying before age 20 are the recorded deaths plus the additional deaths produced by the assumption that the "unknowns" die in the same proportion as the known population

(E) Interaction of age-specific proportions married and marital fertility:

	15-19	20-24	25-29	30-34	35-39	40-44	45-49
(i) Difference in pct. married	.053	.351	.226	.141	.094	.073	.080
(ii) Difference in marital fertility	.032	.023	.057	.077	.022	.028	−.016
(iii) Interaction = 5Σ(i)(ii)	.0017	.0081	.0130	.0031	.0072	.0020	−.0013 = .169

(F) Mean age of mothers at birth, T:

(i) New England: Estimated as age 30 from assumption that the New England mean age at first marriage was 22.0 years; Watertown women who married at this age in 1761-1800 had a mean age at childbirth of 29.98 years.

(ii) Sweden: Mean age at marriage assumed to be 25.0; hence T would be 31.5; this rough estimate probably understates the difference in mean age and hence the mean age at birth.[f]

Sources:

[a] Yasukichi Yasuba, Birth Rates of the White Population of the United States 1800 to 1860 (Baltimore: Johns Hopkins Press, 1961), p. 114.

[b] For a convenient summary of pre-industrial west-European data on the distribution of deaths within the first year, see E. A. Wrigley, "Mortality in Pre-Industrial England: The Example of Colyton, Devon, over three Centuries," Daedalus, 97, No. 2 (Spring 1969), Table 14, p. 568.

[c] Method adopted from Louis Henry, "Interval between confinements in the absence of birth control," Eugenics Quarterly, VIII, No. 2 (June 1961), 200-11. Two-thirds of the families whose variance of birth intervals exceeded 150 were assumed to have had a child not recorded.

[d] H. Gille, "The Demographic History of the Northern European Countries in the Eighteenth Century," Population Studies, III, No. 1 (June 1949), 27, 31.

[e] Ansley J. Coale and Paul Demeny, Regional Model Life Tables and Stable Populations (Princeton: Princeton University Press, 1966), pp. 11, 16.

[f] H. Gille, "The Demographic History of the Northern European Countries in the Eighteenth Century," Population Studies, III, No. 1 (June 1949), Table 7, p. 28.

estimation of a net reproduction rate exist.[4] The contrast in Table 1 rests on the Swedish mortality experience of 1751–1800, the marital fertility of 1776–1800, and the marital structure in 1800; estimates for New England are drawn from a colonial census and a local community. From the reconstitution of the civil and religious vital records of Hingham, Massachusetts, adjusted estimates of mortality and marital fertility were calculated. Since the marital structure of the town was quite atypical by the middle of the eighteenth century, the age-specific proportions of women married estimated by Yasuba from the Connecticut census of 1774 provide the final parameter needed to calculate a reasonable approximation of a net reproduction rate.[5] Since no reasonably accurate estimate of illegitimacy in New England could be made, its contribution to population growth in each society is ignored in the calculation.

By interchanging Swedish and New England parameters in the calculation of the net reproduction rate, the quantitative importance of each may be assessed. The proportion of the difference in NRR's that can be attributed to lower New England mortality depends on the assumptions simultaneously made about the fertility and marriage variables. In the adjusted estimates (left columns of Table 1) mortality accounts for only 0.140 points in the differential between NRR's if the Swedish gross reproduction rate (GRR) serves as the initial point in the calculation. Beginning with the New England GRR, on the other hand, mortality differences are responsible for 0.228 points in the NRR or a quarter of the gap between the rates. In the adjusted model between one-half and three-fifths of the difference in NRR's may be attributed to the higher proportion of women married in New England. The third major component, higher marital fertility in the colonies, explains from a fifth to a sixth of the difference.

While the conclusions for the adjusted data do not conflict with the conventional wisdom concerning New England population growth in the colonial period, the calculation does suggest a more complex and pluralistic pattern of causation than is usually conceived. More importantly the contrast specifies the quantitative importance of each component; instead of a list of causes of higher growth in New England, the procedure provides something better than a rank-ordering of the demographic mechanisms involved. Before these conclusions can be accepted, the reliability of the order of magnitude of the NRR estimate must be assessed, the assumptions underlying the calculation must be justified, the representativeness of the Hingham data and the Swedish contrast must be defended and the problem of under-registration in the colonial data must be considered. With thirty as the mean age at childbirth the estimated adjusted New England NRR of

Daniel Scott Smith   402

1.99 implies an intrinsic growth rate of 22.4 per 1,000, slightly below the crude long-term eighteenth century rate of 24.6 per 1,000. Thus *net* migration into New England has but a minor role in eighteenth century growth. During the eighteenth century the middle and southern colonies absorbed most of the European immigration. Furthermore, the last three decades of the century were almost certainly characterized by net migration from New England.

With unadjusted fertility and mortality data the identical calculation substantially increases the significance of lower mortality in the explanation of the more rapid growth rate of New England. The unadjusted NRR of 2.28 implies an intrinsic growth rate of 27.6 per 1,000, well above the crude long-term increase. If we assume that the registered fertility and mortality rates are correct, then Yasuba's method overstates the proportions married in the 1774 Connecticut census. Under-registered or not, the fertility and mortality pattern for all of New England has been estimated from the demographic experience of a single town. Are the data for Hingham both reliable and representative?

(A) *Mortality.* The proportion of females dying before the mean age at childbirth was estimated by projecting, by means of model life tables, the adjusted mortality of both sexes before age twenty. Adjusted mortality before twenty (328 per 1,000) was more than twice the registered rate (160 per 1,000). Even with this radical upward adjustment (see notes to Table 1), life expectation at birth was forty-one years for both sexes. On the other hand, the recorded childhood mortality figure implies an expectation at birth in excess of fifty-five years. In the overlapping Wigglesworth and McKean collections of late eighteenth-century New England mortality data, the age pattern of deaths more nearly approximates the adjusted model than the recorded. In the Wigglesworth table (4,893 deaths), 66.5 percent of persons dying over five died over age thirty while in the McKean collection (6,756 deaths) the comparable figure is 67.6 percent. In the stable population with the parameters of the adjusted estimate (Model West, Mortality Level 10, GRR = 3.00), 67 percent of the population dying over age five, die over age thirty, but in the stable population corresponding to the recorded data (Model West, Mortality Level 15, GRR = 3.00), the figure is 71 percent. Even though less (34 percent) of the living population over age five is over age thirty in the recorded model than in the adjusted (36 percent), a higher proportion of deaths occur at advanced ages in the low mortality life table.[6]

(B) *Marital fertility and proportions married.* Was the fertility experience of 155 Hingham women married in the two decades from 1761 to 1780 reasonably representative of all eighteenth-century New England women? Total unadjusted fertility for women marrying at exact age twenty was already 9 percent below the peak Hingham cohort of 1721–1740; the secular trend toward low fertility within marriage had already begun in the town by the end of the colonial period. Still, marital fertility probably varied only slightly on a geographic basis. Child-woman ratios, lowest in the densely settled areas of eastern New England, reflect adult age-structure and mortality as well as fertility. For example, the coefficient of variation of the ratio of children under ten per woman aged twenty to sixty-nine among Connecticut counties in 1774 was 8.2 percent; for children per married woman, the ratio was only 4.7 percent.[7] Age-structure, if known in detail for adults, would probably account for still more of the inter-county variation in the child-woman ratio. Although marital fertility was high in eighteenth-century New England, it was not extraordinary by contemporary west European standards. Unadjusted total fertility for women marrying at exact age twenty in Hingham between 1761 and 1780 was only 4 percent above the 1776–1800 Swedish level, below that found in most reconstituted French parishes, and considerably lower than the marital fertility rates of early eighteenth-century French Canada. Even with extreme assumptions about under-registration (7.9 percent for the 1761–1780 cohort), the marital fertility of Hingham still was not unusual by west European standards.[8]

The proportion of adult women who were married in New England approaches what Hajnal has defined as the non-European pattern. In Connecticut in 1774, 73.5 percent of women aged twenty to sixty-nine were married, while two-thirds of New Hampshire females in 1767 and 1773 were wed.[9] In order to use the census data on marital status in the calculation of the NRR, age-specific proportions must be estimated. Yasuba's method basically assumes that the percentage nonmarried changed proportionately in the various age groups between 1890 and 1774.[10]

(C) *Age-Structure in the Recorded Model.* If we assume that Yasuba's method overstates the proportion married, particularly in the crucial high fertility decade from twenty to twenty-nine, and that the true NRR for New England was 2.00, then the corresponding gross reproduction rate would be slightly over 2.50. With the above parameters and mortality level 15 in the Coale-Demeny "West" tables only 28.9 percent of the population would be under ten years of age. However, in the Connecticut census of 1774, 32.1 percent of the population was under ten, and for New England as a whole in 1800 the percentage was 32.2. The extremely low mortality of the unadjusted estimate is incompatible with the rate of population growth, if we assume that the marital and fertility patterns have been estimated accurately. If the calculated NRR is approximately correct, then the unadjusted estimate is incongruent with the extremely youthful age composition of the population. Although precision is not possible with the limited data available on the demographic structure of New England, the adjusted model obviously approximates reality more perfectly than the recorded estimate. In addition it should be noted that the choice of the Swedish contrast influences the relative magnitude of the differences in the components of the NRR. If national data existed for eighteenth-century France, characterized by somewhat higher mortality and lower marriage ages than Sweden, the French contrast with New England would naturally show mortality of greater importance and marital structure of lesser significance in explaining the differences in the net reproduction rates.

The Pattern of New England Growth, 1670–1790

To some extent the decadal estimates of total population in New England in Table 2 exhibit the consistently high rates of increase corresponding to a stable population interpretation of constant birth and age-specific death rates. To be sure, the assumptions of stable population theory do not conform precisely to the annual experience of pre-modern populations.[11] Following the initial extreme growth rates of the period of original settlement in New England, the decadal growth rate from 1670/80 to 1780/90 averaged 26.6 percent in the Rossiter series and 27.4 percent in the Sutherland estimates. Both series were constructed by aggregating estimates for each colony and each total is independent of the preceding and following figures. Since high growth rates tended to follow increases below the trend, some of the variation is doubtless due to the imprecision of the estimates of total population. The necessarily inexact sources available to Rossiter and Sutherland render it impossible either to accept or reject the notion that the rate of growth was constant.

Decades of more rapid growth also tended, inasmuch as impressionistic evidence permits a conclusion, to be periods of relatively high immigration to the colonies.[12] From the existing evidence on colonial mortality, no conclusions connecting high or low decadal growth rates to periods of lesser or greater mortality can be made. Reconstitution studies of towns and genealogies, the chief source of colonial mortality data, typically include so few families that their authors do not disaggregate their data into periods as short as a decade. Extensive under-registration and the probability of significant local and regional variation in death rates make the subject the most unknown and difficult area of colonial demographic history. Finally there may be generational cycles in population growth disturbing the generally smooth pattern of increase. In the absence of detailed age-structure in eighteenth-century censuses, this hypothesis is probably unverifiable above the local level. New settlements contained an unusually large number of persons in the young adult ages which potentially could produce an "echo" a generation later.[13] Natural population growth (births minus deaths) was undoubtedly more even than the crude decadal growth rates indicate. Despite these qualifications concerning the reliability of the total population estimates, two successive decades in each series stand out as a distinct period of less rapid growth, that is, 1690–1710 in the Sutherland totals and 1700–1720 in the Rossiter estimates.

The turn of the eighteenth century marks an interlude between two eras of very rapid growth and a watershed in the evolution of the traditional demographic structure of New England. The first decades of settlement were characterized by a low age at first marriage for women and a high or essentially European marriage age for men. This differential, originally generated by the high sex ratio among the original settlers, narrowed considerably by the end of the seventeenth century and the beginning of the eighteenth by an increase in marriage age for females.[14] In Hingham the age at marriage for both sexes increased between 1680 and 1720 before declining in the eighteenth century (Table 3).

More surprising than the increase in age at first marriage is the behavior of total fertility during this interlude. Hingham women marrying from 1691 to 1715 who survived, still married, to age

TABLE 3

AGE AT FIRST MARRIAGE IN ALL RECONSTITUTED FAMILIES, AGE AT LAST BIRTH AND NUMBER OF CHILDREN PER COMPLETE FAMILY IN HINGHAM, MASS., 1641-1800

| Marriage cohort | Age at first marriage | | Age at last birth | | Children per complete family |
	Men (1)	Women (2)	M<25 (3)	M25+ (4)	Mean (5)
Before 1691	27.4(77)	22.0(97)	39.6	41.3	7.59(69)
1691-1715	28.4(76)	24.7(84)	36.5	39.7	4.61(52)
1716-1740	27.0(125)	23.8(157)	40.3	41.1	6.74(91)
1741-1760	26.0(117)	22.8(135)	39.1	41.5	7.16(94)
1761-1780	24.6(126)	23.5(155)	39.6	40.0	6.39(104)
1781-1800	26.4(159)	23.7(188)	38.4	40.1	6.23(119)

Note: Sample sizes in parentheses.
Source: Daniel Scott Smith, "Population, Family and Society in Hingham, Massachusetts, 1635-1880" (Unpublished Dissertation, University of California, Berkeley, 1972).

Daniel Scott Smith   406

forty-five had only 4.6 children in contrast to the 7.6 in the previous cohort and 6.7 and 7.2 in the succeeding marriage groups. The increase in female marriage age explains less than half of the decline in completed fertility.[15] As would be expected in the case of deliberate family limitation, the drop in fertility was greater for those marrying young; the difference in the mean age at last birth, significant at the 0.05 level, for women marrying before and after age twenty-five was not surpassed until the Hingham cohort marrying from 1821 to 1840, a group well-advanced into the transition to a modern level of low fertility. Overall the fall in age-specific fertility over age thirty for women marrying between 1691 and 1715 compared to the cohort wed before 1691 is statistically significant at the 0.005 level.[16] In addition there is a marked differential in marital fertility rates after thirty between women marrying before and after age twenty-five in the 1691–1715 cohort, although both marriage groups had lower fertility than preceding and succeeding cohorts (Table 4.)

Evidence from other New England population groups suggests that the decline in total fertility in Hingham was not unique to that community. There is a less dramatic but substantial decrease in fertility among New England college graduates, third-generation residents of Andover, and the descendants of the early settlers of Watertown.[17] The decline in fertility in Hingham was not the result of worsening conditions on the immediate local level. Although little is known of

TABLE 4

RECORDED AGE-SPECIFIC MARITAL FERTILITY FOR HINGHAM WOMEN
IN COMPLETED FAMILIES MARRYING
BEFORE AND AFTER AGE TWENTY-FIVE

Marriage cohort	Age-specific marital fertility				
	25-29	30-34	35-39	40-44	45-49
Before 1691					
(a) married < 25	415(272)	389(272)	290(279)	157(274)	012(255)
(b) married 25+	250(16)	509(55)	350(60)	204(64)	024(83)
(c) ratio b/a	———	1.31	1.21	1.31	2.00
1691-1715					
(a) married < 25	333(120)	233(120)	150(120)	083(120)	000(105)
(b) married 25+	366(60)	371(102)	290(124)	133(135)	008(126)
(c) ratio b/a	1.10	1.59	1.93	1.60	
1721-1780					
(a) married < 25	414(951)	352(944)	283(944)	138(951)	016(910)
(b) married 25+	492(94)	449(222)	304(920)	161(304)	022(318)
(c) ratio b/a	1.19	1.27	1.07	1.17	1.37

Note: Women-years of experience in parentheses.
Source: See Table 3.

the economic situation in the town during this period, the last of its proprietary lands were not distributed until the 1730s. A land shortage for sons could have been met either by the allotment of these undivided lands or by increased outmigration of the excess members of the younger generation. However, from King Philip's War in 1675 to the Peace of Utrecht in 1713, the geographic expansion of settlement in New England was extremely limited. Some new towns were formed within the periphery of existing settlement. Although military danger from the Indians and French during this period was a significant element in the limitation of expansion, perhaps the major impact of these external pressures was their feedback on the marital patterns and fertility behavior of the population.[18]

The relative shutting off of the frontier in conjunction with the equalization of the sex ratio among young adults kept the age at marriage for men high and thereby increased the female age at marriage. An alternative scenario of population change can easily be constructed. Without the narrowing of opportunities for geographical expansion, the age at marriage for men might have dropped, with that for women remaining low at the mid-seventeenth century level. Instead of limitation of fertility through higher marriage ages for females and restraint within marriage, population and land could have been maintained at the social equilibrium by a combination of more outmigration and the greater use of primogeniture. With the addition of higher mortality in the immediate decades after 1715 this particular demographic drama was in fact enacted in the next half century in Hingham. The temporary "fertility solution" to the population problem at the turn of the eighteenth century was the product of a unique conjunction of external constraints on migration, the continuation of a marriage pattern established in an era of male surplus, and a family structure in which fathers had considerable control over the demographically important decision of when their children could marry. As the eighteenth century progressed, fathers increasingly lost control of the marriage process.[19]

Demographic Determinants of Marital Fertility

In all three cohorts in Table 4 women in marriages of shorter duration exhibited higher fertility over the age of thirty than women who married before the age of twenty-five. The 1691–1715 cohort is particularly unusual both for its higher marriage ages and its extreme differential in fertility between early- and late-marrying women. The higher fertility of late-marrying women is partially a spurious product of the relatively short interval between marriage and first birth, which inflates the age-specific fertility of women marrying over age twenty-five. This effect can be removed by contrasting the fertility after age thirty of women marrying before age twenty-five with those marrying from twenty-five to twenty-nine. Furthermore, late-marrying women are more likely to have younger husbands than women who marry at a younger age. Nearly one-third of all women marrying between twenty-five and twenty-nine from 1721 to 1800 had younger husbands in contrast to 6 percent of women marrying before the age of twenty-five (Table 5). The lower coital frequency in marriages with older husbands has a substantial effect on the fertility of wives over age thirty.[20] Nevertheless, this unconscious mechanism does not completely erase the differential in fertility in Table 5. If the women marrying before twenty-five in the period from 1721 to 1800 had husbands whose ages were distributed the same as the husbands of the twenty-five to twenty-nine marriage group, the increase in the fertility of the early-marrying women would be only 35.4 percent of the difference between the recorded post-thirty means of 3.78 and 4.26. If advancing age of the husband lowers coital frequency, then marriages of longer duration presumably could also be characterized by reduced levels of sexual activity compared to more recently formed marriages. The apparent statistical evidence for the conscious control of marital fertility (the higher age-specific rates in marriages of shorter duration) may derive instead from nonfertility related differences in sexual behavior.

TABLE 5

EFFECT OF THE RELATIVE AGE OF THE HUSBAND ON
THE AVERAGE NUMBER OF CHILDREN BORN TO
HINGHAM WOMEN AFTER AGE THIRTY IN COMPLETE FAMILIES

	Period married						
	Before 1691		1691-1715		1721-1800		
Wife's marriage age	<25	25-29	<25	25-29	<25	25-29	All
Age of husband relative to wife:							
Husband younger	4.75	6.33	0.00	4.14	4.56	4.37	4.46
	(4)	(3)	(1)	(7)	(16)	(19)	(50)
Husband same age or	4.47	4.75	2.82	4.50	3.94	4.85	4.03
1-4 years older	(15)	(4)	(12)	(4)	(141)	(20)	(196)
Husband 5-9	4.23	—	1.50	3.00	3.55	3.89	3.50
years older	(13)	(0)	(8)	(1)	(80)	(9)	(111)
Husband 10 or more	3.92	6.00	2.50	2.75	3.16	3.20	3.34
years older	(13)	(1)	(2)	(4)	(25)	(10)	(55)
Totals	4.27	5.50	2.22	3.81	3.78	4.26	3.85
	(45)	(8)	(23)	(16)	(262)	(58)	(412)

Note: Sample sizes in parentheses.
Source: See Table 3.

Additional data confirm the interpretation of the absence of family limitation for eighteenth-century Hingham women. If couples had rationally aimed for a given family size, then the death of a child would presumably cause them to increase their fertility to make up the loss. The so-called replacement hypothesis, recently advanced for colonial New England in a study of the diptheria epidemic of the 1730s,[21] is not supported by the comparison of the fertility behavior of couples who had lost a child before the wife reached age thirty and the couples without a known death in their family (Table 6). More surprising is the fact that women with more children by age thirty had still more births in their remaining fertile life than women with fewer children at age thirty (Columns 4 & 5 of Table 6). The positive correlation of early and late fertility may result from substantial variation in fecundity among women or from nonfertility related behavioral differences in nursing practices or coital frequency. It is compatible with the existence of conscious family limitation only under the hypothesis that some of the couples had small target family sizes from the inception of marriage that were achieved by the deliberate prolon-

TABLE 6

EFFECT OF THE MORTALITY OF CHILDREN DYING BEFORE THE MOTHER REACHES AGE 30 ON FERTILITY BETWEEN AGE 30 AND THE TERMINATION OF CHILDBEARING (HINGHAM WOMEN IN COMPLETE FAMILIES WHO MARRIED BEFORE AGE 25 IN THE PERIOD FROM 1721 TO 1780)

Number of children born before age 30	No. (1)	Women with child dying before she reached age 30		Mean number of children born after age 30 No. deaths < 30		Difference (5) − (4)
		No. (2)	Pct. (3)	Zero (4)	1 or more (5)	(6)
0	8	—	—	0.12	—	—
1	4	0	0.0%	2.25	—	—
2	27	7	25.9	2.80	3.86	+1.06
3	40	13	32.5	3.41	3.31	−0.10
4	42	14	33.3	4.85	3.93	−0.92
5	43	25	58.1	4.56	4.48	−0.08
6	19	10	52.6	5.11	5.60	+0.49
7	5	4	80.0	5.00	4.75	−0.25
8	1	1	100.0	—	7.00	—
9	0	—	—	—	—	—
10	1	1	100.0	—	11.00	—
Totals	190	75	39.5%	3.37	4.73	+1.16
Weighted average of differences (parity 2 to 7)						→ (−0.05)
Total born before age 30				3.71	4.33	
All children born				7.08	8.86	

Source: See Table 3.

Daniel Scott Smith

gation of the interval between births. Increases in child spacing, certainly consciously attained, were more important in the nineteenth-century decline in marital fertility in Hingham than the concomitant trend toward an earlier completion of childbearing. Long and irregular intervals between births would be expected if a partially effective means of contraception, such as coitus interruptus, were employed by couples seeking to limit their ultimate family size.[22]

Although there are significant reasons to doubt the existence of conscious limitation of fertility within marriage during most of the colonial period, the experience of the 1691–1715 cohort demonstrates the potential of an early modern population to respond to a perceived disequilibrium between numbers and resources. The threat of relative deprivation can be as powerful a motivating force as the impending reality of subsistence or starvation. The discovery of the influence of relative age of the husband on the fertility of the wife confirms again, as if anyone needed a reminder, the subtlety and complexity of the historical behavior of human populations.[23]

Notes

1   For data on colonial and contemporary European population growth rates, see J. Potter, "The Growth of Population in America, 1700–1860," in D. V. Glass and D. E. C. Eversley, eds., *Population in History* (London: Edward Arnold, 1965), pp. 639–43; and J. T. Krause, "Some Implications of Recent Work in Historical Demography," *Comparative Studies in Society and History,* I, No. 2 (June 1959), 173.

2   Forty-nine percent of the American population was under age sixteen in 1790 and the mean white family size was 5.7. In New York in 1771 there were 105 males under sixteen and over sixty per 100 males sixteen to fifty-nine. Data are taken from W. S. Rossiter, *A Century of Population Growth* (New York: Johnson Reprint Corporation, 1966; orig. pub. 1909), pp. 94, 96, 183. Only three of sixty-four nations over 100,000 population in censuses from 1955 to 1963 had mean family sizes above 5.7. See Thomas K. Burch, "The Size and Structure of Families: A Comparative Analysis of Census Data," *American Sociological Review,* 32, No. 3 (June 1967), p. 353. Mean English family size was nearly one person less than the 1790 American figure over three centuries of stability from 1574 to 1911. See Peter Laslett, "Size and Structure of the Household in England over Three Centuries, Part I, Mean Household Size in England since the Sixteenth Century," *Population Studies,* XXIII, No. 2 (July 1969), 199–223.

3   Two series of colonial population totals at decadal intervals have been constructed: by Rossiter, *A Century* . . . , pp. 9–10 and by Stella H. Sutherland in U.S. Bureau of the Census, *Historical Statistics of United States, Colonial Times to 1957* (Washington, D.C.: GPO, 1960), Series Z1–19, p. 756. Potter, "The Growth of Population . . ." uses the Rossiter estimates.

4   H. Gille, "The Demographic History of the Northern European Countries in the Eighteenth Century," *Population Studies,* III, No. 1 (June 1949), 3–65, was the source for the Swedish data.

5   Yasukichi Yasuba, *Birth Rates of the White Population of the United States, 1800–1860* (Baltimore: The Johns Hopkins Press, 1960), p. 114. With heavy male outmigration in Hingham, nearly 15 percent of all women born to reconstituted marriages of 1721 to 1760 survived to age forty-five as spinsters.

6   The stable population and ratios of deaths by age are from Ansley J. Coale and Paul Demeny, *Regional Model Life Tables and Stable Populations* (Princeton: Princeton University Press, 1966), pp. 92–3, 188–89 and 102–03, 198–99. Edward Wigglesworth, "A Table Showing the Probability of the Duration, the Decrement, and the Expectation of Life, in the States of Massachusetts and New Hampshire, formed from sixty-two Bills of Mortality on the files of the American Academy of Arts and Sciences, II, pt. I (1793), 132. Reverend Joseph McKean, "Synopsis of Several Bills of Mortality," *Memoirs of the American Academy of Arts and Sciences,* II, pt. II (1804), 65. For the deficiencies of the Wigglesworth material, see Maris A. Vinovskis, "The 1789 Life Table of Edward Wigglesworth," *The Journal of Economic History,* XXXI, No. 3 (Sept. 1971), 570–90. Some 1,113 of the 4,893 deaths in the Wigglesworth sample were taken from the records of Ebenezer Gay, minister of the first parish in Hingham.

7   Calculated from the census data for Connecticut counties in Rossiter, *A Century . . . ,* pp. 166–69. For state variations in child-woman ratios within New England in 1800, see Yasuba, *Birth Rates . . . ,* p. 61.

8   Gille, "The Demographic History . . . ," p. 31. For a summary of age-specific fertility data from reconstitutions of French parishes and French-Canadian genealogies, see A. Chamoux and C. Douphin, "La contraception avant la Revolution française: L'exemple de Châtillon-sur Seine," *Annales, Economies, Sociétés, Civilisations, 24,* No. 3 (May–June 1969), 668–69. Yasuba, *Birth Rates . . . ,* p. 115, calculated that marital fertility was 26 percent higher in Connecticut in 1774 and New Hampshire in 1773 than in Sweden from 1776 to 1800.

9   Generalizing from European censuses from 1850 to 1910 Hajnal concluded that, "On the European pattern, the percentage of women over 15 who were married in a country as a whole was below 55 and usually below 50 in the nineteenth century." J. Hajnal, "European Marriage Patterns in Perspective," in *Population in History,* p. 119. Only 50.3 percent in 1750 and 50.1 percent in 1800 of the female population over 15 in Sweden was married. Gille, "The Demographic History . . . ," p. 25.

10   For details of Yasuba's method, see *Birth Rates . . . ,* pp. 111–15.

11   The average annual net reproduction rate from 1751 to 1800 in Sweden was 1.172; however, there was considerable variation from year to year with a standard deviation of 0.1719 and thus a coefficient of variation of 14.7 percent. Calculated from Hannes Hyrennius, "Reproduction and Replacement: A Methodological Study of Swedish Population Changes during 200 Years," *Population Studies,* IV, No. 4 (March 1951), Table 2, 424.

12   Potter notes that the decades of most rapid growth in all the colonies (the 1720s, 1740s and 1780s) were also periods of heavier immigration. "The Growth of Population . . . ," pp. 638–39.

13   For recent suggestive approaches using generational hypotheses in colonial studies, see Kenneth A. Lockridge, "The Population of Dedham, Massachusetts, 1636–1736," *Economic History Review,* 2d ser., XIX (Aug. 1966), 328, 341–42; Philip

J. Greven, Jr., *Four Generations: Population, Land and Family in Colonial Andover, Massachusetts* (Ithaca: Cornell University Press, 1970), esp. pp. 17–18, 180–81, 205–06; and P.M.G. Harris, "The Social Origins of American Leaders: The Demographic Foundations," *Perspectives in American History*, III (1969), pp. 220–34, 311–33.

14 There were 157 males per 100 females among the passengers to New England from 1620 to 1640. See Herbert Moller, "Sex Composition and Correlated Culture Patterns of Colonial America," *William and Mary Quarterly*, 3d ser., II (1945), 115–17. In a sample of Plymouth Colony couples the age at marriage converged from 27.0 and 20.6 for men and women respectively born 1600, 25 to 24.6 and 22.3 for those born 1675–1700 (sample size of 650 persons in five birth cohorts). John Demos, *A Little Commonwealth, Family Life in Plymouth Colony* (New York: Oxford University Press, 1970), p. 193. In Andover, the male age at first marriage did not decline until after 1730; averages for the second, third, and fourth generation male descendants of the original settlers are 26.7 (104), 27.1 (224) and 25.3 (294). For Andover women the corresponding generational averages are 22.3 (81), 24.5 (210) and 23.2 (282), with the increase coming after 1704. Greven, *Four Generations*, pp. 188–90, 206–10. In Ipswich, a larger, more commercial town near Andover, marriage ages were 27.2 (34), 26.5 (73) and 24.0 (88) for men and 21.7 (17), 23.6 (70) and, 23.3 (98) for women marrying in the periods 1652–1700, 1701–1725 and 1726–1750. Susan L. Norton, "Population Growth in Colonial America: A Study of Ipswich, Massachusetts," *Population Studies*, XXV, 3 (Nov. 1971), p. 445. Older studies based on family genealogies confirm these trends. In Jones' sample, male age dropped from 27.0 to 24.8 while female age at marriage increased from 21.4 to 22.2 between 1651–1700 and 1701–50 (27 and 176 marriages respectively). Carl E. Jones, "A Genealogical Study of Population," *Publications of the American Statistical Association*, XVI (1918), p. 208. In the genealogical study by Frederick S. Crum, "The Decadence of the Native American Stock: A Statistical Study," *Publications of the American Statistical Association*, XIV (1914), 220, the age at first marriage increased from 21.4 (30) before 1700 to 21.7 (147) for women married from 1700 to 1749.

15 Using pre-1691 marital fertility rates for women aged 20–24, the increase of 2.76 years in the average age at first marriage for women can account for only 1.29 of the total decline of 2.98 children (43.3 percent) per complete family in the 1691–1715 cohort compared to the women married before 1691.

16 Marital fertility over age thirty was tested by the same analysis of variance method used by E. A. Wrigley, "Family Limitation in Pre-Industrial England," *Economic History Review*, 2d ser. XIX, No. 1 (April 1966), pp. 90–91. The test yielded a F of 20.38 with 1 and 430 degrees of freedom.

17 The average number of births per Harvard or Yale alumnus declined from 5.96 (186) for graduates aged 34 in 1656 to 1698 to 5.21 (289) for graduates aged 34 in 1699–1722, before rebounding to 5.98 (1,153) for alumni aged 34 in 1723–1758. Harris, "The Social Origins . . . ," Table 14, p. 317. In Andover there was a drop from 8.7 (37) children per complete family, 1685–1704, to 7.4 (67) for families formed from 1705 to 1724; a very small sample of those married from 1725 to 1744 averaged 7.5 (17) children per complete family. Greven, *Four Generations*, Table 21, p. 202. The increase in marriage age in Andover between 1685–1704 and 1705–24 explains between 69 percent and 83 percent of the total decrease in mean family size. The number of children per complete family among the descendants of the original settlers of Watertown, was 8.85 (20), 7.48 (105), 8.63 (150) and 7.84 (168) respectively for marriages formed before 1670, 1671–1720, 1721–1760 and

1761–1800. Calculated from Henry Bond, *Genealogies of the Families and Descendants of the early Settlers of Watertown, Massachusetts* (Boston: N.E. Historic-Genealogical Society, 2d ed., 1860). Internal evidence suggests a substantial upward bias in these figures with the author concentrating on the ancestors of his mid-nineteenth century generation.

18 On the halt to New England expansion from 1675 to 1713, see Lois Kimball Matthews, *The Expansion of New England* (New York: Russell and Russell, Inc., 1962), pp. 43–75, and Douglas Edward Leach, *The Northern Colonial Frontier* (New York: Holt, Rinehart and Winston, 1966), pp. 109–25. Both Matthews and Leach emphasize the direct security impediments to frontier expansion.

19 The complex socio-demographic evolution uncovered in post-1715 Hingham can only be hinted at here. Premarital pregnancy, outmigration, daughters not marrying in order of birth, and primogeniture are among the indicators which show increases in frequency as the eighteenth century progresses. Tension between generations probably increased as fathers were unable to maintain their dominance on the old seventeenth century basis; however, it is not until after the Revolution that marriage was established as a "free" act of the couple being wed.

20 It may appear highly speculative to conclude that the effect of husband's age on the fertility of the wife operates through coital frequency. Between the ages of 20 and 45 at least, the fecundity of the male does not decline. See John MacLeod and Ruth Z. Gold, "The Male Factor in Fertility and Infertility. VII. Semen Quality in Relation to Age and Sexual Activity," *Fertility and Sterility,* 4, No. 3 (1953), 194–209. Furthermore, modern studies indicate a marked decrease with age in rates of sexual intercourse. John MacLeod and Ruth Z. Gold, "The Male Factors in Fertility and Infertility. VI. Semen Quality and Certain Other Factors in Relation to Ease of Conception," *Fertility and Sterility,* 4, No. 1 (1953), 10–33; and Alfred C. Kinsey, Wardell B. Pomeroy, Clyde V. Martin and Paul H. Gebhard, *Sexual Behavior in the Human Female* (New York: Pocket Books ed., 1965), pp. 392–94. Finally empirical data confirm a strong relationship between frequency of intercourse and the probability of conception. MacLeod and Gold, "Semen Quality and Certain other Factors . . . ," Table 19, p. 29; John C. Barrett and John Marshall, "The Risk of Conception on Different Days of the Menstrual Cycle," *Population Studies,* XXIII, 3 (Nov. 1969), 455–61. Barrett and Marshall calculate, for example, that the probability of conception during a given menstrual cycle increases from 0.24 to 0.68 for coital patterns of every fourth day and every day respectively.

21 H. Louis Stettler, "The New England Throat Distemper and Family Size," in H. Klarman, ed., *Empirical Studies in Health Economics* (Baltimore: Johns Hopkins University Press, 1970), pp. 17–27. Stettler's conclusions may be questioned since he failed to compare the post-epidemic record of families of the same size or women of the same age at the time of the outbreak. His data (Table 2, p. 23) merely confirm the probabilistic point that the chance a family will lose a child increases with the number of children already born.

22 For emphasis on spacing as an important means in the control of marital fertility and a critique of the classic tests for the existence of family limitation, see J. J. Dupaquier and M. Lechiver, "Sur les débuts de la contraception en France ou les deus malthusianismes," *Annales, E. S. C.,* XXIV, No. 6 (Nov.-Dec. 1969), 1391–406.

Daniel Scott Smith   414

23   For the complexity of the map of pre-demographic transition European fertility, see Ansley J. Coale, "The Decline in Fertility in Europe from the French Revolution to World War II," in S. J. Behrman, Leslie Corsa, Jr., and Ronald Freedman, eds., *Fertility and Family Planning. A World View* (Ann Arbor: University of Michigan Press, 1969), pp. 3–19.

Selected Bibliography

Books

Anderson, Michael. *Family Structure in Nineteenth Century Lancashire.* Cambridge: Cambridge University Press, 1971.

Aries, Phillippe. *Centuries of Childhood: A Social History of Family Life.* New York: Vintage Books, 1960.

Bailyn, Bernard. *Education in the Forming of American Society.* Chapel Hill: University of North Carolina Press, 1960.

Banks, J. A. and Olive. *Feminism and Family Planning in Victorian England.* New York: Schocken Books, 1964.

Bremner, Robert, ed. *Children and Youth in America: A Documentary History.* 2 vols. Cambridge: Harvard University Press, 1970–71.

Calhoun, Arthur W. *A Social History of the American Family.* 3 vols. Cleveland: Clark, 1917.

Carden, Maren L. *Oneida: Utopian Community to Modern Corporation.* Baltimore: Johns Hopkins University Press, 1969.

Demos, John. *A Little Commonwealth: Family Life in the Plymouth Colony.* New York: Oxford University Press, 1970.

Drake, Michael. *Population and Society in Norway, 1735–1865.* Cambridge: Cambridge University Press, 1969.

Farber, Bernard. *Guardians of Virtue: Salem Families in 1800.* New York: Basic Books, 1972.

Flaherty, David H. *Privacy in Colonial New England.* Charlottesville: University of Virginia Press, 1972.

Glass, D. V. and Eversley, D. E. C., eds. *Population in History: Essays in Historical Demography.* Chicago: Aldine, 1965.

Grabill, W. H.; Kiser, C. V.; and Whelpton, P. K. *The Fertility of American Women.* New York: John Wiley, 1958.

Greven, Philip J., Jr. *Four Generations: Population, Land, and Family in Colonial Andover, Massachusetts.* Ithaca: Cornell University Press, 1970.

Hewitt, Margaret. *Wives and Mothers in Victorian Industry.* London: Rockliff, 1958.

Himes, Norman E. *Medical History of Contraception.* New York: Gamut, 1963.

Howard, George E. *A History of Matrimonial Customs.* 3 vols. Chicago: University of Chicago Press, 1904.

Hunt, David. *Parents and Children in History.* New York: Basic Books, 1970.

Kennedy, David M. *Birth Control in America: The Career of Margaret Sanger.* New Haven: Yale University Press, 1970

Laslett, Peter. *The World We Have Lost.* New York: Scribner's, 1965.

Laslett, Peter, and Wall, Richard, eds. *Household and Family in Past Time.* Cambridge: Cambridge University Press, 1972.

Lockridge, Kenneth, A. *New England Town: The First Hundred Years.* New York: Norton, 1970.

Macfarlene, Alan. *The Family Life of Ralph Josselin, a seventeenth-century clergyman.* Cambridge: Cambridge University Press, 1970.

McLachlan, James. *American Boarding Schools: A Historical Study.* New York: Scribner's, 1970.

Marcus, Steven. *The Other Victorians: A Study of Sexuality and Pornography in Mid-Nineteenth-Century England.* New York: Basic Books, 1966.

Monahan, Thomas P. *The Pattern of Age at Marriage in the United States.* 2 vols. Philadelphia: Privately printed, 1951.

Morgan, Edmund S. *The Puritan Family.* New York: Harper & Row, 1966.

O'Neill, William. *Everyone was Brave: The Rise and Fall of Feminism in America.* Chicago: Quadrangle, 1968.

Pearsall, Ronald. *The Worm in the Bud: The World of Victorian Sexuality.* New York: Macmillan, 1969.

Pinchbeck, Ivy. *Women Workers and the Industrial Revolution, 1750–1850.* London: Frank Cass, 1969.

Sennett, Richard. *Families Against the City: Middle Class Homes of Industrial Chicago, 1872–1890.* Cambridge: Harvard University Press, 1970.

Taylor, G. Rattray. *Sex in History.* London: Thames and Hudson, revised edition, 1959.

Wishy, Bernard. *The Child and the Republic.* Philadelphia: University of Pennsylvania Press, 1968.

Articles

Bloomberg, Susan E. *et al.* "A Census Probe into Nineteenth Century Family History: Southern Michigan, 1850–1880." *Journal of Social History* V (1971): 26–45.

Brooks, Carol F. "The Early History of the Anti-Contraceptive Laws in Massachusetts and Connecticut." *American Quarterly* 18 (1966): 3–23.

Cobbledick, M. R. "The Property Rights of Women in Puritan New England." In *Studies in the Science of Society,* edited by George Murdock, pp. 107–16. New Haven: Yale University Press, 1937.

Gordon, Michael, and M. Charles Bernstein, "Male Choice and Domestic Life in the 19th Century Marriage Manual," *Journal of Marriage and the Family* 32 (1970): 665–674.

Furstenberg, Frank F. Jr. "Industrialization and the American Family: A Look Backward." *American Sociological Review* XXXI (1966): 326–37.

Goubert, Pierre. "Historical Demography and the Reinterpretation of Early Modern French History: A Research Review." *Journal of Interdisciplinary History* I (1970): 37–48.

Greven, Philip J., Jr. "Historical Demography and Colonial America." *William and Mary Quarterly* 24 (1967): 438–54.

Habakkuk, H. J. "Family Structure and Economic Change in Nineteenth-Century Europe." *Journal of Economic History* 15 (1955): 1–12.

Hareven, Tamara K. "The History of the Family as an Interdisciplinary Field." *Journal of Interdisciplinary History* 2 (1971): 399–414.

Hershberg, Theodore. "Free Blacks in Ante-Bellum Philadelphia: A Study of Ex-Slaves, Free-Born and Socio-Economic Decline." *Journal of Social History* 5 (1971–72): 183–209.

Higgs, Robert, and Stettler, H. Louis. "Colonial New England Demography: A Sampling Approach." *William and Mary Quarterly*, 27 (1970): 282–94.

Jeffrey, Kirk. "The Family as Utopian Retreat from the City: The Nineteenth-Century Contribution." *Soundings* 55 (1972): 21–41.

Keniston, Kenneth. "Youth as a New Stage of Life." *The American Scholar* 39 (1970): 631–54.

Kephart, William M. "Experimental Family Organization: An Historico-Cultural Report on the Oneida Community." *Journal of Marriage and the Family* 25 (1963): 261–71.

Kett, Joseph F. "Adolescence and Youth in Colonial America." *Journal of Interdisciplinary History* 2 (1971): 283–98.

Knodel, John "Two and a Half Centuries of Demographic History in a Bavarian Village. *Population Studies* XXIV (1970): 353–376.

Lamb, Robert K. "The Entrepreneur and the Community." In *Men in Business*, edited by William Miller. New York: Harper Torchbooks, 1962.

Lantz, H.; Britton, M.; Schmidt, R.; and Snyder, E. "Pre-Industrial Patterns in the Colonial Family in America: A Content Analysis of Colonial Magazines." *American Sociological Review* 33 (1968): 413–26.

Lockridge, Kenneth A. "Land, Population and the Evolution of New England Society." *Past and Present* 47 (1970): 51–70.

McGovern, James R. "The American Women's Pre-World War I Freedom in Manners and Morals." *Journal of American History* 55 (1968): 315–33.

Lindt, Gillian. "Family Surrogates in Colonial America: The Moravian Experiment." *Journal of Marriage and the Family* 31 (1969): 650–58.

Modell, John. "Family and Fertility on the Indiana Frontier, 1820." *American Quarterly* 23 (1971): 615–34.

Monahan, Thomas. "One Hundred Years of Marriage in Massachusetts." *American Journal of Sociology* 56 (1951): 534–45.

Neuman, R. P. "Industrialization and Sexual Behavior: Some Aspects of Working-Class Life in Imperial Germany." In *Modern European Social History*, edited by Robert J. Bezucha, pp. 270–98. Lexington, Mass: D. C. Heath, 1972.

Norton, Susan L. "Population Growth in Colonial America: A Study of Ipswich, Massachusetts." *Population Studies* 25 (1971): 433–52.

Parish, William L. Jr., and Schwartz, Moshe. "Household Complexity in Nineteenth Century France." *American Sociological Review* 37 (1972): 154–72.

Saveth, Edward. "The Problem of American Family History." *American Quarterly* 21 (1969): 311–29.

Shorter, Edward; Knodel, John; and van de Walle, Etienne. "The Decline of Non-Marital Fertility in Europe, 1880–1940." *Population Studies* 25 (1971): 375–93.

Strong, Bryan. "Ideas of the Early Sex Education Movement in America, 1890–1920." *History of Education Quarterly* 12 (1972): 129–161.

Sunley, Robert. "Early Nineteenth-Century American Literature on Child Rearing." In *Childhood in Contemporary Cultures,* edited by M. Mead and M. Wolfenstein, pp. 150–67. Chicago: University of Chicago Press, 1963.

Uhlenberg, Peter R. "A Study of Cohort Life Cycles: Cohorts of Native Born Massachusetts Women, 1830–1920." *Population Studies* 23 (1969): 407–420.

Vinovskis, Maris A. "Mortality Rates and Trends in Massachusetts before 1860." *Journal of Economic History* 32 (1972): 184–213.

Wells, Robert V. "Family Size and Fertility Control in Eighteenth Century America: A Study of Quaker Families." *Population Studies* 25 (1971): 73–82.

Special Journal Issues Devoted To Family History or Historical Demography.

Daedalus 97 (1968) [Demographic Studies].
Journal of Interdisciplinary History 2 (1971).
Journal of Marriage and the Family 35 (forthcoming).

Index

Abbott, Lyman, 255
Adams, Henry, 282, 283
Adler, Felix, 255, 256
Adolescence, 209–210, 212–218
Adultery, 284, 289, 290
"Age-grading," 217

Aggregate data analysis, 4
Alcott, William, 229
Alienation, 9
Allen, Grant, 257
American Sociological Society, 259–260
American women. *See* Women

Anderson, Michael, 11, 59, 100
Anti-Saloon League, 272
Apprenticeship, 186
Ariès, Philippe, 13, 101, 102, 126, 127, 180
Arnold, Sir Edwin, 197, 198
Artisans, 104, 107
Atwater, Caleb, 226
Authority, 7, 86, 103, 198, 201, 211, 217, 311

Bailyn, Bernard, 188, 200
Ballentine, William G., 260
Banfield, E. C., 73
Barker-Benfield, Ben, 336
Battey, Robert, 354, 355, 358, 359
Beard, Mary, 280
Beaujour, Félix de, 376
Beecher, Henry Ward, 212, 213
Bell, Daniel, 254
Bennett, Arnold, 203
Berkner, Lutz K., 10, 19, 34
Birth control, 29, 350, 374, 386, 393, 398, 409
Birth rates, 161, 378, 382–385
Black family, 153–173: birth rate of, 161–162; employment, 158–160, 164–165; fertility of, 389–393; migration of, 155–157, 162, 171, 172. See also Family; Family structure
Blau, P., 125
Boarders. See Lodgers
Boorstin, Daniel, 194
Booth, C., 73
Bott, Elizabeth, 127
Bradford, William, 291, 379
Branagan, Thomas, 227
Brigham, Amariah, 337, 338
Brunner, Otto, 46
Bryan, Mary, 273
Burnap, George, 231, 233, 239
Butler, Elizabeth B., 145

Caird, Mona, 257
Calhoun, Arthur, 3
Calvinism, 101
Capitalism, 305, 306
Castration, 354–357, 359–361
Cawelti, John, 128
Chayanov, A. V., 49
Chester, Greville, 193

Chevalier, Louis, 120
Child, Lydia Maria, 212, 230, 238
Childhood, 180–188, 211–212, 214. See also Adolescence; Children
Children, 64, 68–70, 79, 80, 81, 170, 181, 234, 276, 379, 421: aggression in, 183–184; education of, 187, 194, 196–197, 199–201; employment of, 186–188, 216; mortality in, 161, 182, 233, 234, 383–384, 385, 391, 403; "parentless," 68–70, 162; socialization of, 110; views on American, 192–205
Circumcision, 353
Clitoridectomy, 353, 354
Cobbett, Thomas, 291
Coitus, 328–329, 330, 332, 397
Community, 6
Comstock Laws, 330
Conjugal family, 10, 11, 20. See also Family
Contraception. See Birth control
Co-residence, 68, 71, 72, 73
Cotton, John, 283
Crowe, Eyre, 194

Dagg, Mrs. S. L., 226
Danforth, J. N., 240
Darwinism, 215
DeBary, Richard, 202
Deland, Margaret, 256
Demography. See Population, studies
Demos, John, 4, 11, 180, 209
Demos, Virginia, 209
Dicey, Edward, 201
Dictionary of American Biography, 336
Dike, Samuel, 252, 256, 259, 261
Divorce: attitudes toward, 254–262, 331; laws, 252–254; rate, 251–252, 259
Doane, William Croswell, 253, 254, 260
DuBois, W. E. B., 164, 168, 169, 171
Dudley, A. Palmer, 359, 360, 361
Duncan, O. D., 125

Edes, Robert, 360
Education, 308, 309
Elliot, Charles, 230
Ellwood, Charles A., 256

Emerson, Ralph W., 233
Episcopal church, 253, 254
Erikson, Erik, 130, 184, 185, 203
Esquirol, Jean-Dominique, 339
Extended family, 21, 23–24, 28–29, 34, 41–43, 105, 106, 111, 122, 123, 126, 168: modified, 77, 93, 94. *See also* Family

Family, 2, 4, 107–110, 152, 158–159, 194, 210, 255, 276, 311–312: and modernization, 5, 10–12, 22, 26; authority, 7, 86–94, 103, 198–199, 201, 211, 217, 312; development of American, 200–204; economic pressures in, 68–73; effect of longevity on, 81–82; history, 2–4; "intensive," 124, 126–131; life cycle, 34, 36, 41–42, 44, 49, 52–53, 66; size, 25–28, 80–81, 123, 374. *See also* Black family; Conjugal family; Extended family; Household; Nuclear family; Stem family
Family organization. *See* Family; Family structure
Family reconstitution, 3
Family structure, 20–21, 23–29, 44–45, 59–66, 70, 72–73, 77–78, 81, 85, 93, 94, 216–217: black, 152–173; Italian-American, 136–148; middle class, 112, 122–124, 131–132; Puritan, 101–109
Farber, Bernard, 100, 136
Farley, Mrs. S. E., 233
Farnham, Eliza, 228
Farrar, Eliza, 227, 228, 234, 235
Feminism, 262, 269, 350. *See also* Reform movements
Fertility: and household size, 379; and migration, 378–379; declines in, 383–389, 391–394, 404, 405–411; determinants of marital, 407–411; in colonial period, 28, 374–382, 397–398, 402, 403–411
Fertility of American Women, The, 374
Flaxman, Ann, 232
Flower, Benjamin O., 258
Forester, Fanny, 228
Fornication, 284, 288, 289, 290
Franklin, Benjamin, 375, 376, 382
Fraser, James N., 194

Frazier, E. Franklin, 171
Freud, Sigmund, 351
Frustration and Aggression, 121
Fuller, Margaret, 226

Gardner, A. K., 341, 342, 343, 344, 347, 348, 350, 352, 353, 357, 358
George, W. L., 195
Gibbs, Sir Philip, 203
Gilliam, David, 355, 356
Gilman, Caroline, 232
Gilman, Charlotte P., 259
Goode, William J., 7, 10, 11, 12, 29, 137
Goubert, Pierre, 23
Grabill, Wilson H., 374
Graves, Mrs. A. J., 227
Greenwood, Grace, 232
Greven, Philip J., Jr., 77
Guardians of Virtue, 100
Gutman, Herbert, 152, 171
Gynecology, 346, 348, 353–356, 359–361

Hajnal, John, 28
Hale, Sarah Josepha, 226
Hall, G. Stanley, 210, 214, 215, 216, 218
Handlin, Oscar, 140
Hare, William Hobart, 252
Harrington, Henry F., 241
Harris, C. C., 61, 64, 66
Hatton, Joseph, 195
Hawes, Joel, 212
Hayami, Akira, 26
Haymarket Riot, 113–117
Hélin, Etienne, 314
Helmholtz, Hermann von, 341
Hemans, Felicia, 231
Henry, Louis, 3, 23
Hershberg, Theodore, 152, 170, 172
Hofstadter, Richard, 128
Holmes, John H., 261
Holmes, Oliver Wendell, 349
Holyoake, George, 203
Household, 20, 22–29, 45–48, 164, 165: American colonial, 22, 28; size, 26, 52; structure, 23–25, 46, 53, 63, 72–73, 166–173. *See also* Family
Howard, George E., 251, 259, 260
Humphreys, Mrs. Desmond, 194

Identity, 351–352, 356–357
Illegitimacy, 296, 297–299, 306–315, 322, 327, 328, 330, 332: types of, 301–305
Immigration, 378, 379, 380, 383, 398, 403
Industrialization, 8, 10, 11, 26, 59–60, 107
Infant mortality. See Children, mortality in
Inheritance. See Property
Ironside, Charles, 3
Irving, Helen, 236
Irving, Washington, 238

Jacks, L. P., 196, 199
Jackson, J. A., 349
Jacobi, Abraham, 353
James, Janet, 268
Jarvis, Edward, 340
Jefferson, Thomas, 376
Jensen, Richard, 267
Judd, Charles H., 215

Keniston, Kenneth, 217, 218
King, Gregory, 45
King, Irving, 215
Kinsey, Alfred, 330
Kinship, 69–70, 73, 109, 122
Kiser, Clyde V., 374
Kyle, James, 253

Laborers, 106–107
Laslett, Peter, 19, 35, 44, 61, 64, 66
Le Bon, G., 119, 120
Lees, Lynn, 123, 124
Le Play, Frédéric, 35, 36
Life expectancy, colonial, 379–380, 403
Lipset, Seymour Martin, 121
Litwak, Eugene, 127
Lodgers, 50–52, 62, 66, 72, 144, 146, 169

McLaughlin, Virginia Yans, 136
Macrae, David, 193, 205
Manton, W. P., 357
Marriage: age at, 82–85, 375, 406; attitudes toward, 255, 269, 283, 284, 286, 291–293, 308–309
Marriage manuals, 330
Marryat, Captain, 198

Martineau, Harriet, 236, 241
Marx, Karl, 9, 305, 351
Masturbation, 338, 340–346, 349, 353
Mathews, Joseph M. D., 226
Matriarchy, 148
Mead, Margaret, 203, 215
Meigs, Charles, 225, 231, 347
Mercer, Margaret, 234
Merchants, 102, 107
Merton, Robert, 130
Midwives, 354, 357
Migration. See Immigration
Miller, John C., 405
Miller, Samuel, 239
Modernization, 5. See also Industrialization; Social change
Möller, H., 299
Morgan, Edmund S., 3, 282
Morris, Robert, 359
Mortality, 28, 161, 403, 405
Moynihan, Daniel P., 139, 147, 148, 152
Muirhead, James Fullarton, 199, 202
Munger, Theodore T., 213

Nakane, Chie, 27
Negroes, 153–173. See also Black family
New England Divorce Reform League, 252, 261
Nisbet, Robert, 5, 6, 7, 8
Notable American Women, 1607–1950, 268, 273, 279
Nuclear family, 10, 19, 20, 21, 28, 34, 41, 43, 52, 111, 122, 124–128, 167: function, 123. See also Family

Odencrantz, Louise, 146
O'Neill, William L., 251
Orphans. See Children
Osgood, Frances, 225

Parsons, Talcott, 121, 124, 126
Patriarchy, 93
Peabody, Francis, 256
Platt, Gerald M., 305
Pleck, Elizabeth H., 152
Population: distribution, 6; growth, 309, 376, 378–379; studies, 79–81, 382–394, 397–411
Praeger, Arnold, 355, 361

Pregnancy, 322, 323–330. *See also* Illegitimacy
Primogeniture, 408. *See also* Property
Property, inheritance of, 87, 92–93, 103, 311
Prostitution, 254
Protestant Ethic and the Spirit of Capitalism, The, 107
Psycho-history, 4
Puritans, 100–101, 105: and marriage, 283, 284, 286, 291–293; and sex, 184, 282–294; character structure of, 185

Rape, 285, 290
Rapson, Richard L., 192
Ray, Isaac, 337, 338, 339, 343
"Recapitulation," 215
Reform movements, 241, 242, 268, 270–276, 279–281, 347. *See also* Feminism
Religion, 9, 225, 226, 227
Riehl, Wilhelm, 47
Riots, 119, 153
Robertson, William, 193
Robinson, John, 182, 183, 184
Roosevelt, Theodore, 255
Rosser, C., 61, 64, 66
Rudé, George, 120
Russell, William Howard, 196

Sahlins, M. D., 73
Sandford, Mrs. John, 226, 231, 233
Saunders, William, 201
Schmauk, Theodore, 255
School system, 194, 196, 199, 200
Sennett, Richard, 106, 111
Servants, 46–50, 52, 62, 63, 70, 286–288, 307
Sex: attitudes toward, 330–331, 336–361; premarital, 297–299, 301, 302, 304, 321, 322; ratio, 162, 163
Sex manuals. *See* Marriage manuals
Sexual revolution, 296, 297, 301, 308–309, 311–313, 321–332
Shorter, Edward, 13, 296
Sigourney, Lydia H., 231, 233, 235, 240
Simon, William, 300
Sims, J. Marion, 342, 348, 357, 358
Slavery, 27, 154, 166
Slaves, 381

Small, Albion, 260
Smith, Daniel Scott, 5, 13, 321, 397
Smith, Walter George, 259, 260
Social change, 6, 305, 306, 309, 374. *See also* Sexual revolution
Social class, 8, 100, 102–108
Sodomy, 290
Solé, Jacques, 303
Spender, Harold, 205
Stanton, Elizabeth Cady, 258, 261
Stearns, Jonathan F., 229, 242
Steevens, George, 204
Stem family, 21, 28, 34–53. *See also* Family
Stephens, Ann, 236
Storer, Horatio, 347
Stowe, Harriet Beecher, 237
Strathesk, John, 203
Stuart-Wortley, Emmeline, 194
Student's Manual, The, 338–339
Sublimation, 344
Suffragism. *See* Feminism; Reform movements
Sumner, William G., 259, 260
Sussman, Marvin, 127

"Talented Tenth," 159
TenHouten, Warren, 148
Terman, Lewis M., 328
Thernstrom, Stephan, 126
Thorndike, E. L., 215
Tilly, Charles, 120
Tobenkin, Elias, 145
Tocqueville, Alexis de, 306, 337, 344, 346, 347, 351
Todd, John, 337, 338, 339, 340, 343–346, 347, 350, 352

Universal Lexikon, 46
Urban life, 307, 308

Vachell, Horace, 196, 197
Vaile, P. A., 194
Van de Warker, Ely, 356

Walters, J. H., 343
Weber, Max, 101, 104, 107–108
Weinstein, Fred, 305
Wells, H. G., 255, 257
Welter, Barbara, 224
Whelpton, Pascal K., 374

Whitman, Walt, 197, 198
Wiebe, Robert, 352
Willard, Samuel, 283
Williams, Jesse Lynch, 258
Wilmott, Peter, 127
Wollstonecraft, Mary, 241
Women: advice to, 231–232, 238–241; and divorce, 251; and employment, 136, 141–148, 269–280; and sterility, 393–394; attitudes toward, 337, 347–350, 353, 354, 357–358; education of, 226, 236–238, 328, 346; 19th-century views of, 224–243; roles of, 255–256, 267–270; surgical treatment of, 353–357
Woodson, Carter, 155

World We Have Lost, The, 35
Wright, Carrol, 258, 259
Wright, Fanny, 227
Wright, Frances, 241
Wright, Frank Lloyd, 127
Wright, Richard, 169
Wrigley, E. A., 314
Wyse, Francis, 198

Yelverton, Therese, 193
Youth. *See* Adolescence
"Youth culture," 217, 218. *See also* Adolescence

Zadruga, 24, 25
Zincke, Foster B., 201, 202